Houghton Mifflin Company
Editorial Advisory Committee in Education

Herold C. Hunt
Harvard University

C. Gilbert Wrenn
Macalester College

Van Cleve Morris
University of Illinois at Chicago Circle

Samuel A. Kirk
University of Illinois

William Van Til
Indiana State University

Charles S. Benson
University of California, Berkeley

Robert H. Anderson
Harvard University

Kaoru Yamamoto
The Pennsylvania State University

TEACHING
Essays
and
Readings

HOUGHTON MIFFLIN COMPANY
BOSTON
New York
Atlanta
Geneva, Illinois
Dallas
Palo Alto

Copyright © 1969 by Kaoru Yamamoto

The selections reprinted in this book are used by permission of and special arrangement with the proprietors of their respective copyrights.

All rights reserved. No part of this work may be reproduced or transmitted in any form or by any means, electronic or mechanical, including photocopying and recording, or by any information storage or retrieval system, without permission in writing from the publisher.

Printed in the U.S.A.

FOREWORD

Teaching and the teacher have come a long way from the days when the one was a rigid input process and the other was a drudge and public servant. Even the youngest readers of these lines have read some samples of educational Americana—descriptions of teachers who were required to sweep out the room, carry in the wood and water, "keep school" for long hours, teach Sunday School, and attend church all day Sunday. They were forbidden to smoke, drink, play pool, read fiction, or even court a prospective wife (some liberal communities permitted courting one night a week!). The content of teaching was both irrelevant and inflexible, its "learning" enforced by rote and rod.

In 1969, these traditions are archaic in perhaps 90 percent of the United States. What concerns us more today is a healthy but disturbing kind of revolt of both pupils and teachers: pupils revolt against a school curriculum and an adult attitude toward youth and the school that are oriented to the past; teachers revolt against administrative arbitrariness and social unrealities. The student dissent (even though many observers feel there is too little of it) often is unfair to the facts and impatient beyond reason, and it tends to group all adults as members of one oppressive power party. Teacher revolts often make clear that the teachers are putting self above others, and that they are *not* concerned with pupil welfare; in fact, the dissenting teachers sometimes seem to be aiming primarily at making parents and students suffer as much as they have. Both kinds of revolts are real and present and cannot be swept under the rug. Despite their unfavorable aspects, they are more likely to bring about changes in both teaching and learning than did the passivism of the past century—though the byproducts are somewhat toxic to our society.

This book brings a breath of cool, fresh air into the turbulent, smoggy atmosphere of today's schools. Dr. Yamamoto recognizes the idealism toward individuals and toward society that draws most young teachers into the field. But he recognizes, too, that this idealism must operate in an environment of severe social tensions, accommodating itself to the vigorous attempts of teachers' organizations to protect their membership at almost any cost. These conflicts must be bewildering to the initiate! They are confusing even to the experienced.

The conflicts within education have been matters of deep personal concern to the author of this book over the past several years. Dr. Henry Borow and I were the major professors for Dr. Yamamoto when he was a candidate for the Ph.D degree, and he has kept in touch with me over the years through personal correspondence. This book grows out of a concern which I know to be both deeply personal and profession-wide. "The main thing for me," he once wrote, "is how to keep college teaching honest and relevant.... I try to hew a new line in my sections without vainly beating my head against the sacred wall of tradition." And elsewhere he wrote, "Increasingly I realize that I *cannot* 'teach'! You suggest that I play less of a role and simply share myself with my students. I am all for that, but often students' expectations are for neat packages of knowledge and skill, and that is precisely what I do *not* have."

So this book has grown out of the author's struggle to answer profound personal questions about both teaching and learning. He has developed a way of thinking about teaching which is psychologically very meaningful to me. I can think of nothing more basic than to start the prospective teacher out with the "Many Faces of Teaching." In it, Yamamoto draws distinctions between teaching and learning, between learning in school and learning as a life process, between kinds of learning, between the *teaching* of one generation and the *learning* of another generation. These distinctions are crucial. So also are Yamamoto's models of learning. It seems quite appropriate that the "Many Faces" analysis be followed by Margaret Mead's discussions of teaching from the anthropologist's point of view—how we in America have come to stress teaching rather than learning.

As I have worked with this manuscript I have developed a considerable admiration for two dimensions of the book: the character of the selections presented and the organization of these selections within the book. The "Why—Who—Whom—Where and When—What—How—How Well?" section titles cover all the elements of teaching to which the prospective teacher should be introduced. The questions raised are not lightly responded to, however, and Yamamoto has searched the literature well for the best to be found. The selections made are not only representative of the best in teaching; they are astonishingly relevant. Those who teach teachers might well aspire to introduce their students to such a varied array of distinguished authors as Margaret Mead, Alfred N. Whitehead, William James, Gilbert Highet, Gordon Hullfish, Christopher Jencks, John Dewey, Ernest Hilgard, Herbert Thelen, Nathaniel Gage, and many others. With the exception of the classical statements of James (1899), Dewey (1902), Whitehead (1929), Mead (1943), and Highet (1950) the selections are products of the 1960's—and two-thirds of the twenty-three selections have been written or published within the last five years. It is significant that Yamamoto has written critically on most of the topics of the book. His eight selections were all written within the past two years. This book is not merely a collection of readings—it represents the integrated thinking of one deeply concerned scholar who has drawn upon some giants in the field to help him answer his own questions.

Seven sets of Discussion Questions and Further Readings are included as aids to learning. Many students will gloss over these, but the strongly committed and the intellectually curious, the very students whose attention a teacher of teachers wants to capture, may well be stimulated by these suggestions. It is likely, too, that the extensive references which conclude the author's own selections may arouse the interest of some of the more curious students, and teachers.

This is a carefully designed book, substantial but provocative, classical and current. I commend it to the thoughtful committed teacher.

C. Gilbert Wrenn

PREFACE

To teach is to touch someone else's life in progress. To be a teacher is to share human hopes and disappointments with another being. To examine teaching is, therefore, to study the perennial enigma, man himself, in all his grandeur and insignificance.

It may indeed be presumptuous for me to offer this personal look at teaching in such an overwhelming context. Nevertheless, I feel strongly that, unless a teacher tries to develop his own perspective of his profession, he is unlikely to be able to engage with his charges in a search for awareness and appreciation of human capacities. If the individual teacher gains an inclusive vision of teaching early in his training, he may be able to keep sight of his ultimate concern through all of the day-to-day experiences that are to follow in his career.

The need for formulation of a perspective about teaching is the rationale for this volume; it was my wish to offer a starting point for those in search of the meaning of teaching. It is my hope that the book will serve to stimulate students at every level of teacher preparation and experience in their efforts to arrive at a meaningful and comprehensive concept of teaching.

This anthology should kindle both thought and discussion among the students in a variety of education courses: in elementary, secondary, or university teacher preparation; in introduction, principles, curriculum, methods, and practicum courses; and in any other courses which investigate the purpose and process of teaching.

Needless to say, I owe much to those who have taught me that to live is to learn to love. They include Professor Henry Borow of the University of Minnesota, Professor O. L. Davis, Jr., of the University of Texas, Professor Henry F. Dizney of the University of Oregon, Professor Siegmar Muehl of the University of Iowa, Professor C. Gilbert Wrenn of Macalester College, and last but not least, Etsuko, my wife.

Kaoru Yamamoto

CONTENTS

FOREWORD v

PREFACE viii

PROLOGUE

MANY FACES OF TEACHING 3

WHY

1 / OUR EDUCATIONAL EMPHASES IN PRIMITIVE PERSPECTIVE 19
Margaret Mead

2 / EDUCATION YESTERDAY AND TODAY 31
Kaoru Yamamoto

3 / THE AIMS OF EDUCATION 53
Alfred N. Whitehead

WHO

4 / PSYCHOLOGY AND THE TEACHING ART 71
William James

5 / THE TEACHER 77
Gilbert Highet

6 / COMMITTED TO WHOM
AND FOR WHAT?   91
H. Gordon Hullfish
Philip G. Smith

WHOM

7 / CHILDREN UNDER PRESSURE   113
Kaoru Yamamoto

8 / CHILDREN OF THOSE WHO
ARE NOT LIKE US   129
Kaoru Yamamoto

WHEN and WHERE

9 / A NEW LOOK AT READINESS   167
Harry S. Broudy
B. Othanel Smith
Joe R. Burnett

10 / IS THE PUBLIC SCHOOL
OBSOLETE?   179
Christopher Jencks

11 / A REDEFINITION
OF EDUCATION   191
Margaret Mead

WHAT

12 / THE CHILD AND THE
CURRICULUM   203
John Dewey

13 / EDUCATION AND COMMITMENT   221

Solon T. Kimball
James E. McClellan, Jr.

14 / RELIGION AND THE PUBLIC SCHOOLS   239

Marvin Fox

15 / FOR EACH TREE IS KNOWN ...   249

Kaoru Yamamoto

HOW

16 / THE HUMAN DIMENSION IN TEACHING   265

Ernest R. Hilgard

17 / HOW CHILDREN FAIL   279

John Holt

18 / ORGANIC TEACHING   291

Sylvia Ashton-Warner

19 / FOUR MODELS FOR EDUCATION   297

Herbert A. Thelen

HOW WELL

20 / EVALUATION IN TEACHING   317

Kaoru Yamamoto

21 / TEACHING STYLES
AND LEARNING 327
Daniel Solomon
William E. Bezdek
Larry Rosenberg

22 / THEORIES OF TEACHING 337
N. L. Gage

23 / ANALYSIS OF TEACHING—
ANOTHER LOOK 355
Kaoru Yamamoto

EPILOGUE

LOOKING BACK AND AHEAD 369

PROLOGUE

MANY FACES OF TEACHING

Have you ever wondered what makes a teacher a teacher? Forgetting for a moment any social (institutional) requirements for a person to be labeled a teacher, what distinguishes him in substance and in spirit as a teacher? From Socrates through Mrs. Anne Mansfield Sullivan (Helen Keller's teacher) to any of the inspirational, though little famed, teachers of today, what characterizes an individual who, in the name of teaching, conducts himself in such a manner as to induce, facilitate, and maintain others' explorations of the world and the self?

No doubt you know much about this subject-matter or that. Certainly you know far more about things than most of your students do. Under the circumstances, it would be easy for you to let your skills and knowledge flow from your level to that of your students', thus filling the void in their mind. But, is this really what teaching is all about? Would you be trying basically to share *your* wisdom with your students so long as it lasts? Would you have anything left to teach your students once they had acquired about as much skills and knowledge as you possessed? In principle, is a teacher nothing more than a vending machine?

Undoubtedly, too, you know a lot about how children grow and learn. Different learning capacities will be revealed at different points in maturation. As a teacher, you would find out how they learn at each point and then reverse the principle to teach them; right? Or, is it?

TEACHING: SPHERES AND BRIDGES

Teaching versus Learning   It has often been said that teaching and learning are two sides of a coin, thus implying that a single process underlies these two types of activities. Although appealing to common sense, the apparent simplicity of this analysis is deceptive, mainly because it implies that one activity is the reverse of the other. In fact, however, the activity of teaching is not simply one of emanation of knowledge, and learning is not just absorption of knowledge. Under most circumstances, two separate agents perform the activities identified as teaching and learning. Their purposes in engaging in these activities, as well as the kinds of activities, are different for the teacher and the learner.[1] Thus, teaching is one thing, while learning is another.

Nor does understanding of learning, in and of itself, lead to understanding of teaching. This distinction resembles one between the knowledge and skills of a zoologist and those of an equestrian. A zoologist can tell us much about the classification and life cycles of animals, including the horse species. He is also knowledgeable in genetics, physiology, biochemistry, microbiology, and other related branches of study. He certainly understands a horse in one particular context. However, this, in and of itself, does not help him to become a good rider. Good horsemanship is to be mastered in another context, requiring the different body of skills and knowledge of the equestrian. How to handle a horse, within the limits set by biological and environmental factors, in pursuit of certain goals and in the face of some definite hurdles—that is one thing. To understand the origin, development, and ecology of a horse and to study its habits and physiological functioning, both at global and molecular levels—that is another. Similarly, it is one thing to investigate the process and principles underlying behavioral changes not ascribable to maturation (learning), while it is another to study how to nurture transactions so as to facilitate the learner's examination of self, inquiry into human inquiry itself, and creation (or recreation) of cultural heritage and wisdom (teaching).

Thus, for the purposes of discussion here, it seems profitable to consider teaching and learning as two quite separate dimensions of education or, more narrowly, of schooling. A reasonable simile to replace the two-sides-of-a-coin image may be one that embodies teaching and learning as two separate spheres; each must be considered for its own characteristics, and the best means of relating them must be one that takes into account the nature of each.

MANY FACES OF TEACHING
Kaoru Yamamoto

Both teaching and learning may be intentional or unintentional. When teaching is intentional, it usually takes a form of either instruction or demonstration, depending upon the proportion of verbal and behavioral acts. Formal schooling relies heavily on intentional teaching and so does propaganda and proselytization. On the other hand, many activities subsumed under the term "socialization" are examples of unintentional teaching in which sharing and contagion play an important part. The socializing context may range from the family of orientation through peer groups, various social functions, to scholastic colloquia.[2]

Likewise, learning may be either intentional or unintentional. A motivated and interested learner can absorb much of what is offered by a teacher. Such learning may be cognitive or affective in nature, and various theories of learning, as well as those of role playing and language, have been offered to describe the processes.[3] In addition, such learning may be either direct (first-person) or indirect (vicarious or observational). Furthermore, much as we wish all learning to be intentional, children and adults alike show numerous undesirable but entrenched habits to prove otherwise. Unintentional or incidental types of learning, both conscious and unconscious, would appear to represent a large territory yet to be fully explored and skillfully exploited by education. The overall situation may be conveniently summarized as in Table P.1.

Teaching–Learning Contexts It must first be recognized that the discrete dimensions (e.g., teaching vs. no teaching, or intentional learning vs. unintentional learning) are adopted here merely for the sake of convenience and these cannot be anything but a poor approximation to the actual, complex phenomena. Second, a distinction has to be made between education in its general sense and education in its institutionalized form. The latter, namely, schooling, is explicitly committed to intentional teaching. Education in general, however, covers the full spectrum of activities represented in Table P.1.

The cell A in Table P.1 represents the optimum situation for schooling, in either its individual or group form, and in either its instructional or demonstrational modes. Unfortunately, this combination seems rarer than we wish it were and our students tend to learn many things, both relevant and irrelevant, in the condition of cell B. An extreme example here would be the brainwashing operation of prisoners of war who pick up bits and pieces of information, generally in spite of themselves. Any

TABLE P.1
Classification of Teaching–Learning Contexts

		Learning: Yes, Intentional	Learning: Yes, Unintentional	Learning: No
Teaching: Yes	Intentional	A	B	C
Teaching: Yes	Unintentional	D	E	F
Teaching: No		G	H	I

A: Teaching intended—Learning intentional
B: Teaching intended—Learning unintentional
C: Teaching intended—No learning takes place
D: Teaching unintended—Learning intentional
E: Teaching unintended—Learning unintentional
F: Teaching unintended—No learning takes place
G: No teaching takes place—Learning intentional
H: No teaching takes place—Learning unintentional
I: No teaching takes place—No learning takes place

learning which depends heavily upon social (authority or peer) conformity would also fall in this category. Cell C is sadly much too familiar in our classrooms. Daydreaming children, exceptional students of various kinds, and pupils from nonmodal backgrounds frequently nullify the best-intentioned teaching efforts.

Activities falling in cell D are also quite familiar. When we select and read books for knowledge and wisdom, when a music student attentively observes a maestro conducting an orchestra in a crowded concerthall, and when like-minded scholars get together for a colloquium, we see some typical examples of this condition. If a person is motivated to learn what is meaningful to him, he seems to absorb whatever there is to absorb and, in turn, offer whatever he has to offer with much enthusiasm. Frequently, the parties involved are unaware of the fact that they are engaged in teaching–learning interaction, since the situation is more aptly characterized as sharing of the same experience, cognitive and/or emotional.

This informal nature of interaction becomes further accentuated in cell E where both teaching and learning appear to be effected through modeling, contagion, and osmosis, so to speak. What transpires between parents and children, between spouses, and among peers is typical of such relationships. It is interesting to note in this connection that the results of such unintentional learning may not conform to what is being unintentionally taught, as witnessed in those cases in which children unconsciously reject parental values or overcompensate for them. In addition, there can, theoretically at least, be events that correspond to the combination of cell F where no relevant learning takes place despite exposure to unintentional teaching; for example, a baby might see his father drinking coffee from a saucer, but since the child never uses a cup and saucer, he neither picks up the habit nor rejects it.

On the other hand, cell G may represent such efforts as playing golf or piano alone to improve one's skill, while more typical recreational activities tend to fall in cell H which typifies "accidental" learning. Finally, certain clearly noneducational conditions are found in cell I. In schools, we may find examples of this combination in many routines such as collecting milk money or taking a roll call, as well as in such disruptive activities as student riots or mob action. Casual social functions, particularly when they are not carefully incorporated into the total educational scheme, would also fall in this cell.

Looking at Table P.1 again, it becomes clear that any study of learning is in itself insufficient for our understanding of the transactional process of teaching–learning. Knowledge derived from investigation of one dimension of a complex event cannot substitute for that along another dimension. A comparable problem confronts the person who tries to understand the concept of velocity. For full comprehension, he must study each of the three component dimensions (distance, direction, and time) separately first and then all of them together. It is obviously too naive to insist, as some psychologists tend to do, that teaching would be vastly improved *if only* educationists were to apply known principles of learning in their classroom teaching.[4]

Bridges to Build   We have suggested that there are two separate spheres involved in the teaching–learning interaction. Moreover, we must keep in mind that the teacher's sphere was in existence typically much earlier than the learner's. Thus it is crucial for a teacher to be aware of this developmental or generational gap and to close it by building a bridge between the young and the old.[5]

Construction of such a generational bridge is a difficult feat, because the world in which teachers grew up is not the one in which students are now growing up and also because the temporal displacement has been accelerated by rapid and extensive social changes. The challenge is how to attain the goal of "two minds, one thought" across the ever-widening gap.[6]

One facet of this problem is seen in the oft-forgotten observation that we cannot and should not expect our students to make a broad jump from the concrete to the abstract. In other words, it is foolish for a teacher to try to teach a systematized body of knowledge to beginning students in its systematized form. No matter how complete and relevant such structured knowledge may seem to the teacher, he would do well to recall that the systematization is the end product of a long process of abstraction which makes sense to him only because he, himself, has trod the long way from the concrete world of early childhood years to the symbolic world of collegiate and adult life.

Unfortunately, his students are not living in the same abstract world with him and, hence, what is significant and interesting to the teacher is nothing but a dried and dead subject for his students. The teacher's questions are not the students', and the teacher's curiosity is not the students'. How frequently does a teacher kill off the enthusiasm for learning in his students by his insensitive discussion of a discipline which does not mean a thing to them? The teacher must bridge the gap between generations by building from where the students are, rather than from where he himself is. The logical structure of a discipline is rarely so stimulating as the students' own questions. After all, Euclid's theorems and Newton's laws followed, rather than preceded, their more immediate inquiries into what interested and puzzled them. There is no reason for a teacher to expect his students to get excited about axioms and principles from the outset. Why, then, should the teacher always "begin at the beginning"? Why should the students be required always to start their reading from page one, paragraph one, line one?

In the same vein, if we are going to require our young to learn something, it must have some significance to them *here and now.* A delayed-fuse mechanism seldom works with students and it is quite difficult to convince them that what they are taught today will become indispensable two years, five years, or ten years hence. The argument may be perfectly valid but such a long-range goal can hardly sustain a young learner's motivation for any extended period of time. We may paraphrase the slogan, "Freedom now!," to read, "Meaningfulness now!" The students must feel there is some relevance for their immediate life in what they are doing in the school. Herein lies the second challenge for teachers: how to show the students the relationship between the knowledge they acquire in the school and the many other spheres of our society. It is essential that there be a continuity between academic experience and practical experience, and the teacher is in a strategic position to point out the why and how of building the bridges to society.[7]

STUDY OF TEACHING

How, then, should we study teaching? As is true with most other topics of our inquiry, we will not find *the* best, single answer here. For the moment, nevertheless, let us examine the matter first using a cross-sectional approach (at any given time point), next from a longitudinal viewpoint (developmental, or across time), and finally with reference to an overall orientation which may prove to be useful to teachers in their study of teaching.

Questions on Teaching In our efforts to explore teaching and unravel its complexity, it seems convenient to schematize the relevant questions as in Table P.2.

It is immediately clear from Table P.2 that more than one question must be asked to understand teaching and, moreover, that each question can be phrased in two different forms: prescriptive ("What *ought* teaching to be?") and descriptive ("What *is* teaching?").

These questions cover such areas of concern as aims of teaching ("Why?"), agents ("Who?"), clientele ("Whom?"), timing ("When?"), curriculum ("What?"), method ("How?"), and locale ("Where?"). In the prescriptive form, these questions demand deliberation and decision while, in the descriptive form, they call for assessment of the current status. When we compare our answers to the prescriptive questions with those to the descriptive ones, we engage ourselves in evaluation. Thus, for example, the answer to "How are we teaching?," when compared with the answer to "How should we be teaching?," yields an answer to still another (evaluative) question, "How well are we teaching?"[8]

In passing, it seems important to point out that it is misleading

TABLE P.2
Teaching—Schematization of Questions

QUESTION		AREA OF CONCERN
Prescriptive	*Descriptive*	
Why should we be teaching?	Why are we teaching?	Values, goals, intentions, and motives
Who should be teaching?	Who are teaching?	Teacher qualification (recruitment, selection, and preparation)
Whom should we be teaching?	Whom are we teaching?	Student characteristics (recruitment, selection, and distribution)
When should we be teaching?	When are we teaching?	Readiness and logistics (physical, cognitive, and social development, timing, duration and continuity)
What should we be teaching?	What are we teaching?	Curriculum (types and quantity of material, structure, and sequence)
How should we be teaching?	How are we teaching?	Instruction and demonstration (methods, media, climate, and control)
Where should we be teaching?	Where are we teaching?	Ecology and logistics (locale, physical facilities, and geocultural administration)

to speak of *"a"* theory of teaching. This is a mistake familiar to us through our earlier experience with a single, dream theory of learning whose much-touted "superiority" over other theories was expected to be proved by a so-called critical experiment or two.

It is evident, however, that we must develop many theories of teaching to account for the several questions above (aims, method, locale, etc.), as well as for the two different forms of each inquiry (prescriptive and descriptive), and further, for each of the contexts shown in Table P.1. If, after all this, we are going to offer any overall theory of teaching, it will obviously be on a different level of abstraction and must be treated as such.

In the present volume, the classification scheme in Table P.2 is employed to organize the readings. Each area of concern is discussed in these selections to clarify the processes of judgment (prescription) and assessment (description) and also to illustrate the interrelated nature of such inquiries. It will be revealing to examine the basic postulates held by each author and, where disagreements occur among them, to compare the different *models* they employed; such a comparison is more rewarding than trying to settle the specific *contents* of their argument. If the writers seem to ignore some of the questions in Table P.2, or when they seem oblivious to some of the contexts in Table P.1, then it is our task as readers to keep in mind the total context of education and to evaluate the arguments accordingly.

Developmental Models and Teaching How do we relate the cross-sectional analysis of the *contexts* and *facets* (or questions) of teaching with the inescapable phenomenon of human development? And what is meant above by *models?* These two questions may be answered, in an illustrative manner, when we examine various hypotheses on the development of the human mind; these hypotheses have led different teachers to different strategies, tactics, or emphases in their teaching.

The first hypothesis on development we shall consider may be called an *invariant model* and is schematized in Figure P.1.

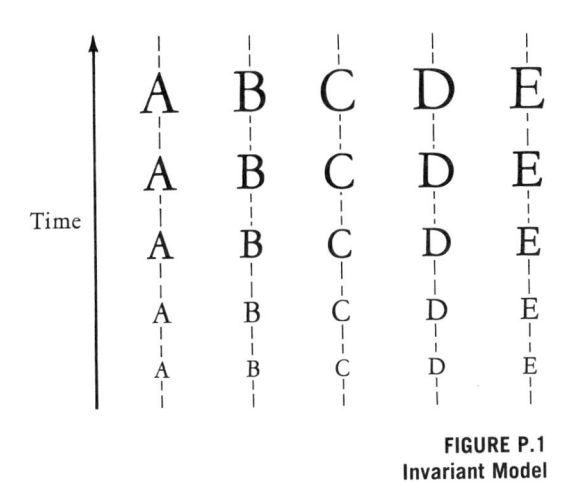

**FIGURE P.1
Invariant Model**

For the moment, interpret the symbols (A—E) quite loosely as components (and/or functions) of the mind. What the diagram tries to convey is the idea that the human mind remains structurally (and/or functionally) the same from one time-point to the next, even though it may grow wider and keener. In other words, oaks are oaks and pines are pines at any age. Accordingly, it is argued that anything can be taught to a student at any time, so long as the task is properly adjusted to his particular level of growth. A teacher's central concern will thus be with structuring of knowledge in such a way that students, from the earliest moment, may be exposed to essential concepts which will be repeated with greater and greater elaborations at successive time-points. The crucial consideration here is the *structure of the curriculum* and its *spiral* presentation. This model can supply answers to all the questions in Table P.2.

Now, contrast this with another model, schematized in Figure P.2, which may be called a *stage model*.

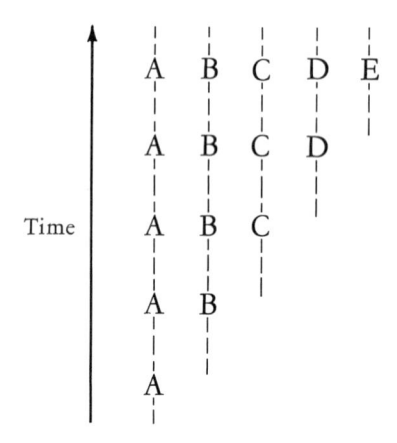

FIGURE P.2
Stage Model

In this formulation, it is believed that various components (and/or functions) of the mind develop in successive stages. Therefore, nothing can be taught until and unless the proper stage has been reached for it. In Figure P.2, for example, a task requiring a component (and/or function) B is teachable only from the second time-point on. The crucial concept here is *readiness*.

Still another case may be called a *file model,* which is diagrammed in Figure P.3. In this model, the development of each component (and/or function) follows that of another in the manner of an Indian file in which, note well, the same element is not repeated twice. Thus, a task (e.g., one corresponding to B) may be taught only when the time is ripe for it (namely, at the second time-point), never before and never after. Unless it is taught at this particular time, it will be lost forever. The crucial consideration is understandably that of the *critical period:* "To every thing there is a season, and a time to every purpose under the heaven" (Ecclesiastes 3:1).

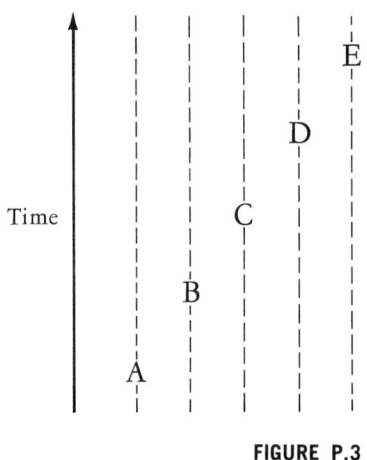

FIGURE P.3
File Model

Let us add just one other model which may be designated as *hierarchical*. As seen in Figure P.4, this model postulates that

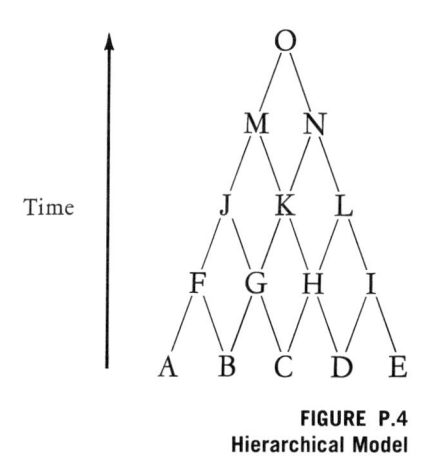

FIGURE P.4
Hierarchical Model

later components (and/or functions) of the mind develop on the basis of earlier ones. Corresponding to such developmental patterns, any teaching must build upon the results of previous learning. There is only one way to reach F and that is to start out with A and B. Educational practices such as fulfillment of prerequisites and accumulation of credits are based upon this model. Another example may be found in the psychoanalytic concept of fixation: in the present example, if a person has not developed L there is no way for him to achieve N and, hence, he is fixated at the third level. His later development thus becomes imperfect.

Alert readers must already have noticed that, even though these four examples are discussed as separate models, they all share common underlying assumptions: that the human mind consists of certain identifiable components (and/or functions), that it develops according to some predetermined schedule, and so forth. Obviously, if one does not share these assumptions, either singly or in toto, his reasoning and conclusions will surely be different from any that evolve into the four models we have been considering. It would be fruitless to argue back and forth about the content of any of these models without first establishing whether the parties agree on the underlying tenets of the models. Each person bases his judgment and assessment on his personal set of assumptions and beliefs which may or may not be shared by others. Many of us seem unaware that our beliefs are arbitrary, thus we waste much time in irreconcilable and irrelevant discussion of content because we have not seen that arguments which spring from different assumptions simply can not confront each other logically. Worse yet than the waste of time is the insistence on indoctrinating students with *the* viewpoint, *the* theory or *the* method. In a learner, this blindness or ethnocentric orientation is deplorable, to say the least, but it is understandable and can be dispelled. In a teacher, however, such blindness is nothing short of frightening and can lead only to a disaster.

Discipline of Teaching When teachers prepare themselves to teach a subject it is important for them not only to become knowledgeable in that particular discipline but also, and more crucially, to become aware of various alternative frames of reference available in the inquiry of the particular aspects of man's experience. Ordinarily, only one of these models is found in any disciplinary treatise at a particular historical juncture and, largely for this very reason, it remains implicit and unexamined. Accordingly, the end product of specialization is often none other than encapsulation.

Under the circumstances, the oft-recommended attempts to upgrade teachers by requiring them to specialize in a single

MANY FACES OF TEACHING
Kaoru Yamamoto

subject to a larger and larger extent is not likely to produce desirable results. Instead, it seems that we need to raise a central question, namely, "What is teaching?," and to study the *teaching of* a discipline, rather than study the discipline itself. An examination of teaching of a subject is not an examination of the subject and it is important that teachers realize the difference.[9]

The realization is important since no other discipline is specifically concerned with *teaching of* that same discipline. Astronomers are mainly interested in the study of celestial matters, not in the study of teaching of astronomy. The latter is the unique contribution of the discipline of teaching, or of education. And to teach astronomy, to continue our example, it is not particularly useful if teachers merely present what they have learned in the name of the most current version of astronomy without being able to interpret it in an overall perspective of the human inquiry into the mysteries of man and nature.

How has humankind, with all its subcultures across time and space, phrased and re-phrased its questions and invented and re-invented its conceptual models to answer them—that is the unique interpretation a teacher can and should convey through his teaching. Otherwise, he may transmit certain skills and knowledge within the restricted scope of his narrow and transient understanding without eliciting in students a wisdom for tomorrow. He may raise a generation of task-oriented technicians without guiding them to examine themselves and to appreciate the interrelatedness of human fate.

With all this in mind, let each reader try first to formulate his own answers to the many *questions* on teaching, to ponder the various *contexts* in which he engages in teaching, and to make his personal *model* explicit. Let him then examine carefully the writings of other teachers, found here and elsewhere, to clarify his thinking. (In several of the author's essays, a large number of footnotes have intentionally been employed to call the reader's attention to available sources of reference.) The reader will go through the process time and again of formulating questions and assessing answers, his own and others', so long as he remains and functions as a teacher. Good luck in the study of the many faces of teaching!

FOOTNOTES

[1] See the later selections in the present volume by Gage (pp. 337–353) and Yamamoto (pp. 355–365).

[2] O. G. Brim. "Socialization Through the Life Cycle," *Items* 18 (No. 1): 1–5; March 1964.

O. G. Brim and S. Wheeler. *Socialization After Childhood.* New York: John Wiley & Sons, 1966.

[3] Albert Bandura and Richard H. Walters. *Social Learning and Personality Development.* New York: Holt, Rinehart & Winston, 1963.

R. M. Gagne. *The Conditions of Learning.* New York: Holt, Rinehart & Winston, 1965.

Ernest R. Hilgard, Ed. *Theories of Learning and Instruction.* (63rd Yearbook, National Society for the Study of Education, Part I) Chicago: University of Chicago Press, 1964.

[4] B. F. Skinner. "The Science of Learning and the Art of Teaching," *Harvard Educational Review* 24: 86–97 (Winter 1954).

[5] Gilbert Highet. *The Art of Teaching.* New York: Vintage Books, Random House, 1950.

[6] Jacques Barzun. *Teacher in America.* Garden City. N.Y.: Doubleday Anchor Books, 1954.

[7] Highet, *op. cit.*

[8] See Yamamoto, pp. 317–325, in the present volume.

[9] For similar viewpoints, see the following:

Daniel Bell. *The Reforming of General Education.* New York: Columbia University Press, 1966.

Marc Belth. *Education as a Discipline.* Boston: Allyn and Bacon, 1965.

Elizabeth S. Maccia. "Logic of Education and of Educatology: Dimensions of Philosophy of Education," In Hugh C. Black, Ed. *The Proceedings of the Twentieth Annual Meeting of the Philosophy of Education Society.* Lawrence, Kansas: School of Education, University of Kansas, 1964. Pp. 99–109.

WHY

OUR EDUCATIONAL EMPHASES IN PRIMITIVE PERSPECTIVE

Margaret Mead

In its broadest sense, education is the cultural process, the way in which each new-born human infant, born with a potentiality for learning greater than that of any other mammal, is transformed into a full member of a specific human society, sharing with the other members a specific human culture. From this point of view we can place side by side the newborn child in a modern city and the savage infant born into some primitive South Sea tribe. Both have everything to learn. Both depend for that learning upon the help and example, the care and tutelage, of the elders of their societies. Neither child has any guaranty of growing up to be a full human

Reprinted from "Our Educational Emphases in Primitive Perspective," by Margaret Mead, *American Journal of Sociology* 48: 633–639 (May 1943); by permission of the University of Chicago Press. [Copyright 1943 by the University of Chicago.]

being should some accident, such as theft by a wolf, interfere with its human education. Despite the tremendous difference in what the New York infant and the New Guinea infant will learn, there is a striking similarity in the whole complicated process by which the child takes on and into itself the culture of those around it. And much profit can be gained by concentrating on these similarities and by setting the procedure of the South Sea mother side by side with the procedure of the New York mother, attempting to understand the common elements in cultural transmission. In such comparisons we can identify the tremendous potentialities of human beings, who are able to learn not only to speak any one of a thousand languages but to adjust to as many different rhythms of maturation, ways of learning, methods of organizing their emotions and of managing their relationships to other human beings.

In this paper, however, I propose to turn away from this order of comparison—which notes the differences between human cultures, primitive and civilized, only as means of exploring the processes which occur in both types of culture—and to stress instead the ways in which our present behavior, which we bracket under the abstraction "education," differs from the procedures characteristic of primitive homogeneous communities. I propose to ask, not what there is in common between America today and a South Sea culture which recently displayed a Stone Age level of culture, but to ask instead: What are some of the conspicuous differences, and what light do these differences throw upon our understanding of our own conception of education? And, because this is too large and wide a subject, I want to limit myself still further and to ask a question which is appropriate to this symposium: What effects has the mingling of peoples—of different races, different religions, and different levels of cultural complexity—had upon our concept of education? When we place our present-day concept against a backdrop of primitive educational procedures and see it as influenced by intermingling of peoples, what do we find?

I once lectured to a group of women—all of them college graduates—alert enough to be taking a fairly advanced adult-education course on "Primitive Education" delivered from the first point of view. I described in detail the lagoon village of the Manus tribe, the ways in which the parents taught the children to master their environment, to swim, to climb, to handle fire, to paddle a canoe, to judge distances and calculate the strength of materials. I described the tiny canoes which were given to the three-year-olds, the miniature fish spears with which they learned to spear minnows, the way in which small boys learned

OUR EDUCATIONAL EMPHASES IN PRIMITIVE PERSPECTIVE
Margaret Mead

to calk their canoes with gum, and how small girls learned to thread shell money into aprons. Interwoven with a discussion of the more fundamental issues, such as the relationship between children and parents and the relationships between younger children and older children, I gave a fairly complete account of the type of adaptive craft behavior which was characteristic of the Manus and the way in which this was learned by each generation of children. At the end of the lecture one woman stood up and asked the first question: "Didn't they have any vocational training?" Many of the others laughed at the question, and I have often told it myself as a way of getting my audience into a mood which was less rigidly limited by our own phrasing of "education." But that woman's question, naive and crude as it was, epitomized a long series of changes which stand between our idea of education and processes by which members of a homogeneous and relatively static primitive society transmit their standardized habit patterns to their children.

FROM LEARNING TO TEACHING *

There are several striking differences between our concept of education today and that of any contemporary primitive society; [1] but perhaps the most important one is the shift from the need for an individual to learn something which everyone agrees he would wish to know, to the will of some individual to teach something which it is not agreed that anyone has any desire to know. Such a shift in emphasis could come only with the breakdown of self-contained and self-respecting cultural homogeneity. The Manus or the Arapesh or the Iatmul adults taught their children all that they knew themselves. Sometimes, it is true, there were rifts in the process. A man might die without having communicated some particular piece of ritual knowledge; a good hunter might find no suitable apprentice among his available near kin, so that his skill perished with him. A girl might be so clumsy and stupid that she never learned to weave a mosquito basket that was fit to sell. Miscarriages in the smooth working of the transmission of available skills and knowledge did occur, but they were not sufficient to focus the attention of the group upon the desirability of *teaching* as over against the desirability of *learning*. Even with considerable division of labor and with

---

* *Editor's Note:* The three headings in this selection were added by the editor for readers' convenience. They are not the author's.

a custom by which young men learned a special skill not from a father or other specified relative but merely from a master of the art, the master did not go seeking pupils; the pupils and their parents went to seek the master and with proper gifts of fish or octopus or dogs' teeth persuaded him to teach the neophyte. And at this level of human culture even close contact with members of other cultures did not alter the emphasis. Women who spoke another language married into the tribe; it was, of course, very important that they should learn to speak the language of their husbands' people, and so they learned that language as best they could—or failed to learn it. People might compliment them on their facility or laugh at them for their lack of it, but the idea of *assimilating* them was absent.

Similarly, the spread of special cults or sects among South Sea people, the desire to *join* the sect rather than the need to make converts, was emphasized. New ceremonies did develop. It was necessary that those who had formerly been ignorant of them should learn new songs or new dance steps, but the onus was again upon the learner. The greater self-centeredness of primitive homogeneous groups (often so self-centered that they divided mankind into two group—the human beings, i.e., themselves, and the nonhuman beings, other people) preserved them also from the emphasis upon the greater value of one truth over another which is the condition of proselytizing: "*We* (human beings) do it this way and *they* (other people) do it that way." A lack of a desire to teach *them* our ways guaranteed also that the *we* group had no fear of any proselytizing from the *they* groups. A custom might be imported, bought, obtained by killing the owner, or taken as part of a marriage payment. A custom might be exported for a price or a consideration. But the emphasis lay upon the desire of the importing group to obtain the new skill or song and upon the desire of the exporting group for profit in material terms by the transaction. The idea of conversion, or purposely attempting to alter the ideas and attitudes of other persons, did not occur. One might try to persuade one's brother-in-law to abandon his own group and come and hunt permanently with the tribe into which his sister had married; physical proselytizing there was, just as there was actual import and export of items of culture. But once the brother-in-law had been persuaded to join a different cultural group, it was his job to learn how to live there; and you might, if you were still afraid he would go back or if you wanted his cooperation in working a two-man fish net, take considerable pains to teach him this or that skill as a bribe. But to bribe another by teaching him one's

OUR EDUCATIONAL EMPHASES IN PRIMITIVE PERSPECTIVE
Margaret Mead

own skill is a long way from any practice of conversion, although it may be made subsidiary to it.

We have no way of knowing how often in the course of human history the idea of Truth, as a revelation to or possession of some one group (which thereby gained the right to consider itself superior to all those who lacked this revelation), may have appeared. But certain it is that, wherever this notion of hierarchical arrangements of cultural views of experience appears, it has profound effects upon education; and it has enormously influenced our own attitudes toward education. As soon as there is any attitude that one set of cultural beliefs is definitely superior to another, the framework is present for active proselytizing, unless the idea of cultural superiority is joined with some idea of hereditary membership, as it is among the Hindus. (It would indeed be interesting to investigate whether any group which considered itself in possession of the most superior brand of religious or economic truth, and which did not regard its possession as limited by heredity, could preserve the belief in that superiority without proselytizing. It might be found that active proselytizing was the necessary condition for the preservation of the essential belief in one's own revelation.) Thus, with the appearance of religions which held this belief in their own infallible superiority, education becomes a concern of those who teach rather than of those who learn. Attention is directed toward finding neophytes rather than toward finding masters, and adults and children become bracketed together as recipients of conscious missionary effort. This bracketing-together is of great importance; it increases the self-consciousness of the whole educational procedure, and it is quite possible that the whole question of methods and techniques of education is brought most sharply to the fore when it is a completely socialized adult who must be influenced instead of a plastic and receptive child.

PROBLEMS OF ASSIMILATION

With social stratification the possibility of using education as a way of changing status is introduced, and another new component of the educational idea develops. Here the emphasis is still upon the need to learn—on the one hand, in order to alter status and, on the other, to prevent the loss of status by failure to learn. But wherever this possibility enters in there is also a possibility of a new concept of education developing from the relationship between fixed caste and class lines and education.

In a static society members of different caste or class groups may have been teaching their children different standards of behavior for many generations without any essential difference between their attitudes toward education and those of less complex societies. To effect a change it is necessary to focus the attention of the members of the society upon the problem, as conditions of cultural contact do focus it. Thus, in Bali, until recently the high castes were sending their daughters to the Dutch schools to be trained as schoolteachers because it was preeminently important that learning should be kept in the hands of the high castes and profoundly inappropriate that low-caste teachers should teach high-caste children. They felt this strongly enough to overcome their prejudices against the extent to which such a course takes high-caste women out into the market place.

As soon as the possibility of shift of class position by virtue of a different educational experience becomes articulately recognized, so that individuals seek not only to better their children or to guard them against educational defect but also to see the extension of restriction of educational opportunity as relevant to the whole class structure, another element enters in—the relationship of education to social change. Education becomes a mechanism of change. Public attention, once focused upon this possibility, is easily turned to the converse position of emphasizing education as a means toward preserving the status quo. I argue here for no historical priority in the two positions. But I am inclined to believe that we do not have catechumens taught to say "to do my duty in that state of life into which it has pleased God to call me" until we have the beginning of movements of individuals away from their birth positions in society. In fact, the whole use of education to defend vested interests and intrenched privilege goes with the recognition that education can be a way of encroaching upon them. Just as the presence of proselytizing religions focuses attention upon means of spreading the truth, upon pedagogy, so the educational implications of social stratification focus attention upon the content of education and lay the groundwork of an articulate interest in the curriculum.

Movements of peoples, colonization, and trade also bring education into a different focus. In New Guinea it is not uncommon to "hear" (i.e., understand without speaking) several languages besides one's own, and many people not only "hear" but also speak neighboring languages. A head-hunting people like the Mundugumor, who had the custom of giving child hostages to temporary allies among neighboring peoples, articulately recognized that it was an advantage to have members of

OUR EDUCATIONAL EMPHASES IN PRIMITIVE PERSPECTIVE
Margaret Mead

the group be well acquainted with the roads, the customs, and the language of their neighbors, who would assuredly at some time in any given generation be enemies and objects of attack. Those who took the hostages regarded this increased facility of the Mundugumor as a disadvantage which had to be put up with. But the emphasis remained with the desirability of learning. Today, with the growth of pidgin English as a lingua franca, bush natives and young boys are most anxious to learn pidgin. Their neighbors, with whom they could trade and communicate more readily if they knew pidgin, are not interested in teaching them. But the European colonist is interested. He sees his position as an expanding, initiating, changing one; he wants to trade with the natives, to recruit and indenture them to work on plantations. He needs to have them speak a language that he can understand. Accordingly, we have the shift from the native who needs to learn another language in order to understand to the colonist who needs someone else to learn a language so that he, the colonist, may be understood. In the course of teaching natives to speak some lingua franca, to handle money, to work copra, etc., the whole focus is on teaching; not, however, on techniques of teaching in the sense of pedagogy, but upon sanctions for making the native learn. Such usages develop rapidly into compulsory schooling in the language of the colonist or the conqueror, and they result in the schools' being seen as an adjunct of the group in power rather than as a privilege for those who learn.

Just as conquest or colonization of already inhabited countries brings up the problems of assimilation, so also mass migrations may accentuate the same problem. This has been true particularly in the United States, where education has been enormously influenced by the articulate need to assimilate the masses of European immigrants, with the resulting phrasing of the public schools as a means for educating other peoples' children. The school ceased to be chiefly a device by which children were taught accumulated knowledge or skills and became a political device for arousing and maintaining national loyalty through inculcating a language and a system of ideas which the pupils did not share with their parents.

It is noteworthy that, in the whole series of educational emphases which I have discussed here as significant components of our present-day concept of "education," one common element which differentiates the ideas of conversion, assimilation, successful colonization, and the relationship between class-caste lines and education from the attitudes found in primitive homogeneous societies is the acceptance of discontinuity between parents and children, even if the actual teacher was not a parent but a maternal uncle or a shaman. Modern education includes a heavy emphasis upon the function of education to create discontinuities—to turn the child of the peasant into a clerk, of the farmer into a lawyer, of the Italian immigrant into an American, of the illiterate into the literate. And parallel to this emphasis goes the attempt to use education as an extra, special prop for tottering continuities. Parents who are separated from their children by all the gaps in understanding which are a function of our rapidly changing world cling to the expedient of sending their children to the same schools and colleges they attended, counting upon the heavy traditionalism of slow-moving institutions to stem the tide of change. (Thus, while the father builds himself a new house and the mother furnishes it with modern furniture, they both rejoice that back at school, through the happy accident that the school is now well enough endowed, son will sit at the same desk at which his father sat.) The same attitude is reflected by the stock figure of the member of a rural school board who says, "What was good enough for me in school is good enough for my children. The three *R*'s, that's enough."

Another common factor in these modern trends of education is the increasing emphasis upon change rather than upon growth, upon what is done to people rather than upon what people do. This emphasis comes, I believe, from the inclusion of adults as objects of the educational effort—whether effort comes from missionaries, colonizers, conquerors, Old Americans, or employers of labor. When a child is learning to talk, the miracle of learning is so pressing and conspicuous that the achievement of the teacher is put in the shade. But the displacement, in an adult's speech habits, of his native tongue by the phonetics of some language which he is being bullied or cajoled into learning is often more a matter of triumph for the teacher than of pride for the learner. Changing people's habits, people's ideas, people's language, people's beliefs, people's emotional allegiances, involves a sort of deliberate violence to other people's developed personalities—a violence not to be found in the whole teacher-child relationship, which finds its prototype in the cherishing parent helping the young child to learn those things which are essential to his humanity.

We have been shocked in recent years by the outspoken brutality of the totalitarian states, which set out to inculcate into children's minds a series of new ideas which it was considered politically useful for them to learn. Under the conflicting currents of modern ideologies the idea of *indoctrination* has developed as a way of characterizing the conscious educational

OUR EDUCATIONAL EMPHASES IN PRIMITIVE PERSPECTIVE
Margaret Mead

aims of any group with whom the speaker is out of sympathy. Attempts to teach children any set of ideas in which one believes have become tainted with suspicion of power and self-interest, until almost all education can be branded and dismissed as one sort of indoctrination or another. The attempt to assimilate, convert, or keep in their places other human beings conceived of as inferior to those who are making the plans has been a boomerang which has distorted our whole educational philosophy; it has shifted the emphasis from one of growth and seeking for knowledge to one of dictation and forced acceptance of clichés and points of view. Thus we see that the presence of one element within our culture—a spurious sense of superiority of one group of human beings over another, which gave the group in power the impetus to force their language, their beliefs, and their culture down the throats of the group which was numerically, or economically, or geographically handicapped—has corrupted and distorted the emphases of our free schools.

TO SET THE FUTURE FREE

But there has been another emphasis developing side by side with those which I have been discussing, and that is a belief in the power of education to work miracles—a belief which springs from looking at the other side of the shield. As long as the transmission of culture is an orderly and continuous process, in a slowly changing society, the child speaks the language of his parents; and, although one may marvel that this small human being learns at all, one does not marvel that he learns French or English or Samoan, provided that this be the language of the parents. It took the discontinuity of educational systems, purposive shifts of language and beliefs between parents and children, to catch our imagination and to fashion the great American faith in education as creation rather than transmission, conversion, suppression, assimilation, or indoctrination. Perhaps one of the most basic human ways of saying "new" is "something that my parents have never experienced" or, when we speak of our children, "something I have never experienced." The drama of discontinuity which has been such a startling feature of modern life, and for which formal education has been regarded in great measure as responsible, suggested to men that perhaps education might be a device for creating a new kind of human being.

Here it is necessary to distinguish sharply between the sort of idea which George Counts expressed in his speech, "Dare the

School Build a New Social Order?"[2] and the idea of education as creation of something new. Dr. Counts did not mean a new social order in the sense of an order that no man had dreamed of, so much as he meant a very concrete and definite type of society for which he and many others believed they had a blueprint. He was asking whether the teachers would use the schools to produce a different type of socioeconomic system. His question was still a power question and partook of all the power ideas which have developed in the long period during which men in power, men with dominating ideas, men with missions, have sought to put their ideas over upon other men. His question would have been phrased more accurately as "Dare the schools build a different social order?" The schools of America have these hundred years been training children to give allegiance to a way of life that was new to them, not because they were children to whom all ways were new, not because the way of life was itself one that no man had yet dreamed of, but because they were the children of their parents. Whenever one group succeeds in getting power over the schools and teaches within those schools a doctrine foreign to many of those who enter those doors, they are building up, from the standpoint of those students, a different social order. From the standpoint of those in power, they are defending or extending the old; and, from the moment that the teachers had seriously started to put Dr. Counts's suggestion into practice, they would have been attempting by every method available to them to extend, in the minds of other people's children, their own picture, already an "old" idea, of the sort of world they wanted to live in.

It is not this sort of newness of which I speak. But from those who watched learning, those who humbly observed miracles instead of claiming them as the fruits of their strategy or of their superior teaching (propaganda) techniques there grew up in America a touching belief that it was possible by education to build a new world—a world that no man had yet dreamed and that no man, bred as we had been bred, could dream. They argued that if we can bring up our children to be freer than we have been—freer from anxiety, freer from guilt and fear, freer from economic constraint and the dictates of expediency—to be equipped as we never were equipped, trained to think and enjoy thinking, trained to feel and enjoy feeling, then we shall produce a new kind of human being, one not known upon the earth before. Instead of the single visionary, the depth of whose vision has kept men's souls alive for centuries, we shall develop a whole people bred to the task of seeing with clear imaginative eyes into a future which is hidden from us behind the smoke screen

OUR EDUCATIONAL EMPHASES IN PRIMITIVE PERSPECTIVE
Margaret Mead

of our defective and irremediable educational handicaps. This belief has often been branded as naive and simple-minded. The American faith in education, which Clark Wissler lists as one of the dominant American culture traits, has been held up to ridicule many times. In many of its forms it is not only unjustified optimism but arrant nonsense. When small children are sent out by overzealous schoolteachers to engage in active social reforms—believed necessary by their teachers—the whole point of view becomes not only ridiculous but dangerous to the children themselves.

Phrased, however, without any of our blueprints, with an insistence that it is the children themselves who will some day, when they are grown, make blueprints on the basis of their better upbringing, the idea is a bold and beautiful one, an essentially democratic and American idea. Instead of attempting to bind and limit the future and to compromise the inhabitants of the next century by a long process of indoctrination which will make them unable to follow any path but that which we have laid down, it suggests that we devise and practice a system of education which sets the future free. We must concentrate upon teaching our children to walk so steadily that we need not hew too straight and narrow paths for them but can trust them to make new paths through difficulties we have never encountered to a future of which we have no inkling today.

When we look for the contributions which contacts of peoples, of peoples of different races and different religions, different levels of culture and different degrees of technological development, have made to education, we find two. On the one hand, the emphasis has shifted from learning to teaching, from the doing to the one who causes it to be done, from spontaneity to coercion, from freedom to power. With this shift has come the development of techniques of power, dry pedagogy, regimentation, indoctrination, manipulation, and propaganda. These are but sorry additions to man's armory, and they come from the insult to human life which is perpetuated whenever one human being is regarded as differentially less or more human than another. But, on the other hand, out of the discontinuities and rapid changes which have accompanied these minglings of people has come another invention, one which perhaps would not have been born in any other setting than this one—the belief in education as an instrument for the creation of new human values.

We stand today in a crowded place, where millions of men mill about seeking to go in different directions. It is most uncertain whether the educational invention made by those who emphasized teaching or the educational invention made by those who emphasized learning will survive. But the more rapidly we can erase from our society those discrepancies in position and privilege which tend to perpetuate and strengthen the power and manipulative aspects of education, the more hope we may have that that other invention—the use of education for unknown ends which shall exalt man above his present stature—may survive.

FOOTNOTES

[1] This discussion, unless otherwise indicated, is based upon South Sea people only.

[2] G. Counts. *Dare the Schools Build a New Social Order?* New York: John Day Pamphlets, No. 11, 1932.

EDUCATION YESTERDAY AND TODAY

Kaoru Yamamoto

Consensus is a difficult thing to achieve. Nevertheless, if we are asked to define the purpose of education, our answer will likely be couched in individualistic and psychological terms rather than in collective and social ones. Thus, we would rather describe the school's function as facilitating each child's self-actualization than characterize it as, for example, mobilization of manpower. Our own schooling saw to it that we would discuss our profession only in certain terms acceptable to us.

When we turn to people wearing different glasses, however, we find that their view of the purpose of education tends to be noticeably different. Here is the statement of a sociologist.

> The message is very simple. Like so many obvious things, it is not only fundamental but also much overlooked. The main busi-

---

This essay is based upon a paper presented at the 1967 fall conference on "Middle School Ideas," at the College of Education, University of Toledo, Ohio, in November of 1967. The original title was, "America in Which Our Children Will Live: An Educational Perspective."

ness of socialization is the training of infants, children, adolescents (and sometimes adults) so that they can ultimately fulfill the social obligations that their society and culture will place on them.[1]

It is often painful for us to recognize that our schools do a remarkable job of screening, homogenization, and distribution of personnel, that schools perform useful punitive and custodial functions to serve the interest of adults who may not love the young so much as they profess they do, and that some of our zeal to teach children may be based more on our selfish, dominative needs than on altruistic, service motives.[2] For us, understandably, the school is the single central institution through which a self-renewing society may be molded into existence.

In a wider perspective, however, it must be admitted that "the history of education in America is one of unmistakable domination by other institutions which education traditionally has existed to serve.... Therefore, as religion, the family, business, and the state successively have dominated society, their influences have been evident in the classroom." [3] These social institutions, among others, are still here and will undoubtedly continue to influence American education in the coming years. Let us, therefore, examine each one of these briefly in the hope that some extrapolation can be made from the past and present to the future.[4]

RELIGION

The Protestant revolt which marked the beginning of modern America represented an effort to escape the control of the organized church. Ironically, the Puritans then established their own domination over the whole society. They developed and maintained a community (and a sense of community) characterized by close association, active participation, and ideological unity. Schools merely followed suit and taught children God's words. Theology, politics, and economics were inseparable, and education was permeated with religious values.[5]

As we now know, this state of affairs did not last too long. For one thing, sectarianism forced each sect to seek protection from domination by others in the form of the principle of the separation of church and state. Through the first amendment to the Constitution, as well as through various state constitutions, legal provisions were made to preserve people's right to hold religious views of their choice. While not intended originally to exclude teaching of religion from the public schools, these safety measures against sectarian teaching in fact accomplished such an exclusion precisely because the numerous sects have never been able to agree on what constitutes a common core of religious belief.[6]

Another reason for the dissipation of Puritan control was that Protestant theology itself gradually changed its character under the broad influence of science, the historical and cultural relativism in cosmology, the increasingly this-worldly emphasis in modern thought, and the shift (back) in Christian ethics from personal purity to social concern. In addition to these Western trends, the pragmatic and optimistic orientation in the United States tended to facilitate secularism. Thus, it was once said of American religion that, from the earliest days of Puritanism, its orientation has always been characterized by a concern for men living and acting here and now in the God-given environment of these great United States.[7]

It is reported that the churches now list the names of two-thirds of all Americans, while the proportion was only one-sixth in the 1850's. In 1957, 66.2 percent of Americans of age 14 and above classified themselves as Protestant, 25.7 percent as Roman Catholic, 3.2 percent as Jewish, 1.3 percent as believers in other religions, a mere 2.7 percent as not affiliating with any religion, and only 0.9 percent did not respond. Within the past half century, furthermore, the number of clergymen increased by more than two-thirds.[8] These figures certainly suggest the institutional strength of religion, and there are some who believe that the church will continue to perform an important function in coming years not only as a blessed community of Christians but also as an intellectual as well as international institution. Doctrines may come and go but the institution can remain to preserve a certain basic continuity.[9]

However, despite the marked increase in church affiliations, there has been a growing divergence in this century between religion and religious awareness. Most observers note a decline in theological concern, or a loss of the dimension of depth, which makes such institutional religion, prosperous as it may be, rather irrelevant to the world of today.[10]

> It [American church] is a "religious" institution of immense power, wealth, and prestige, but one characterized largely by secular values such as recreation, sociability, and sporadic good works in the community. The social value of such an institution is undoubted in our mobile, rootless, suburban culture. Whether it has any real *religious* character—whether it manifests a presence of the holy in its midst or offers a higher ethical standard for man's daily life—is something else again.[11]

The Ultimate Concern and Teaching Trivialization of religion and of its sacred symbols has caused much concern among theologians. Nietzsche's theme, "God is dead," has again given rise to a controversy which centers on the experience of the absence of God, rather than on the absence of the experience of God. Proponents of the God-is-dead philosophy emphasize the impossibility of responding to the classical images of the Creator and his creation and the necessity (or even desirability) of exposing Christian faith to the secular and profane while waiting for the return of God.[12] Social activism and an existential emphasis upon "the ultimate concern" (after Tillich) seem to represent two of the current reactions.[13]

In these efforts to regain meaningfulness of religion, interestingly, "Many Christians are discovering that the Judaeo-Christian world view was an illusory support of their faith, while many atheists are discovering that their own convictions have the structure of a faith." [14] Self-renewal of Christianity may still be possible with "a greater modesty, a greater sense of contingency and darkness, a greater sense of comradeship with non-Christians" [15] among Christians who realize that they are, after all, a decided minority in the multitudes of men.

Where, then, does school stand? What is the duty of teachers vis-à-vis such religious trends of tomorrow? It seems that education is faced with a challenge to restore the true spirit of religion by raising the basic questions that lie at the deepest level of man's existence. In this, we are obviously not concerned with any formal religion, any empty ritual patterns, or any dead symbols. Instead of being a sedative, religion would be regarded as the goad, the prod, and the gadfly to keep man and society alert, aware, and awake to their ideals, their imperfect actualities, and the formidable discrepancies between the two.[16]

It would help if schools were to cultivate children's social experiences so as to lead them to the discovery of religious moods. The richness of human emotion must be re-created in their own life, and the wisdom of the human species must be reconstructed in their own terms. In this process, they will perhaps learn what many of us have never fully recognized in our own lives. One of these ignored lessons is that it is the sin of sins to play God, to delude ourselves in believing we (armed with science and technology) are omniscient and omnipotent, and to forget our limitations and the nature of human existence. Another is that the belief in God as the Creator should symbolize the insight to worship creativity, not the accomplished products of creativity. In other words, "What needs to be sanctified are the processes which create value, not merely the values that have thus far been experienced."[17]

The call for teachers is clear. "At every level and in every subject area, from the first grade through the university, we need teachers who are deeply committed and ultimately concerned—teachers who are troubled by the basic human questions and who have had the courage to find their own direction."[18] The task may not be easy but the reward will be great. When a teacher, through his whole presence, transforms indifference and ignorance in his students into informed concern and commitment, he is indeed a teacher in the truest sense of the word.[19]

Image of Man, Work, and Leisure Closely related to the subject of religion is the matter of values. Many observers have noted the decline in Protestant ethic which emphasizes will, industry, thrift, and self-denial. Such morality, it has been observed, was based on individualism and the economy of privation, both of which have been fast vanishing from the American scene. The emerging value patterns seem to be geared instead to the industrialized and urbanized corporate society which demands a new kind of outlook and commitment.[20]

As the original Puritan concept of the depravity of man gradually gave way to the typical American belief in meliorism, environmentalism, and optimism concerning human nature, and as secure institutional values were slowly replaced by the process-oriented instrumental values of scientism and industrialization, our concepts of work and play have also shown some revealing changes. Rather vain efforts have been made to counteract decreasing intrinsic satisfaction in one's job (motivating factors) with an increase in extrinsic incentives such as higher wages, shorter work hours, longer paid vacation, and better recreational and working facilities (hygiene factors).[21] The end result is to compensate workers with money, time, and other amenities for their sacrifice, namely, their mechanical and insignificant work, so that they may enjoy their leisure which is their own life.

Interestingly, such interpretation of work still fits the Hebraic-Puritan values which regard work as the inescapable fate of cursed human beings forever condemned for their original sin. The Hellenic-Romantic interpretation of work as an inherently rewarding, play-like activity has added much to the educational emphasis upon child-centered curriculum, spontaneity and creativity, and extra-curricular activities; but it has not completely swung people's attitudes away from the hard-labor tradition.[22]

One aspect of this problem is the oft-mentioned fact that Americans work at play, making a serious enterprise out of their leisure activities, placing much importance on active participation and accomplishments in hobbies. This seems to assuage somewhat their guilt feelings about having freedom from imperative work, that is, about having time in order to do nothing.[23] This is a strange and painful paradox indeed:

> ... leisure is coming to occupy for adults something of the position the school already occupies for youngsters, of being the institution which seems "available" to bear the brunt of all society's derelictions in other spheres. Thus, just as schools are asked to become a quasi-parental, quasi-custodial, quasi-psychiatric, and quasi-everything else, filling in for tasks other institutions leave undone or badly done, with the result that the schools often cannot do their job of education adequately; so leisure is now being required to take up the energies left untapped everywhere else in our social order, with the result that it often fails in its original task of recreation for most of us most of the time and of creativity for some of us some of the time.[24]

Thus, while the leisure is ours, the skill to use it is not. And we have thrust upon the school the obligation of satisfying yet another social requirement. Increasingly, schools must teach their charges to develop individual tastes and proficiency in the use of spare time. What we must teach is simply this, "No leisure time will be enough for man to experience the joys of knowledge, of art and poetry, of devotion to great human causes, of communicating with others in the dreams and anxieties of the mind, of silently conversing with himself and silently conversing with God." [25]

In such preparatory efforts, it will be necessary to fuse our concepts of occupation (employed work) and leisure (voluntary or non-employed work) into a new concept of vocation. Vocation means purpose, commitment, and even a calling, for one's whole work life, remunerative or not, occupational or not. One works both for the fulfillment of self and for the fulfillment of others by developing all his capacities and talents, whether marketable or not, and using them in activities which are personally significant and collectively meaningful. Work must again be "love made possible" and this is the sense of vocation which we have to impart to our children.[26]

BUSINESS AND INDUSTRY

Max Weber's analysis of the close association between the Protestant ethic and the values of capitalism is well known. The transition in this country from a religious ideology to a commercial one was facilitated by an interpretation of profit motives as moral virtues. Expanding business, organization of labor, and the rise of state systems of education in the nineteenth century,[27] all worked to displace the earlier school function of religious character formation by the gradual inculcation of business values. It is a matter of record that educational leaders supported the position of businessmen and property owners during the period of early, laissez-faire industrialism.[28]

Education for the masses drew support first from business as a long-range security to placate the growing labor unrest and later from organized labor forces to offset the competition in employment. Thus, "The passage of state compulsory education laws requiring all children to remain in school until the age of sixteen followed closely upon laws establishing the same minimum age requirement for child labor in industry; compulsory education was not instituted until children no longer were needed in the labor market."[29]

Three additional observations must be made of these laws regarding child labor and compulsory attendance: first, the fact that the humanitarian trend at the turn of the century helped the movement to safeguard minors from mistreatment and cruelty; second, that the regulation of these matters remains in the hands of the states and not of the Federal government; and third, that several observers have been urging a re-examination of these earlier legislations in view of the recent social changes.[30]

As the business ideology permeated education, many concepts and practices were borrowed from business and industry. Especially in organizational and administrative spheres, preoccupation with *scientific* management has made the school administrator more an efficiency expert than an educator. Teacher evaluation has often been based on various *productivity* figures; thus, a teacher whose classes register mean achievement-test scores that are higher than national norms (which, as we should know, are not standards of performance at all) is a successful teacher; the teacher who has a number of students go on to college is effective; the teacher who gives out a higher-than-usual proportion of good or poor grades is suspect; the one who can process large classes without fuss or complaints knows how to teach; the one who has published a lot is a better teacher. Similarly, schools are judged on the basis of material and numerical tangibles such as average daily attendance figures, teacher-pupil ratio, assets of physical facilities, proportion of holders of advanced degrees among the faculty, dropout rate, or efficiency of room usage.[31]

Public relations and advertising are regarded as quite important and so are human relations within the school. First and foremost, teachers must fit into a smooth-running organization and children, too, are under much pressure to behave and achieve though they get little encouragement for developing their *competence*.[32]

Industrialization of Education

A more recent and more obvious case of assimilation of business-industrial philosophy in education is the rise of a hybrid specialty called educational technology and an all-out involvement of big corporations, such as the IBM, GE, Xerox, Litton Industries, and Raytheon, in the production and sales of educational goods and services. Teaching machines, audio-visual equipment, computers, and systems approach are expected to work wonders by modernizing the educational thought and practice.[33] Instructional process, when seen as a communication problem, is expected to be stripped of its mysteries and ineptitude through systematic technical analysis and instrumentation by operationally-oriented educational engineers and by efficiency-minded systems administrators who have ample funds at their disposal.[34]

Most leaders in education appear to hail this recent development in the name of progress and admonish teachers not to be old-fashioned and irrational in their reaction.[35] It seems indeed foolhardy not to take advantage of these "labor- and time-saving objective devices"[36] and of resources in research and development, technology, and management offered by industry which vouches to be "motivated by a keen sense of social responsibility and the strong desire to render a truly significant service to the American people by providing a truly significant service to American education."[37] Nevertheless, there are doubts and objections which deserve serious consideration lest activities should become their own justification.

First, there is the matter of ultimate goals or ends of education which scientists and engineers admit is of little concern to them.[38] Educational technology chooses to start its operations from observable and measurable behavioral units assumed to be the intermediate links to any *given* goals. This, however, leaves open the question not only of what these goals should be but also of which persons specify them and how.[39]

The value of "neutrality" claimed here is, further, more apparent than real. It cannot change the fact that science is based on a set of assumptions whose adoption represents a quite personal choice and commitment.[40] Nor can it ignore the oft-repeated observation that certain acknowledged means, by their nature, restrict the attainment of appropriate goals and even become ends in themselves.[41] Thus, it has been said that, as the means become more and more efficient and as the school is judged increasingly in terms of its efficiency as an educational machine, there remains less and less room for any human unpredictability. And "when, finally, there is no room for error there is also no room for insight and discovery."[42]

The predicament we are in becomes clearer if we think of the completion of such technological revolution in education. Assume that industrialization, so to speak, of education has been accomplished and the *business* of education is being run smoothly and seriously by professionals devoted to precision and efficiency. What then? What is there for schools to do other than doing what they are doing now, only faster and with less wastage? What difference would that make for teachers who already regard themselves as the dispensers of neatly packed commodities called facts or knowledge? They may *sell* these in larger quantities than they do now but the "professional" model of teachers (being available to offer service to needy clients), rather than the "artist" model (sharing one's own creative experience with others), will persist.[43] What is different between them and, say, salesmen?

And, finally, what would there be to justify the presence of a separate social institution called the school? After all, and understandably, "In defining the education market, or the knowledge market as it is sometimes called, industry views education in its broadest sense, embracing the full and ever-widening spectrum of learning situations—in the primary and secondary school classroom or on the college or university campus; in business, industry, civilian government, or the armed services."[44] Why should we then need anything over and above well-designed and skillfully-coordinated training programs within each of these institutions?

Even when the so-called technical revolution will have been completed, we will find ourselves still confronted with most of the *old* issues which are made more critical precisely because technology has run its course and thus lost its relevance and attraction. We may then realize, certainly much too late, that instruments and values of technology can not help us go beyond technology or solve any unfinished business in education. What we would need then and what we need now seems to be such human qualities as moral courage, commitment, or dedication, transcending the observable, measurable, manufacturable, or manipulable.[45] The time to think about the world beyond technology is now and, so far as education is concerned, this task may be far more crucial than any discussion within the technological-corporational value context itself.[46]

THE FAMILY

In the Colonial days, the family occupied a central place in the social structure and controlled most of the educational, religious, and economic functions in the community. Children were assets on the farm and many families were, therefore, unwilling to give them up to public education when the latter increased its demands in the mid-nineteenth century. Industrialization exacted further tolls in family autonomy by turning the flow of population from the farms to the cities, taking fathers away from home, assigning wives to strictly housekeeping and child-rearing roles, and making liabilities out of children. However, due to the continuing emphasis on technical sophistication, and due also to social stratification consonant with the new corporate structure, children were soon to regain their importance as agents of family prestige and mobility.[47] Their central position in the family has been strengthened by the fact that now, in the absence of many other familial functions, "sexual relations, childbearing, and child rearing have proportionately a much larger place in total family life than they once had;"[48] American parents seem to have become increasingly more permissive, psychology-conscious, and child-centered;[49] and success or failure as parents is largely judged on the basis of children's performance.[50]

Nevertheless, it is not easy to be a child in the world of today or tomorrow. Evidently, the child is under considerable stress, being required to serve many masters at one time.[51] He is to learn both to "get along with" others and to "get ahead of" others ("bureaucratic" and "entrepreneurial" orientations, respectively[52]). He is to help compensate for all the frustration, anxiety, and humiliation which his father suffers outside in the dehumanized, industrial world, and which his mother experiences in playing the confusing roles of the American female.[53] Living in an urban enclave or in suburban homogeneity, he is expected to learn to make social adaptations with little cross-group experience. He is to learn proper sex, vocational, and life roles when these are not clearly defined and where no adequate models are available.[54] He is encouraged to grow, yes, but grow into what kind of world? A world in which no human significance is felt, no humility is left, and no escape is seen from either the desperate population explosion or the threat of thermonuclear annihilation? Why should the child grow at all, especially when he is not recognized as a full-share participant despite having his whole future at stake?[55]

Schools to the Rescue   Nowadays, schools are supposed to be capable of solving any social issues and the present one is no exception. The school is now perceived as an institution in which the young are prepared for the radical transition from the private world of home and family, personal emotions and private symbols, to the public world of the great social superstructures, impersonal rationality and corporate symbols. The transformation of the child is obviously not a matter of *degree* (learning more of the same) but rather one of *kind* (learning different types of morality). It has been said that no American can escape being an organization man. Even if this observation is true, it does not mean that a man must fit the traditional definition—the cog in a huge and impersonal machine.[56] He may yet learn how to use the immense power of the organization for goals of value, for the good of humanity.

Within the family itself, children are first taught to develop some autonomy and next guided to adopt their proper sex roles. The first is a vertical differentiation, so to speak, on the basis of certain task proficiency, while the second is a horizontal sorting on the basis of the kind of tasks involved. Interestingly, this order of events seems to be repeated at successively higher levels of the educational institution.[57]

Thus, at the primary school level, pupils are confronted with a common set of task expectations and a common scale of evaluation. As a result, they distribute themselves hierarchically along the dimension of achievement, some complying with the external evaluative pressure better than others. Achievers are identified as *good* pupils and given status and encouragement. Unfortunately, in this early process, we may set a self-fulfilling prophecy in motion for *poor* ones and, worse yet, may stamp the sense of competence out of children's mind.[58] The secondary school, on the other hand, is more concerned with a role-type differentiation between those oriented toward scholarly pursuit and those who lean toward interpersonal relations. A leading crowd interested in athletic prowess and popularity is clearly separated from the minority who are academically committed.[59]

At a still higher level, colleges recycle the process by differentiating among students according to a narrower definition of achievement, thus sending the strongly achievement-oriented ones to the next level of formal training while directing the rest to the military, business, government, industry, etc. Finally at the graduate level, a further sifting is done in terms of role types. The results are the familiar distinction between "non-person-directed" and "person-directed" specialties,[60] between researchers and teachers (or administrators), or between performers and dramatizers.[61]

In this manner, we have traditionally followed a spiral process of screening, training, and distribution by differentiating students first vertically on proficiency and second horizontally on the type of activities. Whether this sequence of screening and sifting, or of selection and placement, serves in its present form our future needs is moot in view of the changing social structure and cultural requirements. For example, an emphasis in elementary schools on a limited variety of achievement tends to force many minority children out of any later consideration for a fair vocational sorting. It may also be noted that many novel occupational activities, as yet not clearly defined, would necessitate a reversal of this order, thus initially depending on the whereabouts of a person's interest and then developing certain performance requirements for later programs.

Within the sorting stages themselves, a difficulty may arise if the current specialization trend persists. Certainly the task-oriented and people-oriented activities will continue to appeal to different groups of people but the crucial question for education is how to create "an awareness that they share a common fate," [62] how to develop a sense of "historical identification" [63] among all human beings. Unless we can nurture a larger sense of "we-ness" through the recognition of a "common predicament" facing all of us, all palliative efforts to solve intergroup conflicts across sex, age, ethnic, religious, national, or other divisive lines are doomed to failure.[64] Can and would schools teach this fundamental wisdom?

THE STATE

"Because our government is a representative one, Americans have tended to seek political solutions for social problems. When tasks are not accomplished by private action, we delegate them to the public sector, to be taken care of by public action." [65] Within the past quarter century, governmental involvement in areas long considered outside the direct scope of the state has become increasingly heavier. Today, the proportion of government employees in the total labor force is more than 15 percent while it was less than 3 percent a century ago. Whereas 31 percent of the national income goes to Federal, state, and local taxes now, it was 14 percent a century ago. At the turn of the century, the Federal government received less than 20 percent of all taxes collected, but the amount has grown to 75 percent today.

As part of this general trend, education has been interpreted more and more in terms of the interests of the state and of the national manpower strategy in the current international crisis. Many a decision in education is made on "the assumption that the public school's primary responsibility is to train citizens who are useful to their country, just as certainly as an earlier goal was to train religious zealots useful to the church. Precisely as education has come to play a more important function in the economy, it has become more strategically involved in politics." [66] Schools are increasingly regarded as the principal agents of change for implementing public policies derived through political processes.[67] If we base our prediction upon historical trends, this phenomenon will persist for some time to come.

Several questions arise here. The first is whether any single social institution can perform as many functions as are now delegated to the educational institution. Conservation of social order and transmission of cultural heritage are themselves difficult tasks to accomplish in the fast-changing world. A sense of continuity and identity is indeed hard to find now, precisely when we need it to keep us sane and mindful of the interdependence of human fate. In addition to these tasks, the schools are charged with formulation of strategies for social change, with *selling* these novel ideas for tomorrow to the public of today, with providing trained personnel for execution of these plans, and with serving as custodial and remedial institutions for those who cannot quite make it. Can they really perform all these functions?

A clear, negative answer should perhaps be given to this query so as not to indulge in dreaming an impossible dream. On the other hand, even when the challenge is accepted, it must be recognized that the traditional entity of the institution of school is hard to maintain any more. New organizational, as well as functional, forms of education must be developed to satisfy the needs of the society and to make schooling closer and more relevant to the life and work of tomorrow's citizens. The historical idea of a community of scholars may not serve all these purposes in and of itself.[68]

Such de-institutionalization of schools will undoubtedly be stimulated by the massive efforts expended by the Federal government (Peace Corps, Job Corps, Teacher Corps, etc.), the military, and the business-industry.[69] Nevertheless, it must be seriously questioned whether the desired results are obtainable in any approaches in which the familiar institutional form and its control are left intact.[70] It is also debatable whether education based on strictly national goals is at all defensible in view of the world-wide values necessary to build a viable and just international order.[71]

EPILOGUE

This, then, has been one man's review of what has been, is, and will probably be our society and schools. While neither representative nor exhaustive, it has depicted some of the challenges education is destined to face in coming decades. Although the trends observed were arbitrarily classified according to the four major institutional forces which have influenced American education in the past—religion, the family, business, and the state—it is obvious that they are all interrelated and complex. It is hoped that an awareness of these issues may result in keener discussion and wiser decisions on specific problems within education itself.

Before concluding, however, we should consider one cautionary note. We know that schools, their structure, curriculum, and function, will change because, more than anything else, change is our *Zeitgeist*. It is automatically *good* to try out new ways and things; *not* to change is heretical. On the other hand, it is a fact that many fads and fashions have come and gone without affecting children a bit. Changes may be desirable but, if made only for their own sake, they may be far less than useful.

Many studies in education have tended to suggest that any new method of teaching is about as good as any old one, but no better, when judged in terms of student achievement. At the beginning, the educational innovator always gets much attention and publicity and everyone expects some miraculous increase in student learning. After a few years, and after a few studies, however, his method joins the rank of many, many old methods and is supplanted by still another "new" approach. This cycle has led one educational psychologist to wonder whether any of the rational decisions we make concerning the management of schooling really have much to do with the process of learning itself. The "mechanisms actually responsible for academic growth" may "reside in humble, spontaneous tendencies which are always in operation when an adult consorts with maturing children."[72]

The point is not that various administrative, curricular, and instructional arrangements should be left untouched but that we often forget the most important element in teaching–learning interactions because we are busy worrying about the tangible matters. It may be that not much more is required than the presence of an interested adult for children to feel secure and to grow in wisdom and strength. To replace the popular factory model of schooling where students are manufactured, so to speak, an agricultural model may be more useful in our thinking and practice. That is, our efforts must work *with* and *through* the basic, organic forces already set in motion in children themselves. Farmers may sleep but plants continue to grow. These natural processes must be appreciated, understood, and incorporated into the process of education—this could indeed be the biggest challenge facing the teachers of tomorrow.

FOOTNOTES

[1] Alex Inkeles. "Social Structure and the Socialization of Competence," *Harvard Educational Review* 36:265–283; Summer 1966. Quoted from p. 279.

[2] Burton R. Clark. *Educating the Expert Society.* San Francisco: Chandler Publishing, 1962.

Edgar Z. Friedenberg. *Coming of Age in America.* New York: Random House, 1963.

Jules Henry. *Culture Against Man.* New York: Random House, 1963.

Earl C. Kelley. *In Defense of Youth.* Englewood Cliffs, N.J.: Prentice-Hall, 1962.

Carol LeFever. "Why Teach?," *Elementary School Journal* 66: 121–125; December 1965.

Kaoru Yamamoto. "The Rewards and Results of Teaching," *Education* 87: 67–72; October 1966.

[3] Ronald G. Corwin. *A Sociology of Education.* New York: Appleton-Century-Crofts, 1965. Pp. 69–70.

[4] The danger in this attempt must be recognized at once. Social changes are a certainty but the unprecedented scope, speed, and complexity of these changes make any prediction precarious. This is especially true when it is recalled that our thinking seems characterized by an extrapolative style, namely, an assumption of linear continuity. See, e.g., David Riesman, "Leisure and Work in Post-Industrial Society." In W. Warren Kallenbach and Harold M. Hodges, Jr., Eds. *Education and Society.* Columbus, Ohio: Charles E. Merrill Books, 1963. Pp. 353–373.

[5] Merle L. Borrowman. "Traditiona Values and the Shaping of American Education." In Nelson B. Henry, Ed. *Social Forces Influencing American Education* (60th Yearbook of the National Society for the Study of Education, Part II). Chicago: University of Chicago Press, 1961. Pp. 144–170.

Corwin, *op. cit.*

[6] Ward Madden. "Education for Religious Quality in Experience." In Harold J. Carter, Ed. *Intellectual Foundations of American Education*. New York: Pitman Publishing Corp., 1965. Pp. 161–179.

See also, August W. Steinhilber. "The U.S. Supreme Court and Religion in the Schools," *Theory into Practice* 4: 8–13; February 1965.

[7] Langdon Gilkey. "Social and Intellectual Sources of Contemporary Protestant Theology in America," *Daedalus* 96: 69–98; Winter 1967.

[8] Murray Gendell and Hans L. Zetterberg. *A Sociological Almanac for the United States.* (2nd ed.) New York: Charles Scribner's Sons, 1964.

[9] Krister Stendahl. "Religion, Mysticism, and the Institutional Church," *Daedalus* 96: 854–859; Summer 1967.

[10] William Barrett. *Irrational Man.* New York: Doubleday & Co., 1958.

Donald N. Michael. *The Next Generation.* New York: Vintage Books, Random House, 1963.

Michael Novak. "Christianity: Renewed or Slowly Abandoned?" *Daedalus* 96: 237–266; Winter 1967.

Thomas F. O'Dea. "The Crisis of the Contemporary Religious Consciousness," *Daedalus* 96: 116–134; Winter 1967.

Paul Tillich. "The Lost Dimension in Religion." In Richard Thruelsen and John Kobler, Eds. *Adventures of the Mind.* New York: Alfred A. Knopf, 1960. Pp. 47–56.

[11] Gilkey, *op. cit.*, p. 79.

[12] Daniel Callahan. "The Quest for Social Relevance," *Daedalus* 96: 151–179; Winter 1967.

Emil L. Fackenheim. "On the Self-Exposure of Faith to the Modern-Secular World: Philosophical Reflections in the Light of Jewish Experience," *Daedalus* 96: 193–219; Winter 1967.

Martin E. Marty. "The Spirit's Holy Errand: The Search for a Spiritual Style in Secular America," *Daedalus* 96: 99–115; Winter 1967.

[13] Harvey G. Cox. "The 'New Breed' in American Churches: Sources of Social Activism in American Religion," *Daedalus* 96: 135–150; Winter 1967.

Marvin Fox. "Religion and the Public Schools—A Philosopher's Analysis," *Theory into Practice* 4: 40–44; February 1965.

Gilkey, *op. cit.*

Tillich, *op. cit.*

[14] Novak, *op. cit.*, p. 261.

[15] *Ibid.*, p. 253.

[16] Fox, *op. cit.*

[17] Madden, *op. cit.*, p. 170.

[18] Fox, *op. cit.*, p. 42.

[19] Fox, *op. cit.*

[20] Solon T. Kimball and James E. McClellan, Jr. *Education and the New America.* New York: Vintage Books, Random House, 1966.

Fred M. Newmann and Donald W. Oliver. "Education and Community," *Harvard Educational Review* 37: 61-106; Winter 1967.

David Riesman. "Some Questions About the Study of American Character in the Twentieth Century," *Annals of the American Academy of Political and Social Sciences* 370: 36-47; March 1967.

David Riesman, Nathan Glazer and Reuel Denney. *The Lonely Crowd.* New Haven, Conn.: Yale University Press, 1950.

George D. Spindler. "Education in a Transforming American Culture," *Harvard Educational Review* 25: 145-156; Summer 1955.

Allen Wheelis. *The Quest for Identity.* New York: W. W. Norton, 1958.

William H. Whyte, Jr. *The Organization Man.* New York: Simon & Schuster, 1956.

[21] Frederick Herzberg, Bernard Mausner and Barbara Snyderman. *The Motivation to Work.* New York: John Wiley & Sons, 1959.

Delbert C. Miller and William H. Form. *Industrial Sociology.* (2nd ed.) New York: Harper & Brothers, 1964.

[22] Borrowman, *op. cit.*

[23] Corwin, *op. cit.*

Robert M. MacIver. *The Pursuit of Happiness.* New York: Simon & Schuster, 1955.

[24] Riesman, "Leisure and Work in Post-Industrial Society," *op. cit.*, p. 366.

[25] Jacques Maritain. *Reflections on America.* Garden City, N.Y.: Image Books, Doubleday, 1964. Quoted from p. 90.

[26] C. Gilbert Wrenn. "Human Values and Work in American Life." In Henry Borow, Ed. *Man in a World at Work.* Boston: Houghton Mifflin, 1964. Pp. 24-44.

[27] H. G. Good. *A History of American Education.* (2nd ed.) New York: Macmillan, 1962.

[28] Merle Curti. *The Social Ideas of American Educators.* Paterson, N.J.: Littlefield, Adams, 1959.

[29] Corwin, *op. cit.,* p. 74.

[30] Friedenberg, *op. cit.*

Paul Goodman. *Compulsory Mis-education and the Community of Scholars.* New York: Vintage Books, Random House, 1966.

Kelley, *op. cit.*

[31] Raymond E. Callahan. *Education and the Cult of Efficiency.* Chicago: University of Chicago Press, 1962.

Corwin, *op. cit.*

V. T. Thayer and Martin Levit. *The Role of the School in American Society.* (2nd ed.) New York: Dodd, Mead, 1966.

Thorstein Veblen. *The Higher Learning in America.* New York: B. W. Huebsch, 1918.

[32] Henry, *op. cit.*

Kaoru Yamamoto. "For Each Tree Is Known . . .," pp. 249–260 of this volume.

[33] Phil C. Lange. "Future Developments." In Phil C. Lange, Ed. *Programed Instruction* (66th Yearbook of the National Society for the Study of Education, Part II). Chicago: University of Chicago Press, 1967. Pp. 284–325.

Marshall McLuhan and Quentin Fiore. *The Medium is the Massage.* New York: Bantam Books, 1967.

[34] H. A. Bern. "Wanted: Educational Engineers," *Phi Delta Kappan* 48: 230–236; January 1967.

Desmond L. Cook. *Program Evaluation and Review Technique: Applications in Education.* (OE–12024, Cooperative Research Monograph No. 17) Washington: Bureau of Research, Office of Education, U.S. Department of Health, Education, and Welfare, 1966.

B. F. Skinner. "Why We Need Teaching Machines," *Harvard Educational Review* 31: 377–398; Fall 1961.

[35] Cf., for example, the entire issue of the *Phi Delta Kappan* (Volume 48, Number 5, January 1967) on the topic, "Big Business Discovers the Education Market," edited by Myron Lieberman.

[36] Sidney L. Pressey. "Autoinstruction: Perspectives, Problems, Potentials." In Ernest R. Hilgard, Ed. *Theories of Learning and Instruction* (63rd Yearbook of the National Society for the Study of Education, Part I). Chicago: University of Chicago Press, 1964. Pp. 354–370. Quoted from p. 370.

[37] Edward L. Katzenbach. "Discussion: The Education Industries," *Harvard Educational Review* 37: 119–124; Winter 1967. Quoted from p. 123.

[38] Robert Glaser. "The Design of Instruction." In John I. Goodlad, Ed. *The Changing American School* (65th Yearbook of the National Society for the Study of Education, Part II). Chicago: University of Chicago Press, 1966. Pp. 215-242.

A. A. Lumsdaine. "Educational Technology, Programmed Learning, and Instructional Science." In Ernest R. Hilgard, Ed. *Theories of Learning and Instruction* (63rd Yearbook of the National Society for the Study of Education, Part I). Chicago: University of Chicago Press, 1964. Pp. 371-401.

Skinner, *op. cit.*

[39] Francis S. Chase. "School Change in Perspective." In John I. Goodlad, Ed. *The Changing American School* (65th Yearbook of the National Society for the Study of Education, Part II). Chicago: University of Chicago Press, 1966. Pp. 271-306.

[40] Marc Belth. *Education as a Discipline.* Boston: Allyn & Bacon, 1965.

Marjorie Grene. *The Knower and the Known.* New York: Basic Books, 1966.

Floyd W. Matson. *The Broken Image.* Garden City, N.Y.: Anchor Books, Doubleday, 1966.

[41] Kenneth Melvin. "McLuhan the Medium," *Phi Delta Kappan* 48: 488-491; June 1967.

Kaoru Yamamoto. "A Reflection upon Research in Education," *Journal of Teacher Education,* Winter 1968.

[42] Herbert A. Thelen. *Education and the Human Quest.* New York: Harper & Row, 1960. Quoted from p. 212.

[43] Donald W. Oliver. "Discussion: The Education Industries," *Harvard Educational Review* 37: 110-113; Winter 1967.

Yamamoto, "Rewards and Results of Teaching," *op. cit.*

[44] Katzenbach, *op. cit.,* p. 120.

[45] Kenneth Keniston. *The Uncommitted.* New York: Harcourt, Brace & World, 1965.

Kimball and McClellan, *op. cit.*

[46] Paul Goodman. "Discussion: The Education Industries," *Harvard Educational Review* 37: 107-110; Winter 1967.

Newmann and Oliver, *op. cit.*

[47] Corwin, *op. cit.*

[48] Raymond W. Mack. *Transforming America.* New York: Random House, 1967. Quoted from p. 44.

[49] Urie Bronfenbrenner. "The Changing American Child: A Speculative Analysis," *Journal of Social Issues* 17 (1): 6-18; 1961.

[50] Solon T. Kimball. "Cultural Influences Shaping the Role of the Child," *National Elementary Principal* 40: 28-32; September 1960.

[51] Kaoru Yamamoto. "Children Under Pressure," pp. 113–128 of the present volume.

[52] Daniel R. Miller and Guy E. Swanson. *The Changing American Parent.* New York: John Wiley & Sons, 1958.

[53] Betty Friedan. *The Feminine Mystique.* New York: W. W. Norton, 1963.

Henry, *op. cit.*

[54] Kimball, *op. cit.*

Margaret Mead. "The Life Cycle and Its Variations: The Division of Roles," *Daedalus* 96: 871–875; Summer 1967.

Patricia Minuchin. "Sex-Role Concepts and Sex Typing in Childhood as a Function of School and Home Environments," *Child Development* 36: 1033–1048; December 1965.

[55] John B. Calhoun. "Population Density and Social Pathology," *Scientific American* 206: 139–148; 1962.

Friedenberg, *op. cit.*

Paul Goodman. *Growing Up Absurd.* New York: Vintage Books, Random House, 1960.

Kelley, *op. cit.*

Keniston, *op. cit.*

[56] Kimball and McClellan, *op. cit.*, p. 315.

[57] Talcott Parsons. "General Theory in Sociology." In Robert K. Merton, Leonard Broom and Leonard S. Cottrell, Eds. *Sociology Today.* New York: Harper Torchbooks, 1965. Pp. 3–38.

[58] Yamamoto, "For Each Tree Is Known . . .," *op. cit.*

[59] James S. Coleman. *The Adolescent Society.* New York: The Free Press, 1961.

[60] Anne Roe. "Personality Structure and Occupational Behavior." In Henry Borow, Ed. *Man in a World at Work.* Boston: Houghton Mifflin, 1964. Pp. 196–214.

[61] Erving Goffman. *The Presentation of Self in Everyday Life.* Garden City, N.Y.: Anchor Books, Doubleday, 1959.

[62] Erik H. Erikson. "Memorandum on Youth," *Daedalus* 96: 860–870; Summer 1967.

[63] Milton M. Gordon. *Assimilation in American Life.* New York: Oxford University Press, 1964.

[64] Muzafer Sherif. *In Common Predicament.* Boston: Houghton Mifflin, 1966.

[65] Mack, *op. cit.*, pp. 127–128.

[66] Corwin, *op. cit.*, p. 85.

[67] J. Steele Gow, Jr., Burkart Holzner and William C. Pendleton. "Economic, Social, and Political Forces." In John I. Goodlad, Ed. *The Changing American School* (65th Yearbook of the National Society for the Study of Education, Part II). Chicago: University of Chicago Press, 1966. Pp. 159-199.

Galen Saylor. "The Federal Colossus in Education—Threat or Promise?" *Educational Leadership* 23: 7-14; October 1965.

[68] Harold Orlans. "Educational and Scientific Institutions," *Daedalus* 96: 823-831; Summer 1967.

[69] Appleton-Century-Crofts, Inc. *Guide to Federal Assistance for Education.* New York: 1966.

John Lunstrum. "The Mystique of the Peace Corps: A Dilemma," *Phi Delta Kappan* 48: 98-102; November 1966.

Frank Mankiewicz. "The Peace Corps Without Tears," *Phi Delta Kappan* 48: 103-104; November 1966.

Don W. Robinson, Ed. "Education and the Military," *Phi Delta Kappan* 48: 417-480; May 1967 (the entire issue, Number 3).

Ruth A. Roney. *The Doubleday Guide to Federal Aid Programs: 1966-67.* Garden City, N.Y.: Doubleday, 1966.

Jerry M. Rosenberg. *Automation, Manpower, and Education.* New York: Random House, 1966.

[70] H. Millard Clements. "Cities and Schools," *Phi Delta Kappan* 49: 94-97; October 1967.

Friedenberg, *op. cit.*

Newmann and Oliver, *op. cit.*

Robert H. Salisbury. "Schools and Politics in the Big City," *Harvard Educational Review* 37: 408-424; Summer 1967.

[71] Harold Taylor. "National Goals and International Goals," *Phi Delta Kappan* 47: 175-179; December 1965.

[72] J. M. Stephens. *The Process of Schooling.* New York: Holt, Rinehart & Winston, 1967. Quoted from p. 10.

THE AIMS
OF EDUCATION

Alfred N. Whitehead

                             Culture is activity of thought, and receptiveness to beauty and humane feeling. Scraps of information have nothing to do with it. A merely well-informed man is the most useless bore on God's earth. What we should aim at producing is men who possess both culture and expert knowledge in some special direction. Their expert knowledge will give them the ground to start from, and their culture will lead them as deep as philosophy and as high as art. We have to remember that the valuable intellectual development is self-development, and that it mostly takes place between the ages of

---

Reprinted with permission of The Macmillan Company and of the Cambridge University Press from *The Aims of Education* by Alfred North Whitehead. Copyright 1929 by The Macmillan Company, renewed 1957 by Evelyn Whitehead. This selection was taken from the Mentor Books edition, pp. 13–16 (New York: Mentor Books, The New American Library of World Literature). The selection was based on Whitehead's presidential address to the Mathematical Association of England, 1916.

sixteen and thirty. As to training, the most important part is given by mothers before the age of twelve. A saying due to Archbishop Temple illustrates my meaning. Surprise was expressed at the success in after-life of a man, who as a boy at Rugby had been somewhat undistinguished. He answered, "It is not what they are at eighteen, it is what they become afterwards that matters."

INERT IDEAS IN EDUCATION *

In training a child to activity of thought, above all things we must beware of what I will call "inert ideas"—that is to say, ideas that are merely received into the mind without being utilised, or tested, or thrown into fresh combinations.

In the history of education, the most striking phenomenon is that schools of learning, which at one epoch are alive with a ferment of genius, in a succeeding generation exhibit merely pedantry and routine. The reason is, that they are overladen with inert ideas. Education with inert ideas is not only useless: it is, above all things, harmful—*Corruptio optimi, pessima.* Except at rare intervals of intellectual ferment, education in the past has been radically infected with inert ideas. That is the reason why uneducated clever women, who have seen much of the world, are in middle life so much the most cultured part of the community. They have been saved from this horrible burden of inert ideas. Every intellectual revolution which has ever stirred humanity into greatness has been a passionate protest against inert ideas. Then, alas, with pathetic ignorance of human psychology, it has proceeded by some educational scheme to bind humanity afresh with inert ideas of its own fashioning.

Let us now ask how in our system of education we are to guard against this mental dryrot. We enunciate two educational commandments, "Do not teach too many subjects," and again, "What you teach, teach thoroughly."

The result of teaching small parts of a large number of subjects is the passive reception of disconnected ideas, not illumined with any spark of vitality. Let the main ideas which are introduced into a child's education be few and important, and let them be thrown into every combination possible. The child should make them his own, and should understand their application here and now in the circumstances of his actual life. From

---

* *Editor's Note:* The three headings in this selection were added by the editor for the reader's convenience. They are not the author's.

54

THE AIMS OF EDUCATION
Alfred N. Whitehead

the very beginning of his education, the child should experience the joy of discovery. The discovery which he has to make, is that general ideas give an understanding of that stream of events which pours through his life, which is his life. By understanding I mean more than a mere logical analysis, though that is included. I mean "understanding" in the sense in which it is used in the French proverb, "To understand all, is to forgive all." Pedants sneer at an education which is useful. But if education is not useful, what is it? Is it a talent, to be hidden away in a napkin? Of course, education should be useful, whatever your aim in life. It was useful to Saint Augustine and it was useful to Napoleon. It is useful, because understanding is useful.

I pass lightly over that understanding which should be given by the literary side of education. Nor do I wish to be supposed to pronounce on the relative merits of a classical or a modern curriculum. I would only remark that the understanding which we want is an understanding of an insistent present. The only use of a knowledge of the past is to equip us for the present. No more deadly harm can be done to young minds than by depreciation of the present. The present contains all that there is. It is holy ground; for it is the past, and it is the future. At the same time it must be observed that an age is no less past if it existed two hundred years ago than if it existed two thousand years ago. Do not be deceived by the pedantry of dates. The ages of Shakespeare and of Molière are no less past than are the ages of Sophocles and of Virgil. The communion of saints is a great and inspiring assemblage, but it has only one possible hall of meeting, and that is, the present; and the mere lapse of time through which any particular group of saints must travel to reach that meeting-place, makes very little difference.

Passing now to the scientific and logical side of education, we remember that here also ideas which are not utilised are positively harmful. By utilising an idea, I mean relating it to that stream, compounded of sense perceptions, feelings, hopes, desires, and of mental activities adjusting thought to thought, which forms our life. I can imagine a set of beings which might fortify their souls by passively reviewing disconnected ideas. Humanity is not built that way—except perhaps some editors of newspapers.

In scientific training, the first thing to do with an idea is to prove it. But allow me for one moment to extend the meaning of "prove"; I mean—to prove its worth. Now an idea is not worth much unless the propositions in which it is embodied are true. Accordingly an essential part of the proof of an idea is the proof, either by experiment or by logic, of the truth of the propositions. But it is not essential that this proof of the truth should constitute the first introduction to the idea. After all, its assertion by the authority of respectable teachers is sufficient evidence to begin with. In our first contact with a set of propositions, we commence by appreciating their importance. That is what we all do in after-life. We do not attempt, in the strict sense, to prove or to disprove anything, unless its importance makes it worthy of that honour. These two processes of proof, in the narrow sense, and of appreciation, do not require a rigid separation in time. Both can be proceeded with nearly concurrently. But in so far as either process must have the priority, it should be that of appreciation by use.

Furthermore, we should not endeavour to use propositions in isolation. Emphatically I do not mean, a neat little set of experiments to illustrate Proposition I and then the proof of Proposition I, a neat little set of experiments to illustrate Proposition II and then the proof of Proposition II, and so on to the end of the book. Nothing could be more boring. Interrelated truths are utilised *en bloc,* and the various propositions are employed in any order, and with any reiteration. Choose some important applications of your theoretical subject; and study them concurrently with the systematic theoretical exposition. Keep the theoretical exposition short and simple, but let it be strict and rigid so far as it goes. It should not be too long for it to be easily known with thoroughness and accuracy. The consequences of a plethora of half-digested theoretical knowledge are deplorable. Also the theory should not be muddled up with the practice. The child should have no doubt when it is proving and when it is utilising. My point is that what is proved should be utilised, and that what is utilised should—so far as is practicable —be proved. I am far from asserting that proof and utilisation are the same thing.

At this point of my discourse, I can most directly carry forward my argument in the outward form of a digression. We are only just realising that the art and science of education require a genius and a study of their own; and that this genius and this science are more than a bare knowledge of some branch of science or of literature. This truth was partially perceived in the past generation; and headmasters, somewhat crudely, were apt to supersede learning in their colleagues by requiring left-hand bowling and a taste for football. But culture is more than cricket, and more than football, and more than extent of knowledge.

Education is the acquisition of the art of the utilisation of

THE AIMS OF EDUCATION
Alfred N. Whitehead

knowledge. This is an art very difficult to impart. Whenever a text-book is written of real educational worth, you may be quite certain that some reviewer will say that it will be difficult to teach from it. Of course it will be difficult to teach from it. If it were easy, the book ought to be burned; for it cannot be educational. In education, as elsewhere, the broad primrose path leads to a nasty place. This evil path is represented by a book or a set of lectures which will practically enable the student to learn by heart all the questions likely to be asked at the next external examination. And I may say in passing that no educational system is possible unless every question directly asked of a pupil at any examination is either framed or modified by the actual teacher of that pupil in that subject. The external assessor may report on the curriculum or on the performance of the pupils, but never should be allowed to ask the pupil a question which has not been strictly supervised by the actual teacher, or at least inspired by a long conference with him. There are a few exceptions to this rule, but they are exceptions, and could easily be allowed for under the general rule.

We now return to my previous point, that theoretical ideas should always find important applications within the pupil's curriculum. This is not an easy doctrine to apply, but a very hard one. It contains within itself the problem of keeping knowledge alive, of preventing it from becoming inert, which is the central problem of all education.

The best procedure will depend on several factors, none of which can be neglected, namely, the genius of the teacher, the intellectual type of the pupils, their prospects in life, the opportunities offered by the immediate surroundings of the school, and allied factors of this sort. It is for this reason that the uniform external examination is so deadly. We do not denounce it because we are cranks, and like denouncing established things. We are not so childish. Also, of course, such examinations have their use in testing slackness. Our reason of dislike is very definite and very practical. It kills the best part of culture. When you analyse in the light of experience the central task of education, you find that its successful accomplishment depends on a delicate adjustment of many variable factors. The reason is that we are dealing with human minds, and not with dead matter. The evocation of curiosity, of judgment, of the power of mastering a complicated tangle of circumstances, the use of theory in giving foresight in special cases—all these powers are not to be imparted by a set rule embodied in one schedule of examination subjects.

KEEPING KNOWLEDGE ALIVE

I appeal to you, as practical teachers. With good discipline, it is always possible to pump into the minds of a class a certain quantity of inert knowledge. You take a textbook and make them learn it. So far, so good. The child then knows how to solve a quadratic equation. But what is the point of teaching a child to solve a quadratic equation? There is a traditional answer to this question. It runs thus: The mind is an instrument, you first sharpen it, and then use it; the acquisition of the power of solving a quadratic equation is part of the process of sharpening the mind. Now there is just enough truth in this answer to have made it live through the ages. But for all its half-truth, it embodies a radical error which bids fair to stifle the genius of the modern world. I do not know who was first responsible for this analogy of the mind to a dead instrument. For aught I know, it may have been one of the seven wise men of Greece, or a committee of the whole lot of them. Whoever was the originator, there can be no doubt of the authority which it has acquired by the continuous approval bestowed upon it by eminent persons. But whatever its weight of authority, whatever the high approval which it can quote, I have no hesitation in denouncing it as one of the most fatal, erroneous, and dangerous conceptions ever introduced in the theory of education. The mind is never passive; it is a perpetual activity, delicate, receptive, responsive to stimulus. You cannot postpone its life until you have sharpened it. Whatever interest attaches to your subject-matter must be evoked here and now; whatever powers you are strengthening in the pupil, must be exercised here and now; whatever possibilities of mental life your teaching should impart, must be exhibited here and now. That is the golden rule of education, and a very difficult rule to follow.

The difficulty is just this: the apprehension of general ideas, intellectual habits of mind, and pleasurable interest in mental achievement can be evoked by no form of words, however accurately adjusted. All practical teachers know that education is a patient process of the mastery of details, minute by minute, hour by hour, day by day. There is no royal road to learning through an airy path of brilliant generalisations. There is a proverb about the difficulty of seeing the wood because of the trees. That difficulty is exactly the point which I am enforcing. The problem of education is to make the pupil see the wood by means of the trees.

The solution which I am urging, is to eradicate the fatal disconnection of subjects which kills the vitality of our modern

THE AIMS OF EDUCATION
Alfred N. Whitehead

curriculum. There is only one subject-matter for education, and that is Life in all its manifestations. Instead of this single unity, we offer children—Algebra, from which nothing follows; Geometry, from which nothing follows; Science, from which nothing follows; History, from which nothing follows; a Couple of Languages, never mastered; and lastly, most dreary of all, Literature, represented by plays of Shakespeare, with philological notes and short analyses of plot and character to be in substance committed to memory. Can such a list be said to represent Life, as it is known in the midst of the living of it? The best that can be said of it is, that it is a rapid table of contents which a deity might run over in his mind while he was thinking of creating a world, and had not yet determined how to put it together.

Let us now return to quadratic equations. We still have on hand the unanswered question. Why should children be taught their solution? Unless quadratic equations fit into a connected curriculum, of course, there is no reason to teach anything about them. Furthermore, extensive as should be the place of mathematics in a complete culture, I am a little doubtful whether for many types of boys algebraic solutions of quadratic equations do not lie on the specialist side of mathematics. I may here remind you that as yet I have not said anything of the psychology or the content of the specialism, which is so necessary a part of an ideal education. But all that is an evasion of our real question, and I merely state it in order to avoid being misunderstood in my answer.

Quadratic equations are part of algebra, and algebra is the intellectual instrument which has been created for rendering clear the quantitative aspects of the world. There is no getting out of it. Through and through the world is infected with quantity. To talk sense, is to talk in quantities. It is no use saying that the nation is large,—How large? It is no use saying that radium is scarce,—How scarce? You cannot evade quantity. You may fly to poetry and to music, and quantity and number will face you in your rhythms and your octaves. Elegant intellects which despise the theory of quantity, are but half developed. They are more to be pitied than blamed. The scraps of gibberish, which in their school-days were taught to them in the name of algebra, deserve some contempt.

This question of the degeneration of algebra into gibberish, both in word and in fact, affords a pathetic instance of the uselessness of reforming educational schedules without a clear conception of the attributes which you wish to evoke in the living minds of the children. A few years ago there was an outcry that school algebra was in need of reform, but there was a general agreement that graphs would put everything right. So all sorts of things were extruded, and graphs were introduced. So far as I can see, with no sort of idea behind them, but just graphs. Now every examination paper has one or two questions on graphs. Personally, I am an enthusiastic adherent of graphs. But I wonder whether as yet we have gained very much. You cannot put life into any schedule of general education unless you succeed in exhibiting its relation to some essential characteristic of all intelligent or emotional perception. It is a hard saying, but it is true; and I do not see how to make it any easier. In making these little formal alterations you are beaten by the very nature of things. You are pitted against too skilful an adversary, who will see to it that the pea is always under the other thimble.

Reformation must begin at the other end. First, you must make up your mind as to those quantitative aspects of the world which are simple enough to be introduced into general education; then a schedule of algebra should be framed which will about find its exemplification in these applications. We need not fear for our pet graphs, they will be there in plenty when we once begin to treat algebra as a serious means of studying the world. Some of the simplest applications will be found in the quantities which occur in the simplest study of society. The curves of history are more vivid and more informing than the dry catalogues of names and dates which comprise the greater part of that arid school study. What purpose is effected by a catalogue of undistinguished kings and queens? Tom, Dick, or Harry, they are all dead. General resurrections are failures, and are better postponed. The quantitative flux of the forces of modern society is capable of very simple exhibition. Meanwhile, the ideas of the variable, of the function, of rate of change, of equations and their solution, of elimination, are being studied as an abstract science for their own sake. Not, of course, in the pompous phrases with which I am alluding to them, here, but with that iteration of simple special cases proper to teaching.

If this course be followed, the route from Chaucer to the Black Death, from the Black Death to modern Labour troubles, will connect the tales of the mediaeval pilgrims with the abstract science of algebra, both yielding diverse aspects of that single theme, Life. I know what most of you are thinking at this point. It is that the exact course which I have sketched out is not the particular one which you would have chosen, or even see how to work. I quite agree. I am not claiming that I could do it myself. But your objection is the precise reason why a common external examination system is fatal to education. The process of exhibiting the applications of knowledge must, for its success, essen-

THE AIMS OF EDUCATION
Alfred N. Whitehead

tially depend on the character of the pupils and the genius of the teacher. Of course I have left out the easiest applications with which most of us are more at home. I mean the quantitative sides of sciences, such as mechanics and physics.

Again, in the same connection we plot the statistics of social phenomena against the time. We then eliminate the time between suitable pairs. We can speculate how far we have exhibited a real causal connection, or how far a mere temporal coincidence. We notice that we might have plotted against the time one set of statistics for one country and another set for another country, and thus, with suitable choice of subjects, have obtained graphs which certainly exhibited mere coincidence. Also other graphs exhibit obvious causal connections. We wonder how to discriminate. And so are drawn on as far as we will.

But in considering this description, I must beg you to remember what I have been insisting on above. In the first place, one train of thought will not suit all groups of children. For example, I should expect that artisan children will want something more concrete and, in a sense, swifter than I have set down here. Perhaps I am wrong, but that is what I should guess. In the second place, I am not contemplating one beautiful lecture stimulating, once and for all, an admiring class. That is not the way in which education proceeds. No; all the time the pupils are hard at work solving examples, drawing graphs, and making experiments, until they have a thorough hold on the whole subject. I am describing the interspersed explanations, the directions which should be given to their thoughts. The pupils have got to be made to feel that they are studying something, and are not merely executing intellectual minuets.

Finally, if you are teaching pupils for some general examination, the problem of sound teaching is greatly complicated. Have you ever noticed the zig-zag moulding round a Norman arch? The ancient work is beautiful, the modern work is hideous. The reason is, that the modern work is done to exact measure, the ancient work is varied according to the idiosyncrasy of the workman. Here it is crowded, and there it is expanded. Now the essence of getting pupils through examinations is to give equal weight to all parts of the schedule. But mankind is naturally specialist. One man sees a whole subject, where another can find only a few detached examples. I know that it seems contradictory to allow for specialism in a curriculum especially designed for a broad culture. Without contradictions the world would be simpler, and perhaps duller. But I am certain that in education wherever you exclude specialism you destroy life.

We now come to the other great branch of a general mathematical education, namely Geometry. The same principles apply. The theoretical part should be clear-cut, rigid, short, and important. Every proposition not absolutely necessary to exhibit the main connection of ideas should be cut out, but the great fundamental ideas should be all there. No omission of concepts, such as those of Similarity and Proportion. We must remember that, owing to the aid rendered by the visual presence of a figure, Geometry is a field of unequalled excellence for the exercise of the deductive faculties of reasoning. Then, of course, there follows Geometrical Drawing, with its training for the hand and eye.

But, like Algebra, Geometry and Geometrical Drawing must be extended beyond the mere circle of geometrical ideas. In an industrial neighbourhood, machinery and workshop practice form the appropriate extension. For example, in the London Polytechnics this has been achieved with conspicuous success. For many secondary schools I suggest that surveying and maps are the natural applications. In particular, plane-table surveying should lead pupils to a vivid apprehension of the immediate application of geometric truths. Simple drawing apparatus, a surveyor's chain, and surveyor's compass, should enable the pupils to rise from the survey and mensuration of a field to the construction of the map of a small district. The best education is to be found in gaining the utmost information from the simplest apparatus. The provision of elaborate instruments is greatly to be deprecated. To have constructed the map of a small district, to have considered its roads, its contours, its geology, its climate, its relation to other districts, the effects on the status of its inhabitants, will teach more history and geography than any knowledge of Perkin Warbeck or of Behren's Straits. I mean not a nebulous lecture on the subject, but a serious investigation in which the real facts are definitely ascertained by the aid of accurate theoretical knowledge. A typical mathematical problem should be: Survey such and such a field, draw a plan of it to such and such a scale, and find the area. It would be quite a good procedure to impart the necessary geometrical propositions without their proofs. Then, concurrently in the same term, the proofs of the propositions would be learnt while the survey was being made.

THE GENERAL AND THE SPECIAL

Fortunately, the specialist side of education presents an easier problem than does the provision of a general culture. For

THE AIMS OF EDUCATION
Alfred N. Whitehead

this there are many reasons. One is that many of the principles of procedure to be observed are the same in both cases, and it is unnecessary to recapitulate. Another reason is that specialist training takes place—or should take place—at a more advanced stage of the pupil's course, and thus there is easier material to work upon. But undoubtedly the chief reason is that the specialist study is normally a study of peculiar interest to the student. He is studying it because, for some reason, he wants to know it. This makes all the difference. The general culture is designed to foster an activity of mind; the specialist course utilises this activity. But it does not do to lay too much stress on these neat antitheses. As we have already seen, in the general course foci of special interest will arise; and similarly in the special study, the external connexions of the subject drag thought outwards.

Again, there is not one course of study which merely gives general culture, and another which gives special knowledge. The subjects pursued for the sake of a general education are special subjects specially studied; and, on the other hand, one of the ways of encouraging general mental activity is to foster a special devotion. You may not divide the seamless coat of learning. What education has to impart is an intimate sense for the power of ideas, for the beauty of ideas, and for the structure of ideas, together with a particular body of knowledge which has peculiar reference to the life of the being possessing it.

The appreciation of the structure of ideas is that side of a cultured mind which can only grow under the influence of a special study. I mean that eye for the whole chessboard, for the bearing of one set of ideas on another. Nothing but a special study can give any appreciation for the exact formulation of general ideas, for their relations when formulated, for their service in the comprehension of life. A mind so disciplined should be both more abstract and more concrete. It has been trained in the comprehension of abstract thought and in the analysis of facts.

Finally, there should grow the most austere of all mental qualities; I mean the sense for style. It is an aesthetic sense, based on admiration for the direct attainment of a foreseen end, simply and without waste. Style in art, style in literature, style in science, style in logic, style in practical execution have fundamentally the same aesthetic qualities, namely, attainment and restraint. The love of a subject in itself and for itself, where it is not the sleepy pleasure of pacing a mental quarter-deck, is the love of style as manifested in that study.

Here we are brought back to the position from which we started, the utility of education. Style, in its finest sense, is the last acquirement of the educated mind; it is also the most useful. It pervades the whole being. The administrator with a sense for style hates waste; the engineer with a sense for style economises his material; the artisan with a sense for style prefers good work. Style is the ultimate morality of mind.

But above style, and above knowledge, there is something, a vague shape like fate above the Greek gods. That something is Power. Style is the fashioning of power, the restraining of power. But, after all, the power of attainment of the desired end is fundamental. The first thing is to get there. Do not bother about your style, but solve your problem, justify the ways of God to man, administer your province, or do whatever else is set before you.

Where, then, does style help? In this, with style the end is attained without side issues, without raising undesirable inflammations. With style you attain your end and nothing but your end. With style the effect of your activity is calculable, and foresight is the last gift of gods to men. With style your power is increased, for your mind is not distracted with irrelevancies, and you are more likely to attain your object. Now style is the exclusive privilege of the expert. Whoever heard of the style of an amateur painter, of the style of an amateur poet? Style is always the product of specialist study, the peculiar contribution of specialism to culture.

English education in its present phase suffers from a lack of definite aim, and from an external machinery which kills its vitality. Hitherto in this address I have been considering the aims which should govern education. In this respect England halts between two opinions. It has not decided whether to produce amateurs or experts. The profound change in the world which the nineteenth century has produced is that the growth of knowledge has given foresight. The amateur is essentially a man with appreciation and with immense versatility in mastering a given routine. But he lacks the foresight which comes from special knowledge. The object of this address is to suggest how to produce the expert without loss of the essential virtues of the amateur. The machinery of our secondary education is rigid where it should be yielding, and lax where it should be rigid. Every school is bound on pain of extinction to train its boys for a small set of definite examinations. No headmaster has a free hand to develop his general education or his specialist studies in accordance with the opportunities of his school, which are created by its staff, its environment, its class of boys, and its endowments. I suggest that no system of external tests which

THE AIMS OF EDUCATION
Alfred N. Whitehead

aims primarily at examining individual scholars can result in anything but educational waste.

Primarily it is the schools and not the scholars which should be inspected. Each school should grant its own leaving certificates, based on its own curriculum. The standards of these schools should be sampled and corrected. But the first requisite for educational reform is the school as a unit, with its approved curriculum based on its own needs, and evolved by its own staff. If we fail to secure that, we simply fall from one formalism into another, from one dung-hill of inert ideas into another.

In stating that the school is the true educational unit in any national system for the safeguarding of efficiency, I have conceived the alternative system as being the external examination of the individual scholar. But every Scylla is faced by its Charybdis—or, in more homely language, there is a ditch on both sides of the road. It will be equally fatal to education if we fall into the hands of a supervising department which is under the impression that it can divide all schools into two or three rigid categories, each type being forced to adopt a rigid curriculum. When I say that the school is the educational unit, I mean exactly what I say, no larger unit, no smaller unit. Each school must have the claim to be considered in relation to its special circumstances. The classifying of schools for some purposes is necessary. But no absolutely rigid curriculum, not modified by its own staff, should be permissible. Exactly the same principles apply, with the proper modifications, to universities and to technical colleges.

When one considers in its length and in its breadth the importance of this question of the education of a nation's young, the broken lives, the defeated hopes, the national failures, which result from the frivolous inertia with which it is treated, it is difficult to restrain within oneself a savage rage. In the conditions of modern life the rule is absolute, the race which does not value trained intelligence is doomed. Not all your heroism, not all your social charm, not all your wit, not all your victories on land or at sea, can move back the finger of fate. To-day we maintain ourselves. To-morrow science will have moved forward yet one more step, and there will be no appeal from the judgment which will then be pronounced on the uneducated.

We can be content with no less than the old summary of educational ideal which has been current at any time from the dawn of our civilisation. The essence of education is that it be religious.

Pray, what is religious education?

A religious education is an education which inculcates duty and reverence. Duty arises from our potential control over the course of events. Where attainable knowledge could have changed the issue, ignorance has the guilt of vice. And the foundation of reverence is this perception, that the present holds within itself the complete sum of existence, backwards and forwards, that whole amplitude of time, which is eternity.

DISCUSSION QUESTIONS
AND FURTHER READINGS

In examining the why of teaching, it behooves us to raise our sights from a familiar discussion of the here and now to that of broader temporal and spatial perspectives. Have you ever pondered what really makes human beings human? In his *Teacher in America* (Garden City, N.Y.: Anchor Books, Doubleday, 1954), Jacques Barzun observes that, "The reason teaching has to go on is that children are not born human; they are made so" (p. 17). How has the human race developed into a unique species among animals? What differentiates *The Phenomenon of Man* (by Pierre Teilhard de Chardin, New York: Harper & Row, 1959) from all the rest? Where and how does the act of teaching fit into the overall scheme of things? Trace *The Immense Journey* of man (New York: Vintage Books, Random House, 1957) with Loren Eiseley. Consider what it means to attempt to teach a being to become human by reading Jean-Marc-Gaspard Itard, *The Wild Boy of Aveyron* (New York: Appleton-Century-Crofts, 1962).

Would you agree with this observation by Teilhard de Chardin, in *The Future of Man* (New York: Harper & Row, 1964)? "In the passage of time a state of collective consciousness has been progressively evolved which is inherited by each succeeding generation of conscious individuals, and to which each generation adds something.... It seems that where Man is concerned the specific function of education is ... to extend and ensure in collective mankind a consciousness which may already have reached its limit in the individual" (p. 32). Why should *you*, of all people, become and be a teacher? Have you yourself developed a transcendental goal for your own teaching, one which makes your daily activities as a teacher ultimately meaningful?

Needless to say, each cultural group in each historical period has translated such a macroscopic insight into more microscopic ideas and operations. How do these philosophies and procedures vary among various societies and why? See, for example, Gordon C. Lee, *Education and Democratic Ideals* (New York: Harcourt, Brace & World, 1965) and Robert J. Havighurst, editor, *Comparative Perspectives on Education* (Boston: Little, Brown, 1968.) What, in your opinion, is the rationale for teaching in American schools today? Tomorrow?

WHO

4

PSYCHOLOGY AND THE TEACHING ART

William James

In the general activity and uprising of ideal interests which every one with an eye for fact can discern all about us in American life, there is perhaps no more promising feature than the fermentation which for a dozen years or more has been going on among the teachers. In whatever sphere of education their functions may lie, there is to be seen among them a really inspiring amount of searching of the heart about the highest concerns of their profession. The renovation of nations begins always at the top, among the reflective members of the State, and spreads slowly outward and downward. The teachers of this country, one may say, have its future in their hands. The earnestness which they at present show in striving to enlighten and strengthen themselves is an index of the nation's probabilities of advance in all ideal directions. The outward organization of education which we have in our United

---

From William James, "Psychology and the Teaching Art," pp. 21–27 in *Talks to Teachers* (New York: W. W. Norton & Company, 1958). This selection was originally a lecture, delivered in 1892.

States is perhaps, on the whole, the best organization that exists in any country. The State school systems give a diversity and flexibility, an opportunity for experiment and keenness of competition, nowhere else to be found on such an important scale. The independence of so many of the colleges and universities; the give and take of students and instructors between them all; their emulation, and their happy organic relations to the lower schools; the traditions of instruction in them, evolved from the older American recitation-method (and so avoiding on the one hand the pure lecture-system prevalent in Germany and Scotland, which considers too little the individual student, and yet not involving the sacrifice of the instructor to the individual student, which the English tutorial system would seem too often to entail),—all these things (to say nothing of that coeducation of the sexes in whose benefits so many of us heartily believe), all these things, I say, are most happy features of our scholastic life, and from them the most sanguine auguries may be drawn.

Having so favorable an organization, all we need is to impregnate it with geniuses, to get superior men and women working more and more abundantly in it and for it and at it, and in a generation or two America may well lead the education of the world. I must say that I look forward with no little confidence to the day when that shall be an accomplished fact.

No one has profited more by the fermentation of which I speak, in pedagogical circles, than we psychologists. The desire of the schoolteachers for a completer professional training, and their aspiration toward the 'professional' spirit in their work, have led them more and more to turn to us for light on fundamental principles. And in these few hours which we are to spend together you look to me, I am sure, for information concerning the mind's operations, which may enable you to labor more easily and effectively in the several schoolrooms over which you preside.

Far be it from me to disclaim for psychology all title to such hopes. Psychology ought certainly to give the teacher radical help. And yet I confess that, acquainted as I am with the height of some of your expectations, I feel a little anxious lest, at the end of these simple talks of mine, not a few of you may experience some disappointment at the net results. In other words, I am not sure that you may not be indulging fancies that are just a shade exaggerated. That would not be altogether astonishing, for we have been having something like a 'boom' in psychology in this country. Laboratories and professorships have been founded, and reviews established. The air has been full of rumors. The editors of educational journals and the ar-

PSYCHOLOGY AND THE TEACHING ART
William James

rangers of conventions have had to show themselves enterprising and on a level with the novelties of the day. Some of the professors have not been unwilling to co-operate, and I am not sure even that the publishers have been entirely inert. 'The new psychology' has thus become a term to conjure up portentous ideas withal; and you teachers, docile and receptive and aspiring as many of you are, have been plunged in an atmosphere of vague talk about our science, which to a great extent has been more mystifying than enlightening. Altogether it does seem as if there were a certain fatality of mystification laid upon the teachers of our day. The matter of their profession, compact enough in itself, has to be frothed up for them in journals and institutes, till its outlines often threaten to be lost in a kind of vast uncertainty. Where the disciples are not independent and critical-minded enough (and I think that, if you teachers in the earliest grades have any defect—the slightest touch of a defect in the world—it is that you are a mite too docile), we are pretty sure to miss accuracy and balance and measure in those who get a license to lay down the law to them from above.

As regards this subject of psychology, now, I wish at the very threshold to do what I can to dispel the mystification. So I say at once that in my humble opinion there *is* no 'new psychology' worthy of the name. There is nothing but the old psychology which began in Locke's time, plus a little physiology of the brain and senses and theory of evolution, and a few refinements of introspective detail, for the most part without adaptation to the teacher's use. It is only the fundamental conceptions of psychology which are of real value to the teacher; and they, apart from the aforesaid theory of evolution, are very far from being new.— I trust that you will see better what I mean by this at the end of all these talks.

I say moreover that you make a great, a very great mistake, if you think that psychology, being the science of the mind's laws, is something from which you can deduce definite programmes and schemes and methods of instruction for immediate schoolroom use. Psychology is a science, and teaching is an art; and sciences never generate arts directly out of themselves. An intermediary inventive mind must make the application, by using its originality.

The science of logic never made a man reason rightly, and the science of ethics (if there be such a thing) never made a man behave rightly. The most such sciences can do is to help us to catch ourselves up and check ourselves, if we start to reason or to behave wrongly; and to criticise ourselves more articulately after we have made mistakes. A science only lays down lines within which the rules of the art must fall, laws which the follower of the art must not transgress; but what particular thing he shall positively do within those lines is left exclusively to his own genius. One genius will do his work well and succeed in one way, while another succeeds as well quite differently; yet neither will transgress the lines.

The art of teaching grew up in the schoolroom, out of inventiveness and sympathetic concrete observation. Even where (as in the case of Herbart) the advancer of the art was also a psychologist, the pedagogics and the psychology ran side by side, and the former was not derived in any sense from the latter. The two were congruent, but neither was subordinate. And so everywhere the teaching must *agree* with the psychology, but need not necessarily be the only kind of teaching that would so agree; for many diverse methods of teaching may equally well agree with psychological laws.

To know psychology, therefore, is absolutely no guarantee that we shall be good teachers. To advance to that result, we must have an additional endowment altogether, a happy tact and ingenuity to tell us what definite things to say and do when the pupil is before us. That ingenuity in meeting and pursuing the pupil, that tact for the concrete situation, though they are the alpha and omega of the teacher's art, are things to which psychology cannot help us in the least.

The science of psychology, and whatever science of general pedagogics may be based on it, are in fact much like the science of war. Nothing is simpler or more definite than the principles of either. In war, all you have to do is to work your enemy into a position from which the natural obstacles prevent him from escaping if he tries to; then to fall on him in numbers superior to his own, at a moment when you have led him to think you are far away; and so, with a minimum of exposure of your own troops, to hack his force to pieces, and take the remainder prisoners. Just so, in teaching, you must simply work your pupil into such a state of interest in what you are going to teach him that every other object of attention is banished from his mind; then reveal it to him so impressively that he will remember the occasion to his dying day; and finally fill him with devouring curiosity to know what the next steps in connection with the subject are. The principles being so plain, there would be nothing but victories for the masters of the science, either on the battlefield or in the schoolroom, if they did not both have to make their application to an incalculable quantity in the shape of the mind of their opponent. The mind of your own enemy, the pupil, is working away from you as keenly and eagerly as is the mind of

PSYCHOLOGY AND THE TEACHING ART
William James

the commander on the other side from the scientific general. Just what the respective enemies want and think, and what they know and do not know, are as hard things for the teacher as for the general to find out. Divination and perception, not psychological pedagogics or theoretic strategy, are the only helpers here.

But, if the use of psychological principles thus be negative rather than positive, it does not follow that it may not be a great use, all the same. It certainly narrows the path for experiments and trials. We know in advance, if we are psychologists, that certain methods will be wrong, so our psychology saves us from mistakes. It makes us, moreover, more clear as to what we are about. We gain confidence in respect to any method which we are using as soon as we believe that it has theory as well as practice at its back. Most of all, it fructifies our independence, and it reanimates our interest, to see our subject at two different angles,—to get a stereoscopic view, so to speak, of the youthful organism who is our enemy, and, while handling him with all our concrete tact and divination, to be able, at the same time, to represent to ourselves the curious inner elements of his mental machine. Such a complete knowledge as this of the pupil, at once intuitive and analytic, is surely the knowledge at which every teacher ought to aim.

Fortunately for you teachers, the elements of the mental machine can be clearly apprehended, and their workings easily grasped. And, as the most general elements and workings are just those parts of psychology which the teacher finds most directly useful, it follows that the amount of this science which is necessary to all teachers need not be very great. Those who find themselves loving the subject may go as far as they please, and possibly become none the worse teachers for the fact, even though in some of them one might apprehend a little loss of balance from the tendency observable in all of us to overemphasize certain special parts of a subject when we are studying it intensely and abstractly. But for the great majority of you a general view is enough, provided it be a true one; and such a general view, one may say, might almost be written on the palm of one's hand.

Least of all need you, merely *as teachers,* deem it part of your duty to become contributors to psychological science or to make psychological observations in a methodical or responsible manner. I fear that some of the enthusiasts for child-study have thrown a certain burden on you in this way. By all means let child-study go on,—it is refreshing all our sense of the child's life. There are teachers who take a spontaneous delight in filling syllabuses, inscribing observations, compiling statistics, and computing the per cent. Child-study will certainly enrich their lives. And, if its results, as treated statistically, would seem on the whole to have but trifling value, yet the anecdotes and observations of which it in part consists do certainly acquaint us more intimately with our pupils. Our eyes and ears grow quickened to discern in the child before us processes similar to those we have read of as noted in the children,—processes of which we might otherwise have remained inobservant. But, for Heaven's sake, let the rank and file of teachers be passive readers if they so prefer, and feel free not to contribute to the accumulation. Let not the prosecution of it be preached as an imperative duty or imposed by regulation on those to whom it proves an exterminating bore, or who in any way whatever miss in themselves the appropriate vocation for it. I cannot too strongly agree with my colleague, Professor Münsterberg, when he says that the teacher's attitude toward the child, being concrete and ethical, is positively opposed to the psychological observer's, which is abstract and analytic. Although some of us may conjoin the attitudes successfully, in most of us they must conflict.

The worst thing that can happen to a good teacher is to get a bad conscience about her profession because she feels herself hopeless as a psychologist. Our teachers are overworked already. Every one who adds a jot or tittle of unnecessary weight to their burden is a foe of education. A bad conscience increases the weight of every other burden; yet I know that child-study, and other pieces of psychology as well, have been productive of bad conscience in many a really innocent pedagogical breast. I should indeed be glad if this passing word from me might tend to dispel such a bad conscience, if any of you have it; for it is certainly one of those fruits of more or less systematic mystification of which I have already complained. The best teacher may be the poorest contributor of child-study material, and the best contributor may be the poorest teacher. No fact is more palpable than this.

So much for what seems the most reasonable general attitude of the teacher toward the subject which is to occupy our attention.

THE TEACHER

Gilbert Highet

So far, we have said that a good teacher should know his subject, and, within limits, know his pupils. There is another necessary qualification. He or she should know much else. The good teacher is a man or woman of exceptionally wide and lively intellectual interests. It is useless to think of teaching as a business, like banking or insurance: to learn the necessary quota of rules and facts, to apply them day by day as the bank-manager applies his, to go home in the evening and sink into a routine of local gossip and middle-brow relaxation (radio, TV, the newspaper, and the detective-story), to pride oneself on being an average citizen, indistinguishable from the dentist and the superintendent of the gas-works—and then to hope to stimulate young and active minds. Teachers in schools and colleges must see more, think more, and understand more than the average man and woman of the society in which they live. This does not only mean that they must have a better command of language and know special subjects, such as Spanish literature and marine biology, which are closed to others. It

---

From *The Art of Teaching* by Gilbert Highet. Copyright 1950 by Gilbert Highet. Reprinted by permission of Alfred A. Knopf, Inc., and Methuen & Company, Ltd., London. Vintage Books edition, pp. 48–65.

means that they must know more about the world, have wider interests, keep a more active enthusiasm for the problems of the mind and the inexhaustible pleasures of art, have a keener taste even for some of the superficial enjoyments of life—yes, and spend the whole of their career widening the horizons of their spirit. Most people, as we see, stop growing between thirty and forty. They "settle down"—a phrase which implies stagnation—or at the utmost they "coast along," using their acquired momentum, applying no more energy, and gradually slowing down to a stop. No teacher should dream of doing this. His job is understanding a large and important area of the world's activity and achievement and making it viable for the young. He should expect to understand more and more of it as the years go by.

He has two special functions that make him different from other professional men and from the business-men and workers in his community.

The first of these is to make a bridge between school or college and the world. It is really very hard for the young to understand why they are shut up in classrooms and taught skills such as trigonometry, while the "real world" hums and clatters and shouts beyond the windows. They submit, poor creatures, but the pressure required to keep them there is intense. If they are allowed to think that school or college is an ingenious prison, a squirrel-cage in which they must whirl uselessly for a few years until they are let out, they will profit little or nothing from it. They may resent it bitterly. They cannot be told directly or convincingly how learning trigonometry will fit into their future existence: partly because no one really knows which of them will turn out to be a bridge engineer or will make some now unimagined discovery in ballistics, partly because they themselves cannot realize the value of mathematical thinking during their adolescence and youth, and partly because they cannot foresee even the outlines of their adult lives. But they should be given to understand in as many ways as possible that the two worlds are closely and necessarily connected, and that light and energy from one flow into the other.

This is often done by "making subjects relevant." Little German boys used to be trained in mathematics by getting problems about the number of pounds of explosive required to demolish a (non-German) viaduct. Some teachers of English use current magazines like *Time* to demonstrate vivid and concise writing. Certainly every teacher of a modern foreign language ought to use the newspapers and films produced in that language. But this idea cannot be applied to all subjects, nor

THE TEACHER
Gilbert Highet

to some of the most valuable subjects, while in others it often leads to superficiality and lowers intellectual standards.

The best way to do it is for the teacher to make *himself* relevant. Nine thousand times more pupils have learnt a difficult subject well because they felt the teacher's vitality and energy proved its value than because they chose the subject for its own sake. If a youth, sizing up the professor of medieval history, decides that he is a tremendous expert in the history of the Middle Ages and a deadly bore in everything else, he is apt to conclude that medieval history makes a man a deadly bore. If on the other hand he finds that the man is filled with lively interest in the contemporary world, that he actually knows more about it because, through his training, he understands it better, that the practice of the intellectual life, so far from making him vague and remote, has made him wise and competent, the youth will conclude without further evidence that medieval history is a valuable interest.

The good teacher is an interesting man or woman. As such, he or she will make the work interesting for the students, in just the same way as he or she talks interestingly and writes an interesting letter. Most teaching is done by talking. If your mind is full of lively awareness of the world, you will never be at a loss for new points of view on your own subject. Novel illustrations will constantly suggest themselves to you. You will discard outworn types of argument and find fresh ones. Allusions and reminiscences will brighten your talk and keep your audience from suffering the awful torture of feeling that it knows exactly what you are going to say next. Much teaching consists in explaining. We explain the unknown by the known, the vague by the vivid. The students usually know so little that they are delighted to hear you explain what you know and tie it up with what they are trying to understand. A colleague of mine in Paris used to have great difficulty, when discussing *Don Quixote,* in convincing his intelligent youngsters that Quixote was not merely a farcical old lunatic who should have been locked up. Then he described a series of bull-fights he had seen on a holiday in Seville, with their cruelty, their pride, their useless courage, which is an art in itself, and the oddity of sixteenth-century costumes in a Roman arena for a twentieth-century entertainment, which struck none of the Spaniards as odd; and he reminded them of the same Spanish pride and idealism as expressed in tragedy by the French master Corneille. Then his pupils began to understand that their own standards had not been complex enough for judging all the world's great books, and that Don Quixote's insanity might be a kind of strange sense. From that point the discussions used to develop in a dozen equally interesting and instructive directions.

The second function of the teacher is to make a bridge between youth and maturity. He has to interpret adult life to the young in such a way as to make them adults. To do this, he should belong to both worlds.

Many teachers find this extremely difficult. Some schoolmasters in Britain "live for the school." This means that their horizon is bounded at one edge by the preparatory institutions from which the youngsters come and on the other by the colleges to which they go. The great events of their lives are school cricket-matches and scholarship examinations. Like some officers of the regular army, they will talk for hours about the flap in Ingoldsby's unit, and "Whatever became of the old Snoggins?" but they grow embarrassed when asked about new books or contemporary politics. At the other extreme are teachers who care less than nothing for the hopes and fears and gaieties of the young, who never open the college magazine or watch a school football game, who feel it is an infringement on their dignity to spend nearly every day with children and adolescents, and who would obviously be happier if all their pupils were fifty years old and graying at the temples.

Difficult though this bridge-building between two worlds may be, it is possible; it is necessary; it is done by the best teachers. After all, no one is entirely and exclusively thirty-three years old, or forty-eight, or whatever his legal age may be. Watch any group of people enjoying themselves, vividly interested, and you will see them growing decades younger. Within every one of us, not far from the surface, lie hidden many personalities, some of them as young as childhood, and only one as old as today. The good teacher will be able to draw vitality and variety from the younger layers of personality which are still alive within him, and to know what it is to be a youth again, or a boy, without ceasing to be a man.

For example, he will notice and remember not only the things that interest him as an adult, but those things which used to interest him as a youngster. If he does, and if he uses them to illustrate his teaching but discusses them from a mature level, his teaching will become easier and his explanations clearer. The young are not very deep and consistent thinkers, but they are highly sensitive to new impressions: so they notice things like fanciful advertising campaigns, eccentric new personalities, peculiar rather than essential pieces of news, far more than grown-ups do. They do not think much about such things, but—

THE TEACHER
Gilbert Highet

since they have not yet become blasé and have no very intense inner life—they do experience them. Allusions to such things therefore can clarify a difficult discussion. At the moment this is being written, for instance, it would be wise for anyone trying to explain the ancient Greek "tyrants," those ambitious independent despots, to begin by talking of Marshal Tito. Although the parallel is not really close, it is helpful.

One of the most important qualities of a good teacher is humor. Many are the purposes it serves. The most obvious one is that it keeps the pupils alive and attentive because they are never quite sure what is coming next. Another is that it does in fact help to give a true picture of many important subjects. Suppose you are discussing English literature of the early nineteenth century. If you confine yourself to talking about Wordsworth's lyrical simplicity, and Shelley pinnacled dim in the intense inane, you will be giving an incomplete picture of the group; whereas if you also d-d-describe Ch-Charles Lamb as both f-funny and ch-charming, and bring out the weird boyish comedy of some of Wordsworth's other poems, and read some of Byron's rougher letters, you will then establish the idea that these men were rich and varied and human personalities, not "classics" cast in a single mold of solid bronze, and you can proceed all the better to explain both the nobility of their achievement and the sadness of their failures.

Of course some subjects, notably the sciences, do not admit humorous treatment. There the wise teacher will continue to introduce flashes of humor extraneously, because he knows that fifty-five minutes of work plus five minutes' laughter are worth twice as much as sixty minutes of unvaried work.

Some teachers speak of humor as a useful instrument with which to control their classes. This is a dangerous notion. Those who harbor it often make the mistake of using humor as nineteenth-century schoolmasters used the cane, to terrify the refractory and spur the slow. They begin by mocking a particular set of mistakes. Then they make fun of the boys who make these mistakes. Then they develop a bitter wit which thrives on every kind of personal defect, ruthlessly exposed. They will even feel aggrieved if no boy in their class happens to be a fit subject for satire, and will single out a perfectly innocuous youth simply because they cannot teach without having a butt. They are like the Oriental monarchs who always had a few malefactors impaled before their gates, to remind the citizenry that the master's word was law. Perhaps they would enjoy that comparison, for they are usually so petty and insecure that they would like to be maharajahs. I should compare them rather to the magpies of the Western states which will find a sore patch on a horse's back and perch on it, picking out raw flesh and squawking with self-satisfaction, until the horse runs mad down a cliff-side.

Kipling, who suffered a good deal of torture during his childhood, got this treatment first from his guardians (see *Something of Myself,* Chapter ii) and then from the master whom he immortalized as "King" (note the regal pseudonym) in *Stalky & Co.* What "King" did to him certainly kept him mentally alert; and he says he enjoyed it and profited from it; but it helped to increase that timidity and hypersensitivity which spoilt much of his adult life, and it did something to produce his very odd belief in the pulverizing force of ridicule as a political weapon (see, for instance, "Little Foxes," "As Easy as A.B.C.," and "The Village that Voted the Earth was Flat"), his absolute trust in authority, and his almost delighted contempt for lesser breeds without the Law. If he had only had a teacher like Kim's Lama, he would have been wiser and much happier. But part of his spirit was sacrificed to a schoolmaster who, perhaps, as some schoolmasters also do, detected and resented the superior intellectual brilliance of the grubby boy with the big glasses, and tried to make himself feel great by making young Rudyard Kipling feel small.

No, humor must not be used to tyrannize a class. It seldom is so used. Usually irony and sarcasm are used, because they imply intellectual domination; but not humor. The real purpose of humor in teaching is deeper and more worthy. It is to link the pupils and the teacher and to link them through enjoyment. A very wise old teacher once said: "I consider a day's teaching is wasted if we do not all have one hearty laugh." He meant that when people laugh together, they cease to be young and old, master and pupils, workers and driver, jailer and prisoners, they become a single group of human beings enjoying its existence.

Jules Romains, the eminent French novelist and dramatist, began his career by working out a theory which he later put into several excellent plays and stories. This is the idea that collections of people remain individuals until a single event or purpose or emotion molds them into groups, and that then the group lives, feels, and thinks in a way of its own, superior in energy and intensity to the activity of any one of its members. Sometimes, no doubt, a collective emotion is silly or degrading, as in a riot or a panic. But sometimes, Romains believes, it can be a truly ennobling experience: it is our duty to understand such experiences fully when they come. To be a member of a meeting

THE TEACHER
Gilbert Highet

which is moved by an energetic speaker to take a generous resolution; to applaud with a crowd of friends when your own team, making a huge effort, wins; to share the emotion of actors and audience at the production of a good new play; to walk through a city and feel yourself part of its beating and driving life—these are worthy emotions, which help us out of our own pettiness.

Romains called this theory Unanimism. Obviously it has its dangers. It leads very easily to the annulment of the individual, to the denial of intelligence, to "thinking with the blood" and believing that the majority is always right. Because it is easy to misapply, and because he knows that no eminent artist has ever been tied to one single theory, Romains has not concentrated on preaching and exploiting the doctrine. But it runs through most of his best work, and has inspired several young writers. Now, Romains was for some time a teacher in French high schools. One of the most winning figures in his *Men of Good Will* is the schoolmaster Clanricard, while several others are in fact teachers though they are ostensibly priests, doctors, and authors. Although he got his first glimpse of Unanimism in a busy Paris street, I am sure that he confirmed it from his experiences as a pupil and as a teacher. For one of the greatest pleasures in teaching comes from those hours when you feel that every word you say is being heard, not by a collection of bored and dutiful individuals, but instead by a group which you create and which in turn creates you; that, instead of repeating facts learnt by rote, to be telephoned through the drowsy air to half-deaf ears and garbled down in notebooks, you are both stirring minds to ask questions and answering them; that you are being driven by the energy of the young on the search for truth, and drawing therefrom the power to lead the search; and in fact, that you and your words and the class which listens and thinks are all part of the ceaseless activity of human Reason.

Your pupils will feel this too. If the feeling exists at all, it will be shared. To create it, or to help it to come into being, is one of the teacher's main tasks. It cannot exist unless there is a rapport, a give-and-take, something like a unanimist relationship between the pupils and the teacher. One of the means of establishing that rapport is humor. When a class and its teacher all laugh together, they cease for a time to be separated by individuality, authority, and age. They become a unit, feeling pleasure and enjoying the shared experience. If that community can be prolonged or re-established, and applied to the job of thinking, the teacher will have succeeded.

This can also be put in terms of traditional psychology. There are two powerful instincts which exist in all human beings, and which can be used in teaching. These are *gregariousness* and *the love of play*. Give fifty men four hours to cross a hill and walk down the valley beyond to the nearest town. If they try it separately, many will come in late, and nearly all will be tired. If they march in groups, they will be far less tired and come in sooner. If they do it in two teams competing with each other, or as a hiking party singing songs in rhythm, they will scarcely be tired at all, they will keep together, and they will enjoy the experience. In just the same way, if you can get a class of thirty youngsters to feel they are all pulling together, and if you can give them some reason to enjoy it, they will do nine times better work than thirty individuals working under compulsion. And one of the best appeals to both gregariousness and the play instinct is a good joke.

We said that one function of the teacher was to make a bridge between youth and maturity. If he has a sense of humor, he can build the bridge. The young think their elders are dull. The elders think the young are silly. This is the basis of that mutual misunderstanding of the ages, on which scarcely anything can get done without compulsion. Yet a clever teacher, who can use his sense of humor in such a way as to show the young that not everyone over twenty-five is dead, will at the same time learn enough about his pupils to see that their silliness is only awkwardness, easy to penetrate and dissolve. Both sides will understand each other better, and work together. Togetherness is the essence of teaching.

Now we have listed the main things that a good teacher will know and like. But what kind of man or woman will the good teacher be? Are there any abilities which are absolutely essential?

Not many. But there are certainly three.

The first is memory. A teacher with a poor memory is ridiculous and dangerous. He is like a musician who announces an ambitious concert and plays innumerable wrong notes; or an actor who begins: "It is the cause, it is the cause, my soul," and then blows up; or a doctor who gives one gram of digitalis instead of one grain; or a policeman who directs three lines of traffic into one another; or a merchant who cannot find the goods his customers want ("I know they were in here somewhere; just a moment, it'll come to me where I left them, let me see now . . ."); or a painter who puts both eyes on the same side of the nose—no, no, hush, for Picasso is still alive and distinguished;

THE TEACHER
Gilbert Highet

but certainly those others. Of course he must remember all the essentials of his subject. So much we have already said; although if he now and then forgets a detail, the class will understand and sympathize. (Let him look it up freely and openly—preferably in his own notes, not in a book.) But his memory is also important in covering what is said in class. If a question is raised and discussed, let him remember it and bring it back a week or two later in another context. If a pupil volunteers a good illustration from his own reading, or from a hobby, let the teacher remember to ask him for another one later. If one little group finds a problem unusually hard, let him give special attention to them when the next such problem appears. Memory is as important for the teacher as for other professional men. A creative memory is one of the qualities that differentiate the good lawyer, doctor, or teacher from the mediocre.

A display of good creative memory by a teacher helps the young in one of their most difficult jobs. Their attention is lively and their perception is keen, but they find it very hard to correlate. Many of the facts they learn merely drop into their minds like blocks of metal, and lie there. At examinations they take out the blocks, polish them, and show them to us. Then they put them back, or sometimes throw them away. If the facts simply remain on deposit, however neatly packed and highly polished, their possessors are not educated. The business of the teacher is to pass currents of interest and energy through the facts, while they are being learnt and afterwards, so that they melt, fuse, become interconnected, acquire life, and grow into vital parts of the minds which hold them. One excellent way to do this is to demonstrate *how* apparently remote facts are organically linked, and that can sometimes be done more happily as improvisation than as a prepared part of a lesson. When it comes off, the teacher's reward is there: he sees face after face light up as two blank areas of the brain, with the connections flashing between them, come alive.

Second to memory comes will-power. A good teacher is a determined person.

This was widely known in the nineteenth century. That was a time of strong-willed parents and tough teachers. Sometimes they were merely tyrants. But sometimes they were wise, firm, and efficient educators; and even if the children they produced did often rebel, they became well-educated rebels. This necessity is not so well known nowadays—at least in the schools of the Western democracies. It was recognized in Germany during the National Socialist regime, when will-power was classed as one of the essential qualifications of a schoolmaster and as one of the essential qualities he had to develop in his pupils. Teachers in America and Britain, France and Italy and elsewhere, often avoid the display of will, and prefer to be "nice"—which often means being cheery and indulgent and evasive on difficulties. On the whole, they do not teach so well as their resolute predecessors.

Yet it is obvious that a teacher needs will power. Everyone who has ever faced a class and seen thirty pairs of eyes turned upon him knows that. Some nervous ladies stand behind their desks, as though they were hunting leopards from a hide, while there are men teachers who stride up and down among their pupils, catching every gaze and holding it, barking out short urgent phrases, lacking only the chair and whip to be lion-tamers. Still, it seems that some teachers do not know why they must have a strong will and exercise it: they are perhaps a little ashamed of the necessity, even afraid of it; they feel that in a perfect society no display of will-power would be needed in the schools. But it would.

Consider how many different kinds of resistance the teacher has to overcome. To begin with, the young do not like work. They would rather be playing football, or sitting in the movies eating popcorn. But they must learn to work, because they will assuredly have to work all the rest of their lives; and to teach them that work is unnecessary or avoidable is to deform their characters. (It is odd, by the way, that the word "school" means "leisure" or "pastime." When that name was coined, people felt that a boy was lucky to be in school, because if he weren't he would be sweeping out his father's shop or milking his father's cows: that was real work, and "school" was "play.")

Nor do the young like authority. They are natural anarchists. They would prefer a world of unpredictable disorder, without duties or responsibilities. Such a world is impracticable now. So the young must be taught to respect the principle of authority; and if they do not learn it in school they will find it very bitter to learn later. A subsequent duty of their teachers will be to teach them to distinguish between different types of authority, to choose the good and reject the bad. Only a determined teacher can teach them the first lesson. If he is both determined and wise, he can teach them both.

Also, the young hate concentration. It is an effort, an unfamiliar and painful effort. Watch a boy doing his home-work when he thinks he is not observed. He will read ten lines, then draw a funny face in the margin, then try to read ten lines more

THE TEACHER
Gilbert Highet

and give up, then stop to whistle two bars of "Blood on the Saddle," then rearrange all the books on his table and sharpen all his pencils, then make a dash at the book and read twenty-five lines, and then sit panting and vacant-eyed for at least three minutes before beginning the struggle once more. Even his moments of true attention are accompanied by all kinds of waste motion and diversion: he taps both heels rhythmically on the ground, bites his nails, shifts his position as though he were sitting in a red-hot torture-seat, and usually keeps the radio on full blast. All this side-effort means that he finds concentration to be so painful that he must mitigate the agony by every possible means. He is pretending to escape.

Yet he learns. By the time he gets to college he will be able to concentrate oftener and keep it up for longer periods. If he enters one of the professions, he will have to increase his ability until he can follow and reproduce nearly every stage of a complex operation, or summarize the essentials of six leading judicial decisions in one evening. If he goes to work on leaving school, life will teach him concentration—or else it will make him a nonentity, the sort of man who hops from job to job and has a constant struggle to keep alive in a world where the bees outnumber the butterflies.

Concentration must be learnt. It should be learnt in school. A good teacher can teach it to his pupils. It should not be imagined as nothing but an effort of the will. Concentration is also an intellectual process. It is choice. Take the same boy who reads his book slowly, grudgingly, five lines at a time, and increase the urgency of his study—somehow, anyhow—make the choice clearer to him, and the importance of his study paramount—put him to work on the prize essay—and then watch. "Turn that radio off!" he shouts. He clears the table, except for one photograph. He sits fixed in one position till he is cramped. Sometimes, when he is really intent, he will miss meals and forget about sleep. All this because he has chosen one aim and discarded others. And that, after all, is what we learn to do throughout life.

Many youngsters also resent the domination of one mind. They reject suggestions just in order to assert their own independence, as a horse will jerk its head and side-step when it is ridden on a tight rein. Indeed, one important and successful method of teaching (which we shall be discussing a little later) is based on the idea of provoking the student's resistance. This is the tutorial method used in Oxford and Cambridge and in special classes elsewhere. The student writes an essay on a complex and difficult subject—say the political influence of the nobility in modern Italy, or the relativity of color—and reads it to his tutor. One other student, who knows something of the subject, listens. The tutor may agree with nearly everything in the essay, but it is his duty to tear it to pieces. Ruthlessly he exposes the defects in its arguments. Relentlessly he searches out the passages copied from books and encyclopedias. Surgically he dissects every page, every paragraph: sometimes he will spend an hour on a single important sentence. But the student answers every criticism as far as he can, defends every assertion, and gradually, instead of allowing his essay to become a mass of quivering fragments, can, if he has thought out his subject, build it during the conversation into a fully documented and soundly reasoned paper. Should he do this, the tutor will be well satisfied. Should he make no reply to the tutor's criticisms, should he sit down under them without attempting to resist, he is a poor student, and, probably, the tutor is a poor teacher.

So then, the young naturally resist the domination of their elders' minds. It is good that they should do so. It is one of the aims of teaching to provoke their resistance, and then to direct it into the right channels. But when they are lively and energetic, or when their resistance is particularly strong, their teacher needs a great deal of solid will-power to control them and to retain his own independence.

Again, in some countries, although not in all, schoolboys and schoolgirls put up a strong resistance to the very idea of learning. They feel it as an attack on their own integrity. They think that their own natural endowments—good sense, courage, and vitality—will take them as far as they want to go. They believe, not only that it is useless to learn a lot of stuff out of books, but that it might be positively harmful—very much like the old army cook who declared: "All them vitamines only weakens the system." This is a point of view which is often found in the central and western United States, in Australia, in the English Midlands, and in certain other areas where toughness and energy are much prized. It is difficult for the educator to cope with, and will be discussed later. Meanwhile it can be marked as a common source of resistance to the teacher in his work.

To face all these resistances, then, the teacher needs a strong will. If he is to be a good teacher, he will master them and guide them, instead of merely meeting them head-on and wrestling with them; and for that he will need an even stronger and more mature will. Also, as well as definite currents of resistance, there is always perceptible in big schools and colleges a directionless, anarchist upsurge of revolt and idiocy. You know how, every now and then, three or four boys will break into an empty build-

THE TEACHER
Gilbert Highet

ing and wreck the place as though a regiment of Cossacks had camped in it? And, when they are questioned, they always appear quite normal, in fact rather timid and subdued—as though they themselves were afraid of the forces that had possessed them? Well, in just the same way a whole class or a whole school can go *haywire*—the word comes from the wild whirling and tangling confusion of the wire in a broken hay-baling machine—and do unbelievable damage to themselves, to their teacher, to property, and to morale before they can be stopped. Wise teachers allow the young a large number of outlets through which this energy can escape. To draw it off into helpless, cheerful laughter is another of the functions of humor in teaching. But it takes a strong-minded teacher to resist its constant threat and to control it when it does reach the bursting point.

Memory, then, and will-power are two of the qualities that make a good teacher. The third is kindness. It is very difficult to teach anything without kindness. It can be done, of course, by the exercise of strong compulsion—as lion-tamers teach their beastly pupils—but there are not many types of pupil on which such compulsion can be exercised. Lions are imprisoned, and partially cowed by hot irons and guns. Boys learning religious texts like the Koran and the Talmud are caged within generations of previous examples and prodded on by their own (and their families') ambition. Pupils at officer's schools, and certain other institutions where attendance is a guarded privilege, will drive themselves on within the tight disciplinary mechanism of the school even if the master hates them as much as they hate him. But in nearly all other kinds of learning the pupils should feel that the teacher wants to help them, wants them to improve, is interested in their growth, is sorry for their mistakes and pleased by their successes and sympathetic with their inadequacies. Learning anything worth while is difficult. Some people find it painful. Everyone finds it tiring. Few things will diminish the difficulty, the pain, and the fatigue like the kindness of a good teacher.

This kindness must be genuine. Pupils of all ages, from careless children up to hard-working graduates, easily and quickly detect the teacher who dislikes them, as easily as a dog detects someone who is afraid of him. It is useless to feign a liking for them if you do not really feel it.

On the other hand, it is not at all necessary to show it by pats on the shoulder, by nods and becks and wreathed smiles. A serious-faced lecturer, who seldom addresses a pupil by name and thinks only about the job of making the basic principles of economics or the powers of the Supreme Court absolutely clear and memorable, will often be recognized as a teacher genuinely interested in the job of teaching and anxious for the welfare of his classes. It is not enough for him to be interested in the subject. Many a man is interested in a subject without wanting to teach it to anyone else. But if he is really interested in making the subject better known and more correctly understood, and if he does not expect all his pupils to grasp its elements at the first attempt but will help the slow and correct the confused, then he will be counted kind, although his face remains immovably grave and his manner unemotional and impersonal.

Still, the kindness must be there. It may be the kindness of an elder brother or sister, even of a parent. It can well be the kindness of a fellow-student. Sometimes it is a sympathy based on local patriotism, where the teacher feels he is helping the younger generation of his own fellow-citizens to grow and prosper. (This is at the basis of the admirable plan for conquering illiteracy in Mexico, by getting every Mexican who can read to teach one other of his countrymen.) But if the teacher feels none of these emotions, nor anything like them, if he or she regards the students merely as a necessary evil, in the same way as he regards income-tax forms, then his or her job will be far more difficult to do, far more painful for the pupils, and far less effectively done. Every teacher dislikes *some* pupils—the cheeky lipsticked adolescent girls, the sullen hangdog youths, the cocky vulgar little comedians, how loathsome they can be, all the more so because they do it deliberately! But if any teacher finds himself disliking *all* his pupils, he should change his character, and if that fails, change his job.

COMMITTED TO WHOM AND FOR WHAT?

H. Gordon Hullfish

Philip G. Smith

This book has been written in the firm conviction that history has revealed men to have reached their greatest humane achievements when cultural conditions fostered reflective ability. The authors realize that as men have overcome impeding conditions the presence of restriction has often seemed to be a necessary soil for the cultivation of thought. They realize, further, that under the best conditions of the past only a small percentage of men have had the opportunity to grow fully under the guidance of reflective capacity. They should add, also, their realization that many men, for reasons that range from simple laziness to deep-grained fear, have been complacent when facing opportunities for self-realization.

Reprinted by permission of Dodd, Mead & Company, Inc., from *Reflective Thinking* by H. Gordon Hullfish and Philip G. Smith, chapter 15, pp. 247–265. Copyright © 1964 by Dodd, Mead & Company, Inc.

The pages of history present no simple story of man progressing from a wilderness of ignorance to a high level of civilization and sophistication. His road has been a long one, beset with difficulties, involving some backsliding and much wandering on plateaus, as well as the occasional scaling of hitherto unconquered mountains. Difficulties yet abound. Indeed, within the twentieth century, just when the best of all possible worlds appeared to be within his reach, some of his greatest intellectual achievements were turned against him as a totalitarian power emerged in new and more restrictive forms. Totalitarian power in one section of the world breeds defensive power in other sections; and as this struggle continues, intelligence is used more and more to perfect instruments of terrifying destructive potential. This situation is not relieved, unfortunately, by the fact that the majority of men wish to develop the social instruments, both quantitatively and qualitatively, they know to be needed for survival.

A stalemate of power may hold off destructive forces long enough for man to turn his new-found energies to peaceful uses. This is but the promise of a precarious future; yet, in truth, man's only road to survival is precarious. Stalemated power will not establish a static condition, however. Power at this level will be dynamic, having consequences of political, economic, and social character, quite as much as it will have military consequences. It is in the latter area, of course, that the continuing struggle to gain scientific and technological advantage will be most obvious. Meanwhile, the very effort by free men to gain the strength needed to survive may slowly erode the essential meaning of freedom. We have witnessed how anxiety and fear have led men to destroy what they professed to be protecting. Security is a hard taskmaster, often dulling man's sensitivity.

Teachers Are People We must ask ourselves: What are the alternatives? To pit power against power in open warfare is not a decision that sane men will make through deliberate choice. The extent of destruction at Hiroshima and Nagasaki sensitized even the most ruthless among us to what lies ahead in using the known power of the "better" weapons nations have fashioned since the initial atomic experimentation. The threshold of sanity is unclearly marked, however, and no one can look to the future with the certainty that an unreasoned act of total destruction will not occur.

Nor is it to be expected that men who have enjoyed freedom in whatever measure will accede to pressure, becoming weary of the struggle, and permit totalitarian power to rule the world. They are aware of the fact that communism has the lure of a siren's song for those who have lain destitute on the floor of life for generations. They know, therefore, that they confront a formidable opponent. But one fact has not escaped them. They have observed that those who heard the siren promise them the right to stand erect are themselves yet heavily burdened. They realize, moreover, that these burdens are eased or increased at the command of those in power. There is no alternative here.

The meaning of this situation for the education of free men is clear enough. Knowing that it takes time for the educative process to bear cultural fruit, educators can only hope that a condition of stalemated power will be accompanied by the imaginative thrusts of men who are determined to save the world from the consuming flames of a nuclear hell. This does not mean that educators are to sit complacently on the side lines of life with a "Let George do it" attitude. Educators are people. They are not, as public reaction toward them on occasion suggests, representatives of a strange and ineffective third sex. They are people; and they are citizens, too. It is to be anticipated that each will have his commitments and will work in every way a citizen may to achieve them. The commitments, as citizens, of those responsible for education will reveal, moreover, all of the differences to be found among citizens in general.

What we need to be concerned about, having assured ourselves that educators are not transformed into a minority group by being denied the elementary rights of citizenship, are their *professional* responsibilities. Is the school an agency that may participate directly in remaking and reshaping its world? The school is comparable neither to a political party nor to an association of citizens who have banded together to secure political action to correct a specific social evil. On the other hand, the school has positive work to do in relationship to life as it is, as well as in relationship to those visions of an improved life which demand constant critical attention.

The effects of education are profound. These effects emerge only in the long run, however. They must await the later participation of young people in the affairs of their culture. (We are speaking, of course, of education in the free world, not of the manipulation of young people by totalitarians who may, as it suits their purpose, use the schools as propaganda fronts or as cheering sections.) What teachers have young people do in the daily work of the classroom will make a difference later on as young people become active citizens. This is why the school should never withdraw from life, or what amounts to the same thing, remain enmeshed in habits that glorify only the practices of the past.

Professional Responsibility and Citizenship It is not always easy to trace the line that divides the professional responsibility of the educator as educator and the privileges which are his as citizen. This difficulty leads, in turn, to a failure, in particular instances, to differentiate between a proper professional stance on the part of associated educators and the right of the educator, as a free citizen, to hold whatever views he finds good, even those which most of his fellows reject.

It is easy enough to compartmentalize knowledge; indeed, under the compulsion of special interests, it is easy to fragment life, all unwittingly, as many a businessman has discovered when the church interest he has long taken for granted suddenly forces him to reflect upon the quality of his weekday practices. But the educator is in the business—as he is sure to conclude when he gives serious thought to his primary task—of helping individuals put their lives together through a constant reflective reconstruction of their knowledge, insights, and values. He does not wish, therefore, to fragment his own life. Nor should he. Nor does the suggestion that he should differentiate between his professional and political activities compel him to do so. A proper conception of the function of the school in the free society should lead to the creation of helpful guiding principles, though, of course, no abstractions may ever finally substitute for his personal involvement intellectually in determining, situation by situation, where the line should be drawn.

It may be useful to return to the view of the classroom considered in earlier chapters, remembering that the character of the classroom should be but a reflection of the school as a whole. What we have urged is the creation of an atmosphere in which the reflective and critical consideration of knowledge promotes a continuing reconstruction of experience. Nothing less than the recognition that the development of thinking on the part of students is the thread that unites the work of teachers in all fields of instruction, and on all levels of education, will make this atmosphere possible. This emphasis was placed neither for sentimental nor esoteric reasons but in recognition of the fact, to repeat a phrase that has guided this writing, that *thinking is the method of an educative experience.* We are concerned with the improvement of learning (and, of course, of the teaching that will make this improvement possible); and, in view of our further commitment, it is fortunate that this end of improved learning coincides with the improved humane conditions toward which the democratic aspiration points. More than coincidence is involved here, however. Our understanding of learning and our understanding of democracy have advanced together, exactly to the degree that men have been free to make each an object of study. Further growth will depend upon the maintenance of this freedom.

The continuing professional responsibility, therefore, is to protect the atmosphere of the classroom against the many elements that may befoul it. Always, in a plural culture, we may anticipate that individuals and groups will conceive of the schools as instruments for the promoting of their special purposes or, failing this, will suspect them of being the tools of others. We may hope that pressures to hold education within the narrowing limits of special and group interests will decrease as public understanding increases. But we should not count on this, except in relation to the long haul. It will take time to create attitudes on the part of young people that will lead them to sustain a respect for freedom throughout their adult years.

A professional commitment to the creation and maintenance of conditions that make possible the freedom of teachers to teach and the freedom of students to learn (and, of course, these freedoms are inseparable) is the solid ground which professional organizations may share. It is important, therefore, that such organizations as the American Association of University Professors, on one level, and the Commission for the Defense of Democracy through Education of the National Education Association, on another, be supported. It is equally important that this professional commitment serve as the measure by which to judge the activities of these and other professional organizations of educators.

What is even more important, however, is the development of a professional awareness on the part of state and local educational organizations of their responsibility to create and guard in each classroom those conditions that make freedom of thought possible. It is at these more intimate levels of school and community relationships that schools, or individual classrooms, feel the full force of restricting pressure. It is there that a commonly held professional understanding should compel the community to consider why it is that free people create schools. No teacher or administrator should be deserted by colleagues when his difficulties arise because he has attempted to advance what all should hold as a shared professional commitment.

A Possible Professional Stance   The situation educators work within is complex and confusing. Yet it is within the specifics of the situation that the meaning of this professional commitment has to be developed. A school system, an individual school, or a particular teacher may, for instance, be asked to withdraw a book (say, one by a Magruder, a Muzzey, or a Rugg), or be asked to refrain from dealing with a specific topic (say, the New Deal, evolution, labor unions, the Catholic Church, or TVA). The professional response in such situations in the past has varied all the way from defending an author, in the case of books, or advocating a given position, in the case of an issue, to complacency and indifference.

A proper position, from a professional point of view, should not be difficult to locate. All such demands should be dismissed politely but firmly. If they persist, as they almost certainly will, they should be brought before representative groups of citizens for discussion. The pressure group may be too strong under such circumstances for the educators to offset, but if this proves to be the case, the onus for changing the educational program in ways that violate the professional commitment of schoolmen in the free world should be publicly established.

If some fear that positions may be lost under these circumstances, the fear will frequently be warranted. It is difficult to dismiss the profession as a whole, however. In any event, the chance of gaining friends for education in an open situation of discussion, with its representatives supporting a purpose that is demonstratively professional, is worth taking. So far as the health of education and of society are concerned it is a better risk than to conciliate representatives of prejudice. In the latter instance, potential friends will be bypassed, and, moreover, an invitation to apply pressure will be issued to other groups.

What should be avoided in such situations is professional pronouncements in support either of a particular author, designed to reveal that he is a veritable flame of truth, or of a particular "position" on a controversy, for the purpose of proving that all who differ are ignorant or misguided. Individual members of professional organizations are sure to be in disagreement when this approach is made. Many an organization has suffered internal agonies when some of its members have insisted on such a course. Specific authors are not at issue. The right to use books is. A given side of a controversy is not at issue. The right to discuss topics—any topic relevant to the subject matter of the class—is. The right to parade prejudice before children has no claim to professional support. The right to examine prejudice has. The profession should never act through its official bodies (and there are as many of these as there are shared professional interests) unless it is sure that it does so from the unimpeachable ground that its dominant interest is the creation of an effective climate of learning.

Not all events or conditions that affect the atmosphere of the school or classroom are, at first glance, matters of educational concern. Many are, however. The conditions of economic and social life that deprive some children of a fair chance to participate in normal activities of youth along with others, or those that lead to a spread of fear and conformity; an increase within society generally, or of a segment of it, of disregard of law; a continuing adult emphasis upon material gains, so strong as to suggest that no other motives are quite respectable; the denial by a community of a basic interest in education by giving generous support only to school athletic programs—these and comparable situations raise problems the profession has to consider in professional terms. Irwin Edman once pointed out that the "temper of intelligent criticism is the essential not only of a liberal culture but even of a free society." And to this he added, "this temper can be cultivated only in those sufficiently well clothed, well housed, and well fed to be able to think with composure and alertness and to sense a share in the general welfare."[1]

The profession cannot remain insensitive to the movement and direction of its culture. It has demonstrated this many times—seeing that children whose limited diets did not include milk received it (using contributions from meager salaries before school lunch programs were adopted); contributing or securing clothing for children whose potential nakedness kept them at home; and permitting those whose hours at home led only to exhaustion to rest at school. In each instance, apart from the normal sympathy of sensitive adults, the professional interest has been paramount. Children lacking in these essentials are not free to learn, whatever the classroom atmosphere. It is not easy in such instances to keep the professional interest to the fore, however. The pursuit of the political interest may seem to be the shortest route to what appears to be the same end, if it is forgotten, which is easy when feeling runs deep, that a shift in the means will bring a comparable shift in the end.

Conflict of Views Normal Individual members of professional groups are not cut from the same cloth. Some may earnestly believe, for example, that an open socialization of the economy—indeed, of the government—is the only way to deal adequately with disturbing economic conditions. Others are sure to insist that a return to a completely free economy is a better way. Many others will be equally certain that the end to hold in view is a steady progression toward the creation of cultural and educational conditions which provide a maximum opportunity for all to be free in their thinking, permitting the chips of economic, political, and social forms to fall as they will.

This last group will insist that *all* should have the opportunity, as *citizens,* to have their views prevail. It will insist equally, however, that none use the schools as instruments of political warfare. And, comparably, it will use the weight of the profession, in professional terms, to inform the public of the need to remember that miseducative conditions in a culture will cancel out the educative efforts of the schools. The professional function at this level is to engage the public mind in serious reflection upon the problem created by the paradox of asking schools to carry out programs which cultural conditions undermine. This paradox is nowhere better illustrated than in the public demand for an increased emphasis by the schools on moral and spiritual (or even religious) instruction, when its own actions deny the validity of the ideals involved.

The difficulty we are considering is one that has plagued professional educational organizations continuously. Tough- and adventurous-minded members are in constant conflict at the point of organizational policies with members more tender- and less adventurous-minded. Each wants to live in a good society and to create good schools. The one is anxious to use the modern limited-access highway; the other seems determined to prod along on well-worn roads where improvements are made only when further travel becomes impossible. When their differences become too marked, the only solution may be an open break, with new organizations emerging. In this respect teachers do not differ from their fellow citizens, and for a very good reason: they share with other citizens, as citizens, all of the shadings of values of an open, plural culture. As professional people they should share, however, the commitment that the schools of the free world are not to be used as propaganda agencies, either for a new society or an old one.

Where individual and social values are plural, schools cannot serve as representatives of a single point of view. They have to represent, rather, the condition that makes plurality possible: the protection of freedom in thinking against the beguiling certainties of visions so clear to adherents as to blind them to claims of other visions. Schools, of course, should examine all visions, doing so under reflective, educative conditions. Only thus may we hope to remove the blinders worn by the ignorant, the prejudiced, or the devoted and dedicated reformer.

This is neither the weak position the tough-minded believe it to be nor the dangerous one the tender-minded fear that it is. It takes strength to insist that no vision of social good is beyond examination, especially when one is personally convinced that the good life is really dependent upon one rather than upon others. This strength the profession has to muster, however, if it hopes to escape the parochialism of those whose thinking is turned exclusively to problems of *strategy* on behalf of values previously accepted as final.

To stand firm for the right to create educational conditions within both the school and culture on which the continuing growth of free men depends is to take a positive position, a professional, if not a political, one. It represents neither weakness nor retreat. It represents, as only an institution free of specific political commitment may, the acceptance of the unique and difficult assignment given the schools by free men: (1) the transmission of knowledge and values, in order that the gains of the past may not be lost, and (2) the reconstruction of knowledge and values, in order that the gains of the past and the present may become thresholds to an improved future, not doors closed against one.

A Sentiment Toward Freedom The reader may well ask why it is that the authors, whose commitment to democracy must have been evident throughout, do not state that the profession has the responsibility of creating an education which prepares young people intellectually and emotionally for their entry into democratic citizenship, and be done with it? Why torture the problem? Such an approach is tempting. It is not helpful, however. To ask the schools to advance the cause of democracy is, no doubt, in accord with the prevailing sentiment of the culture and, in this sense, is proper. But direction is not gained from vague expressions of sentiment. Democracy means many things and takes many forms, a fact that the Japanese, for instance, discovered when they were suddenly placed on the pathways of democracy by "Occupationnaires." [2]

The emissaries of democracy had risked their lives to protect it and, in the end, to bring it to Japan. Had democracy been a single, simple thing, the Japanese, dazed by defeat and ruin, would have grasped it appreciatively. Indeed, they made the effort; but, unfortunately, democracy and occupation by military force are strange companions. Moreover, since democracy is in essence an opportunity to use intelligence and not a substitute for it, the "Occupationnaires" presented no uniform social pattern. At times what some suggested conflicted with the suggestions of others; at times their actions denied their expressed ideas; at times they reversed themselves in both ideas and actions. All of this may seem normal enough to the American. It did not to the Japanese, however, and the people of Japan still struggle with the problem of discovering the meaning of democracy for the conduct of their lives. They continue this struggle because the "Occupationnaires," whatever their faults, represented a *sentiment toward freedom* and this sentiment remains.

Democracy, though meaning much specifically to many people, is nevertheless, at another level, all things to all men, the epitome of vagueness. A certain vagueness at this level may be salutary, however. No one has the right to prescribe meaning for others. Among some people, a frequent consequence of this vagueness is a tendency to apologize whenever they use the term. Such apology suggests the presence of a prevailing sentiment that dare not be ignored—a sentiment that favors the absence of a fixed meaning for democracy. For some, of course, the term has always carried the idea of mob control of political and, hence, of social life. They have substituted, whenever possible, their favored term, *republic*. But this term has not prevented the spread of the democratic sentiment far beyond its initial political limits; nor has it prevented, under the impact of the extension of the sentiment to encompass the entire range of man's relationship to man, transformation within the political field itself.

All of this is deplorable to those whose temperaments drive them to pin down meaning with finality. Life would often be less confusing were these individuals successful. The fact seems to be, however, *as long as we are aware of what we are about,* that an open life is more viable than a closed one. As T. V. Smith,[3] writing from his experience as an academic philosopher and an active politician, has said: "It is a simple token of the pluralistic nature of political virtue that from the beginning in America we have on Monday, Wednesday, and Friday, as it were, called our country a republic, and on Tuesday, Thursday, and Saturday called it a democracy."

"Way of Life" Deceptive The question democratic men confront in the face of determined totalitarian men is whether they can afford to continue vague and ambiguous ways. Many consider this to be the road to certain doom. The Communist way of life, as they see it, is a dire threat to the democratic way of life because it involves its citizens, and especially its young people, in the emotional support of specific ends toward which their lives are directed, ends, which if achieved (and no possibility of failure is admitted when the course of history is compelled to run according to dogma), will bring the millennium to all. Democracy, they feel, should not do less, else it will leave its young people helpless, without purpose. The fact that the same argument was put forward when Nazi Germany and predefeated Japan posed a threat for free men is not a counterargument, though it may appear to be one at first glance. Neither possessed resources, however, comparable to those of the Communist world, nor had either the scientific knowledge and technical skills the latter now possesses.

But a critical point remains to be examined. What is meant by *a way of life,* either democratic or communistic? As one of the authors [4] noted on another occasion,

> Do we mean that each has an internal substance that all who live in relationship to it grasp and understand? If so, neither qualifies as a way of life. Was communism equally communism under Lenin and Stalin? ... Was democracy no democracy before women were granted the vote? And what of our way of life when it was legal to conduct segregated schools? Was our way of life more in evidence on the frontier, when the individual took the law in his own hands? At what point do we stop and say, "There it is; have a go at it"? Was democracy nonexistent when unions were unheard of? Is our way of life more in evidence now that the stock market is watched by government than when bullish and bearish movements were its private business? And who among us is our authority—historian, politican, businessman, churchman, educator, farmer, miner, or factory worker? What, then, is in conflict when we speak of competing and conflicting ways of life? Do we select a single feature (say, the two-party system) or a central tendency (say, belief in a divine being) or an historic fact (say, a general dependence on individual initiative in economic matters) as our point of contrast?

If life in America differs from life in England, France, Sweden, Denmark, or Norway—and it does—do we share *a* democratic way of life with them? If revisionists, deviationists, or Titoists are anathema to the Russian or Chinese leaders—and they are— who, in Marxian terms, is communistic? These questions make clear, at least in relationship to the Communist world, that to the degree a way of life is at issue deviation is not tolerated. And this, we fear, is inescapable when those who have the power to do so set the pattern of loyalties individuals and institutions must follow. With equal significance, however, the questions raise a doubt that the phrasing "a way of life" is as useful as it has seemed to be. The phrasing turns out to be a blanket that obscures the many differences it covers and leads men to assume a unity of belief and practice where none exists, or, realizing this, to insist that one be achieved.

To question the usefulness of referring to democracy as a way of life is not to question the distinctiveness of the democratic sentiment. We have noted above the presence of a prevailing sentiment among those who nevertheless differ in significant ways in their specific interpretations of democracy and in their proposals for advancing it. Ways of life are surely involved in democracy. *A* way of life is not. Nor is the democratic sentiment a simple sentimentalism. What is involved is a pervading disposition or quality of human relationships which leads men to share the belief that there are better ways to settle the normal differences arising among them than to resort to the techniques of power, whether these be subtly or ruthlessly exercised.

This belief has led to the creation of instruments of conference and consultation, to an appreciation of the function of compromise in the settling of disputes, and to dependence upon law as a continuing stabilizer in the midst of difference. From this ground the realization has grown that government, while it may not command, may properly exercise leadership in any aspect of national life where custom or suddenly achieved power suggests to some that they are privileged to deny democratic opportunities to others. It is no accident that we look to the courts to declare democracy-denying tendencies illegal—in education, in employer-employee relationships, in labor unions and in business practices, in discriminations of whatever sort against minority groups. Even so, we are notoriously inconsistent both in our expressions of belief and in our development of practices. And we are seldom fully articulate.

The Basic Commitment That we must build on our past, whatever its faults, is obvious. Still, to build a way of life (if this means more than what we have called "a pervading sentiment") would threaten the enriching results of association our differences have woven into the unities we have progressively achieved. To halt this process now in favor of a final unity would hardly be a bargain. To build such a way of life would be an exciting challenge to some, a challenge already accepted by good people on the right and left. They are prepared to produce in quantity their blueprints for reconstruction and, following them, to organize, perhaps manipulate, the rest of us. There is nothing wrong with blueprints for reconstruction, of course, as there is nothing wrong with planning to ameliorate social ills. It is our good fortune that our forebears were free to plan, to stretch their imaginations by choosing among life's alternatives. It will be the good fortune of future generations, if we guard this same freedom.

Thus we find our basic commitment: no plan or blueprint should be arbitrarily dismissed as unworthy of examination; all who plan should have the right to be heard. But this commits man only to be as wise as he can be as he chooses among plans. He is not committed in advance to any specific plans, and he reserves the right to use as much intelligence in deciding his commitment as was used in developing the plan. This we take to be the essence of the democratic sentiment. It involves a distinctive *way of coming at life.* It relies upon a continuing opportunity for all citizens to participate appropriately in the decisions that build the common life, and at the same time to share an attitude of honoring and protecting differences. Those who *come at life* in this spirit know that no gain has been made when finality and force are substituted for flexibility and intelligence.

A further point, one pertaining to the students, remains to be considered. If teachers (as teachers) are committed to the act of thinking rather than to specific social values which thought should advance, what manner of student will result? If in their school experience students are always asked to examine and re-examine ideas and propositions, will they not finally come to believe that thinking is always insufficient for decision? May not the result be that students will come to look upon thinking as but a required school exercise which, like so many others, has no meaning for life outside?

These are not idle questions. A school program that left students with no guide lines to action would be a sorry one, indeed. But where are these guide lines to come from in a plural culture? Of the many which are available, is the school to make a selection and then arrange that students develop commitments to these? If so, will it wet a finger and hold it aloft, in the manner of a golfer, to see which way the wind of social emphasis is blowing at a given time? These are not idle questions, either.

The fact is that an education appropriate for a democratic world is not easily fashioned. But one point seems clear. An experience in reflective valuing is at least as promising a base on which to erect the mansions of free men as is either an authoritarian control of the value experience or dependence at the point of decision upon a nonreflective, irrational quality of this experience. The authors, of course, believe it to be more promising, holding the view that no culture has ever possessed too much intelligence. They believe with John Dewey that to "claim that intelligence is a better method than its alternatives, authority, imitation, caprice and ignorance, prejudice and passions, is hardly an excessive claim." [5] They do not believe, nor did Dewey, that "intelligence will ever dominate the course of events," that it comes with a built-in guarantee which will save man from "ruin and destruction." But as Dewey noted, "The issue is one of choice, and choice is always a matter of alternatives." [6]

If we think of the student for a moment, rather than of the values certain adults wish to have perpetuated, the situation may appear in differing perspective. To begin with, students are not, at any stage of their school experience, devoid of values. They are born into families that value them and that value certain experiences both for them and for the family as a whole. And the families are within communities, the communities within states, the states within the nation, the nation within the world. They are assailed, so to speak, with many value vectors as they mature. They do not grow up with the neutrality of a vegetable or a machine. This fact is revealed in any classroom that gives students an opportunity to express their beliefs.

A further fact is revealed in such situations, a fact that is critical in our considerations. It is this: in our plural culture young people develop beliefs (a belief being at this level a readiness to act), and they develop commitments (a commitment at this level being an announced determination to act, even though it may be only the individual himself who hears the expression of determination). And these beliefs and commitments frequently deny one another. In short, students reflect the inconsistencies or disharmonies of their adult world. It is no accident that in the name of democracy some white students have harassed Negro students who attempted to enter "their" schools. Their acts have reflected the commitments of most adults within their communities—on the streets, at church, at patriotic gatherings, in pool halls. Nor is it an accident that other students, within the same communities, have reflected the generous and tolerant commitments of other adults. Young people do not grow up in a value vacuum; nor do they (nor should they) check their values outside the schoolroom door when they enter it.

Now such a situation is messy. It is small wonder that dedicated individuals want to do something about it. But what is proper to do? Indoctrination on behalf of *the* right commitments may be immediately dismissed. No one seriously concerned about the educative process could support this approach. May we not, however, within a rational, reflective program, add an emotional coloring that will gain adherents for those humane values decent men should hold? The question is proper, with the future of humane values as precarious as it is. Yet it does suggest the creation of unreasoned commitments. It further suggests, moreover, a separation of thought from action, and this is in conflict with the position of the authors—namely, *reflection is itself a mode of behaving.*

Reflection comes into being, not as the act of a cold, clear logical machine, but as a consequence of an individual's inability to go forward with an action (explicit or implicit) he is concerned to bring off. It is within the ongoingness of his experience (and this includes feelings, aesthetic sensitivities, body tensions, nonverbalized drives, and the like) that the reflective act occurs.

It is a mistake to assume that emotional, tensional factors must be *added* to the results of reflective inquiry in order to spur the thinker (viewed as a sort of reflective spectator of the confusing, emotionally charged behavior in which men engage) into action. This view keeps thought removed from the human arena in which it should gain its character. If we may put the matter somewhat crudely, the function of reflective behavior is to keep the emotional or nonrational elements of action from hogging the show. The latter are always present; they do not need to be introduced into experience.

What does need to be introduced is a commitment to thinking itself, a reasoned commitment to reasoned beliefs. This can only be done within an experience that gives thinking work to do, work that brings about a reflective, *and prized,* difference in behavior. No exhortation is involved, only the dogged and steady examination, under educative conditions, of beliefs already held, of the consequences of continuing to hold them in the face of evidence that challenges their validity, of the outreach of the consequences that would follow their reasoned reconstruction. There is commitment here aplenty, both for teachers and students.

In Summary To develop fully at this point the consequences for schools and the culture generally of acting in terms of the commitments expressed in this chapter would be but to repeat what has gone before. This is surely unnecessary. Several purposes have been served, however, by our explicit formulation of a statement of commitment.

First, the notion that teachers who emphasize thinking may not themselves have positions on critical issues that confront members of the public is false and misleading. The professional responsibility simply obligates teachers to help young people achieve an understanding of such issues and to arrive at conclusions independently. On this score, teachers are expected to be partisans on the side of initiating and defending the educative conditions upon which the significant growth of students finally depends. This is the basic professional commitment that should guide teachers even when they have to curb, in the interest of freeing their students from either open or insidious restriction, their own partisanship as active, concerned citizens.

Second, the notion that schools may serve as political instruments leads to the false assumption that schools can do what, in a democracy, is beyond their power. The acceptance of this assumption would remove from the culture the one agency it has created which is not committed in advance, as issues arise within society, to the support of special interests. Schools represent only the social interest in the large—an admittedly difficult task. Their responsibility is to contribute to society, through their graduates, an increasingly informed, sensitive, and critical intelligence.

Third, the notion that schools may do their proper work either by withdrawing from the social scene or by complacently following its shifting and conflicting leads would deprive democracy of a needed balance wheel for its plural components. When cultural conditions impede the efforts of schools to create the reflective conditions necessary for the development of the citizens of a free world, it is the responsibility of the profession to make this fact known widely and in ways that extend its educative practices beyond the walls of its classrooms. Educators have positive and challenging work to do within a democratic culture. It is time they found a professional base to share.

Our suggestion for such a base recognizes the fact that the democratic sentiment does not force men into a common mold but, rather, frees them to work out their commitments and their destiny through the interplay of enlightened interests. Its seeming restriction, that each adhere to a full recognition of the right of every individual to speak his piece and of each idea to be given a fair examination, is a restriction only on those whose interests are not in freedom but in dominating others. The right of individuals and of ideas to be heard, in these terms, represents a social conception; it is not an individualistic position inherently opposed to all forms of social planning. It is opposed to the unreasoned acceptance of any particular scheme for social conformity.

The individual does not gain his freedom by first submitting himself to ideas others claim to be true. He gains it, when he does, by enlisting in the common effort to create social instruments that facilitate the sharing of a reflective approach to the problems all confront. It is this fact which provides the base for the professional growth of educators. It is this fact which creates the imperative that educators use what is known about the nature of thinking and learning to advance the thinking capacity of students and, in ways that are professionally proper, to advance respect for thought within the culture. It creates an imperative because it joins the best we know about learning with the best we know about man's relationship to man.

FOOTNOTES

[1] Irwin Edman, *Fountainheads of Freedom* (New York: Reynal & Hitchcock, 1941), p. 189.

[2] This term was used by Harry Emerson Wildes in his description of the occupation and its aftermath. One of the distressing consequences of conflicting and shifting actions by responsible occupation officials was far worse than confusion, bad as this was. Some Japanese doubted the integrity of the whole operation and saw in this an opportunity to use the conqueror's lack of a clear program for personal or cultural gain. See *Typhoon in Tokyo—The Occupation and Its Aftermath* (New York: The Macmillan Company, 1954).

[3] T. V. Smith, *The Democratic Tradition in America* (New York: Farrar & Rinehart, Inc., 1941), p. 12.

[4] H. Gordon Hullfish, "Educating for Democracy," an address presented at The Cooper Union, New York City, Jan. 19, 1955, American Association of University Professors *Bulletin,* Vol. 41, No. 2 (Summer, 1955) pp. 261-262.

[5] John Dewey, *Experience and Nature* (Chicago: Open Court Publishing Company, 1929), p. 437.

[6] *Ibid.,* p. 437.

DISCUSSION QUESTIONS AND FURTHER READINGS

What makes a great teacher great? How many of your own teachers do you consider to be good? For what reasons? Why do you think you will be another good teacher? If you believe that some of the necessary qualities can be systematically developed, what are you doing right now to develop them? A teacher's responsibilities are indeed awesome and he cannot start too early in his efforts to improve himself. "Day in and day out, he enlightens and strengthens, or poisons and mutilates. 'A parent gives life, but as parent gives no more,' said Henry Adams. 'A murderer takes life, but his deed stops there; a teacher affects eternity; he can never tell where his influence stops'" (p. xvi in Houston Peterson, editor, *Great Teachers,* New York: Vintage Books, Random House, 1946). Think a little about the implications of this bold statement.

To be a good teacher is partly a matter of professional preparation. What do you see as prerequisite experiences for teaching? When should children begin thinking about and planning for a career as a teacher? Should elementary and secondary teachers explicitly discuss with their students the idea of teaching as a way of life and as a profession? How should teachers be recruited, selected, and prepared? Compare several analyses and proposals on teacher education, including Arthur W. Combs, *The Professional Education of Teachers* (Boston: Allyn and Bacon, 1965), James B. Conant, *The Education of American Teachers* (New York: McGraw-Hill, 1963), James D. Koerner, *The Miseducation of American Teachers* (Boston: Houghton Mifflin, 1963), and Seymour B. Sarason, Kenneth Davidson, and B. Blott, *The Preparation of Teachers* (New York: John Wiley, 1962). What are your recommendations?

No matter how thorough professional preparation may be, it cannot transform everyone into a good teacher. A question of relevance here is asked by Sylvia Ashton-Warner in her book, *Myself* (New York: Simon and Schuster, 1967): "Do you too aim to be a worthwhile person or only a worthwhile teacher?" (p. 11). Pursuit of identity, self-esteem, and maturity is a serious business. Study such sources as Robert C. Burkhart and Hugh M. Neil, *Identity and Teacher Learning* (Scranton, Pa.: International

Textbook, 1968), Robert E. Nixon, *The Art of Growing* (New York: Random House, 1962), and Allen Wheelis, *The Quest for Identity* (New York: W. W. Norton, 1958). How have you been doing in your own quest?

Miss Ashton-Warner herself gives this advice: "You must be true to yourself. Strong enough to be true to yourself. Brave enough, to be strong enough, to be true to yourself. Wise enough, to be brave enough, to be strong enough, to be true enough to shape yourself from what you actually are" *(op. cit.,* pp. 12–13).

WHOM

CHILDREN UNDER PRESSURE

Kaoru Yamamoto

"Get lost and stay there!"—that is a student's advice to his teacher in a current best-seller, *Up the Down Staircase*.[1] We do not know who this outspoken child really was, because he merely signed his name, "Poisen," and added the traditional symbol of death and danger, the skull and crossbones. The message itself, however, is loud and clear, "Get lost, you teachers, and stay there!"

Granted that such a suggestion sounds unnecessarily harsh and shocking when heard out of context, granted also that not all students are in the chorus all the time, and granted further that teachers tend to become a ready target of youngsters' negative reaction against older generations and institutions in general, this terse command still reveals much about how our children perceive the world they were born into and its oft-unwelcome "natives."

This essay is based on a paper read at the twenty-second annual conference of the Association for Supervision and Curriculum Development at Dallas, Texas, in March of 1967 under the title, "Children Under Pressure."

Unfortunately, we natives do not have any other place to get lost to and we must thus share the same world with our "invaders." So far as we are concerned, this land of ours, of our fathers, and of our fathers' fathers, is a comparatively familiar place, though still full of unexplored territories. But how does the land appear to the newcomers? Do they see the same green valleys, snow-capped mountains, bounteous plains, and sky-blue lakes that we see? Or do they only see hostile hills, barren deserts, polluted rivers, and smoggy cities? That is the main question.

Yesterday, Today, Tomorrow It is admittedly difficult to put ourselves in others' shoes and describe their thoughts and feelings. Even with such quantified measures as the incidence statistics of school dropout, physical ailment, mental illness, drug addiction, delinquency, crime, suicide, and other forms of social deviance, it is probably futile to argue that present-day children are exposed to a greater *amount* of social and psychological pressures or stress than that experienced by earlier generations. No matter where or when, human existence has never been free of uncertainty, anxiety, and despair. Man has always been a mysterious being who experiences himself both subjectively and objectively, a transcendental slave of here and now, and a finite bearer of infinity.[2]

Further, several studies indicate the operation of a self-protective mechanism which screens out the incomprehensible and the untouchable so as not to overload our psychic channels. Thus, it has been shown that most Americans, young and old alike, do not let themselves get worried to death by international tensions, fear of atomic extinction, problems of world population and food supply, or philosophical implications of the human exploration of space.[3] Call this escapism if you like, there is no denying that such a mechanism helps to keep human experiences within a manageable range and to preserve our sanity in the face of the ever-threatening universe.

Accordingly, it would be more to the point to interpret the situation in terms of different *kinds,* rather than amounts, of pressures. If today's pressures were of the same variety as yesterday's, we should know how to guide our children, giving them more of the same prescription which worked reasonably well for ourselves. Alas, today is not yesterday and tomorrow cannot be a duplicate of today. Social change is not only rapid but also complicated. The scope is unprecedentedly broad and the locus unpredictable.

CHILDREN UNDER PRESSURE
Kaoru Yamamoto

In spite of this basic difficulty, we are charged with the task of transmitting our past heritage to children, sharing with them the present life, and preparing them for the challenges of tomorrow. Therefore, we would do well to be keenly aware of the different nature of stress which is felt by our young. "However imprecise our estimate of the pressures may be, knowing that they exist helps us to a better realization of the complexity of some of the forces that affect peoples' lives." [4]

STRESS AND TRAUMA

Effects of stress, which may be defined as an actual or potential danger of either physiological or psychological nature, appear to be a complex function of both the characteristics of demand itself (intensity, multiplicity, and duration of stress; importance of threatened needs or goals; degree of suddenness and unfamiliarity of the challenge) and the characteristics of the individual under pressure (general competence; frame of reference; emotional makeup and involvement; and stress tolerance), and their interactions.[5]

When a person is placed under stress, there usually is an alarm reaction, often accompanied by resistance to diagnose the situation accurately and to accept the seriousness of the threat. Next comes an emergency mobilization of organismic resources (emotional, visceral, cognitive, etc.) to cope with the situation. If stress is mild, the increased alertness may bring forth some improvement in performance and, as a result, the individual may adapt himself to the pressure, recover from the shock, and regain control of himself after a due lapse of time. If, however, the stress is too severe or if it persists too long for the individual, fatigue sets in and his responses become increasingly more erratic, rigid, and disintegrated. Hostility, fear, and anxiety are often observed and, in extreme cases, the breaking point may be reached and the person collapses.

Although the general reaction is comparatively easy to delineate, the effects of a stressful experience are quite difficult to predict for any specific person because of the marked individual differences in competence, attitudes and assumptions, and stress tolerance. There is some evidence to suggest that deliberate training or sensitization can prepare a person better for later performance under pressure,[6] and, hence, past experiences also make a difference. Moreover, stresses "usually do not come singly or operate independently of one another. The total stress pattern at any time determines the part any one stress will play and has much to do with how skillful we will be at resolving it."[7]

Although behavior under severe stress conditions tends to attract more attention owing to the dramatic syndrome such as apathy or DDD (debility, dependency, and dread),[8] it is important to remember that, within limits, "mild but prolonged stress is more damaging and requires a longer time for recovery than brief but intense stress."[9] This "mild but prolonged" variety is precisely what we are discussing here and what Davis called "the truly troubling pressures" which "remain nearby, unseen and frustrating."[10]

Sustained stress, even when not intense, may take a heavy toll by lowering a person's tolerance to other stresses and by using up the deeper, irreplaceable reserve of his adaptive energy. Luckily, not all stress experiences result in traumatic effects, even though every exposure to severe stress is believed to leave an indelible scar which, with the other scars, manifests itself in the form of aging.[11]

What characteristics, then, make an experience particularly damaging and traumatic? Torrance interpreted the central dynamics to be the loss of contact with the environment, absence of anchor in reality, and lack of structure in the experience,[12] while Liddell identified four specific conditions which are inclined to lead to traumata.[13] These are: (1) loneliness (lack of social contact), (2) monotony, (3) confusion, and (4) overstimulation.

Loneliness Are there any social trends which may nurture the sense of loneliness in children? Are there any predisposing factors which make them feel deprived of anchors in reality?

The answer is "yes" if we heed the words of critics who point to the "alienated" nature of our society and its probable effects on children and adolescents.[14] Modern man's relationship to his fellow man has been described by Fromm as a relationship "between two abstractions, two living machines, who use each other."[15] This results from man's attitude toward himself which is characterized as a "marketing orientation."

> In this orientation, man experiences himself as a thing to be employed successfully on the market. He does not experience himself as an active agent, as the bearer of human powers. He is alienated from these powers. His aim is to sell himself successfully on the market. His sense of self does not stem from his activity as a loving and thinking individual, but from his socio-economic role.[16]

It seems certain that these feelings of inner estrangements and uprootedness have always been with us and, perhaps, they are "intrinsic to man's ontogenesis as an individual." [17] When we speak of alienation, however, we mean the loneliness of self-rejection and despair, rather than the experience of the existential and potentially creative aloneness.[18]

According to Seeman, there are five general meanings attached to the term *alienation*.[19] The first of these refers to the sense of powerlessness, of deprivation of both prerogative of decision and the means for it, and of defeatistic expectancy that one does not control the outcomes of his actions. We are familiar with this orientation in our "what can I do?" attitude toward international crises and national problems, as well as in our transposition of individual accountability with biological, psychological, and social determinism.[20]

A second meaning of alienation is exemplified by the individual's perception of ongoing events as meaningless or incomprehensible. The alienated person feels uncertain as to what he ought to believe and he is unable to act insightfully and purposefully. He senses that it is impossible to predict the outcomes of his actions and feels that he lives in an unintelligible world.

While the rapid social change, with its companion condition of tumultuous social order, tends to give a person this feeling of meaninglessness, the impact of the disorder is nowhere clearer than among the members of minority groups. Many things in this world "do not make sense" to them and they rightly feel both meaningless and powerless. If this is their cultural heritage, is it any wonder that minority children—colored, Jewish, poor, migratory, or whatever—reveal a strong inclination to be hostile, destructive, or apathetic towards themselves and others? [21]

Often forgotten but of equal importance is the fact that children who are taught prejudices against such minority members must similarly suffer from the sense of meaninglessness since they are given "a distorted perspective of reality and of themselves and are being taught to gain personal status in unrealistic ways." [22] Discrepancies between the American creed and the social reality will become increasingly difficult to ignore, thus exacting more and more adaptive energy from the majority children as well as from those of the minorities.

The remaining three usages of "alienation" are briefly mentioned merely to conclude Seeman's discussion. The third meaning is that of normlessness or anomie (high expectancy that socially unapproved behaviors are required to achieve given goals), while the fourth covers adaptation by isolation (assignment of low reward value to goals or beliefs which are typically highly valued in the given society). The fifth meaning of alienation is the sense of self-estrangement in which the term was used by Fromm in earlier quotes.

Social trends thus far mentioned are naturally reflected within education itself. When pupils are mass processed, when personal interactions between teachers and pupils or among pupils are kept to a minimum, and when the cult of efficiency is highly valued, our formal schooling does not seem to help assuage loneliness in children.[23]

Confusion and Monotony Social variables which tend to make stressful experiences traumatic seem to be characterized not only by their alienating features but also by their disorganized and unstable nature. Absolutes are gone, sacred institutions and values have been found lacking, and instrumental or emergent solutions are untested and suspect.[24]

A rather obvious source of confusion for younger generations is the absence of clearly-formulated standards to follow and adult models to emulate. In fact, some observers believe that even a poor model is better than none at all, since the former at least gives youngsters some ideas about how or how not to behave.[25] This confusion applies to many roles a child must assume; he needs appropriate sex-role models, work (or vocational) models, and life models.[26] It is true that youth must sooner or later find their own way rather than blindly accept the traditional models of ascribed potency,[27] but they still need some guidelines from adults at the outset, that is, something to grow out of, a sort of security blanket.

In addition to their confusion about adult models, children seem to be handicapped also by insufficient, unclear, or improper feedback from adults concerning their efforts. Thus, for example, Boehm and White recently reported on elementary pupils' perception of school marks, suggesting that children are in fact quite sensitive to teacher evaluation, even though unsure of the exact basis for such appraisal.[28]

As another example, a recent cross-national survey of children's views of foreign peoples had this to say about the sources of information utilized by youngsters in eleven countries.

> Thus, the young child (6 years old) generally learns about others through parents, mainly, or through television and movies. However, there is a very clear change from 10 years on; judging from the sources they recall when questioned, the older children in general receive little or no information about foreign nations from people in their environment, not even from their parents....
> Thus, for older children the major sources of information about

foreign peoples are impersonal ones—television and movies, books, school course work, textbooks, magazines, and, to a lesser extent, direct contact.[29]

Have you ever noticed how blissfully and innocently (I hope) various stereotypes of foreigners and of American minorities have been repeated daily and nightly on TV and radio, in the movies, plays, comic books, magazines, and worst of all, in textbooks?[30] Misrepresentation and magnification of differences are obviously not the best way to dispel confusion in the mind of our students who are destined to grow into an international world, instead of into an isolated community.

Let us next turn to monotony. When the same stress condition is sustained without much variation or reprieve, a person is robbed of gauges for comparison and the monotonous condition can lead to his collapse. One of the ready examples here is the persistent parental pressure on children to make good, to excel, to succeed.[31] Excellence is, at one and the same time, a desirable goal and a currently fashionable magic word among parents and the community at large. Unfortunately, however, "anything short of excellence bears stigma of failure. Excellence, too, has come to be judged against a public, rather than a personal criterion."[32] No wonder some of our students break under the pressure, while others rebel.

A peculiar counterpoint of this theme of success and achievement is the equally persistent insistence by some adults that our children are spoiled, lazy, and irresponsible, and that our adolescents are a lost generation.[33] Such characterization may or may not be accurate,[34] but what concerns us in the present context is the possible effects of the monotonous repetition of these negative comments. "One's reputation, whether false or true, cannot be hammered, hammered, hammered, into one's head without doing something to one's character. A child who finds himself rejected and attacked on all sides is not likely to develop dignity and poise as his outstanding traits."[35]

Overstimulation Finally, there is the matter of overstimulation. This may take the form of demands for speed, accuracy, or complexity beyond an individual's capacity. No one can persist indefinitely in pursuit of an impossible goal without suffering heavy damage. We are all familiar with cases where unreasonable parental expectation or personal ambition brought unhappy results to students.[36] Further, our lock-step system of schooling, anchored to the chronological age scale, is not known for its receptiveness to individual variations.

It is true that some efforts have been made in recent years to innovate (or renovate) school curricula and to synchronize instruction and development. It is also true that, "Almost twenty-five years ago John Anderson, appraising the research on child development and the curriculum, said that scientific concepts can be introduced into the curriculum at any point provided the concepts are presented in appropriate form to younger children." [37]

Nevertheless, when the now-familiar slogan, "any subject may be taught to anybody at any age in some form," [38] is made into a universal edict to be applied indiscriminately, the results are far from beneficial. Thus, for example, "To instruct all children in reading, in kindergarten, in first grade, or at another level, without respect for their readiness and other factors, is professional irresponsibility." [39] Human beings are unique and there is no reason for us to believe that any child can learn anything if he merely applies himself to the task or that every pupil will achieve the same results by studying the same thing.[40]

Another possible mechanism of stress was suggested in a recent study: teachers may unintentionally set expectations too high or too low for children. College students, reacting to filmed behaviors of elementary pupils, revealed a general tendency to give more favorable ratings to girls than to boys. Further, the women were more positive in their ratings than the men, and the older students judged the same pupil behaviors more favorably than the younger students.[41] Implications of these findings are indeed interesting to ponder.

In sum, then, many social forces appear to be operating to make children's experiences particularly stressful and traumatic. Human dignity itself is endangered by fragmentation of experience, impersonalization of human relationships, and encapsulation of individuals.[42]

CAN ANYTHING BE DONE?

What, then, can we do to improve the situation for our children? As usual, problems are alarming but the solutions are not at all obvious and depend heavily upon individual teachers' ingenuity and personal qualities. Seemingly, there are, among others, three possibilities.

Alleviation of Pressure The first is to try to alleviate the effects of stress by giving support and inducing insight. Reduction of unnecessary pressure is possible through elimination of needless sources of tension, clarification and structuring of demands, and provision of reassurance, encouragement, and means for emotional release.[43] Such efforts must be made at all levels and phases of education, namely, in policy formulation, administrative processes, parent-school relations, curricular and instructional decisions, classroom interactions, and others. It is obviously impossible to expect teachers to "take care of kids," when everything else is working to build up tension in children, rather than to reduce or buffer it.

It may be that the cherished system of compulsory education has arrived at a stage at which it needs a major revision.[44] We know full well that differences among individuals within any given group tend to be as great as differences among groups. It may be that the current evaluative procedures, which are geared to inter-individual competition rather than to either intra-individual or inter-group competition, require a basic re-examination.[45] It seems, in any case, dangerous to build up tension in children without allowing them more than the single, socially sanctioned outlet of the school achievement route. Most of us came that route and can attest to the fact that it nearly wrecks the whole, thinking human being; but we should keep in mind that we are the "lucky" minority in the strange race along that course, for many "drop out" for reasons that make sense, in context, at least.[46]

Identification of various coping strategies and preparation in advance may also be useful to our children. It is known that we use numerous methods to manage environmental variables as well as emotional effects of stress, such as: filtering of input, denial of reality, avoidance, tolerance, all-out efforts, and compensation.[47] Not all these are adaptive under all circumstances. Nevertheless, in the absence of a rational analysis and personal insight, we tend to persist in our respective styles of coping, even when they are irrelevant and even self-defeating.[48] By identifying these idiosyncratic patterns, examining other available strategies, and experiencing some of them in the safety of thought and action, children may prepare themselves for later stresses and emergencies. Flexibility and reasonable risk-taking ought to be nurtured as carefully and specifically as any other desirable human qualities.

Nurturance of Competence The second possibility was tacitly implied in the last sentence above. Since human life is full of frustrations, conflicts, and pressures, we are bound to live under pressure most of the time. Thus, "mental health and effective functioning come not from lack of stress but from learning to cope with it and the problems it presents."[49] Since palliative measures are often expensive and their effectiveness uncertain, anticipatory and preventive steps should be taken to bolster children's capacity to handle themselves in stressful situations.

This brings us to the concept of competence or efficacy which has admittedly been underplayed in the dominant homeostatic models of human action, be they behavioristic or psychoanalytic in orientation.[50] These models, as you may know, all base their interpretation of human behavior on the concept of balance. Individuals themselves are more or less pawns of their own inherent elements (instincts, drives, or Id) and they react to stimuli, events, or experiences only when the balance has been disturbed for some reason. When balance is regained in the form of drive reduction (which is said to be reinforcing) or in the form of a delicate truce among Id, Superego, and Ego, the person comes, at least theoretically, to a rest. But people do not merely *react;* they also *act.* They are not simply pushed by some uncontrollable forces, but they also pull themselves toward a certain goal. They are not satisfied in regaining and maintaining a balance; they actively disturb their own balance; they explore and search.

"Competence means capacity, fitness, or ability. The competence of a living organism means its fitness or ability to carry on those transactions with the environment which results in its maintaining itself, growing, and flourishing."[51] Competence is not derived from external incentives but rather is dependent upon an intrinsic effectance motivation which shows itself in behaviors characterized by curiosity, spontaneity, and autonomy. In spite of their initial appearance of playful randomness, such activities in fact show direction, selectivity, and persistence. They are aimed at exploration and mastery of our environment and, when successful, lead to the feeling of efficacy or the sense of competence.

> White emphasizes that the child will experience efficacy most clearly when the achievement is his own, perhaps even attained against the pressures of socializing agents. The strategy of desirable socialization practice that seems to follow is one that encourages and supports the child in solving his problems for himself rather than providing him with solutions. Such a strategy counts on the emergence and deepening of the intrinsic motivation that comes from the gratifications of effective action. If the socializing agents rely heavily on the extrinsic rewards of approval or disapproval, the child's potential intrinsic motivation may be stultified; he may continue to be governed by external

incentives like grades, money, or prestige rather than by the intrinsic satisfactions that he gets from dealing effectively with his world.[52]

The parallel between this concept and the general idea of creativity must be obvious to any observer.[53] It should also be pointed out that competence motivation is not the same as achievement motivation. "Strivings for competence appear long before social evaluation is set on them [children]. Need for achievement is a late, highly socialized, narrowly channeled form of competence motivation. Achievement motivation ... involves performance for the sake of social approval; competence motivation involves being able to risk disapproval in order to do what one wants." [54]

Reconsideration of Educational Policies We cannot, naturally, speak of preparation for competence without discussing the social implications, and this is indeed the third aspect of our children's situation which we can try to improve. Although generic in origin, competence expresses itself through channels that may be culturally and situationally specific.[55] Evidently, then, schools cannot do the job alone and education must be redefined in terms of community-wide and life-long activities. De-institutionalization of education must be seriously considered to allow fuller utilization of community resources and talents; we must also evaluate lateral transmission, in addition to the traditional vertical transmission, of knowledge and skills.[56]

As a matter of fact, some observers seem to feel that development or revitalization of a viable local community in a form not unlike that of the city-state in ancient Greece may be crucial in resolving the apparent stalemate in the formulation of imaginative and functional educational policies.[57] It could be that only such a context permits us to reduce various discontinuities among the nuclear family, school, and corporate worlds in our life; to resolve needless conflicts; and to make learning more meaningful for our children.

The task is certainly an overwhelming one. If, however, we are unable and/or unwilling to "Get lost and stay there," only one thing remains for us to do—accept the challenge and face up to it. Perhaps, with our concerted efforts and a little bit of luck, we may attain the enviable status of the young teacher, one of whose students anonymously but kindly wrote: "Don't worry—We're behind you 85%!" [58]

FOOTNOTES

[1] Bel Kaufman. *Up the Down Staircase.* New York: Avon Books, 1964. P. 185.

[2] Rollo May. *Psychology and the Human Dilemma.* Princeton, N.J.: D. Van Nostrand, 1967.

Allen Wheelis. *The Quest for Identity.* New York: Norton, 1958.

[3] James M. Gillespie and Gordon W. Allport. *Youth's Outlook on the Future.* New York: Random House, 1955.

Rose K. Goldsen, Morris Rosenberg, Robin M. Williams, Jr., and Edward A. Suchman. *What College Students Think.* Princeton, N.J.: D. Van Nostrand, 1960.

Gerald Gurin, Joseph Veroff and Sheila Feld. *Americans View Their Mental Health.* New York: Basic Books, 1960.

H. H. Remmers and D. H. Radler. *The American Teenager.* Indianapolis: Bobbs-Merrill, 1957.

[4] O. L. Davis, Jr. "Pressure on Pupils in the School," *Educational Leadership* 21: 423–428; April 1964. Quoted from p. 423.

[5] James C. Coleman. *Personality Dynamics and Effective Behavior.* Chicago: Scott, Foresman, 1960.

Richard S. Lazarus, James Deese and Sonia F. Osler. "The Effects of Psychological Stress Upon Performance," *Psychological Bulletin* 49: 293–317; July 1952.

E. Paul Torrance. *Constructive Behavior.* Belmont, Calif.: Wadsworth Publishing, 1965.

[6] Karl U. Smith and Margaret F. Smith. *Cybernetic Principles of Learning and Educational Design.* New York: Holt, Rinehart & Winston, 1966.

E. Paul Torrance. "Sensitization Versus Adaptation in Preparation for Emergencies: Prior Experience with an Emergency Ration and Its Acceptability in a Simulated Survival Situation," *Journal of Applied Psychology* 42: 63–67; January 1958.

[7] Coleman, *op. cit.,* p. 163.

[8] I. E. Farber, Harry F. Harlow and Louis J. West. "Brainwashing, Conditioning, and DDD (Debility, Dependency, and Dread)," *Sociometry* 20: 271–283; 1957.

Harvey D. Strassman, Margaret B. Thaler and Edgar H. Schein. "A Prisoner of War Syndrome: Apathy as a Reaction to Severe Stress," *American Journal of Psychiatry* 112: 998–1003; 1956.

[9] Torrance, *Constructive Behavior, op. cit.,* p. 28.

[10] Davis, *op. cit.,* p. 424.

[11] Hans Selye. *The Stress of Life.* New York: McGraw-Hill, 1956.

[12] Torrance, *Constructive Behavior, op. cit.*

[13] H. S. Liddell. *Emotional Hazards in Animals and Man.* Springfield, Ill.: Charles C Thomas, 1956.

[14] Paul Goodman. *Growing Up Absurd.* New York: Vintage Books, 1960.

Nathaniel Hickerson. *Education for Alienation.* Englewood Cliffs, N.J.: Prentice-Hall, 1966.

Karen Horney. *Neurosis and Human Growth.* New York: Norton, 1950.

Earl C. Kelley. *In Defense of Youth.* Englewood Cliffs, N.J.: Prentice-Hall, 1962.

Kenneth Keniston. *The Uncommitted.* New York: Harcourt, Brace & World, 1965.

C. Wright Mills. *White Collar.* New York: Oxford University Press, 1951.

David Riesman. *The Lonely Crowd.* New Haven, Conn.: Yale University Press, 1950.

[15] Erich Fromm. *The Sane Society.* New York: Rinehart, 1955. P. 139.

[16] *Ibid.,* pp. 141-142.

[17] Erik H. Erikson. *Insight and Responsibility.* New York: Norton, 1964. P. 101.

[18] Viktor E. Frankl. *Man's Search for Meaning.* New York: Washington Square Press, 1963.

Talcott Parsons. "Youth in the Context of American Society," *Daedalus* 91: 97-123; Winter 1962.

[19] Melvin Seeman. "On the Meaning of Alienation," *American Sociological Review* 24: 783-791; December 1959.

[20] John R. Seeley. "The Sociological Revolution." An unpublished paper presented at the Second Annual Conference on "Social and Behavioral Sciences as They Impact Upon Counseling," University of Florida, May 1962.

[21] Kenneth B. Clark. *Prejudice and Your Child.* (2nd ed.) Boston: Beacon Press, 1963.

Thomas F. Pettigrew. *A Profile of the Negro American.* Princeton, N.J.: D. Van Nostrand, 1964.

Arnold Rose. *The Negro in America.* New York: Harper Torchbooks, 1964.

Morris Rosenberg. *Society and the Adolescent Self-Image.* Princeton, N.J.: Princeton University Press, 1965.

Kaoru Yamamoto. "Children of Those Who Are Not Like Us," pp. 129-163 of this volume.

[22] K. B. Clark, *op. cit.,* p. 81.

[23] Burton R. Clark. *Educating the Expert Society*. San Francisco: Chandler Publishing, 1962.

David A. Goslin. *The School in Contemporary Society*. Chicago: Scott, Foresman, 1965.

Martin Meyerson. "The Ethos of the American College Student: Beyond the Protests," *Daedalus* 95: 713-739; Summer 1966.

Donald N. Michael. *The Next Generation*. New York: Vintage Books, 1965.

[24] Cora DuBois. "The Dominant Value Profile of American Culture," *American Anthropologist* 57: 1234-1238; December 1955.

John W. Gardner. *Self-Renewal*. New York: Harper Colophon Books, 1965.

O. Hobart Mowrer. *The Crisis in Psychiatry and Religion*. Princeton, N.J.: D. Van Nostrand, 1961.

Robert E. Nixon. *The Art of Growing*. New York: Random House, 1962.

George D. Spindler. "Education in Transforming American Culture," *Harvard Educational Review* 25: 148-156; Summer 1955.

Paul Tillich. "The Lost Dimension in Religion." In Richard Thruelsen and John Kobler, Eds. *Adventures of the Mind*. New York: Alfred A. Knopf, 1960. Pp. 47-56.

William H. Whyte, Jr. *The Organization Man*. New York: Simon and Schuster, 1956.

[25] Reuel Denney. "American Youth Today: A Bigger Cast, A Wider Screen," *Daedalus* 91: 124-144; Winter 1962.

Edgar Z. Friedenberg. *The Vanishing Adolescent*. New York: Dell Publishing, 1959.

[26] Winton M. Ahlstrom. "Masculine Identity and Career Problems for Boys." In William W. Wattenberg, Ed. *Social Deviancy Among Youth* (65th NSSE Yearbook, Part I). Chicago: University of Chicago Press, 1966. Pp. 135-163.

Erik H. Erikson. *Childhood and Society*. (2nd ed.) New York: Norton, 1963.

Geoffrey Gorer, *The American People*. (2nd ed.) New York: Norton, 1964.

Catharine V. Richards. "Discontinuities in Role Expectations of Girls." In William W. Wattenberg, Ed. *Social Deviancy Among Youth* (65th NSSE Yearbook, Part I). Chicago: University of Chicago Press, 1966. Pp. 164-188.

C. Gilbert Wrenn. "Human Values and Work in American Life," In Henry Borow, Ed. *Man in a World at Work*. Boston: Houghton Mifflin, 1964. Pp. 24-44.

[27] Parsons, *op. cit.* (Also see a slightly revised version of the same paper

in Henry Borow, Ed. *Man in a World at Work.* Boston: Houghton Mifflin, 1964. Pp. 237-256.)

[28] Anne E. Boehm and Mary Alice White. "Pupils' Perceptions of School Marks," *Elementary School Journal* 67: 237-240; February 1967.

[29] Wallace E. Lambert and Otto Klineberg. *Children's Views of Foreign Peoples.* New York: Appleton-Century-Crofts, 1967. Pp. 157 and 160.

[30] Gordon W. Allport. *The Nature of Prejudice.* New York: Doubleday Anchor Books, 1958.

George E. Simpson and J. Milton Yinger. *Racial and Cultural Minorities.* (3rd ed.) New York: Harper & Row, 1965.

[31] Solon T. Kimball. "Cultural Influences Shaping the Role of the Child." *The National Elementary Principal* 40: 28-32; September 1960.

V. T. Thayer and Martin Levit. *The Role of the School in American Society.* (2nd ed.) New York: Dodd, Mead, 1966.

[32] Davis, *op. cit.,* p. 426.

[33] Kelley, *op. cit.*

[34] Kenneth Keniston. "Social Change and Youth in America," *Daedalus* 91: 145-171; Winter 1962.

Parsons, *op. cit.*

[35] Allport, *op. cit.,* pp. 138-139.

[36] Irving D. Harris. *Emotional Blocks to Learning.* New York: The Free Press, 1961.

Fritz Redl and William W. Wattenberg. *Mental Hygiene in Teaching.* (2nd ed.) New York: Harcourt, Brace & World, 1959.

[37] Harry S. Broudy, B. Othaniel Smith, and Joe R. Burnett. *Democracy and Excellence in American Secondary Education.* Chicago: Rand McNally, 1964. P. 95.

[38] Jerome S. Bruner. *The Process of Education.* New York: Vintage Books, 1960. P. 12.

[39] Davis, *op. cit.,* p. 426.

[40] Kelley, *op. cit.*

[41] Harold W. Stevenson, Kennedy T. Hill, Gordon A. Hale and Barbara E. Moely. "Adult Ratings of Children's Behavior," *Child Development* 37: 929-941; December 1966.

[42] Fred M. Newmann and Donald W. Oliver. "Education and Community," *Harvard Educational Review* 37: 61-106; Winter 1967.

[43] Wesley Allinsmith and George W. Goethals. *The Role of Schools in Mental Health.* New York: Basic Books, 1962.

[44] Edgar Z. Friedenberg. *Coming of Age in America.* New York: Random House, 1965.

Paul Goodman. *Compulsory Mis-education and the Community of Scholars.* New York: Vintage Books, Random House, 1966.

[45] James S. Coleman. *The Adolescent Society.* New York: The Free Press, 1961.

[46] Daniel Schreiber, Ed. *Profile of the School Dropout.* New York: Vintage Books, Random House, 1968.

[47] Lois B. Murphy. *The Widening World of Childhood.* New York: Basic Books, 1962.

Torrance, *Constructive Behavior, op. cit.*

[48] James C. Coleman. *Abnormal Psychology and Modern Life.* (3rd ed.) Chicago: Scott, Foresman, 1964.

Nathan Kogan and Michael A. Wallach. *Risk Taking.* New York: Holt, Rinehart & Winston, 1964.

[49] Coleman, *Personality Dynamics and Effective Behavior, op. cit.,* p. 164.

[50] Robert W. White. "Motivation Reconsidered: The Concept of Competence," *Psychological Review* 66: 297–333; 1959.

Robert W. White. "Competence and the Psychosexual Stages of Development." In Marshall R. Jones, Ed. *Nebraska Symposium on Motivation, 1960.* Lincoln: University of Nebraska Press, 1960. Pp. 97–141.

[51] Robert W. White. "Sense of Interpersonal Competence." In Robert W. White, Ed. *The Study of Lives.* New York: Atherton Press, 1963. Pp. 72–93; quoted from p. 74.

[52] M. Brewster Smith. "Socialization for Competence," *Items* (Newsletter of the Social Science Research Council) 19: 17–23; June 1965. Quoted from p. 18.

[53] For example: E. Paul Torrance. *Rewarding Creative Behavior.* Englewood Cliffs, N.J.: Prentice-Hall, 1965.

[54] Smith, *op. cit.,* p. 20.

[55] Alex Inkeles. "Social Structure and the Socialization of Competence," *Harvard Educational Review* 36: 265–283; Summer 1966.

[56] Kimball and McClellan, *op. cit.*

Margaret Mead. "A Redefinition of Education," *NEA Journal* 48: 15–17; October 1959.

Newmann and Oliver, *op. cit.*

David T. Turney. "Educational Technology and the Disadvantaged Adolescent." A paper prepared for the Educational Media Council, Inc., Washington, D.C., January 1967.

[57] James E. McClellan. *Toward an Effective Critique of American Education.* Philadelphia: J. B. Lippincott, 1968.

[58] Kaufman, *op. cit.,* p. 186.

CHILDREN OF THOSE WHO ARE NOT LIKE US

Kaoru Yamamoto

Words are, at best, inadequate carriers of our thoughts and emotions. Therefore, in spite of the facility with which we speak nowadays of children who are *culturally deprived, disadvantaged,* or *underprivileged,* it is not always clear specifically whom we designate by such a phrase. And who are *we*, to begin with?

Identification of someone as *culturally deprived* certainly involves postulation of some standard style of cultural life and a value judgment. Loosely speaking, *our* life is assumed to be culturally replete and hence is fit to be the criterion in judging

---

This essay is based on a working paper prepared for the Educational Media Council, Inc., Washington, D.C., in January of 1967 under the title, "Media and Children of *Those Who Are Not Like Us*," and resulted from a contract with the U.S. Office of Education, #OE 5-16-032, "A Study of the Concentration of Educational Media Resources to Assist in Certain Education Programs of National Concern—Final Report, Part I: Education of the Culturally Disadvantaged." This selection is in the public domain and is not covered by the copyright that applies to the rest of this volume.

those who are *not like us*. Naturally, there is nothing absolute about such a comparison, but we seldom adopt as the standard the life style of someone more culturally refined than we are and count ourselves among the culturally deprived!

One of the dangers of this self-centered maneuver appears to be the familiar "gung-ho syndrome," or the well-intentioned but naive proselytization of our own values and practices.[1] Missionary work has long stood accused of the adverse effects of proselytizing; while education and social work, which have had their share of zealous evangelists, have increasingly come under fire. It would not be an overstatement to say that the newest versions of this phenomenon are observable in such celebrated campaigns as the Peace Corps and the War on Poverty.

Another difficulty with the oft-used phrase, *cultural deprivation,* is its implication of absence of culture along a single continuum. Nothing is further from reality: "We have to understand the fact that culturally different does not mean devoid of culture, and that children of Negro, Mexican, uneducated, bookless, and houseless families do not come to us with nothing. Let me repeat —they come with selves and with a sense of belonging to whatever group is theirs...."[2]

In other words, what is in question is not *deprivation* or *deficit* in a monolithic culture, but rather the state of subcultures with their particular values, objectives, norms, and behaviors which disagree with the modal patterns of the general culture.[3]

Finally, the generalized use of the summarizing term, *the culturally deprived,* does not acknowledge the existence of the large inter- and intra-group differences among those so designated.[4] No matter what generic term one applies to such people, he risks imminent overgeneralization and oversimplification. They may be equally impoverished and underprivileged, but the Puerto Rican Americans and the Negro Americans and the white slum dwellers all have different problems. Tasks facing Southern hillbillies or reservation Indians are quite dissimilar to those of the white farm laborers or of migrant workers of Mexican descent. Obviously no single label does justice to the varied groups, their subcultures and the unique ways in which they differ from our norms; and no simple solution is available to meet the divergent issues involved.

PARAMETERS OF DIFFERENCE

Whom, then, should we keep in mind when we discuss *those unlike us?* Havighurst believes that these groups are at the bot-

CHILDREN OF THOSE WHO ARE NOT LIKE US
Kaoru Yamamoto

tom in American income hierarchy, have a rural background, suffer from social and economic discrimination, and are distributed widely throughout the United States. In ethnic terms, he estimates that these groups are about evenly divided between whites and nonwhites and enumerates the following groups as the major ones: Negro and white migrants from the rural South to the Northern industrial cities; Mexican migrants of a rural background moving to the West and Middle West; and European immigrants of a rural background from eastern and southern Europe.[5]

In such a list as this, it is immediately clear that the parameters which characterize the variant populations include, among others, (1) ethclass, (2) economic, and (3) ecological factors. Let us take a brief look at each of these now.

Ethclass Factors The concept of "ethclass" was proposed by Gordon to "refer to the subsociety created by the intersection of the vertical stratifications of ethnicity with the horizontal stratifications of social class."[6] Warner had earlier (1953) observed the interaction between caste and class systems in the society of America;[7] nevertheless, the fact of social classes *within* and *across* various ethnic groups still tends to be underemphasized. We have increasingly come to recognize the importance of social-class status in defining behavior, at least within the dominant Anglo-American population; but to many people, a Chinese is a Chinese and a Negro is a Negro, regardless of what class position they happen to occupy within their own subculture. In reality, however, a Chinese American just does not associate with any and all Chinese Americans merely because they are Chinese. Chances are that in his behavioral patterns he would be more like other members of the same social class, regardless of their ethnicity, than like Chinese in different classes.

In other words, a person feels a sense of peoplehood, or historical identification, with his ethnic group, while his social class is the locus of a sense of behavioral identification. But, in terms of his primary-group relationships, he feels really congenial and relaxed only with those in his particular ethclass. The ethclass, then, gives him a sense of participational identification. This is the only group of people which accords an individual both the sense of interdependence of fate and that of behavioral similarities.[8] Further, due to the multiple melting-pot condition or the structural pluralism of the American society, it is unlikely that the same external appearances and material possessions necessarily represent the same class status within every ethnic group. A minority member with graduate degrees, for example, may live in a dilapidated tenement, driving a taxicab for his livelihood. Still, his tastes, values, and interests may be far closer to those of the majority professionals than to those of his co-workers. Thus, both his ethnicity and class intricately and simultaneously affect his style of life.

The heuristic value of this concept was demonstrated unwittingly by Lesser, Fifer, and Clark in their exploration of mental abilities of Jewish, Negro, Puerto Rican, and Chinese children representing the lower and middle social classes in the city of New York.[9] The authors reported that the interaction of social-class and ethnic-group membership, namely, the ethclass, was significantly associated with the *level* of each of four mental abilities (verbal, reasoning, numerical, and spatial), while the *pattern* of these abilities was more or less specific to each ethnic group, the social class not altering the basic organization. Seemingly, then, "low ability" means one thing to an ethclass, e.g., middle-class, protestant, Swedish Americans, while it means something different to another ethclass, e.g., lower-class, Catholic, Italian Americans.

The alleged class variations in child-rearing practices have been well documented by several authors.[10] In general, these data suggest that middle-class parents have been becoming more permissive and tolerant and that working-class (upper-lower class) parents are also following this trend, thus closing the gap observed earlier between these two adjacent social classes. Here again, however, this generalized picture may be more misleading than revealing. For one thing, ethnic variations in such practices, and their interactions with the class status, have not been systematically studied. For another, even within the Anglo-American majority, it is a fact that not much is known about the attitudes and practices of the bottom group, namely, the lower-lower class. Even among those living in the slum, moreover, one can detect some rather distinct types, for example, Galbraith's "case poverty" and "insular poverty."[11] The former represents those lazy, drunk, or mentally deficient ones who are demoralized, other-blaming, and unconcerned about their children's future. Those who are victims of insular poverty, on the other hand, are cognizant of their fate and engaged in a hard-fought, though admittedly futile, war for themselves and their offspring. This is the group about which Vontress said that "the people most dissatisfied with slum conditions are the people who live in them."[12]

Take, further, the case of Mexican Americans. These people,

CHILDREN OF THOSE WHO ARE NOT LIKE US
Kaoru Yamamoto

the third largest minority group in the United States, are known for their homogeneity in terms both of their religion and language and of their internal social differentiation (occupation, income, and schooling).[13] Contrast this with the second largest minority group, American Indians. It is generally observed that Indians are, in most regions, without a highly developed social-status system, while being quite heterogeneous with regard to their cultural patterns.[14] If, in addition, we recall the complex nature of ethnic assimilation, with several discernible variables (physical features, population, distribution, language, religion, degree of subjugation, strength of subsystems, rate of assimilation, etc.),[15] it becomes obvious that a simple-minded pronouncement, "Let us save the *under-privileged!*," is far from helpful in clarifying the issue and, indeed, not particularly meaningful.

Economic Factors It is nowadays fashionable to speak of *poverty* as a magic word which explains most everything: crime, delinquency, mental illness, learning difficulties, divorce, population increase, or what have you. And, it even appears, some of the non-poor people (in education and politics) are getting less poor by concentrating upon the poor!

Cynicism aside, the economic factors seem to be closely associated with the ethnic variable. Thus, "if a person is poor, there is a fair chance—1 chance in 5—that he is Negro, or Puerto Rican, or Mexican, or Indian." [16]

But, how do we define the poor? Economists and sociologists tell us that the mean gross family income in 1962 was $7,140, while the median family income (1961 figure) was roughly $5,000. In 1961, five percent of American families were annually earning less than $1,000 and five percent earned more than $15,000. The latter families may be called affluent, although few of them are truly wealthy. On the other hand, any typical family (a couple and three children) whose annual gross income is less than $4,000 would find it difficult to get by and may hence be classified as poor. Between the affluent and the poor, "we can designate families as deprived if their yearly income is more than $4,000 but less than $6,000, and as comfortable if their income ranges between $6,000 and $15,000." [17]

Using these definitions, it is observed that about 31 percent of the nation's families, or over 14 million families and 36 million people, are to be classified as poor. In addition, about 22 percent, or 10 million families, fall in the category of the deprived. Thus, the poor and the deprived together constitute 53 percent of the American families, while the remaining 47 percent are in the comfortable or affluent range.

Now, it can certainly be argued that all this is a matter of definition. The fact is, however, that the effect of using different definitions on the overall estimate of the size of the poverty problem is "very little." [18] It may further be contended that even the poorest of American families are still far better off than millions living in other lands.

Unfortunately, however, "poverty . . . has a special significance in a wealthy society" which values financial success highly and measures a person's worth on this criterion.

> When one must watch his children go to bed hungry or go to school with ill-fitting, worn clothing, it is little comfort to be told that they are better fed and clothed than many children in the world. When one's early teenage son or daughter drops out of school to look for a job, it is really no answer to be told that already he has had more education than millions of adults in other countries. It is no answer, because our poor are not living in these "other countries." It is this society, and not some underdeveloped country on the other side of the globe, that our poor know best and whose standards of living they use as a point of comparison with their own.[19]

The awareness of this contrast is keener because of the societal shift from the Protestant ethic or the morality of want (hard labor, thrift, saving, and delay of gratification) to the morality of affluence (the buy-now-pay-later philosophy, and a belief in consumption and waste). Such a trend affects the attitudes of the poor and, at the same time, the fact of economic unproductivity of these people tends to make the rest of the society discuss the matter in utilitarian or pay-off terms, thus contradicting the plausible dream of American individualism and egalitarianism.[20]

Ecological Factors In defining the culturally variant groups, it also appears important to specify where they came from, where they are, and where they are going. For example, Havighurst's list mentioned earlier indicated that migrants or immigrants of rural background who move to industrialized areas represent a sizable portion of the disadvantaged population. Had they stayed around on the farm, would they have been better off? The answer, unfortunately, seems negative and these people are in that unenviable "damned if they do and damned if they don't" situation.

First, it is well known that there has been a consistently decreasing trend in the U.S. farm population. At the turn of the century, one in three workers in the nation was employed on a farm, but the figure today is less than one in ten. With this shift in the form of industry came the abandonment of tenant farming, consolidation of land into larger operating units, and mechanization of agriculture. These resulted in, among other things, a sharp reduction in the number of available farm occupations, especially in the semiskilled and unskilled categories.[21]

This transition from rural areas and jobs to urban residence and employment naturally affected many ethnic groups, notably, Negroes. In 1900, 77.3 percent of the Negro population were classified rural, while the proportion in 1960 was 26.6 percent. The movement from the South, estimated at four million people or more over the period, raised the colored population of the North to nearly 30 percent and of the West to nearly four percent of the total Negro population.

Many of these emigrants left their native states under the pressures of high fertility rate, surplus farm labor, and limited industrial opportunities in the South, but also in the search of a promised land with less discrimination and better living conditions. Unfortunately, however, what awaited most of them in the North was marginal living with family disorganization, congested and segregated economic insecurity, malnutrition, and ill health.[22]

Second, although they tend to be forgotten in the shadow of the more dramatic plight of their big-city brothers, the nation's farmers are poor. It is said that about one-third of the counties in the United States suffer from low-income farm problems. In 1960, the median gross income of the whole experienced civilian labor force was reported at $4,621 (male) and $2,257 (female). On the other hand, the figures for farmers and farm managers were, for male and female respectively, $2,169 and $836; those for farm laborers and foremen were only $1,066 (male)*and $602 (female).[23]

Naturally, great variations are observed among rural areas themselves. For example, in 1956, the index of rural level of living was 145 for the entire nation, 169 in the Northeast, 167 in the West, 165 in the North-Central States, and a mere 119 in the South. Large differences were observed between the families in the South and those in the rest of the farming areas in their possession of such facilities as running water, flush toilet, and telephone.[24] In any case, the impoverished conditions of rural America should not be ignored in our discussion of the disadvantaged. The much-talked-of mountain folk of Appalachia are just a symbol of the rural population in need.

In addition to those who moved, more or less permanently,

from farms to cities, we have a large number of migratory workers as a distinctly variant group. Among the three categories of hired farm workers, namely, the regular workers (employed for more than 150 days a year by a single employer), seasonal workers (employed less than 150 days and by more than one employer), and migratory workers; the most precarious is the status of the last, the itinerant farmhands. Between 1950 and 1960, the total number of these workers remained under 500,000.[25]

In general, there are six streams of migratory farm laborers identified:

1. About 60,000 workers on the Atlantic coast, most of whom are Negro, supplemented by workers from Puerto Rico and Mexican-Americans.

2. Approximately 60,000 workers, nearly all Mexican-Americans, in the sugar-beet stream which starts in Texas and goes North into the North Central and Mountain States.

3. About 30,000 men of Mexican descent who come up from Texas to Montana and North Dakota, mainly as combine teams, to harvest wheat and small-grain.

4. About 80,000 workers of Mexican descent plus Negroes to harvest cotton; starting in Texas—one group goes to the Mississippi Delta and a larger one goes into New Mexico, Arizona, and southern California.

5. Approximately 30,000 people of early American stock who move north and west from Oklahoma, Arkansas, and western Tennessee to pick fruit and tomatoes.

6. About 120,000 workers of all backgrounds who work up and down the Pacific coast.[26]

There was, in addition, a group of imported foreign workers numbering up to about 70,000, but the largest source of these was closed in 1964 by the Congressional action to discontinue the Mexican Contract Labor (Bracero) Program of 1951.

In a sense, the life of these itinerant farmhands typifies the failure end of the continuum in a society oriented to success in the form of visible things and achievement. The average income of the migrant worker was only $902 in 1961. Most of the workers travel with their families, living in primitive quarters with few modern facilities. *The Grapes of Wrath* is not an old, forgotten story. Transient and isolated, these people are not

CHILDREN OF THOSE WHO ARE NOT LIKE US
Kaoru Yamamoto

protected by any minimum wage standards or by health, medical, and social care. Formal education has yet to reach the majority of their children.[27] No stable job, no money, no house, no property, no status, no nothing—here is a people which has not moved from rags to riches, has not climbed the ladder to the stars, and has betrayed the American dream. But who, indeed, is to blame?

Finally, let us remember the fact that the transient nature of the *underprivileged* is not restricted to the migrant farm workers. "One of the problems of inner city poor children is the residential mobility of their families that continually disrupts their school life.... Children of the inner city have often moved many times during their school lives and more frequently than middle-class children.... Much of the residential mobility is a reaction to frustration and is without design or purpose except for a vague hope of a new chance." [28] But the search never ends and the periodic moves continue forever.

WHAT IT MEANS TO BE ONE OF *THEM*

Parameters are not determinants and they are obviously not mutually independent in the American society. Being a member of a minority group, belonging to the lower-lower social stratum, occupying the lowest economic position, or joining the occupationally and residentially migrant population—these telling signs, either singly or in combination, do not necessarily justify our concluding that the person is doomed from our viewpoint. There are enough exceptions to caution us against a blanket diagnosis. However, none of these conditions bespeaks a favorable environmental setting for a person in this nation.

Assuming, for the moment, that you are *one of them,* what is it like? The answer may be approximated from Hollingshead's notable description [29] of those on the bottom in "Elmtown:"

A person may be of American stock, early or late, or of *foreign* descent, e.g., Polish, German, or Norwegian. Perhaps it does not make much difference to outsiders who he is but, within the "scum of the city" itself, this more or less pinpoints the particular subarea he lives in.

A dilapidated, box-like home; a wood-coal stove or a kerosene burner for both heating and cooking; a sagging sofa and/or an iron bed for living and sleeping; an old mirror and several magazine cutouts on the wall; a row of nails to serve as a wardrobe; an abused table and a few poorly-fixed chairs; a radio and a bare light bulb or two; assorted dishes and pans; no books and no phone (less than one percent have it); no independent bath-toilet facilities (about one in seven homes has these); city water (three out of four within the city limits), wells, springs, or creeks.

Privacy in the home is almost nonexistent; the house is rented in four cases out of five; one in two families owns a car which is more than 7 years old; the father is the chief breadwinner in three out of five homes but his employment is unskilled and irregular; the income is meager (the range in Elmtown was $500 to $1,500, with a mode of $850) and personal loans from brokers (in the order of $50) are difficult to obtain.[30] The marital relationship is unstable; 20 to 25 percent of all births are estimated to be illegitimate; close to 80 percent of the mothers gave birth to their first child before the age of 20; little pre- and post-natal care of either mother or child; the number of children is large (the mean in Elmtown was 5.6 per mother, the range being 1 to 13); the mother-child relation is the strongest and most enduring family tie.

Nearly 60 percent of the families have been broken up by death, desertion, separation, or divorce; formal education is largely limited to the elementary school; religious ties are quite tenuous and often hostile ("The 'Everyone Welcome' signs in front of the churches should add 'except people like us....' "); leisure time, extensive because of unemployment and illness, is spent in loafing around the neighborhood, informal visits, gossipping, petty gambling, cheap theaters, drinking, sex plays, and fights; no organized community activities or social functions; residents are well acquainted with the police, sheriff, prosecuting attorney and judge, but only slightly known to the ministers and school officials. People are passive, fatalistic, resigned to the life of frustration and defeat in a community which despises them for their disregard of morals, lack of "success" goals, and dire poverty. They are *non-people*.

Hope, Time, and Identity One thing which characterizes this kind of life is the hopeless quality of human existence, despair, resignation, and bitterness.[31] When a person is struggling for survival and living "in a world of anxiety about the immediate provisions for his basic needs of food, clothing, and shelter, he learns to seek immediate gratification in whatever he does.... Lower-class behavior, which may be regarded as delinquent or shiftless and unmotivated by other groups, is usually realistic and responsive to the cultural situation."[32] He thus develops a strong present-time orientation.

What else does lacking the "essential *strength of hope*" imply? Henry believes that "those who cannot *hope* for achievement or security can have no concept of the organization of behavior through time toward goals.... His behavior, having neither background nor direction, is disorganized. What is left of him is the irreducible ash—the *survival self*—the flight from death."[33] Not only does he lose the sight of time but also his perception of self, since, as pointed out by Heidegger, self-identity is dependent upon the continuity and movement through time: namely, what I was yesterday, what I am today, and what I will be tomorrow. Truncation of any part of this temporal organization is bound to affect the sense of I-ness. When a child says, "I'm nobody, who are you? Are you nobody too?," in the words of Emily Dickinson,[34] he seems to be revealing some fundamental insight over and beyond mere reflection of societal appraisal of him. He does not think of the uncertain future and he stifles all memories of the past, thus fixating in the present. He does not have a clear sense of goals and purposes, nor that of human history and heritage. He is indeed nobody.

Time perspective provides an alternative to impulsive action by freeing a person from the domination of the immediate situation and, further, allows a more accurate assessment of people and events. This, then, is the quality often found to differentiate between middle-class and lower-class members, between normal and schizophrenic adults, between delinquent and non-delinquent adolescents, and between father-present and father-absent children.[35]

Chances are that the *unfortunate* children never develop an adequate sense of futurity, both in its personal aspects (personal projection for the future; living in the future; feeling about and investing in the future) and in its cognitive aspects (working with the future as an abstract cognitive category; utilizing time to organize and interpret experiences).[36] This, in turn, would result in an incomplete differentiation between what is expected (level of reality in the future) and what is dreamed of or wished for (level of unreality in the future).[37] It is recalled in this connection that Hollingshead found among the Elmtown children of unskilled workers a very large amount of uncertainty in vocational aims.[38] Also pertinent is the following observation by Janowitz:

> Children who cannot achieve adequately often compensate by exaggerating the extent of their abilities. There is often real confusion about what they can do.... Studies have been done showing that non-achieving children of sixteen to seventeen still express ambitions of wanting to be doctors, lawyers, and engi-

neers. Such findings have been used to argue that they have the same aspirations that so-called middle-class children have. Actually, it proves nothing of the kind. It only proves that these children are guilty of very wishful thinking.[39]

Two additional things must be mentioned before we leave the topic of time perspective. First, it is a fact that some of the characteristics of the *disadvantaged* in the United States resemble those in different cultures. For example, the present-time orientation, subjugation-to-nature (fatalism and resignation) rather than mastery-over-nature philosophy, and *existing* (low mobility aspiration and achievement need) rather than *doing* personality type, all remind us of the cultural patterns of Latin-American people who, by chance or because of their way of life, find themselves largely among the poor in this country.[40] Whether the impoverished and segregated living conditions first molded such values or the process worked in reverse at the outset is an academic question for our immediate purposes. The important points are that values are sharply in conflict and that they tend to perpetuate themselves.[41]

Second, there are some indications that the loss of the sense of the past and future, and of the goals and purposes are becoming an experience not exclusively of those unlike ourselves. For one thing, in spite of our vigorous pursuit of happiness in the form of tangible fruits of modern science and technology and in spite of our affluence, we have been beset by the uneasy feelings of alienation, anxiety, and lack of meaning. This forces us back into the vicious cycle of activity again and invites an observer to remark that "a serious discussion of the future is just what is missing in the United States," owing to our fear of something worse than total destruction—*"total meaninglessness."* [42]

For another, the accelerating pace of social changes and the resultant generational discontinuities cause the past to grow "progressively more different from the present in fact" and "more remote and irrelevant psychologically.... the future, too, grows more remote and uncertain.... the present assumes a new significance as the one time in which the environment is relevant, immediate, and knowable." [43] What long-range implications this phenomenon possesses, for the American society as a whole and for its subgroups, are unknown at the moment.

Transmission of Culture   It has been noted that many of the *unfortunate* children "(a) question their own self-worth; (b) feel inferior, particularly in the school situation; (c) fear new situations rather than feeling that they are a challenge to their growth; (d) desire to cling tenaciously to the familiar; (e) have many feelings of guilt and shame; (f) have limited trust in adults; and (g) respond with triggerlike reactions to apparently minor frustrations."[44] As we intimated above, all these and other patterns of thought and behavior are *solutions* to their problems and not problems themselves in the first instance. These are functional, coping responses and will persist so long as the overall conditions of life require them of the people.[45]

It is, therefore, small wonder for us to find, for example, that 80 percent of the parents in the relief families have grown up in families of the same type.[46] The culture has to perpetuate and transmit itself to help prevent the participants from perishing. Still, we have to agree with Wortis and his colleagues in their poignant observation:

> Other elements in the environment were preparing the child to take over a lower class role. The inadequate incomes, crowded homes, lack of consistent familial ties, the mother's depression and helplessness in her own situation, were as important as her child-rearing practices in influencing the child's development and preparing him for an adult role. It was for us a sobering experience to watch a large group of newborn infants, plastic human beings of unknown potential, and observe over a 5-year period their social preparation to enter the class of the least skilled, least-educated, and most-rejected in our society.[47]

These children must learn to live with frustration and loneliness, to hit the balance between affiliation need and fear of involvement, and to "be good" in the sense of physical inactivity, verbal nonparticipation, and cognitive nonobservance in the overcrowded living space.[48] They must be exposed early to such realities of life as hunger, heat and cold, noise, hostility, violence, addiction, sexual intimacy, sickness, and death. They are to obey their parents and look after their younger siblings, imitate the parental patterns of aggression so as to be able to fight off any outside offenders, acquire familiarity with law in its negative connotation, and develop strong peer-group identification.[49]

Certain generalized morals of solidarity must be inculcated: "Within this culture of poverty it is perfectly all right to take things from the outgroup as long as you never take from the in-group. If you take from the in-group, then you're really a low-down bastard; if you take from the out-group and get away with it, you're smart."[50] Say nothing to the cops and social workers, they are the worst enemies. Be loyal and reciprocate help when the occasion arises.

At its best, then, such cultural orientation builds self-sufficient, courageous, pragmatic, patient, and compassionate human beings

—Tolstoy knew them and so did Dostoyevsky and Dickens. Unfortunately, however, the odds are increasingly against their emerging as the ultimate victors in the American urban society and mass culture.

Experience and Preparation The life of the *underprivileged* is not geared to its symbolic aspects. Not much writing, reading, or counting is practiced, speaking or listening is not their art, and formal and informal rituals are infrequent. No wonder, then, that a psychiatrist who interviewed lower-class parents reported the impression that conversing with them would neither stimulate nor exercise the intellect. "They are more preoccupied with the 'What is it?' and 'How can I use it?' aspects of human existence than the 'Why is it?' aspects. The brute necessities of economic survival compel them to be basically practical—not to wonder about the meaning and the interrelatedness of life." [51] It is in this sense that Hess and Shipman declared the meaning of deprivation to be a deprivation of meaning.[52]

Understandably, their children tend to be oriented to the concrete and physical. They approach problems, express feelings, and establish social relationships in a motoric, rather than conceptual, mode.[53] Words stand for tangible objects and explicit action; they do not represent the general, the possible, and the hypothetical. Learning is physical and often slow, but the learner can be surprisingly articulate in role-playing situations.[54] These children do not depend on mediated responses, either schematic or thematic, and their reactions are stimulus- or immediacy-controlled.

Their language is (or, to be exact, is hypothesized to be) more informal and restricted than formal and elaborate. It is a language of implicit meaning. Its short, grammatically simple, syntactically poor sentences do not narrow the range of possible significance for the common, multireferential words and, hence, do not facilitate the communication of ideas and relationships requiring any precise formulation.[55]

It is sometimes argued that poverty results in sparsity of observable and manipulable objects and scarcity of cultural experiences. Let us not, however, believe that this is a case of stimulus deprivation in which the amount of stimulation drops below a certain threshold. The difference is not so much in the quantity of input as in its range (variability), quality (content and tone), and organization (patterns and sequencing).

Paucity of artifacts in his early life and lack in diversity of experiential categories would allow a child only a limited exercise of his visual and tactile senses. On the other hand, possibly because of the high noise level of his environment, his auditory discrimination does not highly develop and the resultant inattentiveness also affects his memory function.[56]

Likewise, his restricted environment, coupled with the relative absence of pertinent adult models and structured guidance, would hamper development of his concept formation (collection of things and facts, comparison, and classification), decision making (reflection, weighing consequences, and selection among alternatives), and scientific attitude (planned, problem-solving orientation).[57]

Language and thought are closely intermeshed. Where the former tends to be concrete and particularized, so would be the latter. Accordingly, it is surmised that one of the most important consequences of limited environment is slow and incomplete transition from the concrete, nonverbal, and particularized mode of thought and comprehension to the abstract, verbal, and more precise (differentiated) one. Manipulation of symbols, either numerical, linguistic, or schematic, and handling of abstract concepts and their relationships also tend to be restricted.[58]

In essence, the *unfortunate* children are not raised in a setting favorable to the development of competence. They may receive enough sensory stimulation quite early in their life but this is followed by a poverty of objects and a lack of consistency in perceptual experiences when these become crucial in the formation of linguistic-conceptual intelligence and competence motivation.[59]

Is there any wonder, then, why these children become poor and unwilling pupils? Is there any reason why we should expect anything in school but "cumulative deficit," or exacerbation of their original difficulties?[60] Should we be surprised to find a dropout rate in the lowest-income schools more than 20 times that in the highest-income schools?[61] Is it not also significant that lower social-class standings are associated with higher prevalence rates of mental illness among children?[62]

REACHING TO *THEM*, EDUCATIONALLY—BUT HOW?

In educational spheres, we often hear an admonition, doubtless well meant, that, if culturally variant pupils do not react favorably, schools and more specifically teachers are failing them, rather than the other way around. With due respect to this reminder of our responsibility, let us not be too eager and too ambitious. No matter how strongly we believe in formal education as an ultimate hope for America, we should remember that education cannot get everything done which all other institutions left undone in the society. Education may be a powerful medicine but it is evidently not a panacea.

> Generally, the schools are being asked to improve the economic and social position of deprived children through education, to break through the vicious circle of low education–low socioeconomic status that now exists. Specifically, the schools are being asked to compensate for the massive deprivations from which these children have suffered and to stimulate and motivate them to learn and achieve. Such a program, it seems to us, can be of tremendous significance if careful distinctions are made between what the schools can and cannot do.[63]

Most certainly, schools cannot reverse the tide single-handedly when no sustained help is forthcoming politically, economically, legally, and socially from the community. Teachers cannot be fulltime parent substitutes and models, and children should not be expected to live successfully in two contradictory worlds, home and school, one real and the other unreal.

Confrontation A teacher carries his own heritage with him, just as a pupil does his. When the two meet, it is not a matter merely of two individuals facing each other but also of confrontation between two cultures. With their respective and oft disparate mores, customs, folkways, and taboo, the communication is never easy. Each participant in the interaction has a dual task of finding the other's identity and his own identity as perceived by the other. In other words, the teacher's questions are: "Who is this pupil? And, who does he think I am?" The pupil, in return, asks: "Who is this teacher? What is he like? And, how does he see me?"

Even when each party is certain of his own identity, he still must present it in some form to the other party and must also define the other's identity so as to structure the interactional setting. In this attempt, several types of contexts can arise: a closed context (A does not know who B is, while B knows who A is); a suspicion context (A has some inkling of B's identity but is still uncertain, while B knows who A is); an open context (A knows who B is and B knows who A is); and a pretense context (both A and B are fully aware of the other's identity but pretend not to be).[64]

Chances are that an incoming pupil is unaware of his teacher's identity or of how the latter perceives him. The teacher is a stranger whom the child meets in an unfamiliar place under

CHILDREN OF THOSE WHO ARE NOT LIKE US
Kaoru Yamamoto

uncommon circumstances.[65] This closed awareness is not the most relaxing atmosphere of all. The pupil, uncomfortable and rather powerless, restructures the setting by trying to find out something about the other party. He sulks, balks, hollers, yells, shows off, or challenges the adult. In so doing, he gets the teacher's attention, discovers the limits to which the latter lets him go, and diagnoses the strange fellow. He may not be able to monopolize the interaction to himself but he can gather additional information by watching the teacher's reaction to other pupils.

Pretty soon, he starts suspecting certain things about the stranger and the suspicion context prevails. Is he a regular guy? Is he tough? Does he mean business? Is he a snooper? Is he a prosecutor? A warden? Does he understand me? Does he like me? After a while, the awareness context may become, for better or for worse, open. The teacher cannot help revealing himself over an extended period of time and there remains no question in the pupil's mind of who the teacher is and what he thinks of the student.[66]

When two discrepant cultures meet, it takes rare individuals to bridge the two. Some may be able to integrate the new experiences into their new self, while others become marginal men. Most, however, take the safest way out by clinging to their old identity; this is the pattern followed by the majority of teachers and, not surprisingly, by the majority of children. Both sides may be willing to (or have to, under the law or employment strictures) play along a little longer as if they were still feeling each other out and allowing some benefit of doubt. But in fact both may simply be operating in a pretense context, awaiting the first break for getting away clean.

The picture is, nevertheless, not entirely bleak. Notwithstanding their "shocking" expressions and behaviors, the children are usually more serious, honest, and sensitive than adults. They are quick to divine the genuine and the fake. They are keen about the difference between love and respect which are given freely and willingly and bait which serves intentionally or unintentionally to make a sucker out of them. And, thank heaven, children are willing to understand consistent and reasonable adults.[67] Teachers' attitudes seem to influence children more than the children's attitudes influence teachers and, further, teacher attitudes seem to count more heavily in lower-class schools than in middle-class schools.[68] Granted the difficulty in selection, preparation, and placement of sincere, perceptive, and mature teachers for the *disadvantaged* pupils, the possibility for effective teaching does exist and the omen is not all bad.[69]

Communication: Oral Many of us are poor at comprehending and conversing in a foreign language. Thus, there is good reason to suspect that the "social-class determination of linguistic styles and habits" serves "as an effective deterrent to communication and understanding between child and teacher."[70]

Peisach's study on this point, however, seems to suggest rather complex relationships among relevant variables. For example, working with first- and fifth-grade children, both Negro and white, of lower- and middle-class background, she reported that neither the social-class difference nor the ethnic difference mattered much in the pupils' understanding of teacher speech at the first-grade level. Sex differences (favoring girls), social-class differences (favoring the middle-class), and ethnic differences (favoring the white) all became salient at the fifth-grade level, but the sex difference was the only one which remained significant even after an adequate adjustment was made for the IQ differences involved.

When, in addition, the comprehension of peer speech was studied among fifth graders, it was found that the social-class differences (favoring the middle-class) existed but no ethnic differences were detected. Quite interestingly, when the speech samples represented either lower-class speech or Negro speech, the lower-class pupils understood it (in the sense that they got the meaning of the communication in spite of certain intentional omissions) as well as the middle-class pupils did. But when the speech samples represented either middle-class or white children, the lower-class pupils understood significantly less well than the middle-class children. While the overall ethnic differences were not significant, the Negro pupils tended to do less well than white unless the speech samples were from either boys or Negro children. In looking at these results, let us recall the variable of ethclass we discussed earlier. Finally, among the fifth graders, Peisach reported that the auditory form of sample presentation was much more difficult than the visual (written) mode for both teachers' and children's speech. However, contrary to other evidence (see footnote 56), she obtained no significant interaction effects between the mode of presentation and any other variables, namely, social class, ethnicity, or sex.[71]

This study certainly bears replication and extension. One of its precious qualities is that it studied children's understanding in simulated teacher-pupil and peer interactions. Most other studies have investigated the structure, either logical or functional, of children's or teachers' verbal behavior in isolation, or the whole pattern of verbal communication. Few, if any, have used the culturally variant children as subjects. For example, Loban's longitudinal study of kindergarten children was accomplished by analysis of tape-recorded interviews; verbal reaction of the children was elicited mainly by a standard set of questions and a picture-story task.[72] The analysts then transcribed the speech and investigated its structure. No dialogue, either real or structured, was involved, and in this sense, the analysis was made "in isolation." The counterpart of this approach, concentrating on teacher talk, has been pursued by, among others, Smith.[73]

In contrast, there are schemes of analysis which purport to describe the total configuration of teacher-pupil interaction. Some, like Flanders', explore the affective and content-free characteristics of the verbal behavior,[74] while others try to grasp the strategic intention and moves in teaching.[75] In either case, the analysis transcends the flesh-and-blood level of human communication. It is, by analogy, one thing to investigate the traffic patterns in a large metropolis to improve daily transportation and safety, while it is another to learn how individual drivers feel, think, and react with regard to the problems of their automobiles, driving, and traffic. Make no mistake about this: accumulation of systematic knowledge concerning the culturally variant is close to nil and we certainly need strategic research. However, such research could not obviate either tactical studies or reconnaisance.

Communication: Written and Graphic Earlier we said that the concept of time is not particularly meaningful among the *underprivileged* people. This may be one of the reasons why their children have difficulty handling verbal materials, either spoken or written. Verbal communication is a temporally-ordered method of abstraction, description, and interpretation, which is at best an incomplete translation of a person's perception of world, both internal and external.[76] The perception is an experience in whole and it is spatially, rather than temporally (linearly), organized.

This does not, of course, imply any superiority of a non-temporally oriented person in his spatial perception and cognitive mapping. It may simply mean that transition from spatial to temporal structuring of his experience may not be successful until his exploration of the spatial mode is sufficiently advanced to prepare him for the abstraction and symbolization necessary for the temporal mode.

Such a viewpoint seems comprehensible if we recall the stages of development of spatial concept postulated by Stone and Church:

> We can recognize five major stages in the development of spatial concepts, although any one person (at any age) may operate on several different levels. First, there is *action space,* consisting of the locations to which the child anchors his movements, and the regions in which he moves. Second, there is *body space,* based on the child's awareness of directions and distance in relation to his own body. Third, there is *object space,* where objects can be located relative to each other in terms of directions and distances transferred from body space, but now without direct reference to the child's body. . . . The fourth stage we shall call *map space,* the elaboration and unification of concrete spatial experiences into more or less extensive 'mental maps' dependent on some system of co-ordinates or cardinal directions which may apply to rooms or regions, to towns or nations. Although map space may be concrete in the sense that it relies on visual images, it is abstract both in the sense that it involves principles of organization independent of particular objects and in the sense that a great deal of conceptual understanding is brought to bear in formulating mental maps. A final stage, *abstract space,* . . . comes with the ability to deal with abstract spatial concepts necessary to mapping or navigational problems, geographical or astronomical ideas, or problems of solid geometry, even including, at the most abstract level, multidimensional space beyond our experienced three dimensions.[77]

Chances are that the *disadvantaged* children experience difficulties with the later stages of this ladder which complement the development of verbal communication. This is obviously another area where close observation is sorely needed to help clarify the picture. In any case, it is likely that a person must build the basic structure before aiming at the sky, and reparation is always painful and time consuming.

Assuming that we have finally gotten the children interested in tackling the printed materials, what about books for reading? What do children seek? Here are some tips given by themselves: (1) Books about animals, aviation, careers, hobbies, sports, the sea, and westerns. In other words, books with lots of adventure, plenty of excitement, and many interesting facts of science and nature. (2) Books with many good pictures, good drawings, and big print. (3) Books which push the readers to go on to the next page and the next page and the next. No kid stuff, please.[78]

How solid are these recommendations of children from a technical point of view? Preference is one thing and effectiveness in teaching is often another. Not many people would deny that interest and meaningfulness play an important role in sustaining a learner's efforts; but how about the matter of graphic communication and verbal-nonverbal textbook design? Do illustrations really help? What kind of illustrations are to be preferred?

Evidence available on this point is scanty, to say the least, and studies pertinent to the culturally variant children are still harder to locate. Rather surprisingly, the answer to our first question, "Do illustrations help?," seems to be at best ambiguous among the literature, so long as the effects are measured on verbal tests. Several studies comparing illustrated texts with unillustrated ones indicated that the illustrations do not facilitate learning,[79] but coupling of pictorial and oral presentations appears to yield positive increments in learning over oral presentation alone.[80]

The answer to the second question, "What kind of illustrations are to be preferred?," seems a little clearer. It has been shown that considerable intelligence and training are necessary for the readers to understand diagrams, charts, and graphs and that different types of material require different types of diagrams.[81]

Working with newly literate adults and rural youth in Latin American countries, some authors have found that interpretation of illustrations tended to be extremely literal and structured by past experience of the subjects. For this type of reader, therefore, pictorial illustrations should be as realistic as possible and color should not be used unless it is realistic. Nevertheless, the amount of detail and action in a picture should be limited to the important points to be illustrated and should not contain too much extraneous detail.[82]

Even though simulation of reality and spatial organization of temporal (verbal) material are two of the obvious functions of book illustration, the most complete reproduction of reality by photographs and by life-like paintings and drawings may not be the best means to reach the goal. Identification and accentuation of critical points (graphic segregation), as well as promotion of generalization and transfer (graphic integration), may be better accomplished by line and impressionistic drawings. These types of illustrations may also serve to arouse curiosity and imagination among the readers.[83]

What about the social reality of the reading material? A call for new types of books is by now a familiar one, urging us to adapt them to lower-class urban industrial (or rural) settings rather than to the traditional, middle-class, suburban environment and adjust them to the realities of economic, ethnic, occupational, and familial facts of the *disadvantaged* children's life.[84] No one is likely to quarrel with this argument. Nevertheless, we must be careful in not going overboard in the emphasis on realism. Janowitz explains this as follows:

> The advantage of standard reading materials, however, is that everyone can share the common dreams and wishes they represent. The value of reading about families that are intact and people who have exciting adventures is that children identify with the story and vicariously share these experiences. In the development of new materials, realism about city life should not lose all the values of vicarious enjoyment. There is now great interest in developing special materials for deprived children. No material can be good for deprived children unless it is good for all children. We cannot afford to further alienate these youngsters by denying them the right to share the same dreams and hopes of other children. A culturally ghettoized curriculum would destroy the opportunity to bring them into the mainstream of American life. If they need more active experiences in learning, as many authorities feel they do, this is no different from the needs of all other children who spend too much time in passive learning, being quietly bored.[85]

In other words, if it is carried to an extreme, "being restricted to current reality could in itself be very unreal."[86]

Communication: Multi-Sensory Within certain limits, it appears that simultaneous use of more than one sensory mode in material presentation helps the learner.[87] Since individual variations in the development of sense modalities (visual, aural, tactile, olfactory, and kinesthetic) are to be expected and since no one channel of communication can convey all pertinent information to a receiver, simultaneous input through several channels would ensure, at least theoretically, more comprehensive learning. The precise characteristics of the human information-processing mechanism and its interaction with materials presented are, however, not thoroughly investigated.[88]

With run-of-the-mill students, especially those in the upper-elementary and junior-high grades, some suggestive evidence is available to show that educational television may be useful in facilitating school learning.[89] Unfortunately, no parallel studies with the *underprivileged* children have yet come to the reviewer's attention.

As for the use of commercial television programs, several investigations indicate that television-viewing has different implications for middle-class and working-class (upper-lower) adults. Watching television is regarded by the former as a symbol of passive entertainment, of withdrawal from productive social activity, and of escape from constructive responsibility.

As such, television conflicts with the traditional middle-class values of sociability, goal-seeking activity and reality orientation. In contrast, the same activity serves for working-class people the functions of immediate gratification, escape from reality (fantasy seeking and vicarious experience), and release of frustration (catharsis and displaced aggression). These functions correspond well with the basic value pattern of the working class, and television-viewing does not pose for their children the developmental discontinuity which affects middle-class children.

It has been found that television, when it comes into a child's life, tends simply to replace other sources of fantasy experiences such as movies, radio, comic books, and escape magazines, while not affecting appreciably the sources of reality experiences such as newspapers, books, and general magazines. Maturation is characterized by a shift from fantasy-seeking activities to reality-seeking activities though, among the high-socioeconomic children, the proportion who shift in their early teens is greater than among the low-socioeconomic children. By their behavior, both groups of children meet parental sanction—the middle-class children for not watching television as much and the working-class children for continuing to watch it; [90] both groups align themselves with the basic value pattern of their class. Again, the reviewer knows of few studies conducted with culturally variant individuals as subjects.

Likewise, the application of programmed materials and auto-instructional devices to the culturally variant population seem to be largely absent from the literature. Although it has been argued that these devices allow sequential presentation of the basics, ensure subject-matter readiness, promote the feeling of mastery over an unfamiliar environment, and help to individualize teaching, [91] actual evidence is not available. Furthermore, in view of the rather ambiguous status of the contribution of auto-instructional technique,[92] it does not seem justifiable to generalize about the usefulness of the technique in education of the *disadvantaged.*

In passing, two things must be mentioned. First, in spite of the obvious implications for our work with the *unfortunate* children, little systematic effort has been expended to cultivate the basic sense modalities by, for example, the Montessori method.[93] Likewise, explorations of behavioral communication (postural and other nonverbal forms as well as empathic and intuitive channels) have been largely neglected.

Second, any simple-minded application of the pre–post test design with or without a control group to investigate the effects of any medium leaves much to be desired.[94] This is especially true if the only criterion measures are of the verbal performance type (intelligence, achievement, language, etc.). Difficulties are numerous and well known but seldom heeded. Theses tests assess merely a fraction, and often a marginal one at that, of the target behavior—a result we should have anticipated in view of the hard struggle waged over the culture-fair tests.[95] Even when the desired changes are measurable on these tests, the sleeper effects or the element of delayed action are frequently overlooked. With *underprivileged* children, it must be expected that much of our initial educative effort is expended in raising the level of their reserve power for living. Such a reservoir-filling operation does not often register on our typical performance tests. Only when they have accumulated a sufficient amount of spare energy can these children become open to our type of teaching and learning. Finally, the process of learning is frequently far more significant than the product, especially when individual differences are great. To measure progress, we must judge each subject against himself, comparing his present level with his past level, not with that of others. Any collective measures may be quite unsatisfactory to describe the actual efforts and results.

EPILOGUE

I think I have taxed the readers' patience long enough. In discussing these children, I cannot help recalling one case of relatively pure *cultural deprivation* recorded in history. As you know, in the fall of 1799, the year seven in the new calendar of the French Revolution, a child of 11 or 12 was caught in the Caune Woods. Completely naked, dirty, and alone, roaming in the mountains, the "Wild Boy of Aveyron" was described as indifferent to everything and attentive to nothing in the civilized society. His senses underdeveloped and intellectual functions atrophied, he was destitute of all means of human communication. "In a word, his whole life was a completely animal existence."[96]

A young doctor, Jean-Marc-Gaspard Itard—devoted, idealistic, and patient—took on the responsibility of caring for the boy and of converting him into a social and cultural being. In his monumental work, Itard set five principal aims of "the mental and moral education of the Wild Boy of Aveyron" as follows:

> 1st Aim. To interest him in social life by rendering it more pleasant to him than the one he was then leading,

	and above all more like the life which he had just left.
2nd Aim.	To awaken his nervous sensibility by the most energetic stimulation, and occasionally by intense emotion.
3rd Aim.	To extend the range of his ideas by giving him new needs and by increasing his social contacts.
4th Aim.	To lead him to the use of speech by inducing the exercise of imitation through the imperious law of necessity.
5th Aim.	To make him exercise the simplest mental operations upon the objects of his physical needs over a period of time, afterwards inducing the application of these mental processes of the objects of instruction.

These are words published in 1801—any comments, gentle readers?

FOOTNOTES

[1] John Lunstrum. "The Mystique of the Peace Corps: A Dilemma." *Phi Delta Kappan* 48: 99–102; 1966.

Also see the following:

Ernest H. Austin, Jr. "I. Cultural Deprivation—A Few Questions." *Phi Delta Kappan* 47: 67–70; 1965.

James W. Guthrie and James A. Kelly. "II. Compensatory Education—Some Answers for a Skeptic." *Phi Delta Kappan* 47: 70–74; 1965.

Ernest H. Austin, Jr. "III. A Parting Shot From a Still Skeptical Skeptic." *Phi Delta Kappan* 47: 75–76; 1965.

Dudley Seers. "Why Visiting Economists Fail." In David E. Novack and Robert Lekachman, Eds. *Development and Society*. New York: St. Martin's Press, 1964. Pp. 375–391.

Kaoru Yamamoto. "The Rewards and Results of Teaching." *Education* 87: 67–72; 1966.

[2] Charles J. Calitri. "The Nature and Values of Culturally Different Youth." In Arno Jewett, Joseph Mersand and Doris V. Gunderson, Eds. *Improving English Skills of Culturally Different Youth in Large Cities*. (OE-30012, Bulletin 1964, No. 5) Washington: U.S. Government Printing Office, 1964. Pp. 1–9.

[3] Florence Rockwood Kluckhohn. "Dominant and Variant Value Orientations." In Clyde Kluckhohn, Henry A. Murray and David M.

Schneider, Eds. *Personality in Nature, Society, and Culture.* New York: Alfred A. Knopf, 1953. Pp. 342–357.

Richard A. Kurtz. "The Public Use of Sociological Concepts: Culture and Social Class." *American Sociologist* 1: 187–189; 1966.

[4] Eleanor P. Wolf and Leo Wolf. "Sociological Perspective on the Education of Culturally Deprived Children." *School Review* 70: 373–378; 1962.

[5] Robert J. Havighurst. "Who Are the Socially Disadvantaged?" *Journal of Negro Education* 33: 210–217; 1964.

[6] Milton M. Gordon. *Assimilation in American Life.* New York: Oxford University Press, 1964.

[7] W. Lloyd Warner. *American Life, Dream and Reality.* (rev. ed.) Chicago: University of Chicago Press, 1962.

[8] Gordon, *op. cit.*, pp. 51–54.

[9] Gerald S. Lesser, Gordon Fifer and Donald H. Clark. "Mental Abilities of Children from Different Social-Class and Cultural Groups." *Monographs of the Society for Research in Child Development*, 30, No. 4 (Whole No. 102); 1965.

[10] Urie Bronfenbrenner. "Socialization and Social Class Through Time and Space." In Harold Proshansky and Bernard Seidenberg, Eds. *Basic Studies in Social Psychology.* New York: Holt, Rinehart & Winston, 1965. Pp. 349–365.

Bettye M. Caldwell. "The Effects of Infant Care." In Martin L. Hoffman and Lois W. Hoffman, Eds. *Review of Child Development Research.* (Vol. 1) New York: Russell Sage Foundation, 1964. Pp. 9–87.

Daniel R. Miller and Guy E. Swanson. *The Changing American Parent.* New York: John Wiley & Sons, 1958.

[11] John K. Galbraith. *The Affluent Society.* Boston: Houghton Mifflin, 1958.

[12] Clemmont E. Vontress. "Our Demoralizing Slum Schools." *Phi Delta Kappan* 45: 77–81; 1963.

[13] Celia S. Heller. *Mexican American Youth: Forgotten Youth at the Crossroads.* New York: Random House, 1966.

[14] Harold E. Driver. *Indians of North America.* Chicago: University of Chicago Press, 1961.

[15] Cf., for example, W. Lloyd Warner and Leo Srole. *The Social Systems of American Ethnic Groups.* New Haven, Conn.: Yale University Press, 1945.

[16] Alvin L. Schorr. "Filial Responsibility and the Aging." In Hyman Rodman, Ed. *Marriage, Family, and Society.* New York: Random House, 1965. Pp. 186–197.

[17] John F. Cuber, William F. Kenkel and Robert A. Harper. *Problems of American Society: Values in Conflict.* (4th ed.) New York: Holt, Rinehart & Winston, 1964. P. 70.

[18] Helen L. Witmer. "Children and Poverty." *Children* 11: 207–213; 1964.

[19] Cuber, Kenkel and Harper, *op. cit.*, p. 73.

[20] Donald N. Michael. *The Next Generation.* New York: Vintage Books, Random House, 1965.

John R. Seeley. "Guidance and the Youth Culture." *Personnel and Guidance Journal* 41: 302–310; 1962.

[21] William E. Cole and Charles H. Miller. *Social Problems.* New York: David McKay, 1965.

Seymour L. Wolfbein. "Labor Trends, Manpower, and Automation." In Henry Borow, Ed. *Man in a World at Work.* Boston: Houghton Mifflin, 1964. Pp. 155–173.

[22] Harold A. Phelps and David Henderson. *Population in Its Human Aspects.* New York: Appleton-Century-Crofts, 1958.

[23] Murray Gendell and Hans L. Zetterberg, Eds. *A Sociological Almanac for the United States.* (2nd ed.) New York: Charles Scribner's Sons, 1964. P. 69.

[24] Lee Taylor and Arthur R. Jones, Jr. *Rural Life and Urbanized Society.* New York: Oxford University Press, 1964. Pp. 417–428.

[25] *Ibid.,* pp. 298–300.

[26] George E. Simpson and J. Milton Yinger. *Racial and Cultural Minorities.* (3rd ed.) New York: Harper & Row, 1965. Pp. 265–266.

[27] Robert Coles. "What Migrant Farm Children Learn." In Staten W. Webster, Ed. *Knowing the Disadvantaged.* San Francisco: Chandler Publishing, 1966. Pp. 236–243.

Joe L. Frost. "School and the Migrant Child." *Childhood Education* 41: 129–132; 1964.

George E. Haney. "Problems and Trends in Migrant Education." *School Life* 45 (9): 5–9; July, 1963.

Truman Moore. *The Slaves We Rent.* New York: Random House, 1965.

[28] Gayle Janowitz. *Helping Hands: Volunteer Work in Education.* Chicago: University of Chicago Press, 1965. Pp. 31–34.

[29] August B. Hollingshead. *Elmtown's Youth: The Impact of Social Classes on Adolescents.* New York: John Wiley & Sons, 1949.

[30] It may be informative to recall James Baldwin's statement *(Nobody Knows My Name,* New York: Dial Press, 1961): "Anyone who has ever struggled with poverty knows how extremely expensive it is to be poor; and if one is a member of a captive population, economically speaking, one's feet have simply been placed on the treadmill forever. One is victimized, economically, in a thousand ways—rent, for example, or car insurance. Go shopping one day in Harlem—for anything—and compare Harlem prices and quality with those downtown."

Also see:

David Caplovitz. *The Poor Pay More.* New York: Macmillan, 1963.

[31] Lester D. Crow, Walter I. Murray and Hugh H. Smythe. *Educating the Culturally Disadvantaged Child.* New York: David McKay, 1966. Pp. 28–54.

Oscar Lewis. *The Children of Sanchez.* New York: Vintage Books, Random House, 1961.

Schorr, *op. cit.*, p. 192.

[32] Warner, *op. cit.*, pp. 108–109.

Also see the following:

Walter Mischel. "Preference for Delayed Reinforcement: An Experimental Study of a Cultural Observation." *Journal of Abnormal and Social Psychology* 56: 57–61; 1958.

Walter Mischel. "Father-Absence and Delay of Gratification: Cross-Cultural Comparisons." *Journal of Abnormal and Social Psychology* 63: 116–124; 1961.

[33] Jules Henry. "White People's Time, Colored People's Time." In Joe L. Frost and Glenn R. Hawkes, Eds. *The Disadvantaged Child: Issues and Innovations.* Boston: Houghton Mifflin, 1966. Pp. 396–397.

Also see:

Jules Henry. "Hope, Delusion, and Organization: Some Problems in the Motivation of Low Achievers." In Lauren G. Woody, Ed. *The Low Achiever in Mathematics.* (OE-29061, Bulletin 1965, No. 31) Washington: U.S. Government Printing Office, 1965. Pp. 7–16.

[34] Robert D. Strom. "Teacher Aspiration and Attitude." In Robert D. Strom, Ed. *The Inner-City Classroom: Teacher Behaviors.* Columbus, Ohio: Charles E. Merrill, 1966. P. 21.

[35] Robert Kastenbaum. "The Dimensions of Future Time Perspective: An Experimental Study." *Journal of General Psychology* 65: 203–218; 1961.

Robert Kastenbaum. "The Structure and Function of Time Perspective." *Journal of Psychological Research (India),* 8(3): 1–11; 1964.

Lawrence L. Leshan. "Time Orientation and Social Class." *Journal of Abnormal and Social Psychology* 47: 589–592; 1952.

Walter Mischel. "Preference for Delayed Reinforcement and Social Responsibility." *Journal of Abnormal and Social Psychology* 62: 1–7; 1961.

[36] Robert Kastenbaum. "Cognitive and Personal Futurity in Later Life." *Journal of Individual Psychology* 19: 216–222; 1963.

Also see:

Martin Deutsch. "The Disadvantaged Child and the Learning Process." In Harry Passow, Ed. *Education in Depressed Areas.* New York: Teachers College Press, 1963. Pp. 163-179.

[37] Kurt Lewin. "Field Theory and Experiment in Social Psychology: Concepts and Methods." *American Journal of Sociology* 44: 868-897; 1939.

[38] Hollingshead, *op. cit.,* p. 469.

[39] Janowitz, *op. cit.,* pp. 34-35.

[40] Heller, *op. cit.*

Kluckhohn, *op. cit.*

[41] Leonard Schneiderman. "Value Orientation Preference of Chronic Relief Recipients." *Social Work* 9: 13-18; 1964.

[42] Cuber, Kenkel and Harper, *op. cit.,* p. 82.

[43] Kenneth Keniston. "Social Change and Youth in America." *Daedalus* 91: 145-171; 1962.

[44] George Simpson. *People in Families.* Cleveland: World Publishing, 1966. P. 290.

[45] Hyman Rodman. "Middle-Class Misconceptions About Lower-Class Families." In Hyman Rodman, Ed. *Marriage, Family, and Society.* New York: Random House, 1965. Pp. 219-230.

[46] Schneiderman, *op. cit.*

[47] Caldwell, *op. cit.,* p. 71.

[48] Fred L. Strodtbeck. "The Hidden Curriculum in the Middle-Class Home." In J. D. Krumboltz, Ed. *Learning and the Educational Process.* Chicago: Rand McNally, 1965. Pp. 91-112.

[49] Eugene McCreary. "Some Positive Characteristics of Disadvantaged Learners and Their Implications for Education." In Staten W. Webster, Ed. *Knowing the Disadvantaged.* San Francisco: Chandler Publishing, 1966. Pp. 47-52.

Also see:

Albert Bandura and Richard H. Walters. *Adolescent Aggression.* New York: Ronald Press, 1959.

[50] Bruno Bettelheim. "Teaching the Disadvantaged." In Staten W. Webster, Ed. *Educating the Disadvantaged Learner.* San Francisco: Chandler Publishing, 1966. P. 427.

Also see:

Marjorie Smiley. "Research and Its Implications." In Arno Jewett,

Joseph Mersand and Doris V. Gunderson, Eds. *Improving English Skills of Culturally Different Youth in Large Cities* (OE-30012, Bulletin 1964, No. 5). Washington: U.S. Government Printing Office, 1964. Pp. 35-61.

[51] Irving D. Harris. *Emotional Blocks to Learning.* New York: The Free Press, 1961. P. 19.

[52] Robert D. Hess and Virginia Shipman. "Early Blocks to Children's Learning." *Children* 12: 189-194; 1965.

Robert D. Hess and Virginia Shipman. "Early Experience and the Socialization of Cognitive Modes in Children." *Child Development* 36: 869-886; 1965.

[53] Daniel R. Miller and Guy E. Swanson. *Inner Conflict and Defense.* New York: Henry Holt, 1960.

[54] Frank Riessman. "The Culturally Deprived Child: A New View." In E. Paul Torrance and Robert D. Strom, Eds. *Mental Health and Achievement.* New York: John Wiley & Sons, 1965. Pp. 312-319.

[55] Basil Bernstein. "Social Class and Linguistic Development: A Theory of Social Learning." In A. H. Halsey, Jean Floud and C. Arnold Anderson, Eds. *Education, Economy, and Society.* New York: The Free Press, 1961. Pp. 288-314.

Donald Lloyd. "Subcultural Patterns Which Affect Language and Reading Development." In Arno Jewett, Joseph Mersand and Doris V. Gunderson, Eds. *Improving English Skills of Culturally Different Youth in Large Cities* (OE-30012, Bulletin 1964, No. 5). Washington: U.S. Government Printing Office, 1964. Pp. 110-119.

Walter Loban. "Language Proficiency and School Learning." In J. D. Krumboltz, Ed. *Learning and the Educational Process.* Chicago: Rand McNally, 1965. Pp. 113-131.

[56] Deutsch, *op. cit.*

Charles E. Silberman. *Crisis in Black and White.* New York: Random House, 1965.

[57] Hess and Shipman, *opuses cit.*

Alex Inkeles. "Social Structure and the Socialization of Competence." *Harvard Educational Review* 36: 265-283; 1966.

[58] David P. Ausubel. "Effects of Cultural Deprivation on Learning Patterns." *Audiovisual Instruction* 10: 10-12; 1965.

Hilda Taba. "Cultural Deprivation as a Factor in School Learning." *Merrill-Palmer Quarterly of Behavior and Development* 10: 147-159; 1964.

[59] M. Brewster Smith. "Socialization for Competence." *Items* 19: 17-23; 1965 (Social Science Research Council, New York).

Robert W. White. "Motivation Reconsidered: The Concept of Competence." *Psychological Review* 66: 297-333; 1959.

[60] Martin Deutsch. "The Role of Social Class in Language Development and Cognition." *American Journal of Orthopsychiatry* 35: 78-88; 1965.

[61] Patricia C. Sexton. *Education and Income—Inequalities in Our Public Schools.* New York: Viking Press, 1961.

[62] John Q. Baker and Nathaniel N. Wagner. "Social Class and Mental Illness in Children." *Teachers College Record* 66: 522-536; 1965.

August B. Hollingshead and Frederick C. Redlich. *Social Class and Mental Illness.* New York: John Wiley & Sons, 1958.

[63] Wolf and Wolf, *op. cit.*, p. 378.

[64] Barney G. Glaser and Anselm L. Strauss. "Awareness Contexts and Social Interaction." *American Sociological Review* 29: 669-679; 1964.

[65] Staten W. Webster. "The Teacher as an Alien: Some Theoretical Considerations Regarding Teachers for Disadvantaged Schools." In Staten W. Webster, Ed. *Educating the Disadvantaged Learner.* San Francisco: Chandler Publishing, 1966. Pp. 454-464.

[66] Helen H. Davidson and Gerhard Long. "Children's Perception of Their Teacher's Feelings of Them Related to Self-Perception, School Achievement, and Behavior." *Journal of Experimental Education* 29: 107-118; 1960.

Patrick J. Groff. "Culturally Deprived Children: Opinions of Teachers on the View of Riessman." *Exceptional Children* 30: 61-65; 1964.

A. Harry Passow. "Diminishing Teacher Prejudice." In Robert D. Strom, Ed. *The Inner-City Classroom: Teacher Behaviors.* Columbus, Ohio: Charles E. Merrill, 1966. Pp. 93-109.

[67] Bettelheim, *op. cit.*

Janowitz, *op. cit.*

Bel Kaufman. *Up the Down Staircase.* Englewood Cliffs, N.J.: Prentice-Hall, 1964.

[68] Albert H. Yee. *Factors Involved in Determining the Relationship Between Teachers' and Pupils' Attitudes.* (Final Report, U.S. Office of Education, Cooperative Research Project No. OE-6-10-077) Austin: University of Texas, 1966.

[69] Vernon F. Haubrich. "Teachers for Big-City Schools." In A. Harry Passow, Ed. *Education in Depressed Areas.* New York: Teachers College Press, 1963. Pp. 243-261.

Miriam L. Goldberg. "Adapting Teacher Style to Pupil Differences: Teachers for Disadvantaged Children." *Merrill-Palmer Quarterly of Behavior and Development* 10: 161-178; 1964.

Susan W. Gray and Rupert A. Klaus. "An Experimental Preschool Program for Culturally Deprived Children." *Child Development* 36: 887-898; 1965.

[70] Martin Deutsch. "Some Psychosocial Aspects of Learning in the Disadvantaged." In E. Paul Torrance and Robert D. Strom, Eds. *Mental Health and Achievement.* New York: John Wiley & Sons, 1965. P. 325.

[71] Estelle Cherry Peisach. "Children's Comprehension of Teacher and Peer Speech." *Child Development* 36: 467–480; 1965.

[72] Loban, *op. cit.*

[73] Milton Meux and B. Othaniel Smith. "Logical Dimension of Teaching Behavior." In Bruce J. Biddle and William J. Ellena, Eds. *Contemporary Research on Teacher Effectiveness.* New York: Holt, Rinehart & Winston, 1964. Pp. 127–164.

B. Othanel Smith. "A Conceptual Analysis of Instructional Behavior." *Journal of Teacher Education* 14: 294–298; 1963.

[74] Ned A. Flanders. *Teacher Influence, Pupil Attitudes, and Achievement.* (OE-25040, Cooperative Research Monograph No. 12) Washington: U.S. Government Printing Office, 1965.

Ned A. Flanders. "Some Relationships Among Teacher Influence, Pupil Attitudes, and Achievement." In Bruce J. Biddle and William J. Ellena, Eds. *Contemporary Research on Teacher Effectiveness.* New York: Holt, Rinehart & Winston, 1964. Pp. 196–231.

[75] Arno A. Bellack. "The Language of the Classroom: Meanings Communicated in High School Teaching." A Paper Read at Curriculum Research Institute, Association for Supervision and Curriculum Development, Washington, D.C., March 1964.

Hilda Taba and Freeman F. Elzey. "Teaching Strategies and Thought Processes." *Teachers College Record* 65: 524–534; 1964.

[76] Karl U. Smith and Margaret F. Smith. *Cybernetic Principles of Learning and Educational Design.* New York: Holt, Rinehart & Winston, 1966. P. 350.

[77] L. Joseph Stone and Joseph Church. *Childhood and Adolescence.* New York: Random House, 1957. P. 185.

[78] Charles G. Spiegler. "Give Him a Book That Hits Him Where He Lives." In Arno Jewett, Joseph Mersand and Doris V. Gunderson, Eds. *Improving English Skills of Culturally Different Youth in Large Cities* (OE-30012, Bulletin 1964, No. 5). Washington: U.S. Government Printing Office, 1964. Pp. 91–99.

[79] Frank R. Hartman. "Recognition Learning Under Multiple Channel Presentation and Testing Conditions." *AV Communication Review* 9: 24–43; 1961.

Seth Spaulding. "Research on Pictorial Illustration." *AV Communication Review* 3: 35–45; 1955.

M. D. Vernon. "The Value of Pictorial Illustrations." *British Journal of Educational Psychology* 24: 180–187; 1953.

M. D. Vernon. "The Instruction of Children by Pictorial Illustration." *British Journal of Educational Psychology* 24: 171–179; 1954.

Paul R. Wendt and Gordon K. Butts. "Audiovisual Materials." *Review of Educational Research* 32: 141–155; 1962.

[80] Frank R. Hartman. "Single and Multiple Channel Communication: A Review of Research and a Proposed Model." *AV Communication Review* 9: 235–262; 1961.

Carl H. Ketcham and Robert W. Heath. "Teaching Effectiveness of Sound with Pictures That Do Not Embody the Material Being Taught." *AV Communication Review* 10: 89–93; 1962.

[81] Hugh M. Culbertson and Richard D. Powers. "A Study of Graph Comprehension Difficulties." *AV Communication Review* 7: 97–110; 1959.

O. L. Davis, Jr., Linda C. Hicks and Norman D. Bowers. "The Usefulness of Time Lines in Learning Chronological Relationships in Text Materials." *Journal of Experimental Education* 34: 22–25; 1966.

Gloria D. Feliciano, Richard D. Powers and Bryant E. Kearl. "The Presentation of Statistical Information." *AV Communication Review* 11: 32–39; 1963.

Morton S. Malter. "Children's Ability to Read Diagrammatic Materials." *Elementary School Journal* 49: 98–102; 1948.

Lewis V. Peterson and Wilbur Schramm. "How Accurately Are Different Kinds of Graphs Read?" *AV Communication Review* 2: 178–189; 1954.

M. D. Vernon. "Presenting Information in Diagrams." *AV Communication Review* 1: 147–158; 1953.

[82] L. Fonseca and Bryant E. Kearl. *Comprehension of Pictorial Symbols: An Experiment in Rural Brazil.* Madison: Department of Agricultural Journalism, University of Wisconsin, 1960.

Seth Spaulding. "Communication Potential of Pictorial Illustrations." *AV Communication Review* 4: 31–46; 1956.

Also see:

Whitfield Bourisseau, O. L. Davis, Jr., and Kaoru Yamamoto. "Sense-Impression Responses of Negro and White Children to Verbal and Pictorial Stimuli." *AV Communication Review* 15: 259–268; 1967.

Anne L. Ryle. "A Study of the Interpretations of Pictorial Style by Young Children." Paper Read at the American Educational Research Association, Chicago, February 1966.

[83] T. A. Ryan and Carol B. Schwartz. "Speed of Perception as a Function of Mode of Presentation." *American Journal of Psychology* 69: 60–69; 1956.

Smith and Smith, *op. cit.*

[84] Carl L. Byerly. "A School Curriculum for Prevention and Remediation of Deviancy." In William W. Wattenberg, Ed. *Social Deviancy*

Among Youth. (65th Yearbook of the National Society for the Study of Education, Part I) Chicago: University of Chicago Press, 1966. Pp. 221-257.

Allison Davis. "Society, the School, and the Culturally Deprived Student." In Arno Jewett, Joseph Mersand and Doris V. Gunderson, Eds. *Improving English Skills of Culturally Different Youth in Large Cities* (OE-30012, Bulletin 1964, No. 5). Washington: U.S. Government Printing Office, 1964. Pp. 10-21.

G. Orville Johnson. "Motivating the Slow Learner." In Robert D. Strom, Ed. *The Inner-City Classroom: Teacher Behaviors.* Columbus, Ohio: Charles E. Merrill, 1966. Pp. 111-130.

Panel on Educational Research and Development of the President's Science Advisory Committee. *Innovation and Experiment in Education.* Washington: U.S. Government Printing Office, 1964.

Frank Riessman. *The Culturally Deprived Child.* New York: Harper, 1962.

[85] Janowitz, *op. cit.,* p. 71.

[86] Strodtbeck, *op. cit.,* p. 94.

[87] Robert A. Davis. *Learning in the Schools.* Belmont, Calif.: Wadsworth Publishing, 1966. Pp. 98-111.

Hartman, "Single and Multiple Channel Communication: A Review of Research and a Proposed Model," *AV Communication Review* 9: 235-262; 1961.

[88] Kaoru Yamamoto. "Stimulus Mode and Sense Modality—What's in It for Education?" *Teachers College Record,* 1969.

[89] Ford Foundation and Fund for the Advancement of Education. *Teaching by Television.* (2nd ed.) New York: 1961.

Wilbur Schramm. "What We Know About Learning From Instructional Television." In Lester Asheim et al., Eds. *Educational Television: The Next Ten Years.* Stanford, Calif.: Institute for Communication Research, Stanford University, 1962. Pp. 52-76.

[90] Lotte Bailyn. "Mass Media and Children: A Study of Exposure Habits and Cognitive Effect." *Psychological Monographs* 73 (1, Whole No. 471): 1-48; 1959.

Kent Geiger and Robert Sokol. "Social Norms in Television Watching." *American Journal of Sociology* 65: 174-181; 1959.

Hilde Himmelweit, A. N. Oppenheim and Pamela Vince. *Television and the Child.* London: Oxford University Press, 1958.

Eleanor E. Maccoby. "Why Do Children Watch Television?" *Public Opinion Quarterly* 18: 239-244; 1954.

Wilbur Schramm, Jack Lyle and Edwin B. Parker. *Television in the Lives of Our Children.* Stanford, Calif.: Stanford University Press, 1961.

[91] Ausubel, *op. cit.*

Deutsch, "Some Psychosocial Aspects of Learning in the Disadvantaged," *op. cit.*

[92] John E. Coulson, Ed. *Programmed Learning and Computer-Based Instruction.* New York: John Wiley & Sons, 1962.

John F. Feldhusen. "Taps for Teaching Machines." *Phi Delta Kappan* 44: 265-267; 1963.

Robert Glaser, Ed. *Teaching Machines and Programmed Learning: II. Data and Directions.* Washington: National Education Association, 1965.

Wilbur Schramm. *The Research on Programmed Instruction.* (OE-34034) Washington: U.S. Government Printing Office, 1964.

[93] Maria Montessori. *The Montessori Method.* Cambridge, Mass.: Robert Bentley, Inc., 1965.

[94] Janowitz, *op. cit.*

Smith and Smith, *op. cit.*

Strom, *op. cit.*, p. 38.

For some examples of typical evaluative studies, see:

Doxey A. Wilkerson. "Programs and Practices in Contemporary Education for Disadvantaged Children." *Review of Educational Research* 35: 426-440; 1965.

[95] W. W. Charters, Jr. "Social Class and Intelligence Tests." In W. W. Charters, Jr. and N. L. Gage, Eds. *Readings in Social Psychology of Education.* Boston: Allyn and Bacon, 1963. Pp. 12-21.

[96] Jean-Marc-Gaspard Itard. *The Wild Boy of Aveyron.* New York: Appleton-Century-Crofts, 1962. P. 6.

[97] *Ibid.*, pp. 10-11.

DISCUSSION QUESTIONS
AND FURTHER READINGS

In a land where a nation-wide search is in progress for equality of education for all sectors of the population, it may be difficult to question the basic principle of equality itself. However, any literal application of this principle would be eminently unfair and unjust, so we must ask what constitutes acceptable criteria for equality and fairness. Aristotle once pointed out that injustice results just as much from treating unequals equally as it does from treating equals unequally. It is sometimes necessary to accord differential treatments to different individuals. Within one category, individuals may be equal, but, between different categories, they may be indeed unequal. How should such relevant categories be selected and maintained? Would the criteria be based on age, sex, creed, color, aptitude, status, or what? What is the relationship between the traditional emphasis on individual differences in American education and the principle of equality? For a philosophical discussion of some of these questions, see R. S. Peters, *Ethics and Education* (Chicago: Scotts, Foresman, 1967).

Equality is not identity, you may insist; equality means equity in the distribution of educational opportunities. Would, nevertheless, an equal distribution of opportunities be fair when the population comes from highly varied home and community background experiences? Is this the reason why every student is *forced* to partake of the provided opportunities under the system of compulsory education? What are the merits and shortcomings of this practice? In the name of social justice, why should students be denied the rights to choose and mold their own fate, including the right to withdraw from school when they see fit? Where does the refuted legal principle of "separate but equal" take on relevance? Read Edgar Z. Friedenberg, *Coming of Age in America* (New York: Vintage Books, Random House, 1965), Paul Goodman, *Compulsory Mis-education and The Community of Scholars* (New York: Vintage Books, Random House, 1966), Nathaniel Hickerson, *Education for Alienation* (Englewood Cliffs, N.J.: Prentice-Hall, 1966), and Earl C. Kelley, *In Defense of Youth* (Englewood Cliffs, N.J.: Prentice-Hall, 1962), to gain further perspectives on these issues.

WHEN / WHERE

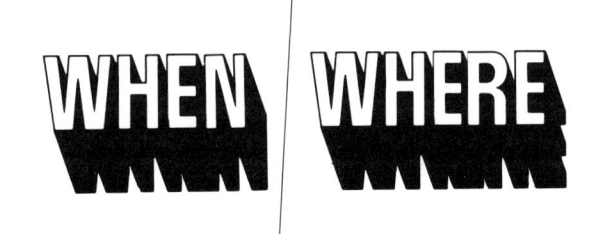

A NEW LOOK
AT READINESS

Harry S. Broudy

B. Othanel Smith

Joe R. Burnett

To be effective, a curriculum must provide learning tasks that students can perform. But the tasks must not be so easy that they offer no challenge, nor so difficult that they are overwhelming.

Today, we are being told, as though it were some new and bold idea, that any subject can be taught effectively and in an intellectually honest fashion to any child at any age. The controversy over what children can learn is an old one. There was a time not so long ago when children were thought to be miniature adults with adult minds on a small scale. Rousseau was one of the first of modern theorists to come to the child's rescue, claiming for him characteristics of mind and body that set him apart

---

From Harry S. Broudy, B. Othanel Smith, and Joe R. Burnett, "A New Look At Readiness," pp. 91–105 in *Democracy and Excellence in American Secondary Education* (Chicago: Rand McNally, 1964).

from adults. The fallacious tendency of adults to overlook the abilities of the child while imposing their image of the world upon him is, and has been, common. This tendency becomes especially strong in a national crisis when adults are anxious to speed up the production of trained brains. When the future of a nation itself appears to depend upon more training for more individuals in less time, the natural tendency for adults to overcrowd the child's mind with their own intellectual products and concerns can easily get out of hand.

As a nation, we are now in such a crisis. We are opposed by a group of aggressive nations whose idealogy makes education a principal feature of their programs. We no longer feel that learning can be taken leisurely. The schools, like the country as a whole, challenged by a group of nations in a hurry to complete the task of world subversion, are now faced by pressures from every direction to speed up their programs of instruction. So we are now trying to settle the age-old question of how much and how fast the young can learn, not in the quiet of the laboratory or in the classroom, but in the halls of debate and controversy, and sometimes in classes being taught by learned individuals who only recently have discovered that children can learn very complex things indeed.

TWO VIEWS OF DEVELOPMENT

The notion that instruction should be coordinate with the child's development, that is, geared to his readiness to learn, has been part of pedagogical lore at least since Rousseau. During this time, two theories of such coordination, one stemming from psychology of development and the other from associative theories of learning, have influenced curriculum planning and development.

Perhaps the oldest view of the individual's development is that based on the notion of progressive emergence of inherent abilities. According to this view, there is latent in the individual at birth all that he is later to become. In its extreme form this doctrine holds that development is independent of instruction. The child's development will run its natural course and reach its highest point independently of adult efforts to instruct him.

As the individual grows older, his potentialities for learning are both extended and actualized. What he learns is simply a veneer overlaying the substructure of his development. In this view, learning depends entirely upon the maturation of the individual. The child cannot learn anything until he has reached the stage of maturity necessary for its attainment. While learning depends upon development, development does not depend upon learning. For development is something which takes place within the organism and is governed by its own laws and conditions, quite apart from outside influences.

Of course, common experience bears out the fact that certain learnings cannot be acquired at any early age. A child six months old does not ordinarily learn to walk or talk. A one-year-old child does not learn to read, and it is quite unlikely that effective methods of teaching him to read will be devised. No one supposes that algebra can be learned by a child three years of age. The child at his age could not learn algebraic operations, or the rules of order and addition which such operations presuppose, in any significant sense.

These common observations give rise to widespread belief that a fixed degree of development is a necessary condition of certain types of learning. Thus, some recent pedagogical views hold that the child is to be taught reading beginning at six years of age when he enters school. He is to be taught to count and to do the simple combinations of arithmetic in the early elementary grades. But, as everyone knows, common observations often lead to erroneous conclusions. It may turn out that some skills and concepts now taught in certain grades will be found to be improperly placed, when all factors are taken into account.

A second view reduces learning and development to one and the same thing. This, too, is an old notion, dating back to the beginnings of the associative school of psychology. According to this school, the development of the individual comes about through an increase in the number of associations among ideas built up through experience. Perhaps the clearest statement of this position has been given by Thorndike. He said that the difference between one individual and another, or between one period of an individual's growth and another period, is simply a difference in the number of synaptic connections which become established. Accordingly, there are no stages of development, but rather a gradual accretion of learnings. Thus, the difference between what an individual is at one chronological age and another is purely quantitative. There are no qualitative changes, no stages of development, but only changes in quantity as measured by the number of synaptic connections. Development is an additive process.

This same view of development is also found in that form of associative psychology based upon the theory of conditioned reflex. Differences between what an individual is at one time and what he is at another are measured in terms of the accumulation of conditioned responses. Again, there are no stages in the growth of the individual, but only a gradual increase in the number and kind of responses he acquires.

All forms of the associative school of psychology rule out stages of development. Any change in the individual is a result of learning, and anything can be learned, provided instruction in it has been prepared for by prior learnings. The problem of meshing instruction with the individual's growth is reducible to the question of what learnings are psychologically prerequisite for new conditionings.

Neither of these views of development is entirely correct. The ability to learn to do certain things is obviously dependent upon the maturation of neural structures. But at the same time, the behavior which the individual takes on is not entirely determined by the development of such structures. For example, no matter how mature an individual's nervous system may become, he would never learn to think mathematically without the influence of a social environment in which mathematical knowledge was present. Maturation and learning are both necessary factors in the growth of the individual, and acquired behavior consists in the coordination of these two factors. Neither by itself is a sufficient condition of human development.

SYNCHRONIZING INSTRUCTION AND DEVELOPMENT

The way in which these two factors may influence curriculum decisions can be seen by exploring them in relation to two topics: (1) the sequential ordering of materials of instruction and (2) the individual's ability to handle materials by progressively more complex operations.

Consider first the ordering of materials of instruction. There can be no quarrel with the view that what an individual can learn is dependent in part upon what he has already learned. But it is often difficult, if not impossible, to specify exactly what must be known already in order to learn a particular concept, generalization, or set of related ideas. One must be able to add and subtract before he can learn to do long division, because these processes are part of the process of doing long division. But it is more difficult to specify what elements of grammar one must know before he can learn to tell whether the subject and the predicate of a sentence agree in number. And it is still more difficult to tell what one must know about history in order to understand the Crusades. For this reason, arguments for prerequisite courses, or for necessary sequences of subject matter for the purpose of instruction, are often difficult to uphold.

Nevertheless, it is possible to arrange concepts, principles, and other sorts of content in a rough order such that they parallel approximately the capacity of the individual to learn them in terms of what he has already achieved. Furthermore, concepts and principles as well as other sorts of content can themselves be expressed in varying degrees of difficulty. For example, it is quite possible for a child at a very early age to understand in a rudimentary way the concept of the atom and the molecular structure of matter. As he acquires more and more learning, he becomes able to grasp the atomic concept in its more complex forms and finally, even as a young adult, to become immersed in the learnings possessed by the specialists in theoretical physics. Almost twenty-five years ago John Anderson, appraising the research on child development and the curriculum, said that scientific concepts can be introduced into the curriculum at any point provided the concepts are presented in appropriate form to younger children. He then went on to point out that the time had come to place emphasis upon determining the methods and materials appropriate for teaching the same concept at various age levels, rather than upon attempts to locate particular skills and concepts in terms of age or maturity.

It is important to note here that no stages have been found in the development of the individual's capacity to acquire information. In learning the atomic concept, as noted above, the individual may begin in his early years with a very rough notion of an atom and little by little add increments of learning until he has acquired an understanding of the atomic concept in its more complex form. There is no marked qualitative difference in the individual's understanding from the beginning until he has acquired the fuller comprehension. He simply understands more and more of a given concept and of its relations to other concepts. Granting that a minimum amount of inherent development is necessary to learn anything at all, one can say that increases in the acquisition of information beyond this point do not seem to be contingent upon some sort of development controlled by laws of its own, but rather upon prior learnings.

COORDINATION OF INSTRUCTION WITH GROWTH IN LOGICAL OPERATIONS

But the story is different when one looks at evidence bearing on the development of the individual's ability to deal with logical operations. The primary logical operations performed by the individual upon the content of his experience are those of classifying, ordering in serial relations, and numbering.[1] As the individual deals with his environment, he classifies the things that make it up. He groups certain objects as chairs, others as tables, and so on. He arranges things in order. He says, "This table is larger than that one," and "This one here is still larger." And then he can go on to say, "We shall call this table 1, this table 2, and so on." Of course, the individual is able to perform most of these operations, in at least a rudimentary sense, by the time he enters school, and the teacher ordinarily takes the ability for granted.

These are the elementary operations upon which are erected the more complex ones that have to do with the handling of propositions and their relations to one another. For example, the deductive operation is based either upon class relationships or upon relations of order. Thus, it follows from the fact that all presidents of the United States have been males that Woodrow Wilson, who was also a president of the United States, was a male. We know this from the proposition that a class contains its members. By a similar deductive operation, we know that if A is taller than B, and if B is taller than C, that A is also taller than C. In this case, the deductive relation depends upon a serial order of height, rather than upon class relations of inclusion. There are many complex operations based upon the simpler operations of classifying and ordering. Many of these do not seem to be within the grasp of the elementary-school child, and even the high-school or college student often performs them very inadequately.

It is evident from the investigations of Piaget and others that it is possible to identify stages of development with regard to these operations. Such stages seem to be relative to the interaction of the child with his environment, and they vary to some extent from one individual to another; but, on the average and for a given social environment, it is possible to identify stages of individual development. Furthermore, transition from one stage to another is gradual. The individual does not go to bed in one stage of development and wake up in another.

Piaget's investigations showed that until approximately two years of age the child is able to perform only overt activities. The child draws objects to himself or moves in the direction of objects which he desires to obtain. At this stage the child has not internalized his actions; he cannot think about them. He apparently cannot think to himself, "Now I will move in the direction of the object." The child simply performs the activity somewhat at the same intellectual level as Köhler's famous chimpanzee, which was able to obtain food outside of his cage and beyond his reach by joining two sticks, thus enabling him to rake the food within reaching distance.

The preschool period of two to six years of age represents the preoperational level. In this age range, the child has learned to use language, although in a very limited degree. He is able to think of his actions; not only can he perform them, but he can also imagine them. Thus, he is able to picture to himself the actions which he wishes to perform. And he can think about actions which he has already performed as well as listen to stories about actions performed by others remote in both space and time. But at this stage, the child cannot express his actions in words, or at least if he attempts to do so, he finds it to be more difficult than to carry out the actions himself.

It is significant that, during this period, the child believes that the amount of a thing is changed as operations are performed on it. He does not grasp the idea that certain features of a thing remain the same through change. If one pours a liquid from one container into another of quite a different shape, the child believes that the amount of liquid has been increased or decreased. He believes that two sticks unequal in length are in fact equal if an end of one stick is placed even with an end of the other; but if the sticks are then placed in such a way that their ends are no longer even, he thinks that the lengths of the sticks have been changed. The child at this age is unable to see that the whole of anything remains the same when its form is changed, when it is displaced in space, or when its parts have been rearranged.

From about seven years of age to about twelve, that is, during the elementary-school years, the child is in what Piaget has called the concrete operational stage. In this stage the child can perform certain operations with concrete things that he can later handle through symbols alone. For example, he can classify actual objects. He can also arrange them in a serial order such that if A is greater than B, and B is greater than C, A is greater than C. The arrangements of things into classes and into a series are logical operations, and in this stage of development the child is able to perform them with concrete things but not with symbols. Of course, he can use symbols. He can represent objects by means of symbols; he can use numbers and perform arithmetical processes. But he cannot perform classificatory and relational operations symbolically. Nor is he able to think in terms of possibility. He cannot take a set of conditions, either formal or concrete, and think systematically of the various possibilities to which they may lead. He seems tied to what is.

The child structures his experience by performing logical operations on various materials as he works in different spheres of activity. He learns from these operations, but he cannot abstract the operations from the concrete context in which they are used: thus, he has no generalized formulation of operations developed in the different areas of his experience.

The child at this stage cannot engage in systematic thinking. He cannot grasp a set of definitions and postulates and then derive propositions from them, nor can he cast them into a pattern of proof after the fashion of proof in plane geometry. He cannot develop a systematic explanation of an historical event or the empirical proof of a proposition in science. As mentioned above, he can grasp intuitively some aspects of these systematic processes, and he can understand almost any part of them that can be represented concretely. For example, he can readily grasp the congruence of triangles when paper models are superimposed upon one another, but he cannot follow the proof of such congruence.

At this stage the child usually has achieved the notions of invariance and reversibility. He sees that a given object remains constant even though it is changed in shape, in space, or in arrangement of parts. If he is presented with a group of objects, say, marbles, and they are divided into two subgroups, he knows that the number of marbles is not changed by dividing them. He knows that there are as many marbles in the two subgroups combined as there were in the total group before dividing them. And he knows also that when the two subgroups are put together, the total group will contain as many marbles as before.

Since mathematics and science are based upon the notions of classification and order, and upon the equally fundamental ideas of invariance and reversibility, the child is at this stage of his development able to learn procedures basic to these fields of knowledge; among others, he can grasp intuitively and concretely some aspects of set theory, traditionally restricted to advanced mathematical study. But, again, he can neither follow nor give a theoretical formulation of the ideas he intuitively grasps. Thus, the effort to move some aspects of higher mathematics into the elementary school is not incompatible with the child's development at this level, as long as he is not required to think systematically. But it should be understood that such curriculum change represents no new knowledge about the intellectual abilities of children, but rather a reassessment of the content itself—a reconsideration of it from the standpoint of its teachability.

At the beginning of junior high school, most individuals enter a period of formal operations. At this point in their development, they are able to manipulate symbols in various logical ways. The average individual is now able to perform with sentences and words the very operations which earlier he could perform only with things. He can now deal verbally with ideas without having to resort to concrete materials, and he can go from a less to a more abstract idea without any intervening manipulation of physical objects. In other words, he is now in the stage at which abstract theoretical thought is possible, and for the most part he is freed from the necessity of working with concrete things. The individual has reached the point at which he is capable of thinking in purely abstract terms, systematically using the sorts of formal operations characteristic of scientists, mathematicians, philosophers, and others who engage in rigorous intellectual work. That the student often fails to think systematically and to perform the intellectual operations of which he is capable is perhaps due more to the failure of curriculum workers and teachers to understand the structure of systematic thought than to the nature of the content of the educational program or to the student's lack of either experience or ability.

During childhood, both content and form are interwoven in the experience of the individual, and he is unable to separate them. But the educative process, from its beginning to its advanced phases, can profitably move in the direction of abstracting the forms of operations from their content. At present, however, the educational program places greater emphasis at all levels upon the concrete rather than the abstract side of operations and content. Consequently, the individual gains little experience in dealing with operations *as such*. He does not reflect upon the operations he performs, or, for that matter, upon those performed by others. Nor is he ordinarily aware of these operations in either high school or college. Although he is capable of doing so, he seldom generalizes these intellectual operations beyond the context in which they are used. Partly for this reason, instruction in one subject probably facilitates the use of higher mental functions in another field only occasionally. Were logical operations to become abstracted from the content of a particular field and understood in their own right, the individual would be more adept at dealing with the great variety of problems and contents that exemplify them. It would appear that as much improvement in the educational program at the high-school level is to be gained by proper instruction in logical operations as in changing the nature and grade location of content.

It is generally held that the individual learns through problem-solving to perform the logical operations that rigorous thought entails. Problems are defined in terms of barriers to action in concrete situations. How to deal with a given barrier is the problem. The solution consists in finding a way of overcoming the barrier and thereby reinstating the impeded action. Considerable research has been carried on to discover ways of increasing the chances that an individual will find a way of dealing with the difficulty when his actions have been blocked. Thus, among other things, it is clear that reduction of fear and inflexibility increases the individual's chances of solving problems.

Problem-solving carried on in strict conformity to logical requirements will doubtless go a long way in the direction of developing a generalized ability to deal with problematic situations, provided the individual is made aware of the methodological and logical elements in his behavior. But the current version of problem-solving has ruled out any explicit reference to the methodological and logical controls of behavior, so that the governance of the individual's thought is reduced to psychological considerations. And, unfortunately, psychology, being a descriptive science, supplies no norms by which to evaluate either the process by which an individual reaches a conclusion or the conclusion itself.

Moreover, the psychological version of problem-solving leaves out the fact that there are many problems in the symbolic as well as in the empirical domain. In other words, not all the significant problems the individual must deal with are those which have to do with concrete situations. The individual is also required to clear up the meaning of expressions, justify decisions, examine arguments, and decide upon their soundness. Analysis of typical contexts calling for thinking reveals a number of distinct kinds of tasks which thinking discharges in the normal course of experience. Among these are deciding upon the meaning of a word, phrase, or statement; deciding upon the soundness of an argument; deciding upon the acceptability of a proposal or proposition; and judging the value of something.

CONTENT AND OPERATIONS IN THE CURRICULUM

It should be clear from the foregoing analysis that the curriculum is comprised of two strands extending from the early grades through the high school, college, and university. One of these strands is the content—factual information, concepts, principles and laws. Certain problems in connection with the determination of the content of the curriculum are considered in later chapters. These problems have to do with the way in which concepts and principles function in human behavior and the further question of whether, and on what basis, some elements of content are more important than others.

The other strand in the curriculum consists in the logical operations which are to be found in behavior generally. Logical operations constitute the rational means by which the individual manipulates content. The intellectual quality of his behavior is dependent not only upon the accuracy of the content which he employs, but also upon the skill with which he performs the various logical operations by which he handles the content itself. By these operations he makes his concepts clear, he puts them into relationship with one another by eliciting laws and principles, and he orders definitions and principles in such a way as to enable him to draw conclusions and make predictions. All of these tasks, together with others too numerous to mention here, the individual performs by means of logical operations.

It has been argued that logical operations develop in the individual progressively, beginning at an early age and extending up to the beginning of the high-school years. By this time the inherent ability of the individual to perform logical operations has been fully developed. But this does not mean that the individual is able to perform these operations adequately at this time. It only means that he is now at the point in his career at which he can begin to refine and perfect the use of these operations in behavior. If the curriculum is to be made more adequate from an intellectual standpoint, it is necessary that the logical operations possible for the individual, at each stage, be identified and adequately catered to by instruction. This also means that content should be properly selected, with emphasis upon more important elements of it, for the purpose of highlighting operational excellence.

This chapter has attempted to show that readiness for learning must be considered with reference to two aspects of the educational program: the subject matter and logical operations by which it is manipulated. It seems apparent that subject matter can be adapted to the level of the individual's ability to learn it by controlling such factors as vocabulary, complexity of sentence structure, and the rate at which information is given to him. But it is different with logical operations. Here, the range of adjustments is not as clearly discernible. Apparently, the logical operations the immature person can perform depend more upon his level of development than the degree to which they can be simplified. It would therefore seem to be inefficient to attempt to adjust these more complex logical operations to his level of development. On the contrary, it would appear to be wiser to let his development catch up with the particular level of logical performance we may wish to demand of him.

These observations about readiness for learning are important in the placement of such materials of instruction as fundamental concepts of science and mathematics. They are also important in connection with the adjustment of instruction to different levels of ability within the same age group. As is discussed in a later chapter, the writers' view of the curriculum calls for children progressing through the educational program at different rates and at different levels of performance. In adjusting the instructional program to differing ability groups, it is important to recognize that there is a rather wide range of adjustments demanded in concepts, principles, norms, rules, and factual information. That is to say, it would be possible to present the same concepts and principles in different ways so as to bring them within the experience of children of different abilities. But the amount of refinement and complexity which a child can take on with respect to logical operations appears to depend less upon his fund of information than upon his level of development.

The readiness factors in learning are extremely important in curriculum development and underlie any and all efforts to improve the educational program. But there are other factors that must be taken into account, such as our conception of the instructional process and the nature and structure of the knowledge to be taught. The next three chapters explore these additional factors.

FOOTNOTE

[1] Since this discussion is based in part upon the works of Jean Piaget, it is important to note that his concept of logical operations is not entirely clear. One interpretation holds that such operations consist in certain fundamental processes of thought: combinativity, reversibility, associativity, and identity. Another interpretation claims that these fundamental processes are the psychological factors necessary to such logical operations as classifying and fitting classes together, serializing or relating asymmetrically and transitively, and so on. The second of these interpretations appears to be more plausible and is the one which is here accepted. See *The Psychology of Intelligence,* trans. by M. Piercy and D. E. Berlyne (London: Routledge & Kegan Paul, 1950), pp. 139–50.

IS THE PUBLIC SCHOOL OBSOLETE?

Christopher Jencks

The problems of education in the slums can be grouped under two broad headings: inadequate public support and excessive bureaucratic timidity and defeatism. Both have been catalogued *ad nauseam* elsewhere, but a brief review is needed to put the remedies I want to discuss in context.

I—THE MONEY PROBLEM

As a rule of thumb, America spends about half as much educating the children of the poor as the children of the rich. The difference derives from two factors. First, the annual expenditure per pupil in a prosperous suburb is usually at least fifty percent more than in a slum in the same metropolitan area. Second, this additional expenditure, in combination with better family and

From Christopher Jencks, "Is The Public School Obsolete?," *Public Interest,* No. 2, Winter 1966, 18–27. © 1966 by National Affairs, Inc.

neighborhood conditions, encourages suburban children to stay in school half again as long as slum children (from kindergarten through college, instead of from first through tenth or eleventh grade). The cumulative result, in round figures, is that the taxpayers typically spend less than $5,000 for the formal education of most slum children compared to more than $10,000 for many suburban children. (All these figures are very rough, varying from individual to individual and from place to place. Thus while we spend twice as much on children born in Scarsdale as on those born in Harlem, we spend perhaps ten times more on the children of Scarsdale than on the children of Tunica County, Mississippi. Conversely, we spend about the same on children born in Harlem as on those born in Montgomery County, Maryland. But allowing for regional and urban-rural variations, the basic rule of thumb is accurate.)

If America were to try to provide all her children with equal opportunity to develop their talents, obtain ample adult incomes, and share in controlling their own and their community's future, this pattern of expenditure would probably have to be reversed. If we wanted to offset the miseducation which takes place in a slum home and neighborhood, we would probably have to spend *twice* as much on formal education in the slums as we do in the suburbs. Instead of starting slum children in school later than suburban children, as we now do, we would have to start them earlier. Instead of keeping slum schools open fewer hours per day than suburban schools, and providing fewer slum children with opportunities to study all year round, we would have to reverse the balance. Instead of creating schools which encourage slum children to drop out as soon as possible, we would have to find ways to keep the slum child learning even longer than suburbanites. Instead of having larger classes, worse books and shoddier buildings in the slums than in the suburbs, we would have to reverse the pattern—aiming, for example, at an average class size in the slums of 15-20 children instead of 35. Instead of spending less—often much less—than $500 per child per year for education in the slums, we would have to spend more like $1500 per year. Hopefully, the result would be that slum children stayed in school longer than suburbanites, qualifying themselves for professional jobs in which skill can offset the wrong background. Instead of a cumulative total of less than $5000 per child, we would have to aim at a total of perhaps $25,000.

In strictly fiscal terms this would not be much of a strain on the national economy. There are something like ten million children now growing up in what the Johnson Administration

IS THE PUBLIC SCHOOL OBSOLETE?
Christopher Jencks

has defined as poverty. Raising expenditures on such children's education to $1500 per year would cost the nation something like $11 billion annually; providing them with pre-schools, kindergartens, and colleges might add another $8 billion to the bill. In the long run there is abundant evidence that this investment would repay itself by raising taxable income and by cutting expenditures for welfare, unemployment, police and other slum symptoms. Even in the short run $11 billion for better education would place comparatively little burden on a well-managed economy. Assuming the President continues to listen to liberal rather than conservative economists, the GNP should increase by at least $150 billion between now and 1970, and federal tax receipts should go up at least $30 billion if the present tax structure is maintained. Unless the Vietnam war spreads, Congress could increase the authorization under Title 1 of the new Elementary and Secondary Education Act, to $20 billion by 1970 without straining the federal budget.

But of course this is not going to happen. Almost nobody really wants to make America an egalitarian society. Ours is a competitive society, in which some people do extremely well and others do equally badly, and most people are willing to keep it that way. For as long as anyone can remember, for example, the richest fifth of the population has earned about ten times as much as the poorest fifth. The ability to influence political and personal events is probably even less equally distributed. As a result, there is enormous competition for the jobs which provide comfort and personal power. And despite a lot of pious rhetoric about equality of opportunity in this competition, most parents want their children to have a more than equal chance of success. Since access to good schools and colleges has become increasingly critical in this struggle, there is constant competition to guarantee one's children access to the "best" schools. This means that if the schools down the road get better, local ideals will rise too. If other schools raise their salaries and begin to lure the best teachers, local schools will respond by doing likewise—if they can. If Washington begins to pour large sums of money into the slums to equalize opportunity, middle class areas will respond by pouring even more money into *their* schools, in order to keep ahead. Or, to be more realistic, they will begin demanding that Washington help middle-class as well as slum schools. If they don't get the money from Washington they will turn to their state legislatures, where they are likely to get a sympathetic hearing.

The fact is that American society, while providing almost unlimited opportunities for particularly gifted individuals, does not provide unlimited opportunity for its people as a whole. On the contrary, American society has always been organized on the assumption that while some will do very well, many will do very badly. Equality of opportunity therefore means not just an equal opportunity for everyone to become President, but an equal opportunity for everyone to end up a street cleaner. No sane family or community wants that kind of equality for *their* children. They struggle to keep *that* kind of opportunity as *unequal* as possible. Inevitably, those who have money and influence struggle more successfully than those who do not. Children who grow up in the slums can see this. They know that America contains failures as well as successes, jobs which pay desperately low wages as well as jobs which pay extremely good ones, styles of life which are miserable as well as styles which are comfortable. Unless they have both unusual faith and unusual talent, they know that their future is, at best, one of comparative failure. It is this comparison, far more than absolute deprivation, which underlies the sickness of today's slums. It is this comparison with the rest of America which makes jobs and living standards that seemed more than adequate a generation ago seem intolerable today. (It is no accident that the "poverty line" shifts from one generation to another. As a rule of thumb, we can predict that any family which makes less than half the national average will *feel* poor, and will be defined as poor by liberal economists.)

This comparative standard must also be kept in mind when evaluating programs for upgrading slum schools. A man's employment prospects are not improved by teaching him ten percent more if, at the same time, all his neighbors are being taught twenty percent more. Increasing a school's budget by fifty percent will not equalize the opportunities open to its students if, at the same time, competing schools also get 50 or even 100 percent more money.

II—THE BUREAUCRACY PROBLEM

It would be politically difficult to equalize opportunity between the slums and the suburbs under the best of circumstances. But not even the better financed slum schools (e.g. those in Harlem, on which more money is spent than in most suburbs outside the New York area) achieve results comparable to suburban systems. This in turn makes it even more difficult to raise the necessary money than it would otherwise be. If an extra $20 billion a year would bring slum children up to the academic level of

IS THE PUBLIC SCHOOL OBSOLETE?
Christopher Jencks

their suburban rivals, some legislators would support the expenditure out of idealism. But many legislators feel—and not without reason—that even if they gave the schools an unlimited budget, the children of the slums would contine to grow up both personally and academically crippled.

These fears may be exaggerated. They certainly ought to be tested empirically before being accepted at face value. The Ford Foundation, for example, instead of sprinkling money around in dozens of different projects and places, ought to try raising school expenditures in one slum area to, say, double the level in nearby suburbs—just to see what would happen. It would, of course, take many years to tell. Children who were more than two or three when the experiment began would already have been scarred, often hopelessly, by the existing system. It would be a generation before the impact of the extra money on today's infants could be fully weighed. But if it turned out that an extra $100 million a year made a dramatic difference in, say, the slums of Washington, D.C., it would become very much easier to get comparable sums from taxpayers in other areas.

Unfortunately, an extra $100 million might not make a dramatic difference in Washington—or in most other places either. Much that has been said and written about slum schools, not only in Washington but in places where race is not an issue, suggests that inadequate funds are only part of their problem. They also have the wrong motives and objectives. Some slum schools seem to be less educational than penal institutions. Their function is more to pacify the young than to teach them. They are ruled by fear, not love, infected by boredom, not curiosity. Such schools should not be given more money; they should be closed.

The roots of the problem go very deep. At times the problem seems to be public control itself. Because the slum school is public, it is accountable to the taxpayer. As in every other public enterprise, this kind of minute accountability to publicity-hungry elected officials leads to timidity among the employees. Public control puts a premium not on achieving a few spectacular successes but on avoiding any spectacular failures. In this respect there is not much difference between education and other fields of public endeavor. Nevertheless, public control over education has achieved a sanctity and respectability which public control over other enterprises has never mustered. Conversely, the ideologists of private enterprise have, with the conspicuous exception of Milton Friedman, been comparatively slow to apply their arguments in behalf of private schools.

Yet public control is not a sufficient explanation of the problems of the slum school, for public control seems to have worked quite well in some suburbs and small towns. The problem seems to be that in the slums public control has been linked to inadequate funds for performing the job assigned. Slum schools have found it difficult to get extra money even when there was reason to believe that the marginal return on this money would be very good. Educators might argue, for example, that doubling expenditures in the slums would treble results. But since we have no good way to measure this, sceptical legislators have been slow to provide extra money. As a result, pay scales in the big city school systems have been too low to compete with most other jobs requiring equivalent training, skill, and masochism. And so, in turn, many slum teachers and administrators have comparatively little competence, confidence or commitment.

In city after city this has led to the creation of a system of education whose first axiom is that *everyone,* on every level, is incompetent and irresponsible. From this axiom comes the corollary that everyone must be carefully watched by a superior. The school board has no faith in the central administration, the central administration has no faith in the principals, the principals have no faith in the teachers, and the teachers have no faith in the students. Decision-making is constantly centralized into as few hands as possible rather than being decentralized into as many hands as possible, in the hope of reducing errors to a minimum. Of course such a system also reduces individual initiative to a minimum, but that is a price which a publicly-controlled bureaucracy, whose aim is not profits but survival, usually seems willing to pay. In such a system it seems natural not to give the principal of a school control over his budget, not to give teachers control over their syllabus, and not to give the students control over anything. Distrust is the order of the day, symbolized by the elaborate accounting system, the endless forms to be filled out for the central office, the time clocks and the two-way radios for monitoring classrooms from the front office, the constant tests and elaborate regulations for students.

In such a system everyone gets along by going along with the man over him. Most come to see themselves as play actors. The student tries to dope out what the teacher wants, and gives it to him. Usually all he wants is a reasonable amount of quiet in class and some appearance of docility in doing assignments. The teachers, in turn, try to figure out what the principal wants. That usually means filing grades and attendance records promptly, keeping trouble over discipline to a minimum, and avoiding complaints from parents or students. The principal, in turn, tries

IS THE PUBLIC SCHOOL OBSOLETE?
Christopher Jencks

to keep the central administration happy (and the administration tries to keep the school board happy) by not sticking his neck out and by damping down "trouble" before it gets "out of hand."

Organizational sclerosis of this kind is extremely difficult to cure. For obvious reasons innovation from the bottom up becomes impossible and unthinkable. But even innovation from the top down is difficult. It is easy to get people to go through the *forms* of change, but it is almost impossible to get them to *really* change, because they are frozen into defensive postures based on years of stand-pattism. If the principal tells the teachers he wants them to revamp the curriculum, they immediately begin looking to him—not to their students in the classroom—for cues and clues about what kinds of changes to propose. If the teachers tell the students to think for themselves, the students interpret this as just another move by the teacher to complicate "the game," another frustration in their efforts to "give the teacher what he wants." If the school board tries raising salaries in order to attract new kinds of teachers, it must still assign them to the same old schools, where they are still treated like filing clerks. So the more imaginative and dedicated teachers leave after a year or two for other schools—often in suburbia—which treat them better. In such circumstances more money may just mean more of the same.

A business which becomes afflicted with this kind of disease either goes bankrupt or else creates a monopoly or cartel to protect itself from more dynamic competition. The same is true of school systems. Were it not for their monopoly on educational opportunities for the poor, most big city school systems would probably go out of business. If, for example, the poor were simply given the money that is now spent on their children's education in public schools, and were told they could spend this money in private institutions, private schools would begin to spring up to serve slum children. In due course such schools would probably enroll the great majority of these children. The case of the parochial schools illustrates this point. These schools are seldom really free, but many parents, including some non-Catholics, make considerable sacrifices to send their children to them. In some cases, of course, this is a matter of religious faith. But if one asks parents why they prefer the parochial schools, the answer is often that they think the schooling itself is better than what the public schools in their area offer. Evidence collected by Peter Rossi and Andrew Greeley of the National Opinion Research Center suggests that the parochial schools usually *do* do more for their students than their public competitors, at least judging by the records of their alumni. This seems to be so despite the fact that they have less money, pay lower salaries to lay teachers, have larger classes, older buildings, and fewer amenities of every sort.

There is, of course, considerable reluctance among non-Catholics (and also among anti-clerical Catholics) to admit that the parochial schools might be doing something of value. Most non-Catholics, including myself, have an instinctive distrust of the Church. We have readily accepted the proposition that its schools were "divisive," despite research evidence which shows that aside from their religious practices parochial school graduates have about the same habits and values as Catholics who attend public schools. A similar prejudice clouds efforts to discuss what have traditionally been called "private" schools. Educators have taught us to use "public" as a synonym for "democratic" or just plain "good", and to associate "private" with "elitist" and "inequality." In part this is because when we think of a "public" school we conjure up a small-town or suburban school which is responsible and responsive to those whom it serves; a "private" school, on the other hand, is imagined as a posh country club for the sons of the rich. Yet using this kind of language to describe the "public" schools of Harlem surely obscures as much as it reveals. The Harlem schools are hardly more responsible or responsive to those whom they nominally serve than the typical "private" school. They are "public" only in the legal sense that the Post Office, for example, is "public," i.e., they are tax supported, open to all, ultimately answerable to public officials who have almost no interest in them. Conversely, while it is true that "private" schools have in the past catered mainly to the well-off, this seems to reflect economic necessity more than social prejudice. If the poor were given as much money to spend on education as the rich, there is every reason to assume that the private sector would expand to accommodate them. Indeed, if we were to judge schools by their willingness to subsidize the poor, we would have to say that private schools have shown *more* interest in the poor than public ones. Has any suburban board of education used its own money to provide scholarships for slum children? Most refuse to admit such children even if their way is paid. Many private boards of trustees, on the other hand, have made such efforts, albeit on a small scale.

Private control has several advantages in a school which serves slum children. To begin with, it makes it possible to attack the

IS THE PUBLIC SCHOOL OBSOLETE?
Christopher Jencks

problem in manageable bites. It is inconceivable that a big city school system can be reformed all at once. Failing that, however, it may be impossible to reform it at all. If, for example, the system is geared to docile teachers who do not want and cannot handle responsibility, how is it to accommodate the enterprising minority who have ideas of their own and want freedom to try them out? The superintendent cannot alter the whole system to deal with a handful of such teachers, even if he wants to. But if he does not alter the system, the better teachers will usually leave—or not come in the first place. Somehow the system must be broken up so that its parts can develop at different paces, in different styles, and even in different directions. Little cells of excellence must be nourished, gradually adding to their own number and excitement. Unusual talent must not be spread so thin over the whole system that no single place achieves the critical mass needed to sustain a chain reaction. Yet this is just what a conventional, centrally controlled system tends to do, for in such a system "special treatment" for a particular school is quickly defined as "favoritism." (This attitude is illustrated in the response of big cities to the offer of federal funds under the new Elementary and Secondary Education Act. Almost nobody wants to concentrate this money in a few places to create really good schools; everyone wants to spread it across the whole system.)

A second virtue of private schools is that they get away from the increasingly irrelevant tradition of neighborhood schools. Every psychologist and sociologist now recognizes that what children learn formally from their teachers is only a small fraction of their overall education. What they learn informally from their classmates is equally or more important. For this reason it is extremely important to expose slum children to classmates who teach them things which will be an asset rather than a liability as they grow older. A school which draws only from the slum itself will not provide this kind of stimulus. Instead, ways must be found to mix slum children with racially and economically different classmates.

In principle, of course, this kind of ethnic and economic mixing ought to be easier within a public system than a private one. But this may not be so in practice. In a publicly controlled system every school is required to follow essentially the same educational policies and practices as every other one. This means that the differences between schools derive largely if not exclusively from the differences in their student bodies. (Ability to hold good administrators and teachers seems to depend largely on this, for example.) So long as the student "mix" is decisive, middle-class parents are understandably reluctant to send their children to school with substantial numbers of lower-class children. White parents feel the same way about schools with large numbers of Negro children. But if the traditions and distinctive identity of a school depend not on the character of the student body but on the special objectives and methods of the staff, middle-class parents who approve of these objectives and methods will often send their children despite the presence of poorer classmates. This is clearest, perhaps, in the parochial schools. It might also be possible in non-sectarian private schools, if these had the money to give poor children scholarships, or if outside groups provided such scholarships to large numbers of children.

Getting rid of the neighborhood school, whether by creating city-wide public schools or private ones, could also have the virtue of providing the poor with a real choice about the kinds of schools their children attend. At present, the neighborhood school must try to be all things to all people in its area. Anything daring is bound to displease somebody, and so must be avoided. But if schools could simply tell those who disliked their methods to look elsewhere, and could look all over a large city for a clientele which wanted a particular brand of education, there would be a better chance both for innovation in the schools and for satisfying the diverse needs of different students. It should be possible, for example, for poor people to send their children to a school which segregates the sexes, or employs the Montessorri method, or teaches reading phonetically, or emulates the Summerhill approach. Not everyone wants such things, but *some* do, and they should be able to get them. Given the present outlook of the men who control big city public schools, the only way to make these choices available is probably in the private sector.

In principle there are two ways to develop a larger measure of private initiative and room for maneuver in educating the poor. One would be to provide tuition grants to children who opted out of the public-controlled schools, equal to what would be spent on them if they stayed in. These tuition grants could be used to pay the bills in private schools. There are not, of course, enough private schools today to handle all the potential applicants from the slums, but more would spring up if money were available. But even without tuition grants it should be possible to create much more diversity and decentralization in the

IS THE PUBLIC SCHOOL OBSOLETE?
Christopher Jencks

schools. School boards could, for example, contract with various groups to manage particular schools in their own system.

A university might be given contract to run a model school system in the slums, as suggested by the Panel on Educational Research and Development of the President's Science Advisory Committee. This is apparently to be tried in New York.

A local business group might also take over the management of a school. (If Litton Industries can run a Job Corps camp, it can surely run a school.)

A group of teachers might incorporate itself to manage a school on contract from the citywide board. This could be done at no expense within the present system, using present personnel and facilities, and it might have appreciable advantages. Suppose, for example, that the New York City Board of Education were to rent its facilities to their present staffs and provide them with a management contract subject to annual review. Ultimate control over the school could be vested in the teachers, who would hire administrators. Hiring and firing teachers, budget-making, programming and so forth would all be decided on the spot. If the school did a poor job—which some surely would—the contract could be terminated. A group of parents, working through an elected board, might also take over a school. This alternative, which should be especially appealing to the New Left and to the prophets of "community action," is perhaps better described as a new kind of public control than as private control. In effect, it would mean replacing responsibility to the taxpayer-stockholder with responsibility to the consumer—a kind of educational cooperative.

All these alternatives aim at a radical decentralization of both power and responsibility. All would liberate the schools from the dead hand of central administration, from minute accountability to the public for every penny, every minute, and every word. They all recognize that so far as the slum child is concerned, the present system of "socialized education" has failed, and that some kind of new departure, either "capitalist" or "syndicalist," is needed.

Either tuition grants or management contracts to private organizations would, of course, "destroy the public school system as we know it." When one thinks of the remarkable past achievements of public education in America, this may seem a foolish step. But we must not allow the memory of past achievements to blind us to present failures. Nor should we allow the rhetoric of public school men to obscure the issue. It is natural for public servants to complain about private competition, just as private business complains about public competition. But if the terms of the competition are reasonable, there is every reason to suppose that it is healthy. Without it, both public and private enterprises have a way of ossifying. And if, as some fear, the public schools could not survive in open competition with private ones, then perhaps they *should* not survive.

A REDEFINITION OF EDUCATION

Margaret Mead

When we look realistically at today's world and become aware of what the actual problems of learning are, our conception of education changes radically. Although the educational system remains basically unchanged, we are no longer dealing primarily with the *vertical* transmission of the tried and true by the old, mature, and experienced teacher to the young, immature, and inexperienced pupil in the classroom.

This was the system of education developed in a stable, slowly changing culture. By itself, vertical transmission of knowledge no longer adequately serves the purposes of education in a world of rapid change.

What is needed and what we are already moving toward is the inclusion of another whole dimension of learning: the *lateral* transmission, to every sentient member of society, of what has

---

From Margaret Mead, "A Redefinition of Education," *NEA Journal* 48: 15–17 (October 1959).

just been discovered, invented, created, manufactured, or marketed.

This need for lateral transmission exists no less in the classroom and laboratory than it does on the assembly line with its working force of experienced and raw workmen. The man who teaches another individual the new mathematics or the use of a newly invented tool is not sharing knowledge he acquired years ago. He learned what was new yesterday, and his pupil must learn it today.

The whole teaching-and-learning continuum, once tied in an orderly and productive way to the passing of generations and the growth of the child into a man, has exploded in our faces. Yet even as we try to catch hold of and patch up the pieces, we fail to recognize what has happened.

We have moved into a period in which the break with the past provides an opportunity for creating a new framework for activity in almost every field—but in each field the fact that there has been a break must be rediscovered. In education there has been up to now no real recognition of the extent to which our present system is outmoded.

Historians point sagely to the last two educational crises—the first of which ended with the establishment of the universal elementary school and the second with the establishment of the universal high school—and with remarkable logic and lack of imagination they predict that the present crisis will follow the same pattern.

According to such predictions, the crisis will last until 1970, when it will end with the establishment of universal college education, accessible in principle to all young Americans.

Implicit in this prediction is a series of other dubious assumptions, such as these:

1. Our educational system has fallen behind in something and should therefore arrange to catch up.

2. Our difficulties are due to the "bulge," the host of babies that tricked the statisticians.

3. The pendulum is swinging back to sense—to discipline and dunce caps, switches and multiplication tables.

But in the midst of the incessant discussion and the search for scapegoats to take the blame for what everyone admits is a parlous state, extraordinarily little attention is being paid to basic issues. Everyone simply wants more of what we already have: more children in more schools for more hours studying more of something.

Likewise, scant attention is paid to the fact that two great new educational agencies, the armed services and industry, have

A REDEFINITION OF EDUCATION
Margaret Mead

entered the field, and there is little awareness of the ways in which operations in these institutions are altering traditional education.

But most important, the pattern itself is hardly questioned, for we *think* we know what education is and what a good education ought to be. However deficient we may be as a people, as taxpayers, or as educators, we may be actualizing our ideals.

An occasional iconoclast can ask: "Wouldn't it be fine if we could scrap our whole school system and start anew?" But he gets no hearing because everyone knows that what he is saying is nonsense. Wishful dreams of starting anew are obviously impractical, but this does not mean that someone should not ask these crucial questions:

Is our present historic idea of education suitable for people in the mid-twentieth century, who have a life expectancy of 70 years, and who live in a world of automation and global communication, ready to begin space exploration and aware of the possibility of bringing about the suicide of the entire human species?

Is it not possible that the problem of the educational system's obsolescence goes beyond such issues as methods of teaching reading or physics, or the most desirable age for leaving school, or the payment of teachers, or the length of summer holidays, or the number of years best devoted to college?

Is not the break between past and present—and so the whole problem of outdating in our educational system—related to a change in the rate of change? For change has become so rapid that adjustment cannot be left to the next generation. Adults must—not once, but continually—take in, adjust to, use, and make innovations in a steady stream of discovery and new conditions.

Is it not possible that an educational system that was designed to teach what was known to little children and to a selected few young men may not fit a world in which the most important factors in everyone's life are those things that are not yet, but soon will be, known?

Is it not equally possible that our present definition of a pupil or a student is out of date when we define the learner as a child (or at best an immature person) who is entitled to moral protection and subsistence in a dependency position and who is denied the moral autonomy that is accorded to an adult?

Looking at our educational system today, we can see that in various ways it combines these different functions:

1. The protection of the child against exploitation and the protection of society against precocity and inexperience.

2. The maintenance of learners in a state of moral and economic dependency.

3. Giving to all children the special, wider education once reserved for those of privileged groups, in an attempt to form the citizen of a democracy as once the son of a noble house was formed.

4. The teaching of complex and specialized skills which, under our complex system of division of labor, is too difficult and time-consuming for each set of parents to master or to hand on to their own children.

5. The transmission of something which the parents' generation does not know (in the case of immigrants with varied cultural and linguistic backgrounds) to children whom the authorities or the parents wish to have educated.

To these multiple functions of an educational system, which, in a slowly changing society, were variously performed, we have added slowly and reluctantly a quite new function: *education for rapid and self-conscious adaptation to a changing world.*

That we have as yet failed to recognize the new character of change is apparent in a thousand ways. Despite the fact that a subject taught to college freshmen may have altered basically by the time the same students are seniors, it is still said that colleges are able to give students "a good education"—finished, wrapped, sealed with a degree.

Upon getting a bachelor's degree, a student can decide to "go on" to a higher degree because he has not as yet "completed" his education, that is, the lump of the known which he has decided to bite off. But a student who has once let a year go by after he is "out of school" does not "go *on*," but rather "goes *back*" to school.

And as we treat education as the right of a minor who has not yet completed high school, just so we equate marriage and parenthood with getting a diploma; both indicate that one's education is "finished."

Consistent with our conception of what a student is, our educational institutions are places where we keep "children" for a shorter or longer period. The length of time depends in part on their intelligence and motivation and in part on their parents' incomes and the immediately recognized national needs for particular skills or types of training.

Once they have left, we regard them as in some sense finished, neither capable of nor in need of further "education," for we still believe that education should come all in one piece, or rather, in a series of connected pieces, each presented as a

A REDEFINITION OF EDUCATION
Margaret Mead

whole at the elementary, secondary, and college level. All other behaviors are aberrant.

So we speak of "interrupted" education—that is, education which has been broken into by sickness, delinquency, or military service—and we attempt to find means of repairing this interruption. Indeed, the whole GI bill, which in a magnificent way gave millions of young men a chance for a different kind of education than they would otherwise have got, was conceived of primarily as a means of compensating young men for an unsought but unavoidable interruption.

Thus we avoid facing the most vivid truth of the new age: *No one will live all his life in the world into which he was born, and no one will die in the world in which he worked in his maturity.*

For those who work on the growing edge of science, technology, or the arts, contemporary life changes at even shorter intervals. Often, only a few months may elapse before something which previously was easily taken for granted must be unlearned or transformed to fit the new state of knowledge or practice.

In today's world, no one can "complete an education." The students we need are not just children who are learning to read and write, plus older students, conceived of as minors, who are either "going on" with or "going back" to specialized education. Rather, we need children *and* adolescents *and* young *and* mature *and* "senior" adults, each of whom is learning at the appropriate pace and with all the special advantages and disadvantages of experience peculiar to his own age.

Each and every one of these is a learner, not only of the old and tried—the alphabet or multiplication tables or Latin declensions or French irregular verbs or the binomial theorem—but of new, hardly tried theories and methods: pattern analysis, general system theory, space lattices, cybernetics, and so on.

Learning of this kind must go on, not only at special times and in special places, but all through production and consumption—from the technician who must handle a new machine to the factory supervisor who must introduce its use, the union representative who must interpret it to the men, the foreman who must keep the men working, the salesman who must service a new device or find markets for it, the housewife who must understand how to care for a new material, the mother who must answer the questions of a four-year-old child.

In this world, the age of the teacher is no longer necessarily relevant. For instance, children teach grandparents how to manage TV, young expediters come into the factory along with the new equipment and young men invent automatic programing for computers over which their seniors struggle.

This, then, is what we call the *lateral transmission* of knowledge. It is not an outpouring of knowledge from the "wise old teacher" into the minds of young pupils, as in vertical transmission. Rather, it is a sharing of knowledge by the informed with the uninformed, whatever their ages. The primary prerequisite for the learner is the desire to know.

To facilitate this lateral transmission of knowledge, we need to redefine what we mean by primary and secondary education. We need to stop thinking that free and, when necessary, subsidized education is appropriate *only* when it is preliminary to an individual's work experience.

Instead of adding more and more years of compulsory education (which would further confuse the meaning of education and the purpose of schools), we need to separate primary and secondary education in an entirely new way:

By *primary education* we would mean the stage of education in which all children are taught what they need to know in order to be fully human in the world in which they are growing up including the basic skills of reading and writing and basic knowledge of numbers, money, geography, transportation and communication, the law, and the nations of the world.

By *secondary education* we would mean an education that is based on primary education, and that can be obtained *in any amount* and *at any period* during the individual's whole lifetime.

After agreeing upon this redefinition, we could begin to deal effectively with the vast new demands that are being made on us. The high schools would be relieved of the nonlearners. (It would be essential, of course, that industry, government, or some other social group accept the responsibility of employing or otherwise occupying these persons.)

But, more important, men and women, instead of preparing for a single career to which—for lack of any alternative—they must stick during their entire active lives, would realize that they might learn something else. Women, after their children became older, could be educated for particular new tasks, instead of facing the rejection that today is related to fear about the difficulty of acquiring new learning in middle age.

Whatever their age, those obtaining a secondary education at any level (high school, college, or beyond) would be in school because they *wanted* to learn and *wanted* to be there *at that time.*

In an educational system of this kind, we could give primary education and protection to children as well as protection and sensitive supervision to adolescents. We could back up to the

A REDEFINITION OF EDUCATION
Margaret Mead

hilt the potentiality of every human being—of whatever age—to learn at any level.

The right to obtain secondary education when and where the individual could use it would include not only the right of access to existing conventional types of schools but also the right of access to types of work training not yet or only now being developed—new kinds of apprenticeship and also new kinds of work teams.

In thinking about an effective educational system, we should recognize that the adolescent's need and right to work is as great as (perhaps greater than) his immediate need and right to study. And we must recognize that the adult's need and right to study more is as great as (perhaps greater than) his need and right to hold the same job until he is 65.

We cannot accomplish the essential educational task merely by keeping children and young adults—whom we treat like children—in school longer. We can do it by creating an educational system in which all individuals will be assured of the secondary and higher education they want and can use any time throughout their entire lives.

DISCUSSION QUESTIONS
AND FURTHER READINGS

Familiar practices tend to be taken for granted. In our educational systems, every child is expected to stay in school from one specified age to another one, supposedly to complete his basic preparation for later life. Granted the desirability for citizens to be able to communicate with each other in a common symbolic language, why should everyone learn the same curriculum in the same order at the same place during the same period of his life? What evidence can you gather to support or refute the current procedures, which specify that a child be initiated into school life at about six, regardless of his sex, physiological type and maturity, psychological development and inclination, social preparation, familial expectations, and community and cultural backgrounds —and that he be retained in school continuously, and essentially *full-time during the day,* until the age of about sixteen? Is this the most economical way to do the training job? Socially efficient? Physiologically reasonable? Psychologically meaningful?

Why not start schooling at the age of two or ten or fifty? Why not end it at seven or fifteen or seventy? Why only daytime for schooling? Why isolate students in the increasingly centralized institution of the school? Why not combine their formal education with some other social, and more immediately productive, activities? If not concurrently, why not at least alternately?

Such discussion is bound to turn its focus to the role of the school as a social institution and to the matter of educational policy. One aspect of these issues is largely internal, that is, what is taking place within the school, how and why? To gain some insight into the dynamics of the institution, see Elizabeth M. Eddy, *Walk the White Line* (Garden City, N.Y.: Anchor Books, Doubleday, 1967) and Willard Waller, *The Sociology of Teaching* (New York: Science Editions, John Wiley, 1965).

Another aspect is external, namely, the relationships between the school and other social institutions. Is the school in a position to fulfill all the expectations held for it by the society? Is the school the best institution to perform these expected tasks? Can, for example, the military, business, and industry do a better job in training personnel? What does the school have to offer which other institutions cannot provide? Are other social institutions, such as the family, church, or social agencies, evading their responsibilities by transferring some of their own tasks to the school? Read Kenneth B. Clark, *Dark Ghetto* (New York: Torchbooks, Harper & Row, 1967), Nathan Glazer and Daniel P. Moynihan, *Beyond the Melting Pot* (Cambridge, Mass.: The M.I.T. Press, 1963), James E. McClellan, *Toward an Effective Critique of American Education* (Philadelphia: J. B. Lippincott, 1968), and Fred M. Newmann and Donald W. Oliver, "Education and Community," *Harvard Educational Review* 37: 61–106 (Winter 1967).

WHAT

THE CHILD AND THE CURRICULUM

John Dewey

Profound differences in theory are never gratuitous or invented. They grow out of conflicting elements in a genuine problem—a problem which is genuine just because the elements, taken as they stand, are conflicting. Any significant problem involves conditions that for the moment contradict each other. Solution comes only by getting away from the meaning of terms that is already fixed upon and coming to see the conditions from another point of view, and hence in a fresh light. But this reconstruction means travail of thought. Easier than thinking with surrender of already formed ideas and detachment from facts already learned is just to stick

---

Reprinted from *The Child and the Curriculum and The School and the Society* (pp. 3–31) by John Dewey by permission of The University of Chicago Press and Mrs. John Dewey. *The Child and the Curriculum,* copyright 1902 by The University of Chicago. *The School and the Society,* copyright 1900, 1915 (revised edition), 1943 by John Dewey. Published in 1956, second impression 1956. All rights to both works reserved. Composed and printed by The University of Chicago Press, Chicago, Illinois, U.S.A.

by what is already said, looking about for something with which to buttress it against attack.

Thus sects arise: schools of opinion. Each selects that set of conditions that appeals to it; and then erects them into a complete and independent truth, instead of treating them as a factor in a problem, needing adjustment.

The fundamental factors in the educative process are an immature, undeveloped being; and certain social aims, meanings, values incarnate in the matured experience of the adult. The educative process is the due interaction of these forces. Such a conception of each in relation to the other as facilitates completest and freest interaction is the essence of educational theory.

But here comes the effort of thought. It is easier to see the conditions in their separateness, to insist upon one at the expense of the other, to make antagonists of them, than to discover a reality to which each belongs. The easy thing is to seize upon something in the nature of the child, or upon something in the developed consciousness of the adult, and insist upon *that* as the key to the whole problem. When this happens a really serious practical problem—that of interaction—is transformed into an unreal, and hence insoluble, theoretic problem. Instead of seeing the educative steadily and as a whole, we see conflicting terms. We get the case of the child vs. the curriculum; of the individual nature vs. social culture. Below all other divisions in pedagogic opinion lies this opposition.

The child lives in a somewhat narrow world of personal contacts. Things hardly come within his experience unless they touch, intimately and obviously, his own well-being, or that of his family and friends. His world is a world of persons with their personal interests, rather than a realm of facts and laws. Not truth, in the sense of conformity to external fact, but affection and sympathy, is its keynote. As against this, the course of study met in the school presents material stretching back indefinitely in time, and extending outward indefinitely into space. The child is taken out of his familiar physical environment, hardly more than a square mile or so in area, into the wide world —yes, and even to the bounds of the solar system. His little span of personal memory and tradition is overlaid with the long centuries of the history of all peoples.

Again, the child's life is an integral, a total one. He passes quickly and readily from one topic to another, as from one spot to another, but is not conscious of transition or break. There is no conscious isolation, hardly conscious distinction. The things that occupy him are held together by the unity of the personal

THE CHILD AND THE CURRICULUM
John Dewey

and social interests which his life carries along. Whatever is uppermost in his mind constitutes to him, for the time being, the whole universe. That universe is fluid and fluent; its contents dissolve and re-form with amazing rapidity. But, after all, it is the child's own world. It has the unity and completeness of his own life. He goes to school, and various studies divide and fractionize the world for him. Geography selects, it abstracts and analyzes one set of facts, and from one particular point of view. Arithmetic is another division, grammar another department, and so on indefinitely.

Again, in school each of these subjects is classified. Facts are torn away from their original place in experience and rearranged with reference to some general principle. Classification is not a matter of child experience; things do not come to the individual pigeonholed. The vital ties of affection, the connecting bonds of activity, hold together the variety of his personal experiences. The adult mind is so familiar with the notion of logically ordered facts that it does not recognize—it cannot realize—the amount of separating and reformulating which the facts of direct experience have to undergo before they can appear as a "study," or branch of learning. A principle, for the intellect, has had to be distinguished and defined; facts have had to be interpreted in relation to this principle, not as they are in themselves. They have had to be regathered about a new center which is wholly abstract and ideal. All this means a development of a special intellectual interest. It means ability to view facts impartially and objectively; that is, without reference to their place and meaning in one's own experience. It means capacity to analyze and to synthesize. It means highly matured intellectual habits and the command of a definite technique and apparatus of scientific inquiry. The studies as classified are the product, in a word, of the science of the ages, not of the experience of the child.

These apparent deviations and differences between child and curriculum might be almost indefinitely widened. But we have here sufficiently fundamental divergences: first, the narrow but personal world of the child against the impersonal but infinitely extended world of space and time; second, the unity, the single wholeheartedness of the child's life, and the specializations and divisions of the curriculum; third, an abstract principle of logical classification and arrangement, and the practical and emotional bonds of child life.

From these elements of conflict grow up different educational sects. One school fixes its attention upon the importance of the subject-matter of the curriculum as compared with the contents of the child's own experience. It is as if they said: Is life petty, narrow, and crude? Then studies reveal the great, wide universe with all its fulness and complexity of meaning. Is the life of the child egoistic, self-centered, impulsive? Then in these studies is found an objective universe of truth, law, and order. Is his experience confused, vague, uncertain, at the mercy of the moment's caprice and circumstance? Then studies introduce a world arranged on the basis of eternal and general truth; a world where all is measured and defined. Hence the moral: ignore and minimize the child's individual peculiarities, whims, and experiences. They are what we need to get away from. They are to be obscured or eliminated. As educators our work is precisely to substitute for these superficial and casual affairs stable and well ordered realities; and these are found in studies and lessons.

Subdivide each topic into studies; each study into lessons; each lesson into specific facts and formulae. Let the child proceed step by step to master each one of these separate parts, and at last he will have covered the entire ground. The road which looks so long when viewed in its entirety is easily traveled, considered as a series of particular steps. Thus emphasis is put upon the logical subdivisions and consecutions of the subject-matter. Problems of instruction are problems of procuring texts giving logical parts and sequences, and of presenting these portions in class in a similar definite and graded way. Subject-matter furnishes the end, and it determines method. The child is simply the immature being who is to be matured; he is the superficial being who is to be deepened; his is narrow experience which is to be widened. It is his to receive, to accept. His part is fulfilled when he is ductile and docile.

Not so, says the other sect. The child is the starting-point, the center, and the end. His development, his growth, is the ideal. It alone furnishes the standard. To the growth of the child all studies are subservient; they are instruments valued as they serve the needs of growth. Personality, character, is more than subject-matter. Not knowledge or information, but self-realization, is the goal. To possess all the world of knowledge and lose one's own self is as awful a fate in education as in religion. Moreover, subject-matter never can be got into the child from without. Learning is active. It involves reaching out of the mind. It involves organic assimilation starting from within. Literally, we must take our stand with the child and our departure from him. It is he and not the subject-matter which determines both quality and quantity of learning.

The only significant method is the method of the mind as it

THE CHILD AND THE CURRICULUM
John Dewey

reaches out and assimilates. Subject-matter is but spiritual food, possible nutritive material. It cannot digest itself; it cannot of its own accord turn into bone and muscle and blood. The source of whatever is dead, mechanical, and formal in schools is found precisely in the subordination of the life and experience of the child to the curriculum. It is because of this that "study" has become a synonym for what is irksome, and a lesson identical with a task.

This fundamental opposition of child and curriculum set up by these two modes of doctrine can be duplicated in a series of other terms. "Discipline" is the watchword of those who magnify the course of study; "interest" that of those who blazon "The Child" upon their banner. The standpoint of the former is logical; that of the latter psychological. The first emphasizes the necessity of adequate training and scholarship on the part of the teacher; the latter that of need of sympathy with the child, and knowledge of his natural instincts. "Guidance and control" are the catchwords of one school; "freedom and initiative" of the other. Law is asserted here; spontaneity proclaimed there. The old, the conservation of what has been achieved in the pain and toil of the ages, is dear to the one; the new, change, progress, wins the affection of the other. Inertness and routine, chaos and anarchism, are accusations bandied back and forth. Neglect of the sacred authority of duty is charged by one side, only to be met by counter-charges of suppression of individuality through tyrannical despotism.

Such oppositions are rarely carried to their logical conclusion. Common-sense recoils at the extreme character of these results. They are left to theorists, while common-sense vibrates back and forward in a maze of inconsistent compromise. The need of getting theory and practical common-sense into closer connection suggests a return to our original thesis: that we have here conditions which are necessarily related to each other in the educative process, since this is precisely one of interaction and adjustment.

TWO LIMITS OF A PROCESS *

What, then, is the problem? It is just to get rid of the prejudicial notion that there is some gap in kind (as distinct from degree) between the child's experience and the various forms of subject-matter that make up the course of study. From the side

---

* *Editor's Note:* The two headings in this selection were added by the editor for readers' convenience. They are not the author's.

of the child, it is a question of seeing how his experience already contains within itself elements—facts and truths—of just the same sort as those entering into the formulated study; and, what is of more importance, of how it contains within itself the attitudes, the motives, and the interests which have operated in developing and organizing the subject-matter to the plane which it now occupies. From the side of the studies, it is a question of interpreting them as outgrowths of forces operating in the child's life, and of discovering the steps that intervene between the child's present experience and their richer maturity.

Abandon the notion of subject-matter as something fixed and ready-made in itself, outside the child's experience, cease thinking of the child's experience as also something hard and fast; see it as something fluent, embryonic, vital; and we realize that the child and the curriculum are simply two limits which define a single process. Just as two points define a straight line, so the present standpoint of the child and the facts and truths of studies define instruction. It is continuous reconstruction, moving from the child's present experience out into that represented by the organized bodies of truth that we call studies.

On the face of it, the various studies, arithmetic, geography, language, botany, etc., are themselves experience—they are that of the race. They embody the cumulative outcome of the efforts, the strivings, and the successes of the human race generation after generation. They present this, not as a mere accumulation, not as a miscellaneous heap of separate bits of experience, but in some organized and systematized way—that is, as reflectively formulated.

Hence, the facts and truths that enter into the child's present experience, and those contained in the subject-matter of studies, are the initial and final terms of one reality. To oppose one to the other is to oppose the infancy and maturity of the same growing life; it is to set the moving tendency and the final result of the same process over against each other; it is to hold that the nature and the destiny of the child war with each other.

If such be the case, the problem of the relation of the child and the curriculum presents itself in this guise: Of what use, educationally speaking, is it to be able to see the end in the beginning? How does it assist us in dealing with the early stages of growth to be able to anticipate its later phases? The studies, as we have agreed, represent the possibilities of development inherent in the child's immediate crude experience. But, after all, they are not parts of that present and immediate life. Why, then, or how, make account of them?

THE CHILD AND THE CURRICULUM
John Dewey

Asking such a question suggests its own answer. To see the outcome is to know in what direction the present experience is moving, provided it move normally and soundly. The far-away point, which is of no significance to us simply as far away, becomes of huge importance the moment we take it as defining a present direction of movement. Taken in this way it is not remote and distant result to be achieved, but a guiding method in dealing with the present. The systematized and defined experience of the adult mind, in other words, is of value to us in interpreting the child's life as it immediately shows itself, and in passing on to guidance or direction.

Let us look for a moment at these two ideas: interpretation and guidance. The child's present experience is in no way self-explanatory. It is not final, but transitional. It is nothing complete in itself, but just a sign or index of certain growth tendencies. As long as we confine our gaze to what the child here and now puts forth, we are confused and misled. We cannot read its meaning. Extreme depreciations of the child morally and intellectually, and sentimental idealizations of him, have their root in a common fallacy. Both spring from taking stages of a growth or movement as something cut off and fixed. The first fails to see the promise contained in feelings and deeds which, taken by themselves, are uncompromising and repellent; the second fails to see that even the most pleasing and beautiful exhibitions are but signs, and that they begin to spoil and rot the moment they are treated as achievements.

What we need is something which will enable us to interpret, to appraise, the elements in the child's present puttings forth and fallings away, his exhibitions of power and weakness, in the light of some larger growth-process in which they have their place. Only in this way can we discriminate. If we isolate the child's present inclinations, purposes, and experiences from the place they occupy and the part they have to perform in a developing experience, all stand upon the same level; all alike are equally good and equally bad. But in the movement of life different elements stand upon different planes of value. Some of the child's deeds are symptoms of a waning tendency; they are survivals in functioning of an organ which has done its part and is passing out of vital use. To give positive attention to such qualities is to arrest development upon a lower level. It is systematically to maintain a rudimentary phase of growth. Other activities are signs of a culminating power and interest; to them applies the maxim of striking while the iron is hot. As regards them, it is perhaps a matter of now or never. Selected, utilized, emphasized, they may mark a turning-point for good in the child's whole career; neglected, an opportunity goes, never to be recalled. Other acts and feelings are prophetic; they represent the dawning of flickering light that will shine steadily only in the far future. As regards them there is little at present to do but give them far and full chance, waiting for the future for definite direction.

Just as, upon the whole, it was the weakness of the "old education" that it made invidious comparisons between the immaturity of the child and the maturity of the adult, regarding the former as something to be got away from as soon as possible and as much as possible; so it is the danger of the "new education" that it regard the child's present powers and interests as something finally significant in themselves. In truth, his learnings and achievements are fluid and moving. They change from day to day and from hour to hour.

It will do harm if child-study leave in the popular mind the impression that a child of a given age has a positive equipment of purposes and interests to be cultivated just as they stand. Interests in reality are but attitudes toward possible experiences; they are not achievements; their worth is in the leverage they afford, not in the accomplishment they represent. To take the phenomena presented at a given age as in any way self-explanatory or self-contained is inevitably to result in indulgence and spoiling. Any power, whether of child or adult, is indulged when it is taken on its given and present level in consciousness. Its genuine meaning is in the propulsion it affords toward a higher level. It is just something to do with. Appealing to the interest upon the present plane means excitation; it means playing with a power so as continually to stir it up without directing it toward definite achievement. Continuous initiation, continuous starting of activities that do not arrive, is, for all practical purposes, as bad as the continual repression of initiative in conformity with supposed interests of some more perfect thought or will. It is as if the child were forever tasting and never eating; always having his palate tickled upon the emotional side, but never getting the organic satisfaction that comes only with digestion of food and transformation of it into working power.

As against such a view, the subject-matter of science and history and art serves to reveal the real child to us. We do not know the meaning either of his tendencies or of his performances excepting as we take them as germinating seed, or opening bud, of some fruit to be borne. The whole world of visual nature is all too small an answer to the problem of the meaning of the child's instinct for light and form. The entire science of physics

THE CHILD AND THE CURRICULUM
John Dewey

is none too much to interpret adequately to us what is involved in some simple demand of the child for explanation of some casual change that has attracted his attention. The art of Raphael or of Corot is none too much to enable us to value the impulses stirring in the child when he draws and daubs.

So much for the use of the subject-matter in interpretation. Its further employment in direction or guidance is but an expansion of the same thought. To interpret the fact is to see it in its vital movement, to see it in its relation to growth. But to view it as a part of a normal growth is to secure the basis for guiding it. Guidance is not external imposition. *It is freeing the life-process for its own most adequate fulfilment.* What was said about disregard of the child's present experience because of its remoteness from mature experience; and of the sentimental idealization of the child's naïve caprices and performances, may be repeated here with slightly altered phrase. There are those who see no alternative between forcing the child from without, or leaving him entirely alone. Seeing no alternative, some choose one mode, some another. Both fall into the same fundamental error. Both fail to see that development is a definite process, having its own law which can be fulfilled only when adequate and normal conditions are provided. Really to interpret the child's present crude impulses in counting, measuring, and arranging things in rhythmic series involves mathematical scholarship—a knowledge of the mathematical formulae and relations which have, in the history of the race, grown out of just such crude beginnings. To see the whole history of development which intervenes between these two terms is simply to see what step the child needs to take just here and now; to what use he needs to put his blind impulse in order that it may get clarity and gain force.

If, once more, the "old education" tended to ignore the dynamic quality, the developing force inherent in the child's present experience, and therefore to assume that direction and control were just matters of arbitrarily putting the child in a given path and compelling him to walk there, the "new education" is in danger of taking the idea of development in altogether too formal and empty a way. The child is expected to "develop" this or that fact or truth out of his own mind. He is told to think things out, or work things out for himself, without being supplied any of the environing conditions which are requisite to start and guide thought. Nothing can be developed from nothing; nothing but the crude can be developed out of the crude—and this is what surely happens when we throw the child back upon his achieved self as a finality, and invite him to spin new truths of nature or of conduct out of that. It is certainly as futile to expect a child to evolve a universe out of his own mere mind as it is for a philosopher to attempt that task. Development does not mean just getting something out of the mind. It is a development of experience and into experience that is really wanted. And this is impossible save as just that educative medium is provided which will enable the powers and interests that have been selected as valuable to function. They must operate, and how they operate will depend almost entirely upon the stimuli which surround them and the material upon which they exercise themselves. The problem of direction is thus the problem of selecting appropriate stimuli for instincts and impulses which it is desired to employ in the gaining of new experience. What new experiences are desirable, and thus what stimuli are needed, it is impossible to tell except as there is some comprehension of the development which is aimed at; except, in a word, as the adult knowledge is drawn upon as revealing the possible career open to the child.

THE LOGICAL AND THE PSYCHOLOGICAL

It may be of use to distinguish and to relate to each other the logical and the psychological aspects of experience—the former standing for subject-matter in itself, the latter for it in relation to the child. A psychological statement of experience follows its actual growth; it is historic; it notes steps actually taken, the uncertain and tortuous, as well as the efficient and successful. The logical point of view, on the other hand, assumes that the development has reached a certain positive stage of fulfilment. It neglects the process and considers the outcome. It summarizes and arranges, and thus separates the achieved results from the actual steps by which they were forthcoming in the first instance. We may compare the difference between the logical and the psychological to the difference between the notes which an explorer makes in a new country, blazing a trail and finding his way along as best he may, and the finished map that is constructed after the country has been thoroughly explored. The two are mutually dependent. Without the more or less accidental and devious paths traced by the explorer there would be no facts which could be utilized in the making of the complete and related chart. But no one would get the benefit of the explorer's trip if it was not compared and checked up with similar wanderings undertaken by others; unless the new geographical facts learned, the streams crossed, the mountains climbed, etc., were viewed, not as mere incidents in the journey of the particular traveler, but (quite apart from the individual explorer's life) in relation to other similar facts already known. The map orders individual experiences, connecting them with one another irrespective of the local and temporal circumstances and accidents of their original discovery.

Of what use is this formulated statement of experience? Of what use is the map?

Well, we may first tell what the map is not. The map is not a substitute for a personal experience. The map does not take the place of an actual journey. The logically formulated material of a science or branch of learning, of a study, is no substitute for the having of individual experiences. The mathematical formula for a falling body does not take the place of personal contact and immediate individual experience with the falling thing. But the map, a summary, an arranged and orderly view of previous experiences, serves as a guide to future experience; it gives direction; it facilitates control; it economizes effort, preventing useless wandering, and pointing out the paths which lead most quickly and most certainly to a desired result. Through the map every new traveler may get for his own journey the benefits of the results of others' explorations without the waste of energy and loss of time involved in their wanderings—wanderings which he himself would be obliged to repeat were it not for just the assistance of the objective and generalized record of their performances. That which we call a science or study puts the net product of past experience in the form which makes it most available for the future. It represents a capitalization which may at once be turned to interest. It economizes the workings of the mind in every way. Memory is less taxed because the facts are grouped together about some common principle, instead of being connected solely with the varying incidents of their original discovery. Observation is assisted; we know what to look for and where to look. It is the difference between looking for a needle in a haystack, and searching for a given paper in a well-arranged cabinet. Reasoning is directed, because there is a certain general path or line laid out along which ideas naturally march, instead of moving from one chance association to another.

There is, then, nothing final about a logical rendering of experience. Its value is not contained in itself; its significance is that of standpoint, outlook, method. It intervenes between the more casual, tentative, and roundabout experiences of the past, and more controlled and orderly experiences of the future. It gives past experience in that net form which renders it most available and most significant, most fecund for future experience. The abstractions, generalizations, and classifications which it introduces all have prospective meaning.

The formulated result is then not to be opposed to the process of growth. The logical is not set over against the psychological. The surveyed and arranged result occupies a critical position in the process of growth. It marks a turning-point. It shows how we may get the benefit of past effort in controlling future endeavor. In the largest sense the logical standpoint is itself psychological; it has its meaning as a point in the development of experience, and its justification is in its functioning in the future growth which it insures.

Hence the need of reinstating into experience the subject-matter of the studies, or branches of learning. It must be restored to the experience from which it has been abstracted. It needs to be *psychologized;* turned over, translated into the immediate and individual experiencing within which it has its origin and significance.

Every study or subject thus has two aspects: one for the scientist as a scientist; the other for the teacher as a teacher. These two aspects are in no sense opposed or conflicting. But neither are they immediately identical. For the scientist, the subject-matter represents simply a given body of truth to be employed in locating new problems, instituting new researches, and carrying them through to a verified outcome. To him the subject-matter of the science is self-contained. He refers various portions of it to each other; he connects new facts with it. He is not, as a scientist, called upon to travel outside its particular bounds; if he does, it is only to get more facts of the same general sort. The problem of the teacher is a different one. As a teacher he is not concerned with adding new facts to the science he teaches; in propounding new hypotheses or in verifying them. He is concerned with the subject-matter of the science as *representing a given stage and phase of the development of experience.* His problem is that of inducing a vital and personal experiencing. Hence, what concerns him, as teacher, is the ways in which that subject may become a part of experience; what there is in the child's present that is usable with reference to it; how such elements are to be used; how his own knowledge of the subject-matter may assist in interpreting the child's needs and doings, and determine the medium in which the child should be placed in order that his growth may be properly directed. He is concerned, not with the subject-matter as such, but with the subject-matter as a related factor in a total and growing experience. Thus to see it is to psychologize it.

THE CHILD AND THE CURRICULUM
John Dewey

It is the failure to keep in mind the double aspect of subject-matter which causes the curriculum and child to be set over against each other as described in our early pages. The subject-matter, just as it is for the scientist, has no direct relationship to the child's present experience. It stands outside of it. The danger here is not a merely theoretical one. We are practically threatened on all sides. Textbook and teacher vie with each other in presenting to the child the subject-matter as it stands to the specialist. Such modification and revision as it undergoes are a mere elimination of certain scientific difficulties, and the general reduction to a lower intellectual level. The material is not translated into life-terms, but is directly offered as a substitute for, or an external annex to, the child's present life.

Three typical evils result: In the first place, the lack of any organic connection with what the child has already seen and felt and loved makes the material purely formal and symbolic. There is a sense in which it is impossible to value too highly the formal and the symbolic. The genuine form, the real symbol, serve as methods in the holding and discovery of truth. They are tools by which the individual pushes out most surely and widely into unexplored areas. They are means by which he brings to bear whatever of reality he has succeeded in gaining in past searchings. But this happens only when the symbol really symbolizes—when it stands for and sums up in shorthand actual experiences which the individual has already gone through. A symbol which is induced from without, which has not been led up to in preliminary activities, is, as we say, a *bare* or *mere* symbol; it is dead and barren. Now, any fact, whether of arithmetic, or geography, or grammar, which is not led up to and into out of something which has previously occupied a significant position in the child's life for its own sake, is forced into this position. It is not a reality, but just the sign of a reality which *might* be experienced if certain conditions were fulfilled. But the abrupt presentation of the fact as something known by others, and requiring only to be studied and learned by the child, rules out such conditions of fulfilment. It condemns the fact to be a hieroglyph: it would mean something if one only had the key. The clue being lacking, it remains an idle curiosity, to fret and obstruct the mind, a dead weight to burden it.

The second evil in this external presentation is lack of motivation. There are not only no facts or truths which have been previously felt as such with which to appropriate and assimilate the new, but there is no craving, no need, no demand. When the subject-matter has been psychologized, that is, viewed as an outgrowth of present tendencies and activities, it is easy to locate in the present some obstacle, intellectual, practical, or ethical, which can be handled more adequately if the truth in question be mastered. This need supplies motive for the learning. An end which is the child's own carries him on to possess the means of its accomplishment. But when material is directly supplied in the form of a lesson to be learned as a lesson, the connecting links of need and aim are conspicuous for their absence. What we mean by the mechanical and dead in instruction is a result of this lack of motivation. The organic and vital mean interaction—they mean play of mental demand and material supply.

The third evil is that even the most scientific matter, arranged in most logical fashion, loses this quality, when presented in external, ready-made fashion, by the time it gets to the child. It has to undergo some modification in order to shut out some phases too hard to grasp, and to reduce some of the attendant difficulties. What happens? Those things which are most significant to the scientific man, and most valuable in the logic of actual inquiry and classification, drop out. The really thought-provoking character is obscured, and the organizing function disappears. Or, as we commonly say, the child's reasoning powers, the faculty of abstraction and generalization, are not adequately developed. So the subject-matter is evacuated of its logical value, and, though it is what it is only from the logical standpoint, is presented as stuff only for "memory." This is the contradiction: the child gets the advantage neither of the adult logical formulation, nor of his own native competencies of apprehension and response. Hence the logic of the child is hampered and mortified, and we are almost fortunate if he does not get actual non-science, flat and commonplace residua of what was gaining scientific vitality a generation or two ago—degenerate reminiscence of what someone else once formulated on the basis of the experience that some further person had, once upon a time, experienced.

The train of evils does not cease. It is all too common for opposed erroneous theories to play straight into each other's hands. Psychological considerations may be slurred or shoved to one side; they cannot be crowded out. Put out of the door, they come back through the window. Somehow and somewhere motive must be appealed to, connection must be established between the mind and its material. There is no question of getting along without this bond of connection; the only question is whether it be such as grows out of the material itself in relation to the mind, or be imported and hitched on from some outside

THE CHILD AND THE CURRICULUM
John Dewey

source. If the subject-matter of the lessons be such as to have an appropriate place within the expanding consciousness of the child, if it grows out of his own past doings, thinkings, and sufferings, and grows into application in further achievements and receptivities, then no device or trick of method has to be resorted to in order to enlist "interest." The psychologized *is* of interest—that is, it is placed in the whole of conscious life so that it shares the worth of that life. But the externally presented material, conceived and generated in standpoints and attitudes remote from the child, and developed in motives alien to him, has no such place of its own. Hence the recourse to adventitious leverage to push it in, to factitious drill to drive it in, to artificial bribe to lure it in.

Three aspects of this recourse to outside ways for giving the subject-matter some psychological meaning may be worth mentioning. Familiarity breeds contempt, but it also breeds something like affection. We get used to the chains we wear, and we miss them when removed. 'Tis an old story that through custom we finally embrace what at first wore a hideous mien. Unpleasant, because meaningless, activities may get agreeable if long enough persisted in. *It is possible for the mind to develop interest in a routine or mechanical procedure if conditions are continually supplied which demand that mode of operation and preclude any other sort.* I frequently hear dulling devices and empty exercises defended and extolled because "the children take such an 'interest' in them." Yes, that is the worst of it; the mind, shut out from worthy employ and missing the taste of adequate performance, comes down to the level of that which is left to it to know and do, and perforce takes an interest in a cabined and cramped experience. To find satisfaction in its own exercise is the normal law of mind, and if large and meaningful business for the mind be denied, it tries to content itself with the formal movements that remain to it—and too often succeeds, save in those cases of more intense activity which cannot accommodate themselves, and that make up the unruly and *declassé* of our school product. An interest in the formal apprehension of symbols and in their memorized reproduction becomes in many pupils a substitute for the original and vital interest in reality; and all because, the subject-matter of the course of study being out of relation to the concrete mind of the individual, some substitute bond to hold it in some kind of working relation to the mind must be discovered and elaborated.

The second substitute for living motivation in the subject-matter is that of contrast-effects; the material of the lesson is rendered interesting, if not in itself, at least in contrast with some alternative experience. To learn the lesson is more interesting than to take a scolding, be held up to general ridicule, stay after school, receive degradingly low marks, or fail to be promoted. And very much of what goes by the name of "discipline," and prides itself upon opposing the doctrines of a soft pedagogy and upon upholding the banner of effort and duty, is nothing more or less than just this appeal to "interest" in its obverse aspect—to fear, to dislike of various kinds of physical, social, and personal pain. The subject-matter does not appeal; it cannot appeal; it lacks origin and bearing in a growing experience. So the appeal is to the thousand and one outside and irrelevant agencies which may serve to throw, by sheer rebuff and rebound, the mind back upon the material from which it is constantly wandering.

Human nature being what it is, however, it tends to seek its motivation in the agreeable rather than in the disagreeable, in direct pleasure rather than in alternative pain. And so has come up the modern theory and practice of the "interesting," in the false sense of that term. The material is still left; so far as its own characteristics are concerned, just material externally selected and formulated. It is still just so much geography and arithmetic and grammar study; not so much potentiality of child-experience with regard to language, earth, and numbered and measured reality. Hence the difficulty of bringing the mind to bear upon it; hence its repulsiveness; the tendency for attention to wander; for other acts and images to crowd in and expel the lesson. The legitimate way out is to transform the material; to psychologize it—that is, once more, to take it and to develop it within the range and scope of the child's life. But it is easier and simpler to leave it as it is, and then by trick of method to *arouse* interest, to *make* it *interesting;* to cover it with sugar-coating; to conceal its barrenness by intermediate and unrelated material; and finally, as it were, to get the child to swallow and digest the unpalatable morsel while he is enjoying tasting something quite different. But alas for the analogy! Mental assimilation is a matter of consciousness; and if the attention has not been playing upon the actual material, that has not been apprehended, nor worked into faculty.

How, then, stands the case of Child vs. Curriculum? What shall the verdict be? The radical fallacy in the original pleadings with which we set out is the supposition that we have no choice save either to leave the child to his own unguided spontaneity or to inspire direction upon him from without. Action is response; it is adaptation, adjustment. There is no such thing as sheer self-activity possible—because all activity takes place in a medium, in a situation, and with reference to its conditions. But, again, no such thing as imposition of truth from without, as insertion of truth from without, is possible. All depends upon the activity which the mind itself undergoes in responding to what is presented from without. Now, the value of the formulated wealth of knowledge that makes up the course of study is that it may enable the educator *to determine the environment of the child,* and thus by indirection to direct. Its primary value, its primary indication, is for the teacher, not for the child. It says to the teacher: Such and such are the capacities, the fulfilments, in truth and beauty and behavior, open to these children. Now see to it that day by day the conditions are such that *their own activities* move inevitably in this direction, toward such culmination of themselves. Let the child's nature fulfil its own destiny, revealed to you in whatever of science and art and industry the world now holds as its own.

The case is of Child. It is his present powers which are to assert themselves; his present capacities which are to be exercised; his present attitudes which are to be realized. But save as the teacher knows, knows wisely and thoroughly, the race-expression which is embodied in that thing we call the Curriculum, the teacher knows neither what the present power, capacity, or attitude is, nor yet how it is to be asserted, exercised, and realized.

EDUCATION AND COMMITMENT

Solon T. Kimball

James E. McClellan, Jr.

We have made our proposals. The final part of our task is to defend our analysis against the obvious charge that commitment is something other than the purely intellectual or cognitive activities we have described under the heading of "disciplines." Commitment is a matter of guts, of will and heart, the objection runs; commitment means a certain state of the emotions and not merely of the mind, as our argument would lead one to believe.

Let us meet this objection head on. It is an idea that is deep-rooted in our culture, and we shall have to make several detours to show why it is entirely misplaced. We shall have to show the radical difference between commitment in our culture and com-

---

From *Education and the New America* by Solon T. Kimball and James E. McClellan, Jr., Chapter 14. © Copyright 1962 by Random House, Inc. Reprinted by permission of the publisher and the authors.

mitment as it exists in other cultures. We shall have to offer an interpretation of individuality and individual responsibility that is different from the one our culture inherited from its agrarian past. With these arguments we shall make our case proof against the objections that seem, at first glance, so destructive.

THE NEW MEANING TO "MORAL"

The world of contemporary metropolitan culture does not manifest itself to its new members as the great forces of the natural world manifested themselves to youths among the Plains Indians. Prayer, fasting, and solitary vigils now produce only giddiness and headaches; they vouchsafe not visions but vertigo. This is a pity, of course, but there it is.

The world today permits itself to be directly seen only in fragments. Its larger, more abiding features are abstract; they must be constructed in the mind, not perceived by the senses. Unlike the world of Irish familism, unlike the Navaho world of personal striving for adulthood, unlike any other world in which a whole society has been forced to live—the world of the contemporary American never permits its basic structure to be reproduced in the ordinary life and affairs of men and women.

Yet all too often we still speak and think of commitment as if it were the sort of dedication shown by the Irish peasant toward the preservation of his family's hold on the land. We see the steady disintegration of this sort of direct relation between a person and the demands of his world, and we complain that the contemporary world creates mass man, lacking in commitment, without roots in the realities of the world he inhabits. We decry conformity; we denounce anomie.[1] In short, we—we who would speak to and for education—fail to see the truth about our own world and the kind of commitment it permits and requires.

Cognitively, our world includes the disciplines by which it can be known. They differ from the disciplines of fasting, prayer, interpersonal loyalty, and self-sacrifice. They are, rather, the wholly impersonal disciplines of scientific experimentation, of natural history, esthetic form and mathematics. They are terrifying disciplines, for they permit no ultimate certainty, no relaxation into the "oceanic feeling" of being at one with the entire universe.[2] Their findings enlarge and change at a dizzying pace: today's most basic theories become uninteresting special cases tomorrow.

But this is no cause for despair. If even our extended lifetime gives us only a small glimpse into *all* the complexities of the world we now inhabit, these glimpses still surpass in richness of texture and order of pattern anything that might have been guessed by our ancestors. What does it matter that our vision of the natural world makes all mankind seem a rather irrelevant cosmic accident? A cognitive grasp of the natural and social world, unfettered by illusions of personal significance, can now be the normal, routine achievement of all men and women. In previous ages and cultures only the extraordinary mystic or scholar could accomplish this. If there is a good in universal education, surely this is part of it.

There are, of course, those who claim that scientific rationality, even in its broadest sense, gives only a partial, even a distorted view of the world. If they mean that there is an illuminative quality in the arts that is different from the light of scientific reason, their claim is true. But it is not damaging to our insistence that, in the purely cognitive sense, scientific rationality is the sovereign, supreme, jealously unique discipline for apprehending the physical and social world. If the truism that there is more to human life than mere cognition seems significant, it may be reiterated as often as one likes. Still our point is this: one aspect of commitment in the contemporary world *is* cognition. It is, moreover, the prerequisite without which all the other relations between a person and his world could not add up to commitment. A man or woman might have the most positive feelings toward this society, might work with assiduous self-sacrifice for its welfare, might pray for it each day, and yet all these would not constitute commitment to our culture in the absence of a rationally disciplined, objective grasp of the fundamentally impersonal structures and processes that constitute our physical and social world.

The world in which we live can be known only by rationally ordered disciplines for which science in its broad sense is the prototype. One could say, then, that the touchstone of our analysis is the relation between the individual and his world, i.e. that scientific, rational knowledge of the world is the basic relation from which conceptions of the world, personality, and symbol systems are derived. One could say this, but we choose to put it the other way for this reason: the objectivity of rational thought means that it *is* a part of the world external to any individual. To learn how the world is organized, what forms, patterns, and regularities are to be apprehended in the environment, means to accept an external discipline for one's cognitions. It isn't necessary that a world be of this sort; the world of Irish familism and Navaho self-proving were different. We believe the difference is better described by saying that these are different social and material worlds, each of which makes its distinctive demands for a particular kind of person and a particular kind of symbolic expression.

What relation, then, between an individual person and his world *is* demanded by the world of contemporary metropolitan culture? Clarity, vigor, and breadth of thought as discussed under the disciplines of education? These, of course, are essential; without them the world is not, and chaos obtains. But is nothing beyond knowledge necessary? Other social and material worlds have demanded obedience, reverence, devotion, self-abnegation, love, sacrifice, prayer.... Does our world demand only disciplined thought?

Not quite. But it doesn't demand any of these other forms of worship. In fact it makes worship very difficult. Awe and respect are almost inevitable concomitants of the disciplined study of anything, but worship is a quite personal relation between worshiper and object worshiped. The world as it reveals itself through the disciplines of science, history, and criticism is not personal. For a person who simply *will* worship, the human imagination can find attributes of personality in virtually anything —a stone, a statue, or constellations of stars. Our world is supremely indifferent in this regard. Its richness and order may be worshiped or not; it neither demands nor prohibits this relation. Freedom of worship is thus to be seen as a structural feature of the world of metropolitan culture.

But are there no demands of a distinctly moral character in the very structure of our culture? Yes and no. Let us state the negative side of the answer first. The recognition of a social system in which social functions are performed irrespective of the personal motives of those who have specific roles in the system was one of Marx's keenest and most enduring insights. (This insight need not be associated with the naive determinism and linear causation found elsewhere in Marx.[3]) A school, a corporation, or political unit simply could not operate if its operation depended on a unanimity of motives in those who perform its functions. It operates on its own internal logic and structure. When it fails to operate well, we seek to improve it by changing its structure: by reorganizing it. We got rid of hereditary kingship and hereditary control of business enterprises because those systems do tend to elevate the personal motives of leaders to greater structural significance than mobile, technological systems can tolerate.

Let us be quite clear about what we are asserting and denying. In one of the usual senses of "moral," when we talk about the moral quality of a man or his actions, we refer to his motives. Now some motives are higher and better than other motives; some motives are narrow and purely self-regarding; others are wider and have regard for other people. But the social functions that are essential to our way of life do not hinge on any person's having one sort of motivation rather than another. Care and diligence in the maintenance of aircraft are essential to our transport system; the motivations of aircraft mechanics are not. Notice that it makes perfect sense to ask a mechanic why he chooses to work for United Airlines. He may answer by reference to the pay, the security, the absence of unwelcome supervision, and so on. But it doesn't make much sense to ask him, "What are your motives for working here?"

We may ask him, quite meaningfully, if the occasion should arise, "What was the motive behind your act of deliberate sabotage?" The difference between these two questions is, in part, that working for United Airlines is a functional activity within a social system. One's motives are largely irrelevant. Only when one acts contrary to the accepted function of a position in a social system does the question of motives become relevant.[4] The point is just this—the system as such does not demand any special motives in those who operate it. Insofar as "moral" has reference to motives, our world, in its larger features, makes no moral demands on individuals. This is the negative answer to the question: Are there no demands of a distinctly moral character in the very structure of our culture?

The positive answer has two parts:

1) All cultures have rules that regulate the behavior of individuals; in our culture these rules must be universal and irrespective of persons as such. This is a distinctly moral demand that arises from the nature of our world.

2) There are very high costs, including the cost of living under impersonal rules, that are inherent in the very structure of our world. There is a distinctly moral demand that every individual accept his share of the cost, however he may feel about having to pay it.

The first point is one we have made many times over. An individual person has a distinct size, shape, color, sex, age, intelligence, ability, religious affiliation, ethnic background, pattern of hates, loves, visions and dreams. Some of the rules under which he must live recognize some of these properties as relevant to the demands made of him. But these rules do not treat him as a unique individual; their demand is not to him as John Smith but to anyone of a certain kind: he must register for military training because he is a member of the class of males over eighteen years in age.

Furthermore, an increasingly narrow range of properties is relevant to the more important demands put on an individual. Beyond a certain minimum point, years of age have relevance to fewer and fewer of the rules to which one is subject. The same is true of sex: at the moment the chief administrative position in Western governments is barred to women, but this rule is in only a few countries a matter of law, and in no country morally justifiable. The same is true of race, religion, social status of parents, etc. Those rules which still operate as vestiges from earlier cultural patterns have no moral significance in our world. But is it not *moral* that such distinctions have no relevance?

It is a bit odd, however, to speak of a *moral* demand when looking at an individual person. Because of the rapid change inherent in our dynamic culture, individuals frequently find themselves in situations in which conflicting rules put conflicting demands on their actions. We say that such a person faces a moral problem. Yet the decision as to which rule ought to be followed is quite frequently made purely by reference to the disciplines of thought discussed earlier.* *Which of these rules actually fits with the nature of the world in which we live?* So put, the question is purely intellectual; it is most usually answered by tracing the natural history of the rules and examining their place in the system in which the actor finds himself.

There are, of course, ultimate moral dilemmas that cannot be solved by intellect, which is to say they cannot be solved at all. These arise most frequently in philosophy classes, not in the context of practical life. If life were for most people most of the

---

* *Editor's Note:* In pp. 297-304 of *Education and the New America*, Kimball and McClellan specify the following four disciplines of thought and action as "the primordial rules of thought that guide our most fundamental interpretations of the world" (p. 303).

    i) The formal disciplines of logic and mathematics.
    ii) The discipline of experimentation.
    iii) The discipline of natural history.
    iv) The discipline of esthetic form.

The authors add: "For one who has learned these disciplines consciously and productively, commitment to American culture is at last possible" (p. 303); "A person who accepts these disciplines as integral to his own thinking and accepts the world as it is revealed through these disciplines has indeed established that relation to the world that deserves the title commitment" (pp. 303-304); and, "We are convinced that the teaching of these disciplines is the prime obligation of our school system, for these are disciplines of the public world" (p. 304).

time merely a series of moral dilemmas, a viable social system would be impossible. For the most part, what we call moral problems are situations in which the rules that we appeal to give conflicting answers, but the decision as to which has more weight is determined by appeal to the disciplines of intellect. It is for this reason that it is a bit odd to speak of a situation like this as posing a moral demand on the individual; the demand is simply for clear thinking.

But how is one to follow the rules when they conflict with his immediate desires? More generally, how is one to act in the way demanded by the world? Is not this kind of action really central to the kind of ordering that we speak of as commitment?

Surely yes. And when we shall have understood this answer, we shall find it contains all that can be said about the other two questions. To explain how and why this is so, we must refer to the final element in commitment: the symbol system by which the individual and his relation to the external world may be understood and interpreted.

Symbols drawn from traditional religions are no longer adequate for the contemporary world. Their origin is in a cultural system based on interpersonal and familial loyalty. Extended to include the impersonal structures of our social and physical world, the symbolic message of Christianity or Judaism becomes attenuated, if not actually unintelligible. This judgment implies no disrespect to the great achievements of twentieth-century theologians, particulary Reinhold Niebuhr, Paul Tillich, and Jacques Maritain. The depth of social sensitivity shown by these men and the enormous ingenuity demonstrated in their efforts to express contemporary social insights in the traditional language of Christianity are worthy of universal admiration. But those achievements in themselves actually help to establish our case: as they stand, that is to say, as they are known and utilized in the common sense world of metropolitan culture, the symbols of the traditional religions are not adequate for understanding and interpreting commitment in a context of impersonal structures. It is no accident that church membership is conceived as an affair of family and locality, that the executives of the electrical companies convicted of corporate collusion were regarded as excellent church members. The symbols of Christianity and Judaism make sense, give adequate expression to the demands for interpersonal commitment within the family and local neighborhood. Within the larger structures of society and nature, no.

In an almost diametrically opposite way, the symbols used to explain and justify politico-economic systems fail to account for commitment within the family and neighborhood. One is not a member of the proletariat or the bourgeoisie in the context of his own home. This was not always so. Self-consciousness about social class or other ideologically expressed relation to the larger structures of the society could be, in some historical moments has been, the central symbolic expression of family and community interaction. But this isn't true now. The symbols for interpreting human behavior in families and neighborhoods are not translatable into the political and economic terms by which we ordinarily describe and justify the large-scale, impersonal, corporate structures of contemporary culture. We have argued this point before; we recall it here only to emphasize that the traditional religious, political, and economic symbol systems are inadequate to express commitment in contemporary culture.

And so we must ask again: What kind of action *is* demanded by the kind of world we live in? How is one to know what the world demands? How is he to learn to act in accordance with his knowledge?

The committed person *knows* what his world demands of him and acts accordingly, because of his knowledge. We have already shown that one can know these demands through the disciplines of thought. Of these disciplines of thought, only the discipline of natural history provides a symbolic medium through which an individual can interpret the complex relations he sustains with his world. And knowing oneself as a part of a social system *is* accepting the moral demands inherent in that system.

Knowing oneself as worker, mother, voter, taxpayer, consumer, and wife is to accept the moral demands arising from each of these roles. Seeing the interconnections among the varied corporate structures in which one's personal life is embedded and knowing how all these are both connected with and also separated from the interpersonal life of family and neighborhood are ways of accepting the world and its demands on conduct.

To ask anything more from commitment is to erect symbol systems into absolutes. Particularly, we should reinterpret what it means to teach young citizens of this nation to love their country. No barrier is imposed to prevent love of family, friends, locality, religion, or even institution, nor does anything prevent our projection of love from the minute part we can see to the whole which we know only through symbols. To know it well is to recognize that America is no longer the kind of place that easily admits of the sort of personal identification we could call "love of country." It is not only too large, too complex, too impersonal an entity for anyone to love, it is also too implacable in its demands. Our nation, beyond any that has ever existed, offers freedom, order, and opportunity. And beyond any other, our nation exacts a price for its goods. Our freedom from material want, from poverty, drudgery, disease, and ignorance will endure only so long as we pay the high price for these great goods, the price of submission to the discipline of a technological culture—not to technology *per se* but to the forms of rational thought and action and to the ordered relations with others in the superstructures which channel and direct our energies. This discipline exhibits itself not only in the time clocks at the production end but also in the need to surround oneself with innumerable physical objects, each of which demands care and attention.

So also is there a cost we must pay for our freedom from arbitrary acts by persons in power. God, we are told, is no respecter of persons, which leads us to believe that God is a bureaucrat. Only in a society which places power in impersonal rules is there a guarantee of freedom from arbitrary personal acts of injustice. This does not deny that there is favoritism, inefficiency, and gross neglect of duty, but these are corruptions of the ideal, and we must be continually alert to eradicate the offenders, otherwise the entire system will come crashing down around us. The price is high, and we have been admonished quite enough by men who would wish to exercise power over other men without rational, impersonal control. Commitment, we would suggest, is the recognition and acceptance of the price we have to pay for freedom from the whimsical, capricious, or malicious acts of persons in power. But let us not be misunderstood on this point either. We argued earlier that the size, complexity, and interdependence of the great superstructures of the public world do not preclude the presence of a great deal more freedom and creativity than these organizations at present allow. Commitment in this particular instance means that one seeks to expand the areas of freedom and exhibit more personal initiative within a system that remains fundamentally *corporate* in form. That a certain price in external regulation and control has to be paid does not mean that all freedom is lost. In fact the values that can accrue from rationalized organization of our public life—not only the material values of mass production but also the ethical values of restraining the power of man over man—will not accrue unless individuals constantly strive to extend the limits of freedom at all levels within the organization.

In short, part of the price of being an American is *being* an organization man. Autonomy is not, as Whyte would have us believe, a viable alternative. On the contrary, the very attempt to discover an alternative is a form of mental and social illness, a denial of reality. The important question is not whether, but what kind of organization man? One who simply occupies a niche on an organization chart? Or one who strives to extend the bounds of his own freedom to act with initiative and resourcefulness at whatever level he finds himself? Truly to understand the reality of the dynamic world we live in is to see that the second sort of individual is not only preferable ethically but that without him our emerging social structure will not stand. Note again that the cognitive grasp of what our world demands furnishes the ground for commitment.

We could continue through the list of social goods and their costs; for example, the omnipresence of the goal of self-fulfillment does indeed broaden and extend the lives of millions of individuals, but it makes any naive contentment in life impossible. But we leave it to the reader to trace this duality in all our values. We turn instead to the final question: Is there any ultimate purpose in this social system?

Order and stability in the social and physical world are essential to personal integrity for the individual. From the simplest expectation that one's footfall will find solidity to the most complex predictive hypothesis in the physical sciences, one stakes his whole integrity as a person on orderliness in the physical world. One or two or even several misjudgments can be tolerated when, as is usually the case, reasons for the misjudgments can be found. But if life presented a preponderance of wholly inexplicable failures of the physical world to accord with expectations, personality would disintegrate.

This need for orderliness in the physical world has exact parallels in the social world. In our day-by-day encounters with other human beings, our expectations are fulfilled: a smile from us elicits a smile from others; a frown, a frown. Approaching a stranger on the street we incline to the right, he does likewise, and our bodies pass without grating contact. Children learn to speak the language of their parents; time and money spent in acquiring the skills necessary for practicing a highly technical vocation are returned with suitable interest during a lifetime of productive work.

Although both nature and society violate our expectations occasionally—the unanticipated earthquake destroys the solidity of the ground; a technological revolution renders hard-won skills economically useless—the more we know, the more our expectations include divergencies from simple uniformity. A sense of self, then, becomes a more differentiated, complex phenomenon as one's image of the natural and social world becomes more complex. "I'm just a farmer" means a different concept of self in an age when agricultural technology has reached the level it has with us as contrasted with what that statement meant in an age when only the grossest expectations of natural processes were part of the conceptual apparatus of the farmer. Just so, "I am a teacher." "I am a mother." One's concept of self is not divorceable from the expectations one has of the world he inhabits.

But the increasing accuracy of our knowledge and the consequent complexity of the natural and social worlds do not assure the integrated relation of a man and his world, the relation we are calling commitment. On the contrary, this very complexity creates a deep fissure in the modern soul; a break between intellect and esthetic sensitivity on one hand and the moral conscience on the other. Intellectually and esthetically modern man delights in diversity and change, in the unusual, the unique. The discipline of experiment has taught us to appreciate the obdurate fact which disproves the neat generalization; we like our order complex and richly textured, not monotonously simple. Modern cosmological theories, the slowly emerging picture of the nucleus of the atom, the story of evolution, the new history—wherever the light of research is allowed to shine, we see not chaos but subtle and diverse patterns that replace the simple mechanical notions that satisfied our ancestors.

A world like this, so delightful to the mind's eye, creates a peculiar problem for the kind of moral conscience we have inherited. It is not that we have created insoluble moral dilemmas for ordinary citizens. For most of us, fortunately, in most of our actions, the right thing to do is not only very obvious, it is also the most natural, the easiest thing to do. As we pointed out earlier, organized civil life would be impossible if truly difficult moral problems were the common experience of ordinary men. A decent society, such as ours is, separates right conduct from wrong in such measure that it is far more likely that right conduct will happen than wrong. This relates also to our point about motives: they are irrelevant except when a person deliberately, willfully violates codes of right conduct.

But our conception of morality has it not only that we should act rightly but that we should do so for some higher reason, to serve some higher purpose, to fulfill some final meaning in the world. *Ad maiorem gloriam Dei,* for the sake of Duty itself, for my Country, my Race, my Class, my Way of Life . . . throughout the history of Western civilization different claimants to be the supreme object of commitment have been heard. But now, as Nietzsche saw, those who are self-consciously literate and attentive to the world can no longer take any such claims seriously.[5] We have created a world in which an individual can find it easy and natural to behave decently toward his neighbors, to practice the classical virtues of temperance, magnanimity, and justice, even the Christian virtue of humility. The price we pay for such a world is that we give up the belief that there is a final reason, an ultimate meaning to justify human existence.

Two questions immediately arise: Is it not true that life is terribly flat, stale, ultimately unsupportable when deprived of final meaning? And what about the unremitting conflict with world communism and our social need, not merely for decent and humane behavior, but for courage, dedication, and sacrifice that go beyond what can be called conventional morality?

Neither of these questions is easily answered. Socrates' noble dictum, "The unexamined life is not worth living," is obviously an intellectualist's conceit (when said by anyone save that person who chose to die rather than stop examining life aloud). But modern men and women have no choice. The very conditions of life—the mobility, the highly symbolic quality of all human action, the widespread literacy—all increase the complexity of the world and the corresponding sense of self in the individual. Thus our life itself leads inevitably to its own examination. The discouraging feature of the present situation is the lack of education to engage in any fundamental examination of life. The historical accident that kept religion out of the public schools is only partly responsible for this. Neither is there evidence that parochial school training in this country or teaching by the "agreed syllabus" in English state schools does a measurably better job than American secular, public schools in giving students the capacity to examine their own existence in the drama of human history.[6]

Perhaps the final step in the democratic experiment is that the society no longer poses an ultimate meaning to life. Instead it builds within each individual such a complex sense of self that the person is forced to create meaning, order, and purpose for himself.

It may be that human beings are incapable of making this experiment a success. Still, having embarked on it, we must not falter simply because there is no guarantee of a favorable outcome. We cannot remake the genetic constitution of the human race, but we can attempt to build the theory and practice of a new kind of education that, if achieved, would make ultimate freedom possible.

But what sort of education would that be? Our answer is in the four intellectual disciplines that we outlined earlier.* We are

---

* *Editor's Note:* See the footnote on page 226.

quite aware that there are aspects of personality that can be reached only with great struggle, if at all, through purely cognitive procedures. We know the frantic efforts that men make to escape from freedom. We are not oblivious to the authoritarian personality and the deeply destructive urges that go with it.[7] Original sin is no quibbling point in theology.

Still we must hold to the principle, even as Mr. Bestor formulated it, that a democratic society is morally required to give its finest, its fundamentally intellectual education to all its citizens. Any citizen so educated may indeed find life flat, stale, ultimately unbearable. The culture has few or no compelling myths, superstitions, or illusions to comfort him. But he may, on the other hand, find the *quest* for meaning, the freedom to *create* his own purposes, the most rewarding life of all. The disciplines of thought and action that we described ever so briefly above we regard as the best education for men and women who will undertake to live a life of ultimate freedom.

But what about the survival of a democratic society? Now that we are faced with the challenge of communism, a system that asserts a monolithic purpose for all its members, a system that is now pressing us with its full power throughout the world, can we afford to set individuals loose to find their own meaning in life? Does not the preservation of freedom require its limitation at least during the critical years of the present world conflict?

Answers to thse questions are not to be found by statistical measures used according to the theory of games.[8] It is not a matter of comparing the freedom we sacrifice for present security against the freedom we might lose if the spread of communism is not halted. This way of looking at the matter assumes what we may call the "rat-race-and-withdrawal" theory of public life. The answer to the demand for commitment and dedication is to replace this obnoxious theory of public life with something more adequate.

The rat-race-and-withdrawal theory of public life is so much a part of the climate of opinion among contemporary intellectuals that its public expression cannot seem other than trite.[9] They proclaim that the public world, the world of great corporate superstructures, is nothing but a rat race. The business corporations exist only to exist: mass advertising creates mass demand to consume the products of mass production, and so around and around forever, all to no purpose other than that the wheels increase in number and speed. Governmental structure is necessary to keep these business corporations from destroying one another domestically and to help spread their influence throughout the world before the (really quite similar) Russian corporate structures spread *their* influence throughout the world. The meaninglessness of the whole competition is nowhere better revealed than in the growth of gigantic military systems which, to justify their existence, will eventually blow the rat race to utter cosmic oblivion.

"Official" education, as received in school, through the mass media, from pulpit and White House makes the rat race sound terribly important; it makes responsibility and authority in the corporate, public world seem exciting and worthy of attainment. But the "informal" education among the *cognoscenti* teaches that the only sensible style of life for man is to exploit that easily exploitable system as efficiently as he can and to use his already acquired leisure and comfort to build a private world in which to pursue self-cultivation until the system blows itself to pieces.

It does not really matter on this theory that television fare is generally inane, vulgar drivel, that urban redevelopment is creating habitation more fit for poultry than human beings, that the natural beauty of our continent is being destroyed with all deliberate speed, that the basic decisions affecting us as a nation are ever further removed from popular inspection and control, that compulsory education for a large proportion of our urban youth is nothing more than custodial supervision, that some public agencies, such as those responsible for transportation and mental health, function at the lowest imaginable level of efficiency—none of these things matter very much since the whole corporate system is a rat race, and anyway there's nothing an individual can do about it. The system, moreover, does provide excellent opportunities for the individual to withdraw and seek his own self-fulfillment through music, literature, arts and crafts that may be pursued in the private world of the home and family. Here indeed, is the way of wisdom, the cultivation of one's own garden, as Voltaire so sagely advised.

And in the present world crisis, on the rat-race-and-withdrawal theory, the society must make certain demands on the individual in order that the system may be preserved. By a combination of force and fraud, it exacts as large a proportion of the individual's time and personality as it can; the individual resisting as hard as he can. By a kind of balance of tensions, depending on internal and external pressures on the system, a compromise is achieved between individual freedom and social survival.

The rat-race-and-withdrawal theory does account for many facts of public life—the graft and corruption revealed daily in the press and the cynicism with which these revelations are greeted, the senselessly huge salaries paid to corporate presidents, signifying the absence of any genuine social reward for socially useful service, and so on. An individual can order his life on the premises of this theory, but he does so at the cost of violating the very realism and disillusionment he cherishes. For this concept of isolated individualism is pure romanticism; self-fulfillment is not to be found in withdrawal into a private world but in productive work in the public world. It does not matter that the public world is imperfect, that its hugeness swallows up the small efforts of individual men and women, that the rapidity of change means that every achievement is soon superseded. For this public, corporate world, despite everything, is *real*. Here there is reality to success and failure; whether the human race survives or not depends on how we learn to work the institutional forms demanded by the density and consumption requirements of *homo sapiens* on this planet.

We hold, therefore, that the key to eliciting excellence in the manifold actions of Americans is not in some phony emotionalism, the use of fraud to persuade individuals to give up their self-enhancing actions in order to perform socially useful services. Rather it is to be found in the intellectual discipline which finally enables the individual to see both his private and public worlds as his own. Distance, change, complexity, mobility—these ineluctable features of modern public life do make it look like a gigantic rat race. The appeals we make to youth, trying to enlist them in causes they do not understand, are transparent to all but the hopelessly stupid. Psychic withdrawal often appears to be the only alternative to madness.

But a firm intellectual grasp of the real nature of this system—with all its complexity, impermanence, dynamism, and freedom—gives the individual a sense of being of, as well as in, his society. That is commitment. Courage, creativity, and leadership spring out of this ordering of an individual, his world, and the symbols by which he understands both. The symbols are those of the appropriate intellectual disciplines.[10]

The obvious alternative is sure to fail. The only way in which we could create a national purpose to match that of communism is by destroying the very freedom we are supposed to serve. We should have to institute controls over the flow of information. We should have to devise all sorts of rewards and punishments to support an orthodoxy. We should have to substitute myth and supersitition for the truth about our natural and social worlds. There are those groups who, out of fear and hostility, would be willing to do just that.

But aside from the moral abhorrence which the suggestion arouses, the appeal to an ultimate meaning served by our national existence would not, in all likelihood, bring our youth to any great pitch of enthusiasm. The young men and women who volunteered to serve as teachers in East Africa and in the Peace Corps made it quite clear that their motives were not those of furthering a particular economic and political system, but overwhelmingly in promoting their own self-growth through the experience of serving other people. They believed, rightly we hope, that what they had to offer was superior to the Russians' contribution because the Americans would be willing to teach, build roads, and improve sanitation without insisting on any particularly American purpose these improvements were to serve. Africans, Asians and South Americans should decide for themselves the ultimate values, if any, to be served by prolonging human life, reducing drudgery, ignorance, and disease.

Perhaps in the long run, the society that agrees to tolerate the tension between public and private worlds, that gives the individual a chance to create his own meaning in both these worlds, that provides him with the tools and symbols to understand the richness and complexity of the world around him without shallow myths and legends—perhaps *that* is the society that can evoke man's highest loyalties and deepest commitments. American education, we believe, ought to be dedicated to that possibility.

NOTES AND REFERENCES

[1] For a very clear-headed critique of this talk about mass nonconformity, etc., see Daniel Bell, *The End of Ideology* (Glencoe: The Free Press, 1960), Chap. 1.

[2] The phrase, "oceanic feeling," was used by Sigmund Freud to mean, "a feeling of indissoluble connection, of belonging inseparably to the external world as a whole." Needless to add, Freud could find no evidence for such a feeling in himself. *Civilization and Its Discontents* (London: The Hogarth Press, 1930), p. 9 *et seq.*

[3] The problem of reconciling a Marxian theory of social system within the allocation of personal responsiblity for concrete actions has not been an easy one for Soviet social philosophy. See Herbert Marcuse, *Soviet Marxism: A Critical Analysis* (New York: Columbia University Press, 1958), chap. 10, "Soviet Ethics—The Externalization of Values."

[4] For a fuller treatment of the distinction between reasons and motives and the place of this distinction in various theories of human nature, see R. S. Peters *The Concept of Motivation* (London: Routledge and Kegan Paul, 1958).

[5] Friedrich Nietzsche, *Beyond Good and Evil,* translated by Marianne Cowan, (Chicago: Henry Regnery Co., 1955), p. 114. "We have

no other choice; we must seek new philosophers, spirits strong or original enough to give an impulse to opposing valuations, to transvalue and turn upside down the 'eternal values'." (Written in 1885). Poor Nietzsche. Those who really did away with the idea of deducing values from the nature of God (or the God of nature), who put man's *will* back to its central place in ethics, were not at all terrifying supermen, but a group of very mild-mannered, innocuous English and Viennese philosophers like G. E. Moore and Moritz Schlick. In a decent orderly society, most human beings eventually, though not without travail, grow up to have decent, orderly *wills*.

[6] Some suggestions for a suitable education in this regard are found in James E. McClellan's "Why Should the Humanities Be Taught?" *Journal of Philosophy,* Vol. LV, No. 23 (Nov. 6, 1958), pp. 997-1108.

[7] Erich Fromm, *Escape from Freedom* (New York: Farrar and Rinehart, 1941). T. W. Adorno, E. Frenkel-Brunswik, D. J. Levinson, and R. N. Sanford, *The Authoritarian Personality* (New York: Harper & Brothers, 1950).

[8] Which is not to say, of course, that statistics and theory of games are *never* useful tools in solving social problems. See James E. McClellan's "Theory in Educational Administration," *School Review,* Vol. 68 (Summer, 1960), pp. 210-227.

[9] Paul Goodman: "The Calling of American Youth," *Commentary,* March, 1960, pp. 217-229. The way Mr. Goodman describes the rat-race is frighteningly familiar; however the world may actually run, surely this is our usual way of talking and thinking about it.

[10] We are aware that others before us have held stark and uncompromising views that bear some resemblance to what we are asserting here. We are aware that in the 1920's, a period that in its apparent affluence superficially resembled our own times, views similar to ours were asserted by men who later recanted in the face of events—depression, Fascism, etc.—they took to be signs of social disintegration. We do not discount the strength of the super-rationalists on one hand and the irrationalists on the other who would attack our theses. See the "Epilogue for 1957" to Morton G. White, *Social Thought in America* (Boston: Beacon Press, 1957), pp. 247-281, and William Barrett, *Irrational Man: A Study in Existential Philosophy* (Garden City: Doubleday and Company, 1958). But we should like to make this much clear: whatever may be the case with others whose views are in some ways like ours, we are not propounding a doctrine of dark despair, we are not praising a soul-less wasteland. We are describing a world with limitations and restrictions, but withal the locus (if there is one) of man's encounter with love and self-fulfillment. In short, the world may be different from our description of it. If so, we welcome new facts that show us where our perceptions were wrong. But we despise, in advance, the critic who objects to our conception of education on the grounds that it lacks a sufficient basis in morality.

RELIGION AND THE PUBLIC SCHOOLS

Marvin Fox

People who talk about agreeing or disagreeing with a decision of the Supreme Court are speaking a very curious language indeed—unless they happen to be legal scholars talking of scholarly agreement or disagreement. For the rest of us, such a decision is, in principle, the law of the land. One must stress, as vigorously as possible, that deliberate efforts to avoid, circumvent, or openly violate the decisions of the Supreme Court are morally deleterious and civically irresponsible. I cannot understand how any public school system can, by its religious practices, deliberately teach its students to violate the law and still claim to be fulfilling its proper functions as an educational system.[1]

If we face a religious crisis in the field of education, it is only a reflection of the general state of religion in our society and, perhaps, of the general confusion about religion as well. Families that do not pray at home and churches whose members are re-

---

From Marvin Fox, "Religion and the Public Schools—A Philosopher's Analysis," *Theory into Practice* 4: 40–44; February 1965.

ligiously illiterate may seek to hide their failures and to salve their troubled consciences by forcing religious exercises on the schools. When they do this, they seem to be not only admitting their own failures, but also closing the doors to any possibility of remedying those failures. One hardly needs to point out the unfairness and the impropriety of using the coercive power of the school authorities to impose upon helpless people religious rites and sectarian practices that violate their consciences and offend their spirits. In my judgment, every sectarian religious practice is offensive in a public school and should be eliminated. I mean not only formal prayers and Bible reading, but also the customary observance of Christmas and Easter as religious holidays in the public schools. If they are not treated as religious holidays, then the religious community should be deeply offended at their secularization; if they are religious holidays, then it seems quite clear that they have no more place in a public school than does public prayer or any other religious ritual. I affirm these views, not as an enemy of religion, but rather because I take religion seriously. Our great and separate religious traditions should not be degraded by dependence upon the police power of the state to maintain their dominance; nor should we lightly compromise the basic principles of human and group equality on which our country was founded.

The current controversy over religion in the schools indicates how much we have trivialized religion. We have misconstrued the true nature of religion, and in so doing we have taken that which is sacred and of inestimable worth and turned it into a series of empty and often comic public rituals. Perhaps my point will be more clear with the help of a magnificent passage from a great thinker, Friedrich Nietzsche, who is considered by some to have been the archenemy of all religious impulses of almost any modern writer. In his *Zarathustra* this passage occurs:

> Have you not heard of that mad man who lit a lantern in the bright morning hours, ran to the market place, and cried incessantly, "I seek God! I seek God!" As many of those who do not believe in God were standing around just then, he provoked much laughter. "Why, did he get lost?" said one. "Did he lose his way, like a child?" said another. "Or is he hiding? Is he afraid of us? Has he gone on a voyage, or emigrated?" Thus they yelled and laughed. The mad man jumped into their midst and pierced them with his glances. "Whither is God?" he cried, "I shall tell you. *We have killed him*—you and I. All of us are his murderers.... God is dead. God remains dead, and we have killed him."

When Nietzsche says "God is dead," he often is accused of being an atheist. We should note, however, that a man who affirms that God is dead, is also affirming that He once was living. A man who affirms that God is dead is not saying that there never was a God nor that there is none. But he is saying that all of the force and all of the power represented in that conception, and for those who believe in that reality, have been lost and made ineffective in contemporary society. And if Nietzsche could say this almost a century ago, I think we have to say it with even greater force in our own time. There is good reason to fear that the external growth of the churches, with their magnificent buildings and burgeoning memberships, and the struggle for the religion in the schools may only be a façade, masking the death of God.

A religion which must use the power of the state to impose its rites on school pupils has emptied itself of its own power and, it seems to me, has admitted that its God is dead. It is not that religious rituals are intrinsically meaningless; I believe the contrary to be true. But if religious rituals, public prayer, and other rites are significant, they are significant because they have a symbolic power found within a historic tradition—a tradition of worship, a tradition of faith, a tradition of practice. The empty imposition of the ritual pattern in public schools, where it has neither the power of its theologico-historical tradition nor its proper symbolic form, is, I think, not only a sacrilege but an ultimate admission of total failure.

What can there be, in the way of religion, in the public schools? I think that to answer this question, one has to ask what we have in mind when we refer to religion in this context. Surely, we must mean something other than rituals and sectarian practices, however precious these may be to individual religious communions. We must seek something more significant than a routinized form of prayer, droned away at a time and under circumstances where nobody listens and nobody participates, something more than watered-down religious neutralism that emasculates the vigor and sucks out the life blood of a living religious tradition and turns it into a kind of empty formal pattern. If religion is significant, it is because, above all else, it is one way of giving meaning, wholeness, and direction to human existence. It is because men who struggle and search are confronted, through the instrumentality of a religious tradition, with the basic questions and are guided in a significant direction in their search for answers. Religion poses those questions that lie at the deepest level of man's being, concerns that point to the very foundation of human existence. It holds out the hope that these deepest puzzles may be solved meaningfully.

If our schools are irreligious or antireligious, it is not because we do not pray in them, but rather because they resist the ultimate questions and are happy to stay on the surface of all basic issues. If our schools are irreligious, it is not because the Bible is not read in them, but because they—the teachers and the institutional structure itself—fear the kind of total commitment that religion demands of us. The position of religion in the public schools is paradoxical. Superficially, we are hospitable to religion, demanding prayers, Bible readings, Christmas and Easter observances, etc. But, fundamentally, I think we oppose everything that religion stands for. Instead of searching for ultimate truth, instead of recognizing the depth of human confusion and of human need, we are satisfied with a kind of endless discussion, which has no direction, gets nowhere, and feeds on itself in a narcissistically cannibalistic way. In this sham, which poses as an exchange of ideas, our thinking gains neither depth nor breadth. We neither give nor receive illumination, but operate under the corrupt notion that there is some magical saving power in "discussion," making it an activity intrinsically worthwhile.

At every level and in every subject area, from the first grade through the university, we need teachers who are deeply committed and ultimately concerned—teachers who are troubled by the basic human questions and who have had the courage to find their own direction. With such teachers we would, in the last analysis, have more religion—and more significant religion—than we shall ever have under present conditions, no matter how much we go through the formalities and the proprieties of prayer, Bible readings, and all the rest. Some will object, "Ah, yes, but committed teachers will indoctrinate." I have been talking about *teachers,* not propagandists. I am talking about teachers who are concerned *not* to impose their own problems or their own solutions upon their students, but who will stand before them as living testimony that men can be engaged at the deepest levels of being. To be a man means, in part, to have this kind of ultimate concern (to use Tillich's famous phrase). Whatever solution, whatever direction a man may find for himself, his humanity is at stake and is enhanced when he operates with this human and, therefore, divine concern.

Let me put it to you in terms of a recent event on my own campus. Not long ago Paul Tillich, one of the most distinguished intellectual figures of our time, came to give a lecture at Ohio State University. The reaction to his coming was, to me, the most astonishing and revealing phenomenon in the whole of my teaching career. For weeks, students were walking around with tremendous excitement. Student groups invited professors to talk

RELIGION AND THE PUBLIC SCHOOLS
Marvin Fox

to them before Tillich's lecture, so that they would be better prepared to understand him. Dozens of students walked through my office asking me to recommend some of Tillich's books that they might read in preparation. The attendance was one of the largest ever seen at a lecture on the campus; the auditorium, which holds about 3,500 people, was jammed to capacity, and large numbers were turned away. Why should this man's coming have had this kind of effect? Certainly his fame was a factor; shortly before, he had been on the cover of *Time* magazine. Even by more meaningful standards, he is a very distinguished person. But equally famous people have come to the University without evoking such a reaction. After thinking about it and talking to other people on the campus, I am convinced that what excited the University community was their feeling that Tillich struggles with the deepest human concerns, the things that matter most to us as human beings, and that he is courageous enough to take a stand. Our students in the universities are tired of being told about all the possible ways to approach every issue without ever being challenged to take their own stand. I believe our students deserve what seems to me to be the most valuable and historic contribution of religion—the confrontation with this kind of ultimate demand and with the commitment that it asks of us.

There was a time in Greek antiquity when philosophy served what is today, I think, the proper function of religion. Plato viewed a teacher, in his own language, as the physician of the soul; and the goal of the teacher was not to impart to his students useless bits and scraps of information. On the contrary, Socrates, the greatest of all teachers, constantly pleaded his own ignorance, because he knew that his task as teacher was simply not to spoon-feed his students with the kinds of information they would memorize, appropriate, regurgitate, and then forget for all time. He challenged them, and he did not challenge them (as we sometimes do) merely to think. A man who thinks has to think about something, and if he is to think significantly, he has to think about something significant. Socrates challenged them to think, at the deepest level, about those questions that affected the whole being. Plato held that it was the business of the teacher to turn his students into independent philosophers, and in this way to help them work out their own salvation.

In more recent times, times that I think were healthier than our own, John Dewey could still view education as primarily moral. He saw it as education of character and spoke of education as the development of every individual to the full stature of his own possibilities. Many people who invoke Dewey's name today trivialize his thought. When he is allowed to speak for himself, it becomes clear that Dewey had the same kind of ultimate concern and struggled with the same ultimate question as Plato did 2,500 years earlier, and as the theologians of the best sort are doing today. Nietzsche, the supposedly antireligious thinker, says in *Beyond Good and Evil:*

> The true philosopher [and I would be inclined to say, the true human being] is a man who demands for himself a verdict, a yea, or a nay, not concerning science, but concerning life and the worth of life. He learns, unwillingly, to believe that it is his right, and even his duty, to obtain this verdict, and he has to seek his way to the right and the belief, only through the most extensive (perhaps disturbing and destroying) experiences, often hesitating, doubting, and dumbfounded.

This is as genuine a representation as I know of the religious dimension of existence. Not a life filled with pat and easy answers; not a classroom situation where we know all there is to know about what doesn't matter anyway, or are fearful, either as persons or as teachers, of standing for something—but on the contrary, "the disturbing and often destroying experiences" which are the heritage of every man who struggles honestly and sincerely to come to terms with himself and with his own being, with the meaning, the purpose, and the direction of his own life.

The religious traditions can offer immensely valuable insight and guidance here, but I do not think anyone can simply hand a man a religion, in a ready-made way, like one would hand him a suit of clothes. If the churches choose to think this way, let them do so on their own terms, on their own time, and on their own property. I grant them the right to think and to practice as they please, but I affirm that this kind of thinking within the classroom is subversive to both religion and education.

How is all of this practically relevant to the schools and to their work? If prayers, Bible readings, Christmas plays, Christmas carols, and all the rest, do not do the job and cannot do the job of religion in the schools, what then? Rabbi Arthur Gilbert has suggested that the objective study of the history and literature of a religion could be a kind of academic discipline.[2] Such study surely deserves a proper place in our curricula. A cultured man should be at least as familiar with the literature of religion as he is with the other major forms of great literature. We should all be distressed when we find we have raised a whole generation totally ignorant even of the elementary facts of Biblical history. It is perfectly clear, however, that the objective study of the history of religion, comparative religion, and religious literature,

RELIGION AND THE PUBLIC SCHOOLS
Marvin Fox

is no solution to the problems we are discussing. If these subjects are taught successfully, they will represent one more academic achievement comparable to learning arithmetic, or English grammar, or history. What is called for is the infusion of a religious perspective and a religious dimension of experience into the whole of our education. This is not a task for theologians or clergymen, nor is it a call for them to invade the public schools. Serious teachers can do the job meaningfully and fruitfully.

A serious teacher must first be a serious human being. A teacher who has mastered some technical discipline is not, by virtue of that alone, worthy of being a teacher. A teacher who has nothing to communicate and nothing to transmit as a person seems, to me, to have failed utterly in the most important aspect of his job. Without any of the formal trappings of religion at all, a school that could transform the indifference, the fearfulness, and the mental flabbiness—which pass for objectivity—into engagement, concern, and commitment, would be a school that does more to advance the cause of religion than any I can think of today.

What of the fear of indoctrination? Do committed teachers threaten us and our children? Not at all. A committed teacher, one who stands for something himself, need not impose his views or his solutions on his pupils. By his very presence, he challenges them, he arouses them, he exemplifies for them the possibilities of human existence itself. Whether his commitment be to some form of historical Christianity, or to secular humanism is of no concern, so long as it is critical, reflective, honest, and genuine. What matters is that his search be genuine and deep, that he use all of his power to make sense out of his own existence and out of that of society. We need have no fear that he will impose his beliefs upon the children entrusted to him. If he seeks to do so in a mechanical and authoritarian way, then he is not really a teacher at all and is doomed to fail.

Anyone who has had the privilege of sitting before even one such true teacher knows how deeply effective such a man can be. The true teacher reaches the depths of his pupils' souls. In this kind of relationship, they begin to become worthy of their own humanity. Martin Buber, in his *Tales of the Hasidim,* tells of one disciple who, returning from a visit to his master, is asked, what did you study? what did you learn? After his friends made various guesses, all wrong, he finally said to them, "I went only to see how my master laces his shoes." What he was saying, of course, is that he had gone to be in the presence of a profound human being, one whose every action—whether he was teaching arithmetic, or Bible, or astronomy, or lacing his shoes, or engaging in dinner conversation—showed the depth of his humanity and the quality of his person. This is the true teacher—one who teaches more by what he is than by formal school exercises.

If only we knew how to present our students with this kind of intellectual and personal opportunity, the danger of indoctrination would be slight. We might, in the process, produce some rebels and nonconformists, but I think, viewed religiously, this would be all to the good. So long as religion is a live and vital force in education, it will make some rebels. But then religious men are supposed to be rebels. Neither Moses nor Jesus were exactly social conformists. Perhaps my point can be made clear through an insight out of Jewish religious tradition. It stands sharply in contrast with today's weak and placid view of religion. There is a Rabbinic comment on a simple Biblical verse. Jacob had left his father's house under very difficult and unhappy circumstances. He was threatened with death by his brother, Esau, and he escaped carrying only his staff and a small knapsack. He was gone for twenty years, and during those years life had not always treated him gently. He acquired a deceiving and rapacious father-in-law, two wives, two concubines, twelve sons, and a daughter. Although he worked desperately hard and was a financial success, he felt homeless and totally uprooted. So he returned home. When he was finally settled, the Biblical text says simply, "And Jacob dwelt in Beersheba." (That is to say, he came home and was at ease.) The Rabbis, commenting on this, imagine the Almighty addressing him and saying to him, "What business do you have being at ease in this world? What business do you have being settled and at peace? Is it not enough for the righteous that peace and serenity may be prepared for them in the world to come? What right do they have to be at ease in this world?"

Religion is viewed here, not as a kind of soporific, whose task it is to put men to sleep and let them be at peace in society, but rather as the goad, the prod, which drives them constantly to see, among other things, how far the actual is from the ideal in themselves and in society around them. Such religion challenges man to be incapable of ease in a world that is less than perfect. I think schools that could communicate this would have communicated more that is religiously significant than the whole conventional pattern (in today's schools) of rituals, prayers, and Bible readings. If we are interested in the place of religion in education, let us move toward the development of teachers, who are themselves in the deepest sense, religious men and women—whether religious in terms of one of the historic traditions, or religious from a perspective and point of view offensive to the historic traditions. We need teachers who are religious men in the sense that they are concerned with the meaning and the purpose of their lives, who seek a direction, who struggle for the truth, who stand openly and without shame before their own failures, who are not afraid to commit themselves, although commitment is always a risk. Let us have teachers who will goad and arouse our students, who will show them what man can be. Let us have teachers who will help our children to see the extent to which our own society is superficial and based on sham, but also how much in our society is sound and genuine and precious. Instead of being patriots by waving the flag, they will be true patriots whose love of America is expressed in their concern for what it means to be a free man in a free society. Instead of being religious by talking vacuously about God, theirs will be the true piety that will exemplify and communicate our conviction that God need not be dead.

Commenting on another Biblical verse, the Rabbis represent God as saying, "Would that the people had abandoned Me, but observed My teachings." If under the guise of religion, at least in public education, we were to talk less about God and worry less about prayer, we might end up taking both God and prayer more seriously. Religion has an important role in education. It should serve to enhance the humanity of each pupil and to help him realize his highest possibilities; to relate teacher and pupil as persons, not as mechanical objects. Viewed in this way, religion can be of inestimable worth in public education. If, however, we force religious observances into the public schools, we make the sacred secular and, therefore, rob prayer and ritual of the power it can have only within a tradition and a communion of faith.

FOOTNOTES

[1] Nothing in this article should be interpreted as opposed to *private* schools which are under the auspices of particular religious communities. There is an important place for such schools in our society, and they serve a highly useful purpose. They are frankly devoted to the propagation of a particular religious tradition; their students have chosen freely to enroll in such a school; they are financed by private or denominational funds. In these circumstances, it is completely proper for them, as the educational arm

of particular religious communities, to set all school activities inside the framework of their own traditional forms of piety. In such school settings, prayers, rituals, catechetical teachings, and the like, are both appropriate and desirable.

[2] *See* Rabbi Gilbert's article, "Major Problems Facing Schools in a Pluralistic Society," Pages 23-28 of this issue of *Theory into Practice* [Vol. 4, February 1965].

15

FOR EACH TREE
IS KNOWN...

Kaoru Yamamoto

An anecdote about the late Dr. William J. Mayo, co-founder with his brother of the famed Mayo Clinic, tells of an invitation he received from the President of the United States to serve as a chairman of a national advisory committee; Dr. Mayo, who was then in his 70's, declined the honor, saying, "I think each generation must settle its own problems and that men along in years who try to project such wisdom as they may have or think they have onto the problems of the future are more likely to do harm than good." [1]

Now, obviously, I am without Dr. Mayo's experience, wisdom, vision, or modesty. Therefore, though I offer for your consideration the following reflection on education of the next generation, I am doing so with considerable hesitation and clear awareness that my analysis may be totally or partially irrelevant and even disruptive. Briefly speaking, my presentation here will be a sur-

---

This essay is based on a paper originally delivered at the Summer Institute, Illinois Plan for Educational Leadership Development, at Urbana, Ill., in July of 1967 under the title, "For Each Tree Is Known...."

vey of what education has come to mean in the American society and where our challenge lies in the overall cultural scheme.

TO BE AN AMERICAN

Several observers have argued that, no matter what we believe human nature to be, we cannot formulate any workable educational scheme for its development (or fulfillment) without fully realizing the nature of social contexts.[2] Since the life of individual beings has always been predicated on the specific combinations of time, space, people, and matter, there is no escaping that our educational efforts must start there, even though the end objective may be to transcend precisely the same restrictions.

Now, it is a rather common observation that, in the early twentieth century, the public school system wrought wonders in transforming the new-arrivals into "true Americans" according to the definitions of the earlier settlers.[3] With the accelerated social change of unprecedented scope and rapidity in the latter half of this century, however, the task of education is to be redefined in terms of a bridge, not between the old world and the new, but between the highly complex, public world of a corporate society and the intimate, private world of a nuclear family.[4] One has no alternative other than living and working in the social superstructure, and the transition from autonomy in the primary group to commitment in the corporate organization must be effected through schooling.

Along this line of analysis, two scholars arrived at the following observation:

> In short, part of the price of being an American is *being* an organization man. Autonomy is not, as Whyte would have us believe, a viable alternative. On the contrary, the very attempt to discover an alternative is a form of mental and social illness, a denial of reality. The important question is not whether, but what kind of organization man? One who simply occupies a niche on an organizational chart? Or one who strives to extend the bounds of his own freedom to act with initiative and resourcefulness at whatever level he finds himself? Truly to understand the reality of the dynamic world we live in is to see that the second sort of individual is not only preferable ethically but that without him our emerging social structure will not stand. Note again that the cognitive grasp of what our world demands furnishes the ground for commitment.[5]

To be an American is, at least in part, to be an organization man! To most of us who have been accustomed to the dream of "rugged individualism" and who have learned to read nothing but negative connotations in the phrase, "an organization man," this is quite a thought. Our first reaction, accordingly, tends to be outright negation of such a statement. Nevertheless, we cannot ignore the consensus of social analysts that, like it or not, we seem to be passing from an era of individual motivation and hard work to that of group efforts and human relations.[6] If this is the world in which our children are going to live, then we should do whatever we can to help them prepare for a full life in that world, not in ours or in our fathers'.

A BALANCING ACT

But, how can we teach our charges to be dedicated and self-renewing organization men? How can we prepare them to be resourceful and motivated members of a corporate society?

We certainly cannot afford to raise a generation of meek, well-conditioned robots. At the same time, however, we cannot simple-mindedly denounce "conformity" and "other-directedness" and praise "inner-directedness" and "autonomy" as a panacea. To begin with, when any of these words is used with no contextual qualifications, our reaction is generally to the symbol itself and not to what is being symbolized. Since a symbol (word) is not the thing and a map is not the territory, it is often futile to argue on the high level of abstraction.[7] Secondly, the problem cannot possibly be resolved by such two-valued, either–or thinking.[8] And, thirdly, the common notion that early Americans were indeed self-reliant individualists or that present-day Americans are more conforming appears to be more an illusion than a realistic observation.[9]

The question, then, is not that of independence (either A or B) but rather that of concomitant or combined outcomes (A and B). In other words, our task, individual as well as collective, is to hit the delicate balance between the feeling of belongingness and that of aloneness. Is such a feat possible?

Many thoughtful men have given an affirmative answer, reminding us of the paradoxical nature of human life. They point out that, while human beings must sacrifice some measure of individual liberty to belong to a society, they owe their humaneness largely to the enriched experience and pooled wisdom of their culture.[10]

Culture most certainly sets certain limits on the available alternatives for individuals. Nevertheless,

> no personality is ever completely molded to the will expressed in the social code, even at high temperature and under constant

pressure. Even if the external molding is outwardly successful, there is much tension within. Culture meets the needs of man with varying degrees of success. Furthermore, what the culture can do to the individual depends on the stuff he is made of.. : . The way in which a person grows into the culture is itself an expression of biological individuality." [11]

Indeed, the paradox here is that "the vaster the organizations of power, industrial or political, the greater the power of the individual who knows how to seize the helm." [12] His success depends on his ability to restructure perception from a detached viewpoint and formulate a relevant conception of the problem and its solutions for himself and his fellow men. In this sense, "individuals can be healthier, even *much* healthier, than the culture in which they grow and live."[13]

Chances are that "most men exercise more control over their own destinies than they know, that many exercise more control than they like to believe, and that most could exercise still more if they would." [14] The problem is how to channel such power for control so as to facilitate individual self-actualization through active and responsible participation in the society. "Many aspects of one's life are of course beyond one's control. But many are not, and those that are not can make a vast difference to oneself, to one's contemporaries, perhaps even to men of the future." [15]

AS TWIGS ARE BENT

Are we, then, encouraging our children to develop a precious sense of group identification, while nurturing a basic belief in the uniqueness and worth of self? Unfortunately, indications are against us.

In the first instance, some of us adults have long since given up the struggle for self-assertion. We have clung to our old, sacred values of Protestant ethic, depending, ironically, on the institutional process to guarantee the significance of life for individuals; and we have lagged considerably in instrumental confirmation of the validity of these values and in the development of new meanings.[16]

Second, we have been quite partial to certainty and absolutism. This is an era of *exact* science in which a single, correct answer is presupposed for every question worthy of the name. This is the age in which anxiety is a cardinal sin and there is a desperate search for the absolute. Seemingly, we try to ignore the finite and uncertain nature of our life. Nevertheless, this fact remains:

> Man's inability to rely upon himself or to have complete faith in himself (which is the same thing) is the price human beings pay for freedom; and the impossibility of remaining unique masters of what they do, of knowing its consequences and relying upon the future, is the price they pay for plurality and reality, for the joy of inhabiting together with others a world whose reality is guaranteed for each by the presence of all.[17]

Third, when we discuss the powerlessness of individuals in the face of the impersonal corporate monstrosity, we tend to exclaim, "Even if I did know who I am, I couldn't make any difference as an individual anyway,"[18] and we do not realize that we are ultimately and inescapably responsible to ourselves for our sense of reality, our definition of situation, and our choice. No one else can live in *my* reality, no one else can make *my* decision (and I must acknowledge that *not* making a decision, or accepting someone else's choice, is itself *my* decision), and no one else can suffer, for me, the consequences of *my* action. In this, I am indeed unique and I am alone.

> No matter how great the forces victimizing the human being, man has the capacity to *know* that he is being victimized, and thus to influence in some way how he will relate *to* his fate. There is never lost that kernel of the power to take some stand, to make some decision, no matter how minute. This is why they [existentialists] hold that man's existence consists, in the last analysis, of his freedom.... Tillich phrased it beautifully in a recent speech, "Man becomes truly human only at the moment of decision."[19]

Finally, it appears that we have been treating the young generation in such a way as to rob them of any sense whatsoever of mastery of their environment. The point is simply this: "We may be of planetary insignificance, but we cannot live by such long views; ..."[20] If we feel completely hemmed in and without control over even a tiny portion of our fate, we become quite vulnerable to the mounting pressure and, sooner or later, we explode or collapse.

Elsewhere I reviewed some of the prevalent conditions which tend to put much stress upon our children,[21] and other observers also attest to the severe limitations on children in their private and social life.[22] Under the circumstances, it is indeed amazing that not more of them turn to violence, sickness, or escapism.

ACHIEVEMENT, SUCCESS AND COMPETENCE

The real difficulty, however, seems to be that, even when our young do not go astray in these extreme forms, they are poorly equipped to cope with future challenges because of our lopsided cultural (and, hence, educational) attention to achievement motivation. Numerous critics, both inside and outside America, have commented on our valuational emphasis on the *doing,* rather than *being* or *being-in-becoming,* orientation and our characteristic preoccupation with *making good.*[23]

"What can be used to succeed in such a society becomes that which is most emphasized during the learning period";[24] and we raise students, ranging from preschoolers to doctoral aspirants, precisely fitted to the concept of achievement which is interpreted as the sole and objective criterion of success and as the necessary prerequisite for being loved. Dependent more on external rewards and punishment than on intrinsic satisfaction, and quite sensitive to normative rather than self (idiographic) evaluation, our students forever seek to find what their teacher wants and to please him at all costs.[25] The American student of today performs for the sake of social approval and would not dare to "risk disapproval in order to do what one wants."[26]

I do not want to be misunderstood here. Many of these are "good," conscientious, and hard-working students. The only trouble is that we define "good" in a particular way, guide their use of intellect into a single channel, and structure our educational activities in such a way as to discourage them (and ourselves) from exploring and searching, from satisfying curiosity, and from evolving a sense of competence, efficacy, and mastery.

In other words, we do everything to stifle their "competence motivation."[27] This becomes clear when we examine reports on our "best" students. In elementary schools, secondary schools, and colleges, we find that many of these elite youngsters feel lost whenever they are expected to find and define their own problems, to pursue these without routine and explicit guidance, to carry the process to closure as they see fit, and to evaluate their own performance without external judgments by others.[28] Thus, it was reported of a bright high school senior who was released for personal inquiry that:

> After two weeks she came to a completely new and unexpected conclusion: she needed to work with other students. She needed them partly for emotional support and reassurance, but mostly to compete with. The meaning of study and learning for Penny resided in the drive to do better than others; without the other students as pace setters, she was confused. And without the reward of knowing that her achievement was superior, she lost her self-confidence.[29]

Being identified as "honest," "independent," "intelligent," or "creative"—depending on our favorite culture symbol of the day,[30] the students faithfully and skillfully perform the expected role of "good" learners, thus allaying their own anxiety and satisfying both themselves and their teachers.

In due course, teachers and students alike come to believe that the content of this performance is an actual expression of the character of the performer, even though some nagging suspicion remains about the real self.[31] Meanwhile, spontaneous and genuine learning tend to be sidetracked. "The attentive pupil who wishes to *be* attentive, his eyes riveted on the teacher, his ears open wide, so exhausts himself in playing the attentive role that he ends up by no longer hearing anything." [32]

BY HIS OWN FRUIT

Indeed, "each tree is known by its own fruit," [33] and we cannot expect to gather figs from thorns or grapes from a bramble bush. So long as we place a premium on the passive and reactive mind, that is precisely what we get. Thus, "the crucial failure of education is in failure to relate achievement demands to the subjective world of the student, or to put it another way, it is the tendency to keep the student working on puzzles rather than on problems meaningful to him." [34]

Not only do we fail to give learning any personal significance, but we also hamstring students' inquiry by exposing them to a single viewpoint concerning the "truth." There is always a right way to do things, to interpret observations, and to handle our feelings and no other alternatives are allowed even to exist, much less to be studied and appreciated. We do not acknowledge that, "The picture is not the look of the world but our way of looking at it: not how the world strikes us but how we construct it. Other people and other ages had different pictures from ours," [35] and for reasons no less logical than ours. Do we examine these different models to learn their respective presuppositions and inherent limitations? The answer seems to be negative.[36] In most instances, we are not even aware of the particular frame of reference we use or of the availability of other approaches. Hence, we behave as if what we see through our glasses were the only reality, the only type of knowledge, transcending time and space. Most assuredly, however, this is not the case.[37]

Granted that our educational system, even in its present form, has sent out a large group of highly efficient, well-trained functionaries, "all the knowledge in the world is worse than useless if it is not humanely understood and humanely used. An intelligence that is not humane is the most dangerous thing in the world."[38] Because of our a-historical orientation and blind faith in science and technology, we tend to produce "encapsulated" beings, clever but not wise, methodical but not sensitive, righteous but not compassionate.[39] In other words, we do a poor job in developing among our students an ultimate sense of identification with the heritage and fate of the human race, or the quality sometimes called "integrity."[40]

Cultivation of competence and search for human identity—these, then, are the paramount tasks set for us, educators. The tasks may be difficult but, apparently, they can be accomplished at the hand of devoted teachers. "The knowledge of self does not teach him to act but to be; it steeps him in the human predicament and the predicament of life; it makes him one with all the creatures."[41]

What should we be teaching our students? Simply two things:

> To believe in their own potentiality for creativity ... [this would be] for the children the first half of their journey towards being educated beings. The other half could be completed only when they could see their own lives surrounded, sustained, and indeed explained by the general experience of all humanity. This part of the journey will take them all the rest of their lives, but to know this is the greatest wisdom they can learn at school."[42]

REFERENCES

[1] Helen Clapesattle. *The Doctors Mayo.* (2nd ed.) Minneapolis: University of Minnesota Press, 1954. Quoted from p. 459 of the Cardinal Giant edition published in 1956 by the Pocket Books of New York.

[2] Nelson B. Henry, Ed. *Social Forces Influencing American Education.* (Part II of the 60th Yearbook of the National Society for the Study of Education) Chicago: University of Chicago Press, 1961.

Solon T. Kimball and James R. McClellan, Jr. *Education and the New America.* New York: Random House, 1962.

Margaret Mead. "A Redefinition of Education," *NEA Journal* 48: 15–17 (October 1959).

Donald N. Michael. *The Next Generation.* New York: Vintage Books, 1963.

Fred M. Newmann and Donald W. Oliver. "Education and Community," *Harvard Educational Review* 37: 61–106 (Winter 1967).

Jerry M. Rosenberg. *Automation, Manpower, and Education.* New York: Random House, 1966.

C. Gilbert Wrenn. *The Counselor in a Changing World.* Washington: American Personnel and Guidance Association, 1962.

[3] D. W. Brogan. *The American Character.* New York: Vintage Books, 1956.

Burton R. Clark. *Educating the Expert Society.* San Francisco: Chandler Publishing Co., 1962.

H. G. Good. *A History of American Education.* (2nd ed.) New York: Macmillan, 1962.

Geoffrey Gorer. *The American People.* (2nd ed.) New York: W. W. Norton, 1964.

V. T. Thayer and Martin Levit. *The Role of the School in American Society.* (2nd ed.) New York: Dodd, Mead, 1966.

[4] Kimball and McClellan, *op. cit.*

[5] *Ibid.* (Vintage Book edition, 1966), p. 315.

[6] Erich Fromm. *The Sane Society.* New York: Rinehart, 1955.

John K. Galbraith. *The Affluent Society.* Boston: Houghton Mifflin, 1958.

Frederick Herzberg, Bernard Mausner and Barbara Snyderman. *The Motivation to Work.* New York: John Wiley & Sons, 1959.

Van Cleve Morris. *Philosophy and the American School.* Boston: Houghton Mifflin, 1961.

David Riesman, Nathan Glazer and Reuel Denney. *The Lonely Crowd.* New Haven, Conn.: Yale University Press, 1950.

William H. Whyte, Jr. *The Organization Man.* Garden City, N.Y.: Doubleday, 1957.

[7] S. I. Hayakawa. *Language in Thought and Action.* (2nd ed.) New York: Harcourt, Brace & World, 1963.

[8] *Ibid.*

[9] Stanley Milgram. "Nationality and Conformity," *Scientific American* 205 (No. 6): 45–51 (December 1961).

David Riesman. "Some Questions About the Study of American Character in the Twentieth Century." In Don Martindale, Ed. *National Character in the Perspective of the Social Sciences* (The Annals of the American Academy of Political and Social Science, Volume 370, March 1967). Pp. 36–47.

[10] Mary Ellen Goodman. *The Individual and Culture.* Homewood, Ill.: Dorsey Press, 1967.

Ralph Linton. *The Cultural Background of Personality.* New York: Appleton-Century-Crofts, 1945.

Henry A. Murray and Clyde Kluckhohn. "Outline of a Conception of Personality." In Clyde Kluckhohn and Henry A. Murray, Eds. *Personality in Nature, Society, and Culture.* New York: Alfred A. Knopf, 1956. Pp. 3–49.

Albert D. Ullman. *Sociocultural Foundations of Personality.* Boston: Houghton Mifflin, 1965.

[11] Gardner Murphy. *Personality.* New York: Basic Books, 1947. P. 905.

[12] *Ibid.,* p. 912.

[13] Abraham H. Maslow. *Motivation and Personality.* New York: Harper & Row, 1954. P. 351.

[14] Mary Goodman. *op. cit.,* p. 245.

[15] *Ibid.*

Also cf. Joseph R. Royce. *The Encapsulated Man.* Princeton, N. J.: D. Van Nostrand, 1964.

[16] Allen Wheelis. *The Quest for Identity.* New York: W. W. Norton, 1958.

[17] Hannah Arendt. *The Human Condition.* Chicago: University of Chicago Press, 1958. Quoted from p. 219 of Anchor Books edition published in 1959 by Doubleday of Garden City, N.Y.

[18] Rollo May. *Psychology and the Human Dilemma.* Princeton, N. J.: D. Van Nostrand, 1967. P. 26.

[19] Rollo May. "The Emergence of Existential Psychology." In Rollo May. Ed. *Existential Psychology.* New York: Random House, 1961. Pp. 11–51. Quoted from p. 42.

[20] Thomas Griffith. *The Waist-High Culture.* New York: Harper & Row, 1959. P. 7.

[21] K. Yamamoto. "Children Under Pressure." Pp. 113–128 in the present volume.

[22] Edgar Z. Friedenberg. *Coming of Age in America.* New York: Random House, 1963.

Paul Goodman. *Growing Up Absurd.* New York: Vintage Books, 1956.

Philip W. Jackson. "The Successful Student," *Teachers College Record* 66: 635–644 (April 1965).

Earl C. Kelley. *In Defense of Youth.* Englewood Cliffs, N. J.: Prentice-Hall, 1962.

Kenneth Keniston. *The Uncommitted.* New York: Harcourt, Brace & World, 1965.

[23] Brogan, *op. cit.*

Fromm, *op. cit.*

Gorer, *op. cit.*

William James. "Talks to Students." In *Talks to Teachers.* New York: W. W. Norton, 1958. Pp. 132–191.

Florence R. Kluckhohn. "Dominant and Variant Value Orientations." In Clyde Kluckhohn and Henry A. Murray, Eds. *Personality in Nature, Society, and Culture.* New York: Alfred A. Knopf, 1956. Pp. 342-357.

Jacques Maritain. *Reflections on America.* New York: Charles Scribner's Sons, 1958.

Lloyd W. Warner. *American Life.* (2nd ed.) Chicago: University of Chicago Press, 1962.

[24] Ashley Montagu. "The Improvement of Human Relations Through Education." In *Race, Science and Humanity.* Princeton, N. J.: D. Van Nostrand, 1963. Pp. 162-171; quoted from p. 163.

[25] John Holt. *How Children Fail.* New York: Pitman Publishing Corp., 1964.

[26] M. Brewster Smith. "Socialization for Competence," *Items* 19: 17-23 (June 1965). Quoted from p. 20.

[27] Alex Inkeles. "Social Structure and the Socialization of Competence," *Harvard Educational Review* 36: 265-283 (Summer 1966).

Smith, *op. cit.*

Robert W. White. "Motivation Reconsidered: The Concept of Competence," *Psychological Review* 66: 297-333 (September 1959).

Robert W. White. "Competence and the Psychosexual Stages of Development." In Marshall R. Jones, Ed. *Nebraska Symposium on Motivation, 1960.* Lincoln: University of Nebraska Press, 1960. Pp. 97-141.

Robert W. White. "Sense of Interpersonal Competence." In Robert W. White, Ed. *The Study of Lives.* New York: Atherton Press, 1963. Pp. 72-93.

[28] Gordon W. Allport. "Crises in Normal Personality Development," *Teachers College Record* 66: 235-241 (December 1964).

Paul Goodman. *Compulsory Mis-Education and the Community of Scholars.* New York: Vintage Books, 1966.

Holt, *op. cit.*

Michael A. Wallach and Nathan Kogan. *Modes of Thinking in Young Children.* New York: Holt, Rinehart & Winston, 1965.

[29] Herbert A. Thelen. *Education and the Human Quest.* New York: Harper & Row, 1960. Pp. 91-92.

[30] Geraldine Joncich. "A Culture-Bound Concept of Creativity: A Social Historian's Critique, Centering on a Recent American Research Report," *Educational Theory* 14: 133-143 (July 1964).

[31] Erving Goffman. *The Presentation of Self in Everyday Life.* Garden City, N.Y.: Doubleday, 1959.

[32] Jean-Paul Sartre. *Being and Nothingness.* New York: Philosophical Library, 1956. P. 60.

[33] Luke 6: 44 (Revised Standard Version).

[34] Thelen, *op. cit.,* p. 95.

[35] J. Bronowski. *The Identity of Man.* Garden City, N.Y.: The Natural History Press, 1966. P. 34.

[36] Marc Belth. *Education as Discipline.* Boston: Allyn and Bacon, 1965.

Royce, *op. cit.*

[37] Bronowski, *op. cit.*

Herbert Marcuse. *One-Dimensional Man.* Boston: Beacon Press, 1964.

Don Martindale. *The Nature and Types of Sociological Theory.* Boston: Houghton Mifflin, 1960.

Floyd W. Matson. *The Broken Image.* New York: George Brazillier, 1964.

Murphy, *op. cit.*

P. Sorokin. *Sociological Theories of Today.* New York: Harper & Row, 1966.

[38] Montagu, *op. cit.,* p. 166.

[39] Royce, *op. cit.*

C. Gilbert Wrenn. "The Culturally Encapsulated Counselor," *Harvard Educational Review* 32: 444–449 (Fall 1962).

[40] Erik H. Erikson. *Childhood and Society.* (2nd ed.) New York: W. W. Norton, 1963.

Erik H. Erikson. *Insight and Responsibility.* New York: W. W. Norton, 1964.

[41] Bronowski, *op. cit.,* pp. 106–107.

[42] Sybil Marshall. *An Experiment in Education.* Cambridge, England: Cambridge University Press, 1963. P. 171.

DISCUSSION QUESTIONS AND FURTHER READINGS

If a class of student teachers are asked what they are going to teach, most will name some skills such as reading, accounting, or athletics, or sets of information, i.e., disciplinary knowledge (science, language, etc.). Would your usefulness as a teacher depend on the fact that your students will never know as much as you know, in spite of your teaching efforts? If your students were to learn everything you have to offer, would you become as useless as an empty vending machine? Do you really cease to be a teacher the moment you have succeeded as a teacher?

Some of you would say instead that students should be taught to learn *how to learn* and that specific subject-matters are merely convenient media to attain this goal. This answer implies, first, that you yourself have learned how to learn so as to be in a position to teach the skills involved. Have you really learned how to learn? Have you come to love wisdom, or have you simply learned how to beat the social system of reward and punishment? Is the latter what you intend to teach your own students? A sort of coaching on how to succeed without really trying?

Second, the answer implies that there are definite ways to learn things. What are these and which ones should be used in learning what? Formulate your teaching strategy.

Still others may respond to the original inquiry by insisting that what you teach is *values and attitudes*. What, then, are the specific values, beliefs, and attitudes you are going to teach? What are the criteria for selecting these from among all imaginable ones the human race has held over the past one million years? Those with which you are familiar? Those about which you are certain? But, would your students be living in the same world as yours? Can a teacher raised in the past teach a child who is going to live in the future? "The only reason the past is certain is that it is dead, and this I consider too great a price to pay for certainty" (p. 45 in Harold Taylor, *Art and the Intellect*, New York: The Museum of Modern Art, 1960). See also John W. Gardner, *Self-Renewal* (New York: Torchbooks, Harper & Row, 1963).

In reality, you will be teaching, without fully realizing it, many many things, some verbally and others nonverbally. Often the values, beliefs, and attitudes you set out to teach have nothing to do with what your students actually learn from you. Can you control the situation at all? Study Kenneth B. Clark, *Prejudice and Your Child* (Boston: Beacon Press, 1964), Vernon W. Grant, *This Is Mental Illness* (Boston: Beacon Press, 1963), Edward T. Hall, *The Silent Language* (Garden City, N.Y.: Doubleday, 1959), and S. I. Hayakawa, *Language in Thought and Action* (New York: Harcourt, Brace & World, second edition. 1964).

HOW

THE HUMAN DIMENSION IN TEACHING

Ernest R. Hilgard

It is surprising that, after all these years of doing it, we know so very little about effective teaching. The payoff of careful studies, such as those reviewed by McKeachie [1] in the Nevitt Sanford volume on *The American College,* is very slight indeed. It is surprising that studies of class size, discussion vs. lecture, and teaching aids such as motion pictures and TV point to so few differences in the effectiveness of teaching. These studies, therefore, give us little guidance.

It is not that these studies are poorly done, and even studies which show little differences in effectiveness leave us with freedom of choice. My guess is that they fail, however, to understand the subtle differences made by kind of student, kind of teaching setting, and kind of long-range goals that are operative. If one looks back on his own experiences, or inquires a little of

---

From Ernest R. Hilgard, "The Human Dimension in Teaching," *College and University Bulletin* 17 (11): 1–3 & 5–6 (March 15, 1965).

others, a number of paradoxes within effective teaching come into view. I shall give a few examples. When I was in high school, they decided to introduce a senior course in economics and assigned it to the history teacher as the only social scientist on the faculty. It so happens that she had great difficulty in understanding economics, but one of my best learning experiences in high school was getting together with other members of the class in order to explain economics clearly to our teacher, who was, in fact, quite ready to learn. I am not joking about this: we went to the bank for statements to *prove* to her that capital was listed as a liability and not as an asset. (She knew capital was an asset because her wealthy aunt occasionally had to dip into capital to pay her bills.) In overcoming her objections, economics became clearer to everybody.

My second illustration is the graduate teaching of psychology at Yale during my student days there. We took only a couple of courses and a seminar, and some of us, like myself, had come without any undergraduate work in psychology. So beyond a course on the history of psychology—which took two years to work up to the time of modern psychology beyond Descartes, and one course on dissecting a dogfish and a human brain—we were largely on our own. So we arranged a little study group without including faculty to work up contemporary psychology. That little group has produced a number of department heads, deans, a university chancellor, journal editors, and four presidents of the American Psychological Association.

One additional illustration. Truman Kelley, an early teacher of statistics at Stanford (later at Harvard), one of the original authors of the Stanford Achievement Tests, and one of the originators of factor analysis, was a very poor but very effective teacher. He was poor in the sense that he always got mixed up in the midst of a derivation he was working out on the blackboard. But, as in the case of my economics teacher, the students learned a great deal in helping him find his errors and putting him back on the track. As a consequence, his students, such as Hotelling, McNemar, Dunlap, Kurtz, Tryon, and Franzen, have gone on to take leadership in statistics in the next generation.

These illustrations are used to point out how occasionally *bad* teaching can have *good* results. This is not to be construed as a recommendation for bad teaching, but only as a warning that we have to be careful about pat answers concerning teaching effectiveness.

I think I could go on almost as well to show how poor students often become our best products. I know a dean in one of our

THE HUMAN DIMENSION IN TEACHING
Ernest R. Hilgard

liberal arts colleges who would almost surely have been rejected for graduate study if the standards of selection in his day were those of today. One of my ex-students failed in college in his sophomore year, came back and was graduated, took a master's degree under my supervision, went on to be the leading Ph.D. student at Harvard in his group, and is now a distinguished professor in a first-rate university.

If then *bad* teachers may in some sense become *great* teachers, and *unsuccessful* students may turn into *successful* professors, we are dealing with a pretty complicated set of relationships.

It is facts such as these that have led me to choose to discuss personal and motivational matters. We are in an age of intellectual and cognitive emphases—but I prefer to stay off that bandwagon, for the present at least.

THE ETHICS OF SELFHOOD

Teaching is an ethical profession; that is, it is concerned with the preservation of historical values, and with their inculcation. No matter how "objective" we become, our ethical responsibilities are inescapable. I wish to discourse a little about ethics, but in order to remain within my role as a psychologist I shall address my remarks to the ethical implications of promoting the growth of *selfhood* in our students.

A popular developmental psychology, one proposed by a leading psychoanalyst, Erik H. Erikson, distinguishes between the *identifications* that help shape a growing personality, and the *identity* that is later achieved.[2] That is, the child incorporates attitudes, ideals, and personality styles from important people around him, chiefly his parents. He develops a conscience based on these internalized values and feels guilty when he does violence to this conscience. But he must eventually become himself, because these influences upon him are not altogether harmonious, nor are they necessarily appropriate to the realities of life as he must live it. This proposal is important for us, because our students come to us still dependent economically, and to some extent emotionally, on their parents and they are here trying to find themselves and to establish their identities.

If we are really helpful in this growth process, we find ourselves in the ethical dilemma of either enforcing parental values, and thus playing safe, or taking the risks of permitting experimentation with life experiences, through which the new identity will emerge. If our teaching is effective, it cannot avoid the awkwardness of being caught in a cross fire at this point, for we can be neither fully on the side of the parents, nor fully on the side of a defiant youth.

Our skill comes in permitting exploration—and error—with a minimum of risk. Erikson speaks of the "moratorium" which many cultures allow during the transition between adolescence and adulthood—a period of wandering about, perhaps sowing a few wild oats, with, for a time, little social responsibility. In America the early years of college often provide something of this moratorium, although we have not learned quite how to manage it without undue risk. One way is, of course, to make as much as we can of vicarious experience. Much great literature has a kind of sordid quality about it; without recommending the degrading experiences it pictures it gives an opportunity for a kind of emotional experimentation that keeps established our own orientation to values. The censorship of literature would often deprive us of this protection against the need for personal experimentation which is provided when our fantasies are worked out and evaluated by others. That great literature and drama is mostly tragic has something of this psychological meaning: The people who die in tragedy, unlike those who die in the who-done-its, are commonly people we wish would not have to die, but often their confused values, as in *Hamlet,* let us examine our own confusions to avoid related pitfalls.

So if we are to do our job for keeps, we must know what we are doing to the self-development of our students. One of the great teachings of psychoanalysis is that self-deception is far more prevalent than was earlier supposed. The mechanisms of defense will preserve self-esteem at all costs; we need, therefore, to bolster self-esteem in realistic ways, so that the mechanisms can dissolve because they are no longer needed, and self-knowledge can replace self-deception.

I know that what I am saying is a mixture of psychology and ethics—we "ought" to do this or that in order to achieve this or that end, recommended, somehow, by psychological considerations. I am not denying the ethical component; I am asserting that it is inevitable, and we had better know that it is a part of teaching.

To carry this assertion a step further: Focus upon self-development and the achievement of identity need not be, indeed must not be, egocentric. How is this dilemma to be avoided, so that enhanced self-esteem remains distinguished from selfishness and self-interest? The answer here is that respect for oneself is a condition for having respect for others—unless one has personal integrity, he doubts, by projection, the integrity of others.

Gregory Vlastos some years ago analyzed this problem and solved it for himself in the concept of mutuality. A mutual relation between two people, he asserted, was on a high ethical plane if each person preserved his identity and derived some growth through the relationship, without one person exploiting the other. This is a good way to characterize the relation between husband and wife, parent and child, or teacher and pupil. That is, the teacher gains satisfaction and becomes enriched through the interplay with students, just as the students, in varying ways, grow under the teacher's influence and become increasingly themselves, in a form acceptable both to themselves and others.

The enhancement of selfhood is, in this sense, a primary aim of education. If this proposition is accepted, some implications follow and to these I now turn.

A PROPER VOCATIONALISM

It is fashionable these days to favor general or liberal education and to deplore vocationalism in education. I wish to talk on the other side and expand a little on the theme of a proper *vocationalism* in education.

Before deploring vocationalism, let us pause to think a little of the original meaning of vocation as a "calling." A vocation as a calling is not a trivial bread-and-butter matter, but an important avenue through which one fulfills one's destiny as an individual.

This is a special problem for women and hence for a college devoted to the instruction of women. I do not propose to plow over the ground covered by the *Feminine Mystique*;[3] it is quite a good book, even though its message would have come through better had it departed more from the defense of the thesis in favor of the analysis of the problem.[4]

As I see it the contrast between the homemaker role and the outside-of-home employment of a woman rests largely on the lack of differentiation *within* the homemaker role. That is, all women are assumed to be essentially alike in their abilities to perform the duties associated with, and in their capacities to derive satisfaction from, rearing children, doing housekeeping, acting as a hostess for the husband, and raising the cultural level of the community through voluntary services. No man's role is so undifferentiated and uniform—not even his lesser responsibilities as a husband and father. Special considerations are made for his share in these responsibilities dependent upon his outside obligations—his office hours, his time in travel, and so on.

By contrast, work outside the home for both men and women is highly differentiated according to the capacities and training of the worker. Some work is itself little differentiated, as in being a typist in a pool, or a routine machine operator, but even those have their own occupational hierarchies, one different from another. If one thinks of marks of individuality as signs of identity and self-esteem, it is no wonder that the homemaker role is not satisfying to many women.

These are not newfangled ideas. The homemaker's role is probably less differential today than in any period of history, when, with home industry, the woman was commonly skilled at making pottery, or baskets, or weaving rugs. In modern life we often have to go to extremes to recover something that was commonplace when technology was at a lower level. I recall an account of a community in the Virgin Islands where a small colony of middle-class people have their homes a few months of the year. There is one caterer who takes turns bringing his hors d'oeuvres and casseroles from one house to another as each in turn has his opportunity to be host by paying the bill. What kind of differentiated role for a housekeeper does this provide? With frozen meals adding to the uniformity of life, there is every reason why some form of self-expression should be sought by the bored housewife.

My own preference is for an early exploration of the vocational problem.[5] There is a danger that should be noted. This I may call *premature vocationalism.* By premature vocationalism I mean the entering early upon a course of narrow training that almost precludes a change of direction. Going to a secretarial school beyond high school, instead of college, for a bright girl would often constitute such a premature vocationalism; perhaps going to an IBM school to train to be a key punch operator would represent the same kind of thing. Premature vocationalism aside, I favor an early effort at reaching a decision, including the exploration of a possible commitment, if only to reject it.

There is an interesting psychology of choice that has recently been explored by one of my colleagues, Alex Bavelas. He finds that a choice actually made is examined much more carefully than one merely contemplated. Let me explain by an illustration, and then return to vocational choice.

One of Mr. Bavelas' demonstrations is as follows. He holds a fairly large book and then riffles through the pages to call the size of the book to the attention of his class or other audience. Now concealing the book behind the lectern he asks each member of the audience to write down his estimate of the number of pages in the book. This having been done, the papers are traded,

270

and he now asks the class members to correct the estimates before them, although they do not see the book again and have no new information. It invariably turns out that the corrected estimates are more accurate than the original ones, even though made by the same people with the same background information. There is no magic in this. The concrete choice having been made and written down, it is examined more carefully than the mere "guess" that was earlier written down. Estimates obviously too great or obviously too small are appropriately changed; plausible ones are preserved, and the total result is a better average estimate than before.

Another problem is given to class members. This is to describe what Professor X will do *tomorrow* if his car breaks down on the way to the airport; these answers are compared with those given by a corresponding class in answer to the question, "What did Professor X do *yesterday* when his car broke down on the way to the airport?" The answers, based on the same information (or lack of it) are very different in the two cases. The answers are very "iffy" and general regarding what he will do tomorrow, but full of vivid detail on what he probably did yesterday.

The suggestion, then, is this. If you act as if you have already chosen, the situation becomes more concrete to you than if you think about it as lying uncertainly in the future. Committed to medicine, the boy or girl who works in the hospital as an orderly during the summer knows "what it feels like" to be a physician in the way an orderly merely earning his living does not. The advantage of early choice is that a negated choice is not costly, and a substantiated choice becomes a focus of integration.

Studies at Yale a number of years ago showed that students, equated for ability, did better in courses perceived as relevant to their major than in other courses.[6] We have postponed some general education courses at Stanford to the junior and senior years on the assumption, for example, that an engineering student will see the relevances of economics as a senior more than he would have seen it while impatient to get on with his engineering.

Hadamard, the distinguished French mathematician, used an expression that I have often quoted. He said that specialization is a good thing, through giving direction and keeping you on the track, provided you learn also to "look aside" as you go down the road.[7] That is the way I feel about having a vocational goal.

A vocational goal need not be a money-earning goal. I suppose a life-plan is what I am talking about, but life-plan has a kind of sentimental sound about it, whereas vocation is getting down to brass tacks. Were we able to get down to brass tacks on life-planning, I would prefer that. Perhaps we can.

TEACHING AS CONTAGION

My theme is a developmental one. I have thus far stressed the growth of the individual and the importance of vocational roles in providing some of the necessary differentiation. Now I wish to get a little closer to the teaching and learning process, for I am sure that you are wondering when I am going to get back into the classroom.

First I am going to wander even further afield, into child training and psychotherapy.

We have been finding out some interesting things about individual development through our research in the personality backgrounds of those susceptible to hypnosis. This phase of our program is largely under the direction of my wife, Josephine R. Hilgard, a medically trained psychiatrist and psychoanalyst. We find that the capacity for deep involvement in novel experiences, so important in hypnotic susceptibility, often has its roots in the close relationship with parents who can themselves become deeply absorbed in music, religion, or communion with nature, and this learning by the child is more a matter of contagion than of instruction.[8]

Basing some of her conjectures on these hypnotic results, Josephine Hilgard and her colleagues have been experimenting with a kind of psychotherapy which she has called *affiliative therapy*. Very disturbed adolescents, who have not been helped by ordinary therapeutic practices and are on the verge of being committed to custodial institutions, have turned the corner toward good adjustment through this procedure. What is done is to find some source of strength, some interest on which to build, such as a skill and interest in swimming, for example. It is important that the college student, as affiliative therapist, must enjoy swimming and think he is getting paid for something that he would like to do without pay. He thus takes the patient along with his enthusiasm but demands consistent effort. The consequence is a spread of self-respect and effort in other areas, such as school work, without the affiliative therapist taking on any interpretive role.

The lessons to be learned from this illustration of contagion are that one way of understanding teacher–pupil relations is through contagion. The strange illustrations of bad teaching that I gave at first can be reinterpreted in this way. Even my high

THE HUMAN DIMENSION IN TEACHING
Ernest R. Hilgard

school economics teacher was intrigued with the new subject she didn't understand; there was no boredom in her interchange with the class. My Yale professors were all strongly identified with psychology, and we got apprentice training in research under them, even though the formal instruction was somewhat casual. What courses we took were never superficial—including the long-drawn-out historical one. And Truman Kelley was teaching on the forefront of statistics as he derived (with errors) statistical formulas that were not yet published.

Reports of great teachers commonly stress their personalities, rather than their scholarship or technical teaching skills. William James used to sit on his desk, dangling his feet, telling the class to read the book while he would share some of his recent thoughts with them. John Dewey put his students to sleep by his delivery, but they took notes avidly to try to keep awake, and these notes on review brought out the freshness of his thought.

Some years ago Boring [9] published in the *American Journal of Psychology* an article on masters and pupils among American psychologists. This has been republished in a book of his collected papers that has recently appeared.[10] I have taken a look at the table to see if any generalizations were possible.

This table consists of eminent psychologists and their eminent pupils—eminence defined by being starred in *American Men of Science*—a practice since cancelled.

While the quantities are not enough to make very firm assertions, it seems possible to classify masters as those who sought *narrow allegiance* and those who produced *divergent* excellence.

Thus Titchener's pupils, while often struggling to throw off his yoke, continue to show his influence on the topics they preferred to study—the Pillsburys, Borings, Dallenbachs, and Bentleys.

James' students diverged as widely as Angell, Thorndike, and E. B. Holt, while Angell produced not only such "animal" men as Watson, Hunter, and Carr, but human learning experts like Robinson, and individual difference people such as Bingham and Downey.

Cattell, too, produced diversity in the first clinical psychologist Witmer, the great experimenter Woodworth, the brain investigator S. I. Franz, and the applied psychologists Strong and Poffenberger.

Thus the enthusiasm of a teacher can encourage breadth or narrowness—the *model* is not defined by its specific content.

I am sometimes puzzled as to what my own students get from me. Most of them who have had an opportunity to reach some eminence in the profession took their degrees with me when I (and they) were working in the experimental study of learning. Yet only one of them, now the editor of a leading psychological journal, has stayed with the experimental study of learning, though another is within learning experiments in education. Several have achieved eminence in social psychology; one department head of a major university is essentially a factor-analyst; one is president of a major private foundation; and another is deputy director of one of the larger governmental foundations. Whether or not my avocational interests in public problems and social responsibility were more influential than the substantive teaching I did would have to be investigated by someone else. I am proud of these ex-students, and in some roundabout way their careers reflect something for which I stand. There is some suggestion that what happens is *caught* rather than *taught.*

SOME PRACTICAL COUNSEL

Now let me see what practical counsel to teachers derives by logic or free association from the things I have been saying.

If we are to be concerned with the student's development of *identity,* in the direction of seeing himself as a competent, effective, creative, and socially responsible person, capable of achieving mutuality in relation to others and *if* we believe that this will come about, in part at least, through a contagious enthusiasm generated by his teacher, then we do, indeed, have some general suggestions for teaching.

1. *Don't try to teach what you aren't interested in: it's no use.* What can this mean? Surely we have "service courses" that we teach because they are assigned to us; surely we have to cover some material that we have been over so often before that the excitement in it has gone out for us. But I say "no" to these "surely's."

If teaching is routine, and material familiar, so that you can't have any enthusiasm for it, assign it for reading, or get it programed; in other words, don't stand in its way. It may be fresh to the student; let the student see for himself. Find something new in it yourself, discover a new angle in which *you* can be interested. A common fallacy in teaching is that the teacher must *cover the ground* in class. This is never essential; there are many ways of "covering the ground," and usually a block-and-gap method, in which *some* ground is well covered and others ignored, is quite satisfactory. The teacher can choose the "blocks" that interest him and leave the dull parts as "gaps" as necessary. If we believe the contagious enthusiasm theory, the best way to *destroy* a topic is to teach it out of duty, without any interest in it.

2. *Don't be afraid of showing feeling.* One advantage of talking together is that the spoken language, accompanied as it is by inflections, gestures, and facial expression, *permits* the communication of feeling. Show that you like something; show that you dislike something. Dislike is not the same as boredom; you may dislike something because you think it limits your freedom for enjoyment or enthusiasm. Objectivity can be served by showing that there are those who believe otherwise, but you need not do obeisance to other viewpoints by sterilizing your own enthusiasm into a vapid eclecticism. Even a little dogmatism will not hurt students; they have to learn to make their own corrections in any case, for they cannot be protected from dogmatism.

What I have said thus far expressed the teacher's attitude toward himself and his subject matter. Now the appropriate attitudes toward the students.

3. *If we accept the contagious enthusiasm theory, celebrate and reward student enthusiasm.* Remember that an idea may be original for a student, even if it is not truly original in the sense that nobody ever had it before. I have known professors so eager to impress students with their knowledge of the history of the subject that as soon as a student says something original he tops it by saying, "You can find the same idea in William James." This may be said in such a way as to put the student in the company of a great mind or to slap him down as an ignoramus. How much better to say, "What a good idea—why don't you see if you can develop it a little further?" Then, later on, you might direct a search for anticipations, after the student's claim to the idea as his own has been anchored.

4. *Finally, encourage growth toward identity by establishing self-criticism based on adequate self-respect.* Modern psychotherapists find their greatest success comes not by first attacking the patient's conflicts and inadequacies, but by first building up his hope through an assessment of whatever objective grounds there are for his own favorable self-image, whatever interest he enjoys. Maybe he was the one his parents always counted on to get the chickens fed, or maybe he taught himself how to swim, or he was brave when big bullies picked on him. Search around, and you always find something, however small, that shows some fiber, some strength, on which to build. Surely our students have a great many accomplishments to their credit, or they would not be here. If an individual, boy or girl, knows he is a

valuable person, to himself or others, he is better able to see and correct defects within himself. "Nothing succeeds like success" is an important dictum.

One of my students once performed an experiment with equated classes of night school students in which one group had weekly quizzes graded, as they commonly are, with the same distribution throughout so that students could come to understand the meaning of an A, B, C, or D grade. But note what this does. Even though all are learning, for every student who moves up a grade, another must move down, in order to keep the distribution the same. In the other section he had an artificial grading scheme in which the proportion of higher grades, beginning low, increased throughout the term, so that the average effect was an *increase*, rather than balancing increases and decreases. The result was that, on the final examination taken by all, those who had been encouraged throughout the term scored significantly higher than those graded by the usual method.

In another experiment, not by a student of mine, it was shown that a sentence written on the paper (in addition to a mark) increased student performance—even if all got the same sentence, such as "It is clear you are trying." [11] Thus there was a motivational significance in increased self-esteem that went beyond any diagnostic significance of the sentence.

Anything that can be said in a paper of this kind is, of course, incomplete. I hope that I have not given the impression of being uninterested in content or instructional devices. My own textbook gives, I believe, evidence of my interest in the details of experiences and theories, and a programed workbook that accompanies it shows that I believe also in teaching aids.

In the statements sometimes made, as by Gilbert Highet in *The Art of Teaching* that teaching is an art and not a science, I believe the position tends to be overstated. For instance he says:

> Scientific teaching, even of a scientific subject, will be inadequate as long as both teachers and pupils are human beings. Teaching is not like inducing a chemical reaction: It is more like painting a picture or making a piece of music or on a lower level like planting a garden or writing a friendly letter.[12]

While I am in sympathy with the flavor of his remarks, I do not like to think of teaching as something so precious and special that we cannot do anything about it.

I believe we ought to find out whether or not our enthusiasms are getting across to our students. If not, the students should not be punished, but our approaches should be changed. I believe that creating a classroom atmosphere by respecting the teachers' interests and enthusiasms, by encouraging students, by building their self-esteem, is something we can go about deliberately, that we can study the effectiveness with which we do it, and we can continue to improve.

FOOTNOTES

[1] W. J. McKeachie. "Procedures and Techniques of Teaching: A Survey of Experimental Studies." In R. N. Sanford, Ed. *The American College.* New York: John Wiley & Sons, 1962. Pp. 312–364.

[2] E. H. Erikson. *Insight and Responsibility.* New York: Norton, 1964.

[3] Betty Friedan. *The Feminine Mystique.* New York: Norton, 1963.

[4] See also the Spring 1964 issue of *Daedalus* devoted to this problem.

[5] Leona E. Tyler. "The Antecedents of Two Varieties of Vocational Interests," *Genetic Psychology Monographs* 70: 177–227, 1964.

[6] A. B. Crawford. *Incentives to Study.* New Haven, Conn.: Yale University Press, 1929.

[7] Jacques Hadamard. *The Psychology of Invention in the Mathematical Field.* New York: Dover, 1954, 145 pp.

[8] E. R. Hilgard. *Hypnotic Susceptibility.* New York: Harcourt, Brace & World, Inc., 1965.

[9] E. G. Boring. "Masters and Pupils among American Psychologists," *American Journal of Psychology* 61: 527–534, 1948.

[10] E. G. Boring. *History, Psychology, and Science: Selected Papers.* New York: John Wiley & Sons, 1963.

[11] E. B. Page. "Teacher Comments and Student Performance." *Journal of Educational Psychology* 49: 173–181, 1958.

[12] G. Highet, *The Art of Teaching.* New York: Alfred A. Knopf, 1950.

HOW CHILDREN FAIL

John Holt

When we talk about intelligence, we do not mean the ability to get a good score on a certain kind of test, or even the ability to do well in school; these are at best only indicators of something larger, deeper, far more important. By intelligence we mean a style of life, a way of behaving in various situations, and particularly in new, strange, and perplexing situations. The true test of intelligence is not how much we know how to do, but how we behave when we don't know what to do.

The intelligent person, young or old, meeting a new situation or problem, opens himself up to it; he tries to take in with mind and senses everything he can about it; he thinks about *it,* instead of about himself or what it might cause to happen to him; he

---

From John Holt, *How Children Fail.* Copyright © 1964 Pitman Publishing Corporation, New York. The selection was reprinted with the publisher's and author's permission from the Dell Publishing Co. edition (New York, 1964), pp. 165–181. Mr. Holt is the author also of the more recent book, *How Children Learn* (New York: Pitman Publishing Corp., 1967).

grapples with it boldly, imaginatively, resourcefully, and if not confidently at least hopefully; if he fails to master it, he looks without shame or fear at his mistakes and learns what he can from them. This is intelligence. Clearly its roots lie in a certain feeling about life, and one's self with respect to life. Just as clearly, unintelligence is not what most psychologists seem to suppose, the same things as intelligence only less of it. It is an entirely different style of behavior, arising out of an entirely different set of attitudes.

Years of watching and comparing bright children and the not-bright or less bright, have shown that they are very different kinds of people. The bright child is curious about life and reality, eager to get in touch with it, embrace it, unite himself with it. There is no wall, no barrier between him and life. The dull child is far less curious, far less interested in what goes on and what is real, more inclined to live in worlds of fantasy. The bright child likes to experiment, to try things out. He lives by the maxim that there is more than one way to skin a cat. If he can't do something one way, he'll try another. The dull child is usually afraid to try at all. It takes a good deal of urging to get him to try even once; if that try fails, he is through.

The bright child is patient. He can tolerate uncertainty and failure, and will keep trying until he gets an answer. When all his experiments fail, he can even admit to himself and others that for the time being he is not going to get an answer. This may annoy him, but he can wait. Very often, he does not want to be told how to do the problem or solve the puzzle he has struggled with, because he does not want to be cheated out of the chance to figure it out for himself in the future. Not so the dull child. He cannot stand uncertainty or failure. To him an unanswered question is not a challenge or an opportunity, but a threat. If he can't find the answer quickly, it must be given to him, and quickly; and he must have answers for everything. Such are the children of whom a second-grade teacher once said, "But my children *like* to have questions for which there is only one answer," and they did; and by a mysterious coincidence, so did she.

The bright child is willing to go ahead on the basis of incomplete understanding and information. He will take risks, sail uncharted seas, explore when the landscape is dim, the landmarks few, the light poor. To give only one example, he will often read books he does not understand in the hope that after a while enough understanding will emerge to make it worth while to go on. In this spirit some of my fifth graders tried to read *Moby Dick*. But the dull child will go ahead only when he knows exactly where he stands and exactly what is ahead of him. If he does not feel he knows exactly what an experience will be like, and if it will not be exactly like other experiences he already knows, he wants no part of it. For while the bright child feels that the universe is, on the whole, a sensible, reasonable, and trustworthy place, the dull child feels that it is senseless, unpredictable, and treacherous. He feels that he can never tell what may happen, particularly in a new situation, except that it will probably be bad.

Nobody starts off stupid. You have only to watch babies and infants, and think seriously about what all of them learn and do, to see that, except for the most grossly retarded, they show a style of life, and a desire and ability to learn that in an older person we might well call genius. Hardly an adult in a thousand, or ten thousand, could in any three years of his life learn as much, grow as much in his understanding of the world around him, as every infant learns and grows in his first three years. But what happens, as we get older, to this extraordinary capacity for learning and intellectual growth?

What happens is that it is destroyed, and more than by any other one thing, by the process that we misname education—a process that goes on in most homes and schools. We adults destroy most of the intellectual and creative capacity of children by the things we do to them or make them do. We destroy this capacity above all by making them afraid, afraid of not doing what other people want, of not pleasing, of making mistakes, of failing, of being *wrong*. Thus we make them afraid to gamble, afraid to experiment, afraid to try the difficult and the unknown. Even when we do not create children's fears, when they come to us with fears ready-made and built-in, we use these fears as handles to manipulate them and get them to do what we want. Instead of trying to whittle down their fears, we build them up, often to monstrous size. For we like children who are a little afraid of us, docile, deferential children, though not, of course, if they are so obviously afraid that they threaten our image of ourselves as kind, lovable people whom there is no reason to fear. We find ideal the kind of "good" children who are just enough afraid of us to do everything we want, without making us feel that fear of us is what is making them do it.

We destroy the disinterested (I do *not* mean *un*interested) love of learning in children, which is so strong when they are small, by encouraging and compelling them to work for petty and contemptible rewards—gold stars, or papers marked 100 and tacked to the wall, or *A*'s on report cards, or honor rolls, or dean's lists, or Phi Beta Kappa keys—in short, for the ignoble satisfaction of feeling that they are better than someone else. We encourage them to feel that the end and aim of all they do in school is nothing more than to get a good mark on a test, or to impress someone with what they seem to know. We kill, not only their curiosity, but their feeling that it is a good and admirable thing to be curious, so that by the age of ten most of them will not ask questions, and will show a good deal of scorn for the few who do.

In many ways, we break down children's convictions that things make sense, or their hope that things may prove to make sense. We do it, first of all, by breaking up life into arbitrary and disconnected hunks of subject matter, which we then try to "integrate" by such artificial and irrelevant devices as having children sing Swiss folk songs while they are studying the geography of Switzerland, or do arithmetic problems about rail-splitting while they are studying the boyhood of Lincoln. Furthermore, we continually confront them with what is senseless, ambiguous, and contradictory; worse, we do it without knowing that we are doing it, so that, hearing nonsense shoved at them as if it were sense, they come to feel that the source of their confusion lies not in the material but in their own stupidity. Still further, we cut children off from their own common sense and the world of reality by requiring them to play with and shove around words and symbols that have little or no meaning to them. Thus we turn the vast majority of our students into the kind of people for whom all symbols are meaningless; who cannot use symbols as a way of learning about and dealing with reality; who cannot understand written instruction; who, even if they read books, come out knowing no more than when they went in; who may have a few new words rattling around in their heads, but whose mental models of the world remain unchanged and, indeed, impervious to change. The minority, the able and successful students, we are very likely to turn into something different but just as dangerous; the kind of people who can manipulate words and symbols fluently while keeping themselves largely divorced from the reality for which they stand; the kind of people who like to speak in large generalities but grow silent or indignant if someone asks for an example of what they are talking about; the kind of people who, in their discussion of world affairs, coin and use such words as megadeaths and megacorpses, with scarcely a thought to the blood and suffering these words imply.

We encourage children to act stupidly, not only by scaring and confusing them, but by boring them, by filling up their days with

HOW CHILDREN FAIL
John Holt

dull, repetitive tasks that make little or no claim on their attention or demands on their intelligence. Our hearts leap for joy at the sight of a roomful of children all slogging away at some imposed task, and we are all the more pleased and satisfied if someone tells us that the children don't really like what they are doing. We tell ourselves that this drudgery, this endless busy-work, is good preparation for life, and we fear that without it children would be hard to "control." But why must this busy-work be so dull? Why not give tasks that are interesting and demanding? Because, in schools where every task must be completed and every answer must be right, if we give children more demanding tasks they will be fearful and will instantly insist that we show them how to do the job. When you have acres of paper to fill up with pencil marks, you have no time to waste on the luxury of thinking. By such means children are firmly established in the habit of using only a small part of their thinking capacity. They feel that school is a place where they must spend most of their time doing dull tasks in a dull way. Before long they are deeply settled in a rut of unintelligent behavior from which most of them could not escape even if they wanted to.

School tends to be a dishonest as well as a nervous place. We adults are not often honest with children, least of all in school. We tell them, not what we think, but what we feel they ought to think; or what other people feel or tell us they ought to think. Pressure groups find it easy to weed out of our classrooms, texts, and libraries whatever facts, truths, and ideas they happen to find unpleasant or inconvenient. And we are not even as truthful with children as we could safely be, as the parents, politicians, and pressure groups would let us be. Even in the most non-controversial areas our teaching, the books, and the textbooks we give children present a dishonest and distorted picture of the world.

The fact is that we do not feel an obligation to be truthful to children. We are like the managers and manipulators of news in Washington, Moscow, London, Peking, and Paris, and all the other capitals of the world. We think it our right and our duty, not to tell the truth but to say whatever will best serve our cause—in this case, the cause of making children grow up into the kind of people we want them to be, thinking whatever we want them to think. We have only to convince ourselves (and we are very easily convinced) that a lie will be "better" for the children than the truth, and we will lie. We don't always need even that excuse; we often lie only for our own convenience.

Worse yet, we are not honest about ourselves, our own fears, limitations, weaknesses, prejudices, motives. We present ourselves to children as if we were gods, all-knowing, all-powerful, always rational, always just, always right. This is worse than any lie we could tell about ourselves. I have more than once shocked teachers by telling them that when kids ask me a question to which I don't know the answer, I say, "I haven't the faintest idea"; or that when I make a mistake, as I often do, I say, "I goofed again"; or that when I am trying to do something I am no good at, like paint in water colors or play a clarinet or bugle, I do it in front of them so they can see me struggling with it, and can realize that not all adults are good at everything. If a child asks me to do something that I don't want to do, I tell him that I won't do it because I don't want to do it, instead of giving him a list of "good" reasons sounding as if they had come down from the Supreme Court. Interestingly enough, this rather open way of dealing with children works quite well. If you tell a child that you won't do something because you don't want to, he is very likely to accept that as a fact which he cannot change; if you ask him to stop doing something because it drives you crazy, there is a very good chance that, without further talk, he will stop, because he knows what that is like.

We are, above all, dishonest about our feelings, and it is this sense of dishonesty of feeling that makes the atmosphere of so many schools so unpleasant. The people who write books that teachers have to read say over and over again that a teacher must love all the children in a class, all of them equally. If by this they mean that a teacher must do the best he can for every child in a class, that he has an equal responsibility for every child's welfare, an equal concern for his problems, they are right. But when they talk of love they don't mean this; they mean feelings, affection, the kind of pleasure and joy that one person can get from the existence and company of another. And this is not something that can be measured out in little spoonfuls, everyone getting the same amount.

In a discussion of this in a class of teachers, I once said that I liked some of the kids in my class much more than others and that, without saying which ones I liked best, I had told them so. After all, this is something that children know, whatever we tell them; it is futile to lie about it. Naturally, these teachers were horrified. "What a terrible thing to say!" one said. "I love all the children in my class exactly the same." Nonsense; a teacher who says this is lying, to herself or to others, and probably doesn't like any of the children very much. Not that there is anything

HOW CHILDREN FAIL
John Holt

wrong with that; plenty of adults don't like children, and there is no reason why they should. But the trouble is they feel they should, which makes them feel guilty, which makes them feel resentful, which in turn makes them try to work off their guilt with indulgence and their resentment with subtle cruelties—cruelties of a kind that can be seen in many classrooms. Above all, it makes them put on the phony, syrupy, sickening voice and manner, and the fake smiles and forced, bright laughter that children see so much of in school, and rightly resent and hate.

As we are not honest with them so we won't let children be honest with us. To begin with, we require them to take part in the fiction that school is a wonderful place and that they love every minute of it. They learn early that not to like school or the teacher is *verboten,* not to be said, not even to be thought. I have known a child, otherwise healthy, happy, and wholly delightful, who at the age of five was being made sick with worry by the fact that she did not like her kindergarten teacher. Robert Heinemann worked for a number of years with remedial students whom ordinary schools were hopelessly unable to deal with. He found that what choked up and froze the minds of these children was above all else the fact that they could not express, they could hardly even acknowledge the fear, shame, rage, and hatred that school and their teachers had aroused in them. In a situation in which they were and felt free to express these feelings to themselves and others, they were able once again to begin learning. Why can't we say to children what I used to say to fifth graders who got sore at me, "The law says you have to go to school; it doesn't say you have to like it, and it doesn't say you have to like me either." This might make school more bearable for many children.

Children hear all the time, "Nice people don't say such things." They learn early in life that for unknown reasons they must not talk about a large part of what they think and feel, are most interested in, and worried about. It is a rare child who, anywhere in his growing up, meets even one older person with whom he can talk openly about what most interests him, concerns him, worries him. This is what rich people are buying for their troubled kids when for $25 per hour they send them to psychiatrists. Here is someone to whom you can speak honestly about whatever is on your mind, without having to worry about his getting mad at you. But do we have to wait until a child is snowed under by his fears and troubles to give him this chance? And do we have to take the time of a highly trained professional to hear what, earlier in his life, that child might have told anybody who was willing to listen sympathetically and honestly? The workers in a project called Streetcorner Research, in Cambridge, Mass., have found that nothing more than the opportunity to talk openly and freely about themselves and their lives, to people who would listen without judging, and who were interested in them as human beings rather than as problems to be solved or disposed of, has totally remade the lives and personalities of a number of confirmed and seemingly hopeless juvenile delinquents. Can't we learn something from this? Can't we clear a space for honesty and openness and self-awareness in the lives of growing children? Do we have to make them wait until they are in a jam before giving them a chance to say what they think?

Behind much of what we do in school lie some ideas, that could be expressed roughly as follows: (1) Of the vast body of human knowledge, there are certain bits and pieces that can be called essential, that everyone should know; (2) the extent to which a person can be considered educated, qualified to live intelligently in today's world and be a useful member of society, depends on the amount of this essential knowledge that he carries about with him; (3) it is the duty of schools, therefore, to get as much of this essential knowledge as possible into the minds of children. Thus we find ourselves trying to poke certain facts, recipes, and ideas down the gullets of every child in school, whether the morsel interests him or not, even if it frightens him or sickens him, and even if there are other things that he is much more interested in learning.

These ideas are absurd and harmful nonsense. We will not begin to have true education or real learning in our schools until we sweep this nonsense out of the way. Schools should be a place where children learn what they most want to know, instead of what we think they ought to know. The child who wants to know something remembers it and uses it once he has it; the child who learns something to please or appease someone else forgets it when the need for pleasing or the danger of not appeasing is past. This is why children quickly forget all but a small part of what they learn in school. It is of no use or interest to them; they do not want, or expect, or even intend to remember it. The only difference between bad and good students in this respect is that the bad students forget right away, while the good students are careful to wait until after the exam. If for no other reason, we could well afford to throw out most of what we teach in school because the children throw out almost all of it anyway.

HOW CHILDREN FAIL
John Holt

The notion of a curriculum, an essential body of knowledge, would be absurd even if children remembered everything we "taught" them. We don't and can't agree on what knowledge is essential. The man who has trained himself in some special field of knowledge or competence thinks, naturally, that his specialty should be in the curriculum. The classical scholars want Greek and Latin taught; the historians shout for more history; the mathematicians urge more math and the scientists more science; the modern language experts want all children taught French or Spanish, or Russian; and so on. Everyone wants to get his specialty into the act, knowing that as the demand for his special knowledge rises, so will the price that he can charge for it. Who wins this struggle and who loses depends not on the real needs of children or even of society, but on who is most skillful in public relations, who has the best educational lobbyists, who best can capitalize on events that have nothing to do with education, like the appearance of Sputnik in the night skies.

The idea of the curriculum would not be valid even if we could agree what ought to be in it. For knowledge itself changes. Much of what a child learns in school will be found, or thought, before many years, to be untrue. I studied physics at school from a fairly up-to-date text that proclaimed that the fundamental law of physics was the law of conservation of matter—matter is not created or destroyed. I had to scratch that out before I left school. In economics at college I was taught many things that were not true of our economy then, and many more that are not true now. Not for many years after I left college did I learn that the Greeks, far from being a detached and judicious people surrounded by chaste white temples, were hot-tempered, noisy, quarrelsome, and liked to cover their temples with gold leaf and bright paint; or that most of the citizens of Imperial Rome, far from living in houses in which the rooms surrounded an atrium, or central court, lived in multi-story tenements, one of which was perhaps the largest building in the ancient world. The child who really remembered everything he heard in school would live his life believing many things that were not so.

Moreover, we cannot possibly judge what knowledge will be most needed forty, or twenty, or even ten years from now. At school, I studied Latin and French. Few of the teachers who claimed then that Latin was essential would make as strong a case for it now; and the French might better have been Spanish, or better yet, Russian. Today the schools are busy teaching Russian; but perhaps they should be teaching Chinese, or Hindi, or who-knows-what? Besides physics, I studied chemistry, then perhaps the most popular of all science courses; but I would probably have done better to study biology, or ecology, if such a course had been offered (it wasn't). We always find out, too late, that we don't have the experts we need, that in the past we studied the wrong things; but this is bound to remain so. Since we can't know what knowledge will be most needed in the future, it is senseless to try to teach it in advance. Instead, we should try to turn out people who love learning so much and learn so well that they will be able to learn whatever needs to be learned.

How can we say, in any case, that one piece of knowledge is more important than another, or indeed, what we really say, that some knowledge is essential and the rest, as far as school is concerned, worthless? A child who wants to learn something that the school can't and doesn't want to teach him will be told not to waste his time. But how can we say that what he wants to know is less important than what we want him to know? We must ask how much of the sum of human knowledge anyone can know at the end of his schooling. Perhaps a millionth. Are we then to believe that one of these millionths is so much more important than another? Or that our social and national problems will be solved if we can just figure out a way to turn children out of schools knowing two millionths of the total, instead of one? Our problems don't arise from the fact that we lack experts enough to tell us what needs to be done, but out of the fact that we do not and will not do what we know needs to be done now.

Learning is not everything, and certainly one piece of learning is as good as another. One of my brightest and boldest fifth graders was deeply interested in snakes. He knew more about snakes than anyone I've ever known. The school did not offer herpetology; snakes were not in the curriculum; but as far as I was concerned, any time he spent learning about snakes was better spent than in ways I could think of to spend it; not least of all because, in the process of learning about snakes, he learned a great deal more about many other things than I was ever able to "teach" those unfortunates in my class who were not interested in anything at all. In another fifth-grade class, studying Romans in Britain, I saw a boy trying to read a science book behind the cover of his desk. He was spotted, and made to put the book away, and listen to the teacher; with a heavy sigh he did so. What was gained here? She traded a chance for an hour's real learning about science for, at best, an hour's temporary learning about history—much more probably no learning at all, just an hour's worth of daydreaming and resentful thoughts about school.

It is not subject matter that makes some learning more valuable than others, but the spirit in which the work is done. If a child is doing the kind of learning that most children do in school, when they learn at all—swallowing words, to spit back at the teacher on demand—he is wasting his time, or rather, we are wasting it for him. This learning will not be permanent, or relevant, or useful. But a child who is learning naturally, following his curiosity where it leads him, adding to his mental model of reality whatever he needs and can find a place for, and rejecting without fear or guilt what he does not need, is growing—in knowledge, in the love of learning, and in the ability to learn. He is on his way to becoming the kind of person we need in our society, and that our "best" schools and colleges are *not* turning out, the kind of person who, in Whitney Griswold's words, seeks and finds meaning, truth, and enjoyment in everything he does. All his life he will go on learning. Every experience will make his mental model of reality more complete and more true to life, and thus make him more able to deal realistically, imaginatively, and constructively with whatever new experience life throws his way.

We cannot have real learning in school if we think it is our duty and our right to tell children what they must learn. We cannot know, at any moment, what particular bit of knowledge or understanding a child needs most, will most strengthen and best fit his model of reality. Only he can do this. He may not do it very well, but he can do it a hundred times better than we can. The most we can do is try to help, by letting him know roughly what is available and where he can look for it. Choosing what he wants to learn and what he does not is something he must do for himself.

There is one more reason, and the most important one, why we must reject the idea of school and classroom as places where, most of the time, children are doing what some adult tells them to do. The reason is that there is no way to coerce children without making them afraid, or more afraid. We must not try to fool ourselves into thinking that this is not so. The would-be progressives, who until recently had great influence over most American public school education, did not recognize this—and still do not. They thought, or at least talked and wrote as if they thought, that there were good ways and bad ways to coerce children (the bad ones mean, harsh, cruel, the good ones gentle, persuasive, subtle, kindly), and that if they avoided the bad and stuck to the good they would do no harm. This was one of their greatest mistakes, and the main reason why the revolution they hoped to accomplish never took hold.

The idea of painless, non-threatening coercion is an illusion. Fear is the inseparable companion of coercion, and its inescapable consequence. If you think it your duty to make children do what you want, whether they will or not, then it follows inexorably that you must make them afraid of what will happen to them if they don't do what you want. You can do this in the old-fashioned way, openly and avowedly, with the threat of harsh words, infringement of liberty, or physical punishment. Or you can do it in the modern way, subtly, smoothly, quietly, by withholding the acceptance and approval which you and others have trained the children to depend on; or by making them feel that some retribution awaits them in the future, too vague to imagine but too implacable to escape. You can, as many skilled teachers do, learn to tap with a word, a gesture, a look, even a smile, the great reservoir of fear, shame, and guilt that today's children carry around inside them. Or you can simply let your own fears, about what will happen to you if the children don't do what you want, reach out and infect them. Thus the children will feel more and more that life is full of dangers from which only the goodwill of adults like you can protect them, and that this goodwill is perishable and must be earned anew each day.

The alternative—I can see no other—is to have schools and classrooms in which each child in his own way can satisfy his curiosity, develop his abilities and talents, pursue his interests, and from the adults and older children around him get a glimpse of the great variety and richness of life. In short, the school should be a great smörgåsbord of intellectual, artistic, creative, and athletic activities, from which each child could take whatever he wanted, and as much as he wanted, or as little. When Anna was in the sixth grade, the year after she was in my class, I mentioned this idea to her. After describing very sketchily how such a school might be run, and what the children might do, I said, "Tell me, what do you think of it? Do you think it would work? Do you think the kids would learn anything?" She said, with utmost conviction, "Oh, yes, it would be wonderful!" She was silent for a minute or two, perhaps remembering her own generally unhappy schooling. Then she said thoughtfully, "You know, kids really like to learn; we just don't like being pushed around."

No, they don't; and we should be grateful for that. So let's stop pushing them around, and give them a chance.

ORGANIC TEACHING

Sylvia Ashton-Warner

It's all so merciful on a teacher, this appearance of the subjects of an infant room in the creative vent. For one thing, the drive is no longer the teacher's but the children's own. And for another, the teacher is at last with the stream and not against it; the stream of children's inexorable creativeness. As Dr. Jung says, psychic life is a world power that exceeds by many times all the powers of the earth; as Dr. Burrow says, the secret of our collective ills is to be traced to the suppression of creative ability; and as Erich Fromm says, destructiveness is the outcome of the unlived life.

So it is of more than professional moment that all of the work of young children should be through the creative vent. It is more than a teaching matter or a dominion one. It's an international matter. So often I have said in the past, when a war is

---

From Sylvia Ashton-Warner, "The Unlived Life," pp. 92–100 in *Teacher* (New York: Simon & Schuster) 1963. Copyright © 1963 by Sylvia Ashton-Warner. Reprinted by permission of Simon & Schuster, Inc.

over the statesmen should not go into conference with one another but should turn their attention to the infant rooms, since it is from there that comes peace or war. And that's how I see organic teaching. It helps to set the creative pattern in a mind while it is yet malleable, and in this role is a humble contribution to peace.

The expansion of a child's mind can be a beautiful growth. And in beauty are included the qualities of equilibrium, harmony and rest. There's no more comely word in the language than "rest." All the movement in life, and out of it too, is towards a condition of rest. Even the simple movement of a child "coming up."

I can't disassociate the activity in an infant room from peace and war. So often I have seen the destructive vent, beneath an onslaught of creativity, dry up under my eyes. Especially with the warlike Maori five-year-olds who pass through my hands in hundreds, arriving with no other thought in their heads other than to take, break, fight and be first. With no opportunity for creativity they may well develop, as they did in the past, with fighting as their ideal of life. Yet all this can be expelled through the creative vent, and the more violent the boy the more I see that he creates, and when he kicks the others with his big boots, treads on fingers on the mat, hits another over the head with a piece of wood or throws a stone, I put clay in his hands, or chalk. He can create bombs if he likes or draw my house in flame, but is is the creative vent that is widening all the time and the destructive one atrophying, however much it may look to the contrary. And anyway I have always been more afraid of the weapon unspoken than of the one on a blackboard.

With all this in mind therefore I try to bring as many facets of teaching into the creative vent as possible, with emphasis on reading and writing. And that's just what organic teaching is; all subjects in the creative vent. It's just as easy for a teacher, who gives a child a brush and lets him paint, to give him a pencil and let him write, and to let him pass his story to the next one to read. Simplicity is so safe. There's no occasion whatever for the early imposition of a dead reading, a dead vocabulary. I'm so afraid of it. It's like a frame over a young tree making it grow in an unnatural shape. It makes me think of that curtailment of a child's expansion of which Erich Fromm speaks, of that unlived life of which destructiveness is the outcome. "And instead of the wholeness of the expansive tree we have only the twisted and stunted bush." The trouble is that a child from a modern respectable home suffers such a serious frame on his behaviour long before he comes near a teacher. Nevertheless I think that

ORGANIC TEACHING
Sylvia Ashton-Warner

after a year of organic work the static vocabularies can be used without misfortune. They can even, under the heads of external stimulus and respect for the standard of English, become desirable.

But only when built upon the organic foundation. And there's hardly anything new in the conception of progress from the known to the unknown. It's just that when the inorganic reading is imposed first it interferes with integration; and it's upon the integrated personality that everything is built. We've lost the gracious movement from the inside outward. We overlook the footing. I talk sometimes about a bridge from the *pa** to the European environment, but there is a common bridge for a child of any race and of more moment than any other: the bridge from the inner world outward. And that is what organic teaching is. An indispensable step in integration. Without it we get this one-patterned mind of the New Zealand child, accruing from so much American influence of the mass-mind type. I think that we already have so much pressure towards sameness through radio, film and comic outside the school, that we can't afford to do a thing inside that is not toward individual development, and from this stance I can't see that we can indulge in the one imposed reading for all until the particular variety of a mind is set. And a cross-section of children from different places in New Zealand provides me with an automatic check on the progress of the one-patterned mind. (I own seventy fancy-dress costumes which I lend.) All the children want the same costumes. If you made dozens of cowboy and cowgirl costumes, hundreds of Superman and thousands of Rocket Man costumes and hired them at half a guinea a go, you'd get every penny of it and would make a fortune vast enough to retire on and spend the rest of your life in the garden. As for my classics—Bo-Peep, the Chinese Mandarin, Peter Pan and the Witch and so on—they so gather dust that they have had to be folded and put away. It's this sameness in children that can be so boring. So is death boring.

To write peaceful reading books and put them in an infant room is not the way to peace. They don't even scratch the surface. No child ever asked for a Janet or John costume. There is only one answer to destructiveness and that is creativity. And it never was and never will be any different. And when I say so I am in august company.

The noticeable thing in New Zealand society is the body of

---

* *Editor's Note:* "pa" means Maori village, according to the author's footnote on page 54 of *Teacher*.

people with their inner resources atrophied. Seldom have they had to reach inward to grasp the thing that they wanted. Everything, from material requirements to ideas, is available readymade. From mechanical gadgets in the shops to sensation in the films they can buy almost anything they fancy. They can buy life itself from the film and radio—canned life.

And even if they tried to reach inward for something that maybe they couldn't find manufactured, they would no longer find anything there. They've dried up. From babyhood they have had shiny toys put in their hands, and in the kindergartens and infant rooms bright pictures and gay material. Why conceive anything of their own? There has not been the need. The capacity to do so has been atrophied and now there is nothing there. The vast expanses of the mind that could have been alive with creative activity are now no more than empty vaults that must, for comfort's sake, be filled with non-stop radio, and their conversation consists of a list of platitudes and clichés.

I can't quite understand why.

From what I see of modern education the intention is just the opposite: to let children grow up in their own personal way into creative and interesting people. Is it the standard textbooks? Is it the consolidation? Is it the quality of the teachers? Is it the access to film and radio and the quality of those luxuries? Or is it the access to low-grade reading material infused through all of these things? I don't know where the intention fails but we end up with the same pattern of a person in nine hundred ninety-nine instances out of a thousand.

I said to a friend, a professor, recently, "What kind of children arrive at the University to you?" He said, "They're all exactly the same." "But," I said, "how can it be like that? The whole plan of primary education at least is for diversity." "Well," he answered, "they come to me like samples from a mill. Not one can think for himself. I beg them not to serve back to me exactly what I have given to them. I challenge them sometimes with wrong statements to provoke at least some disagreement but even that won't work." "But," I said, "you must confess to about three per cent originality." "One in a thousand," he replied. "One in a thousand."

On the five-year-old level the mind is not yet patterned and it is an exciting thought. True, I often get the over-disciplined European five, crushed beyond recognition as an identity, by respectable parents, but never Maoris; as a rule a five-year-old child is not boring. In an infant room it is still possible to meet an interesting, unpatterned person. "In the infant room," I told this professor, "we still have identity. It's somewhere between

ORGANIC TEACHING
Sylvia Ashton-Warner

my infant-room level and your university level that the story breaks. But I don't think it is the plan of education itself."

I think that the educational story from the infant room to the university is like the writing of a novel. You can't be sure of your beginning until you have checked it with your ending. What might come of infant teachers visiting the university and professors visiting the infant room? I had two other professors in my infant room last year and they proved themselves to be not only delightfully in tune but sensitively helpful.

Yet what I believe and what I practise are not wholly the same thing. For instance, although I have reason to think that a child's occupation until seven should not be other than creative in the many mediums, nevertheless I find myself teaching some things.

With all this in mind, therefore, the intent of the infant room is

> the nurturing of the organic idea.
> the preservation of the inner resources,
> the exercise of the inner eye, and
> the protraction of the true personality.

I like unpredictability and variation; I like drama and I like gaiety; I like peace in the world and I like interesting people, and all this means that I like life in its organic shape and that's just what you get in an infant room where the creative vent widens. For this is where style is born in both writing and art, for art is the way you do a thing and an education based on art at once flashes out style.

The word "jalopy" made its fascinating appearance the other day. Brian wrote, "I went to town. I came back on a jalopy bus." This word stirred us. The others cross-questioned him on the character of such a bus. It turned out to mean "rackety" and although the word was picked up at once nevertheless they still ask for it to go up on the spelling list. We haven't had "jalopy" for spelling lately, Brian says. He loves spelling it, which is what I mean when I say that the drive is the children's own. It's all so merciful on a teacher.

Inescapably war and peace wait in an infant room; wait and vie.

True the toy shops are full of guns, boys' hands hold tanks and war planes while the blackboards, clay boards and easels burst with war play. But I'm unalarmed. My concern is the rearing of the creative disposition, for creativity in this crèche of living where people can still be changed must in the end defy, if not defeat, the capacity for destruction. Every happening in the infant room is either creative or destructive; every drawing, every shaping, every sentence and every dance goes one way or the other. For, as Erich Fromm says, "life has an inner dynamism of its own; it tends to grow, to be expressed, to be lived. The amount of destructiveness in a child is proportionate to the amount to which the expansiveness of his life has been curtailed. Destructiveness is the outcome of the unlived life."

I believe in this as passionately as the artist in his brush and the roadman in his shovel. For every work, and first of all that of a teacher, must have its own form, its design. And the design of my work is that creativity in this time of life when character can be influenced forever is the solution to the problem of war. To me it has the validity of a law of physics and all the unstatable, irrepressible emotion of beauty.

19

FOUR MODELS
FOR EDUCATION

Herbert A. Thelen

Somewhere in one of his stories, O. Henry describes the experience of going by train at ninety miles an hour through a small town. The speed was so great, he says, that the watertank and the Episcopal church blended together into the image of a saloon. I am afraid this sort of thing happens not only to small towns but also to survey courses, such as Chapters 2, 3, and 4. We have been traveling pell-mell through an assortment of ideas, and perhaps we had better take the time for a brief review before moving on to the educational implications of the ideas.

Education is a process, a sequence of actions. The participants are teachers and students, individual human beings. Each has a human nature, which in turn is compounded from constituent interacting animal and social natures. The animal heritage

---

"Suppositons: Four Models for Education" (Chapter 5), pp. 74–88 in *Education and the Human Quest* by Herbert A. Thelen. Copyright © 1966 by Herbert A. Thelen. Reprinted by permission of Harper & Row, Publishers, and the author.

tempts us to deal with problems and stresses by acting out reflexively and impulsively, i.e. "emotionally." The social nature, developed through consciousness, language, memory, and learning, inclines us to deal with problems through the effort to comprehend what is involved. These two methods of dealing with situations, acting out and inquiry, have to be reconciled, and they have to be reconciled in every new situation.

The effort to resolve conflict between the two modes of reacting is the central drama of individual human lives. The ideal is neither to compromise nor suppress one or the other, but rather to integrate them within a way of life which is enriched by both—which has the color and richness and involvement that come from emotional response, and that has the control, purposiveness, and effectiveness that come from understanding. The active quest for integration which is most self-realizing in the seeking of autonomy or captaincy of self, goes on in all human beings, regardless, as the saying goes, of race, creed, color, or national origin.

Thus runs the lesson of Chapter 2.

The process of education deals with "subject matter." Subject matter is that part of recorded knowledge which is introduced as material for thought in classrooms. Since subject matter is already written down (for the most part), one way to deal with it is to memorize it. Another way to deal with it is to use it as reference material to answer questions which arise from one's efforts to cope with situations. Memorization produces walking encyclopedias, and it views education as basically a process of consumption. Using subject matter to answer meaningful questions views education as inquiry, and it produces persons who ask questions, connect causes to effects, and learn principles.

When inquiry is consciously guided by method, and when the methods are appropriate to the phenomena being studied, the fruit of knowledge is "discipline," an effective way of life with reference to the phenomena in the field of study. The person who has learned the disciplines of natural science, history, human relations, etc.—and knows when to employ each—may be said to be educated.

The motive power for inquiry is generated in a feeling of perplexity and challenge when one is confronted (under favorable conditions) by things he cannot cope with. The creative aspect of inquiry is in the diagnosis of the problem as it is felt and perceived by each individual. The solution of the problem is the application of rational methods of collecting data, making plans, taking limited action, studying its consequences, modifying plans, acting on these, and so on. The life of inquiry is one in

FOUR MODELS FOR EDUCATION
Herbert A. Thelen

which the experience of each step in problem solving changes one's perceptions and leads to reformulation of the problem. In a literal sense, problems do not get solved, they only get reformulated in terms that are increasingly meaningful.

The various domains of knowledge all enter into life. The knowledge disciplines are learned as part of the quest for autonomy; and in this quest, the person learns to give conscious guidance to his own processes of inquiry.

Thus runs the lesson of Chapter 3.

No man stands alone because his behavior influences other people. It may influence them directly, as when he deals with them face to face; or it may influence them indirectly as when he changes some aspect of the environment with which they also are in contact. Thus people are interdependent, and form a society.

The society coordinates efforts of individuals for the purpose of providing food, shelter, protection, recreation, education, etc., for all. These different purposes are societal functions, and each person, through his job, his hobbies, his votes, his consumption, his participation in activities—has a role with respect to each function. One purpose of education is to enable the student to discover and understand a variety of functional roles within his own society as well as in the adult world. Since roles are defined partly by the expectations of others, one's sense of belonging is contingent upon the roles he occupies—and the extent to which these roles facilitate his own quest for integration and "wholeness."

The development of roles is a joint enterprise. The individual or organization cannot define his or its role in isolation from others. The topic of discussion through which roles are clarified is the job to be done or the function to be carried out and the contribution each can make to this function. When such conversations and consequent mutual accommodations do not occur, the person or organization may react in various ways to the lack of any mechanism for finding a place in the community's functional systems. Thus the school very often withdraws into defensiveness and tries to legitimize its own conception of its role through "public relations" (selling and persuasion) rather than through public discussion of the educational function and the various contributions to the educational function needed from home, church, businesses, schools, and other agencies within the community. Similarly youth, who also do not engage in public discussion through which role expectations can be clarified and defined, form their own society. This is a society in oscillation between two ways of finding self-esteem; through maintaining the privileged status of childhood versus seeking a place in the productive life of the adult community. The resulting behaviors, frequently excessive, reflect the indecision of the youth group and their frustration over the lack of means by which it can be resolved.

Finally we note that the workings of a society are based on some underlying principle, such as that social change will come about through the processes of group anarchy; and that having established its principle of operation, the society is trapped in it. The lesson of Chapter 4 ended with a picture of the vicious circle, and designated the part of the circle where a breakthrough might be possible.

MODELS FOR EDUCATION

On the strength of these ideas, I now propose that there are three fundamental quests going on in the world of man. I shall identify and discuss each one, and will sketch a model of education that can be built around it. Then I shall comment on the common element of inquiry central in all three models, and will end the chapter with a fourth necessary model which is dependent on the other three but which should be implemented separately. In succeeding chapters, I shall consider each model in turn.

Model 1
Personal Inquiry
The first quest is for selfhood or integration. In this quest, we see persons trying to reconcile their tendencies to "acting out" and "to seek reality" in a variety of everyday situations. Note that such seeking has both particular and general aspects: the need, for example, of acquiring not only the abilities of the scientist but also the scientist's way of life; the purpose of testing, not a few prejudices against the world, but an emerging philosophy of life; for seeing, not just a few fascinating ways to make a living or to evaluate the world, but, more fundamentally, discovering alternative ways of life and finding oneself as one creates his own or makes choices among them.

For us to help children in their quest for autonomy, we must first be able to diagnose and understand the nature of this quest. At the present time, with our existing crude diagnostic tools we can identify three sorts of children who should undoubtedly be dealt with on an individual basis.

FOUR MODELS FOR EDUCATION
Herbert A. Thelen

First, there is the child who already knows and is committed to a particular profession, field of study, or way of life within the adult world. He may, at age twelve, be clearly cut out for physical science, music, languages, or mathematics; and he is, by adult standards, "talented." The talents we have so far been able to recognize seem to be with respect to fields of study which can be logically and rationally organized, skills developed through imitation, and artistic expressiveness. We also note such characteristics as an inquiring mind, an impressive fund of all sorts of information, and a startling ability to deal with abstractions. Many (if not most) students can give evidence of great talent, skill, or ability which should, both for their own and society's sake, be encouraged and maximized. According to investigators DeHaan and Havighurst,[1] about one child in five is "gifted" in some way. And we can try to foster such talents.

A second sort of child who is ready to learn is seldom thought of as talented. Such students may be coping, often unsuccessfully, with real and present problems of relationship, of orientation to authority. They may be lacking in overarching goals that can give their lives focus; they may be badly crippled psychologically, and be unable to perceive with any accuracy what goes on around them. Such a child may be continually "acting out" an inadequate theory about the world: he thinks everyone is against him, he regards the world as hostile or unfair, he transmutes every situation into a battle with authority. In short, this is an antisocial child, and he needs to be confronted with situations in which the falsity of his theory is patent, even to him.

(The passive antisocial child, withdrawn and fearful, probably cannot be reached through instructional groups. He is likely to need professional psychiatric help.)

A third sort of child who is ready to learn is the child whose range of experience has been so narrow that he has simply not had the opportunity to try to cope with very many aspects of life. It is fashionable to think of "lower class" children in this way, and to refer to them as "culturally deprived." I would include under this term, in addition, children whose families have been so preoccupied with making a living, achieving social status, being intellectual sophisticates, maintaining piety, etc., that the child has never had the chance to recognize, let alone explore, the possiblities of any other way or kind of life. Such children often appear to have no goal or direction in their own lives, for they have not had to make choices, and therefore they have not had to think through "who they are" and where their commitments lie.

We believe that most normal children have some recognizable degree of talent, of antisocial orientation, and of cultural deprivation. The resulting quest of each child is different, and this calls for individualized instruction. For each quest, a different kind or quality of social opportunity or confrontation by reality is indicated. The talented child, anticipating adulthood, seeks experience in that part of the adult community which uses, challenges, and stretches his talent: the laboratory, studio, library, shop, or counting house. The antisocial child requires confrontation by expectations from the "real" (i.e., adult) community which give the lie to his unsophisticated and partial theory of life. Generally speaking, this confrontation may stimulate the child to seek (or accept) responsibility and reward for functioning as a social rather than as an antisocial person. The culturally deprived child simply needs participant-observer experience in families, groups, and organizations whose existence he could not have dreamed of.

Personal Inquiry with respect to all three needs is inaugurated by selecting an existing spot in the classroom, school, or community which can provide the environment most appropriate to the quest of a particular child. In this spot—shop, studio, store, field, business, work gang—the student participates in the work to be done. He will be encouraged to comprehend his experience to the extent that he is able; and this means thinking about it quite consciously. Thus, in so far as possible we will encourage him to note and mull over his thoughts, feelings, and performance; to try to set his own personal goals for inquiry; to plan strategies for dealing with parts of the job; to consciously collect evidence for his policies. He will be helped to find accounts of the experiences of other people in similar predicaments and circumstances, and to contrast their findings with his own. And, finally, he will be asked to help decide when to bring his inquiry to a close.

Personal Inquiry is the subject of Chapter 6.

Model 2 **Group Investigation** The way each person acts to realize his own biological and psychological needs for self-maintenance and autonomy may very well conflict with like efforts of other persons. House rules are needed, and the most basic one is that "your freedom to swing your fist ends where my nose begins." Thus a social image of man is also needed, a man who builds with other men the rules and agreements that constitute social reality.

FOUR MODELS FOR EDUCATION
Herbert A. Thelen

Interdependent men must and do, in one way or another, develop the agreements they need. In this respect, every collection of people in continual association with each other becomes a "group." Moreover, each individual contributes to the establishment and modification of the rules and thus helps to determine both its prohibitions and freedoms for action.

The rules of conduct, both explicit and implicit, in all fields—religious, political, economic, scientific—are elaborated, rationalized, explained, communicated, and interpreted within a larger body of ideas, purposes, ideals, aesthetic sensibilities, organizational assumptions, material resources, and plans. This larger corpus constitutes the "culture" of the society. It is through continual effort, through reflection, to understand our culture that we become aware of the implicit rules by which we live, the nature of our assumptions about our environment, and the possibilities for freedom.

Thus in groups and societies a cyclical process exists: individuals, interdependently seeking to meet their needs, must establish a social order (and in the process they develop groups and societies). The social order determines in varying degrees what ideas, values, and actions are possible, valid, and "appropriate." Working within these "rules" and stimulated by the need for rules, the culture develops. The individual studies his reactions to the rules and re-interprets them to discover their meaning for the way of life he seeks. Through this quest, he changes his own way of life, and this in turn influences the way of life of others, But as the way of life changes, the rules must be revised, and new controls and agreements have to be hammered out and incorporated in the social order.

The relationship of this dynamic to education has been only half understood. There has been a failure to realize that the development of knowledge, valuable in its own right, is a by-product of the continuously operating dynamic of changing and/or maintaining the social order. The great bulk of knowledge transmitted in schools is legitimized by the assumption that people must and do participate (whether or not they know or like it) in the social order; and they have no choice about this. Motivation for classroom learning should be high when the learner perceives that the restrictions and freedoms in the group are determined by his own state of knowledge and skill. One would expect motivation to be greatest when "rules" and "learnings" reinforce one another; and when increased autonomy can be earned through the gaining of skill, sophistication, intellectual penetration, or other facets of competence. Such relationships would associate the gaining of knowledge to greater opportunities in the way of life in the classroom, and the consequences could be exciting: granted that many students are not initially motivated to acquire some kinds of knowledge, nevertheless all students care about the way of life that develops in the classroom.

The educational model based on these working suppositions is Group Investigation. Given a group of students and a teacher in a classroom, some sort of social order, classroom culture, and "climate" is bound to develop. It may develop around the basic value of comfort, of politeness and middle-class morals and manners, or of keeping the teacher happy and secure. In these all too frequent cases, the gaining of knowledge collapses to the learning of information, and the meaning of the information is respectively to stimulate bull sessions, develop conformity, or provide the teacher with materials to show off with.

We propose instead that the teacher's task is to particpate in the activities of developing the social order in the classroom for the purpose of orienting it to inquiry, and that the "house rules" to be developed are the methods and attitudes of the knowledge discipline to be taught. The teacher influences the emerging social order toward inquiring when he "brings out" and capitalizes on differences in the ways students act and interpret the role of investigator—which is also the role of member in the classroom group. Under these conditions, the gaining of knowledge could serve initially only to validate the student's portrayal of the investigator role; but as the way of life of inquiry comes to dominate the social order, the purpose of gaining knowledge—which by then will be inseparable (but not identical) with meeting personal needs in the group—will have a powerful appeal in itself. And, of course, knowledge learned in its essential, even if microcosmic, social context, will be utilizable in the larger arena as well.

The first requirment for group investigation is a teachable group: one which can develop a sense of common cause, one whose members can stimulate each other, and one whose members are psychologically compatible and complementary. The students are assigned to a consultant (teacher) who confronts them with a stimulus situation to which they can react and discover basic conflicts among their attitudes, ideas, and modes of perception. On the basis of this information, they identify the problem to be investigated, analyze the roles required to "solve" it, train themselves to take these roles; act, report, and evaluate the results. These steps are illuminated by reading, possibly by some short-range personal investigations, and by consultation with experts. The group is concerned with its own effectiveness, but its discussions of its own process are related to the goals of the investigation.

The dynamic of the investigation, as Bion has shown, is the need of the group to maintain itself, and the beginning of investigation is demonstrated incompatibility among assumptions underlying the reactions of the members to the planned stimulus situation. The need to deal with such differences is the primary psychological motivation for investigations by the group, but as the group "develops," many further kinds of gratification become available to individuals, and these add drive to the inquiry. We will expand on these matters later, in Chapters 7 and 8.

Model 3 **Reflective Action** We have been considering the social order as a milieu within which each individual tries to develop and maintain his way of life. Because there is a social order, predictability is possible; one can guess with some accuracy the likely consequences of possible ways of acting, and he can govern himself accordingly. He can see his own behavior as a means to alleviate some immediate condition and, at the same time, as a long-range influence (through changes due to learning) on major social ends.

But in addition to being the social-psychological-humanistic *milieu* of individuals, the social order and culture is the *instrument* through which men provide food, shelter, entertainment, protection, and other conditions necessary for life or demanded by men's aspirations. In its operation as a functional agent, the social order must yield to a higher authority, namely, the demands and facts of the "real" world. In a word, the social order and culture mediates between the individual and his environment; it is the meeting place of desires that come from individuals and the stubborn realities and opportunities that nature makes men face up to.

In Group Investigation, the group transacts business with the environment primarily as a way of finding out how the environment will respond. Thus chemicals are part of the environment and chemical experiments are designed to reveal their properties. Artifacts from another age, such as journals and furniture, are also part of the environment, and the history class collects and studies these objects as part of its effort to reconstruct the life of an earlier period. In both cases the aim is to learn about phenomena whose occurrence depends in no way upon desires of the students.

Our third model, Reflective Action, visualizes the group transacting business with the environment both in order to change the environment and in order to learn the skills and insights necessary for changing the environment. Thus group investigation is directed to the learning of scientific and theoretical propositions, whereas Reflective Action is directed to the learning of working suppositions. Just as a teacher needs both in order to function intelligently, so also does the citizen, chemist, consumer, and everyone else engaged in the practical affairs of the world.

The model of Reflective Action stipulates that the classroom, school, and community are to be thought of as laboratories for the learning of the policy sciences and the engineering arts. Various aspects of the laboratories or of the way of life therein may be reacted to by students: the formal and informal organization of the student society; the methods for legislating and enforcing rules; the physical appearance or convenience of the plant; the program of studies; the lunchroom, gymnasium, library, conference room, and other facilities; and so on. The "climate" of tolerance and freedom will be such that at any given time certain students will feel that certain changes might well be advantageous. Such students will have the opportunity to recruit others to their cause; and a communications system will exist, so that their representations can be channeled in an orderly way to the appropriate deliberative bodies. These will (or will not) arrange for the necessary enabling legislation for the initiating group to act. All steps will be handled with rigorous concern for adequacy of data (e.g., in the sampling of perceptions of the student body); for formulation and weighing of alternatives; for prudence and foresight in planning; for tentativeness in acting; and for periodic assessment of consequences through which further plans and policies can be modified toward greater realism and efficiency. And finally, all action will be seen as illustrative of similar larger actions and underlying significant issues in the larger society. From an educational viewpoint, the student does not "learn by doing." He learns by planning, doing, and reflecting on the doing. This program is to have a first-class intellectual content; and it will demand the learning and exercise of wisdom in affairs impinging directly on the students.

The motivation for Reflective Action by students is the same as for adults: to improve their material and functional way of life and to protect individual rights and liberty in a world whose increasingly complex interdependencies threaten to extinguish individuality. The motivation of the adolescent is considerably stronger than that of the educated intellectual adult who has

FOUR MODELS FOR EDUCATION
Herbert A. Thelen

been taught that social action is "beneath" him and seems, for the most part, quite content merely to complain while his community goes to pieces all around him. For the adolescent has strong need to find, through some sort of participation in the productive community, an avenue to self-esteem. But the fact that this is the driving force in Reflective Action does *not* mean that this is also its educational justification. If students want to get together on their own time and in their own clubs to change the world, let them—and more power to them. But this has nothing to do with the school, which is concerned with social action *only* as a kind of experience indispensable to the learning of certain practical disciplines essential in our times. By and large the school is not out to change society, but only to produce enlightened citizens who will act intelligently. Considering the quality of much of the present operation of society, having people act intelligently would be a sure-fire way to bring about drastic changes; but the changes would come from the force of sound ideas, not from the particular biases or social attitudes of a group of schoolmen.

In the part of the school program concerned with reflective action, consultants from the school and community can serve as trainers in the methodology of action; experts can offer information to be considered and interpreted; working committees can study social, economical, political, and other policies involved in making wise decisions. And there must be continual encouragement and help to ascertain the consequences of actions as perceived by all those touched by the actions, to rediagnose the problem, and to take further and better action.

The educational model of reflective action is spelled out further in Chapter 9.

Inquiry, the Common Element

All three models involve inquiry. Each model is concerned to initiate and supervise the processes of giving attention to something; of interacting with and being stimulated by other people, whether in person or through their writings; and of reflection and reorganization of concepts and attitudes, as shown in arriving at conclusions, identifying new investigations to be undertaken, taking action, and turning out a better product. These characteristics were foreshadowed in Chapter 3.

In these models we have delineated three major situations or contexts of inquiry. Personal Inquiry is close in spirit to the basic human problems of Chapter 2. It is the quest for meaning, the reconciliation of man as animal with man (the same man) as member of society. Group Investigation is oriented to the domains of knowledge, Chapter 3. It is the development of common cause and culture around the pursuit within an interactive group of knowledge. Reflective action is built on the background and processes of Chapter 4. It is the mature effort of the student body (or volunteer fractions thereof) to bring about desired changes in the larger society.

When the three underlying processes—personal integration, development of the social order, and modification of the environment—are kept in balance, with each serving as a check of the other, they become the prime dynamics for achieving the major values of personal autonomy, predictability, lawfulness among groups and nations, and survival of the species.

All of these kinds of inquiry ferret out information and turn it into knowledge (the four domains *) useful for inquiries.

Part of the knowledge of greatest educational value is knowledge of how to participate more effectively in these kinds of inquiry. And through participation in each inquiry, new personal needs, common causes, and action needs will emerge, and lead to further inquiries.

Model 4
Skill Development

I put this last because it is subsidiary to and facilitative of the other kinds of inquiries; if the other inquiries are not in existence, then this fourth type cannot exist. In a way, practice in

---

* *Editor's Note:* In Chapter 3, "Knowledge: The Instinct for the Jugular," pp. 29–53, the author discusses the four domains of knowledge. Thus, on page 35, he states:

> "... I shall assert that there are four different domains of knowledge and that they enable us to comprehend four corresponding kinds of realities. My proposition is that within these several domains of knowledge are implied quite clearly the objectives of education and the kinds of learning activities that schools should be concerned with.
>
> These domains are, by recent tradition, physical science, biological science, social science, and humanistic studies. These four domains can be arranged along a continuum. Physical science is concerned with events and phenomena far out from the self—the stars, for example. Biological science comes in a little closer, and social science still more. In fact we find social knowledge always partly from the point of view of a participant in the phenomena we are studying. Humanistic study is subjective and "inside"; it has to do with the unique thoughts and expressions of individuals. It is the record not of the world "out there" but of the experience that an individual has with the world."

FOUR MODELS FOR EDUCATION
Herbert A. Thelen

skills relieves some of the burden from the other inquiries, but the reason for separating it is purely practical: it is organized differently and probably should involve different and special personnel of its own.

The fact of the matter is that students do have to learn to read, write, listen, memorize the multiplication table and the symbols of the chemical elements, learn the vocabulary of a foreign language, study, and speak effectively. But these learnings are skills which are not ends in themselves. One does not read just to read, he reads for information, to kill time, for enjoyment, etc.; and likewise for the other skills. The motivation for learning skills, then, is to enable one to carry out the other three kinds of inquiry adequately. The most effective pressure for learning skills will be the standard of performance the students themselves require in their own inquiries (with a bit of judicious inspiration and encouragement by adults). To learn skills they must want to learn, for a major requirement is paying attention to practice. Just going through the motions is—simply going through the motions.

The pressures may derive from group standards, but skill learning is an individual matter. Thus some students "pick up" the necessary skills in connection with the larger activity which originated the need. And dragging an already competent reader through the peregrinations of Dick and Jane, or an accurate computer through endless arithmetic problems is probably an excellent way to kill interest and desire to learn.

Students learn skills by different routes. Reading, for example, has been studied quite intensively, and the present conclusion is that the good teacher tailors the approach to each child. For one child, the key seems to be phonics; for another, word study. I suspect the same thing would be found with other skills, such as writing proper sentences. It is possible that grammar is actually useful to some students, but it most certainly is a hindrance to others who learn to write prose the way a "natural" composer writes music—through having something to say and a sensitive ear that tells him when he has said it correctly.

It is proposed to set up a skills laboratory to be attended by individuals when they need more skill—and know that they do. If a student needs more skill and doesn't know it or denies it, he will not go to the practice laboratory because that would do him little good. He will need to be helped, through assessment during inquiry to understand and accept his need.

The laboratory will be manned partly by student consultants; but it will be guided by ingenious teachers who know how to break skills down into manageable parts, and who can help the students make their own flash cards, practice tapes, record charts, test diagnoses, and similar devices.

In the next five chapters I shall attempt to answer: What would a school look like if it took these models seriously and adapted them to education? In anticipation, I assure you that it would look quite different from today's schools. For we propose to separate the three kinds of inquiries which now all go on together in a jumbled and inchoate fashion—deal with each in its own terms, and use the learnings from each to facilitate each other. And in this analysis we shall, whether we like it or not, be forced to see that the school cannot do the educational job alone—a conclusion foreshadowed in Chapter 4. So Chapter 11 will examine in the light of our understanding, the problem of the means by which action can be taken to improve education in the schools and community.

FOOTNOTE

[1] Robert DeHaan and Robert Havighurst, *Educating Gifted Children.* Chicago: University of Chicago Press, 1957, p. 275.

NOTES

The framework of ideas here presented has been emerging for some time. Previous papers by the same author that may help round out the propositions are:

1. Educational Dynamics: Theory and Research. Complete issue of *The Journal of Social Issues,* VI, No. 2 (1950), 96.

2. "Basic Concepts in Human Dynamics," *Journal of the National Association of Deans of Women,* XV, No. 3 (March 1952), 99-111.

3. "The Experimental Method in Classroom Leadership," *Elementary School Journal,* LIII, No. 2 (October 1952).

4. "Emotionality and Work in Groups." In L. D. White, Ed. *The State of the Social Sciences.* Chicago: University of Chicago Press, 1956. Pp. 184-200.

5. With J. W. Getzels, "The Social Sciences: Conceptual Framework for Education," *School Review,* LXV, No. 3 (Autumn 1957), 330-355.

6. "Four Propositions in Search of an Educational Dynamic," *Adult Education,* VIII, No. 3 (Spring 1958), 146-152.

7. La dynamique des groupes sociaux: organisation et group de travail. In *Psychosociologie Industrielle.* Paris: Revue Hommes et Techniques, CLXIX (1959), 72-95.

8. "Work-Emotionality Theory of the Group as Organism." In S. Koch, Ed. *Psychology: A Study of Science* III. New York: McGraw-Hill Book Co., 1959. Pp. 544-611.

9. With J. W. Getzels, "The Class as a Unique Social System." In *Yearbook of the National Society for the Study of Education,* 1960.

10. "Engineering Research in Curriculum Building," *Journal of Educational Research,* XLI, No. 8 (April 1948), 577-596.

**DISCUSSION QUESTIONS
AND FURTHER READINGS**

Where do you usually start teaching? At the beginning, right? You first discuss some fundamental concepts (and words) and then, on these basics, you build more and more advanced concepts. Quite logical. Let us, however, ask: Is the procedure really logical so far as your students are concerned? Are the workings of the human mind in fact logical? Is teaching essentially a logical operation?

Perhaps the procedure appears reasonable to you merely because you are now in the enviable position of enjoying some hindsight on the long process of schooling. Especially in college, the particular way to organize knowledge was shown to you as the culminating system in that discipline. You know what constitutes the basic building components in the total pyramidal structure. It makes sense to you and, hence, you assume that it makes sense to your students. But, does it really?

In the natural course of human development, which comes first: questions or answers? When, for example, some Egyptian men of wisdom were trying to determine the distance from Cairo to Alexandria, or when they were trying to understand the ebb and flow of the Nile, they were simply asking questions. Thanks to their efforts, we now have several systems of axioms, laws, and principles to describe the phenomena under consideration, but the original scholars did not follow the "logical" structure of comprehension. When children ask numerous questions, their inquiries and explorations do not fit in any "logical" sequence in the finished (only temporarily, no doubt) structure of knowledge about the subject. Why, then, should you expect your students to respond enthusiastically to your "logical" teaching? Why should you always begin at the "logical" beginning? See John Dewey, *Experience and Education* (New York: Collier Books, 1963), Sybil Marshall, *An Experiment in Education* (New York: Cambridge University Press, 1966), Hughes Mearns, *Creative Power* (New York: Dover Publications, second edition, 1958), and A. S. Neill, *Summerhill* (New York: Hart Publishing Co., 1960). Also study Joseph J. Schwab, "Structure of the Disciplines: Meanings and Significances," in G. W. Ford and Lawrence Pugno, Eds., *The Structure of*

Knowledge and the Curriculum (Chicago: Rand McNally, 1964), pp. 6–30.

Since the results of a child's earlier, as well as current, experiences may have not been entirely beneficial, it would be useful for you to think of some means to change the patterns of a child's thought and action. How are you going to teach him to replace one style of living and working with another? What educational forces (refer back to the teaching–learning combinations in Table P.1, page 6) in his life space can be mustered to help you in such highly individualized teaching? Consult Virginia M. Axline, *Dibs* (Boston: Houghton Mifflin, 1964), Dorothy W. Baruch, *One Little Boy* (New York: Delta Publishing Co., 1964), and Kaoru Yamamoto, "Planning and Teaching for Behavioral Change" (Chapter 12 in Joe L. Frost and G. Thomas Rowland, Eds., *The Elementary School: Principles and Problems*, Boston: Houghton Mifflin, in press).

HOW WELL

EVALUATION IN TEACHING

Kaoru Yamamoto

We, as active teachers, have wondered about many matters in teaching and raised numerous questions about education and our role in it. Most of these queries have been private in nature, while some remained even subconscious. For the purposes of the present discussion, however, let us make the basic questions explicit.

TEACHING AND ITS QUESTIONS

All our questions point to one central inquiry: "What is teaching?" The latter can be answered in myriad ways, but I submit here (see Table 20.1) a convenient scheme to systematize most

---

The paper was originally discussed at the Preface Plan Project, School of Education, the Ohio State University, Columbus, Ohio, in February of 1967. It was later published in the *Texas Journal of Secondary Education* 21 (No. 3): 4–11; Spring 1968.

TABLE 20.1
Teaching—Schematization of Questions

QUESTION		AREA OF CONCERN
Prescriptive	*Descriptive*	
Why should we be teaching?	Why are we teaching?	Values, goals, intentions, and motives
Who should be teaching?	Who are teaching?	Teacher qualification (recruitment, selection, and preparation)
Whom should we be teaching?	Whom are we teaching?	Student characteristics (recruitment, selection, and distribution)
When should we be teaching?	When are we teaching?	Readiness and logistics (physical, cognitive, and social development, timing, duration and continuity)
What should we be teaching?	What are we teaching?	Curriculum (types and quantity of material, structure, and sequence)
How should we be teaching?	How are we teaching?	Instruction and demonstration (methods, media, climate, and control)
Where should we be teaching?	Where are we teaching?	Ecology and logistics (locale, physical facilities, and geocultural administration)

of these questions and answers. (Table 20.1 appeared in the Prologue as Table P.2 and is reproduced in this essay to facilitate reference to it.) The questions are classified by interrogative pronouns and further divided into normative (prescriptive) and descriptive forms.

For example, one of the fundamental questions takes the form, "Why should we teach?" This asks for the rationale of teaching, probably in terms of cultural values, goals, intentions, and motives, and the answer is expressed as an *ought,* or normative, statement (e.g., "we ought to teach our children to convert them from animals to humans"). Our concept of the nature of the universe and of *Homo sapiens* determines the specific form of the answer to this question.[1]

A variant of the above question is, "Why are we teaching?" This version asks for a description of our present, working rationale, and the answer must therefore clarify the immediate

318

and real reasons for teaching, instead of some ideals. We may insist, in response to the normative form of the question, that our aim is to induce insight and innovation in our students because they are destined to grow up in an unknowable world; but in fact, the actual goal of our teaching may be mere conservation and perpetuation of the past. The two answers, therefore, may or may not agree with each other.

Similarly, when the question, "Whom should we teach?," is raised, we may answer that we should teach every child, regardless of his race, color, sex, creed, social status, and aptitude. If, however, the question is in the descriptive form, "Whom are we teaching?," our answer will be radically different from the above, due to a wide gap between our dream and practice.[2]

Now, my thesis is that we are engaged in "evaluation" whenever we compare our answer to the normative question with that to the descriptive question. In other words, we are evaluating our current activities against what we know or believe we should be doing. Accordingly, if we are conscientious, we will be continuously involved in evaluation which, quite often, we express as feelings of dissatisfaction, insecurity, and anxiety.

In this sense, we cannot escape evaluating various aspects of education, including ourselves as teachers. It is nothing mysterious or threatening. Whether such action is carried out consciously or unconsciously, publicly or privately, constructively or destructively, and systematically or randomly—that is, however, another matter. In any case, evaluation is here to stay as an essential component of teaching activities.

PROCESS OF EVALUATION

We said that evaluation is fundamentally the comparison between our answer to the normative question and that to the descriptive question. Thus, no matter what specific aspects of teaching we are concerned with, evaluation follows the basic pattern shown in Table 20.2.

Let us take an example of the curriculum question, "What should we teach?" The general goal here may be to teach students the use of American language, while a more specific goal could be to teach certain children of the poor[3] how to understand a formal version of this language used by teachers, other children, and textbook writers.[4]

We next answer the descriptive question, "What are we teaching?," by an examination of the current status of curricu-

**TABLE 20.2
An Evaluative Loop**

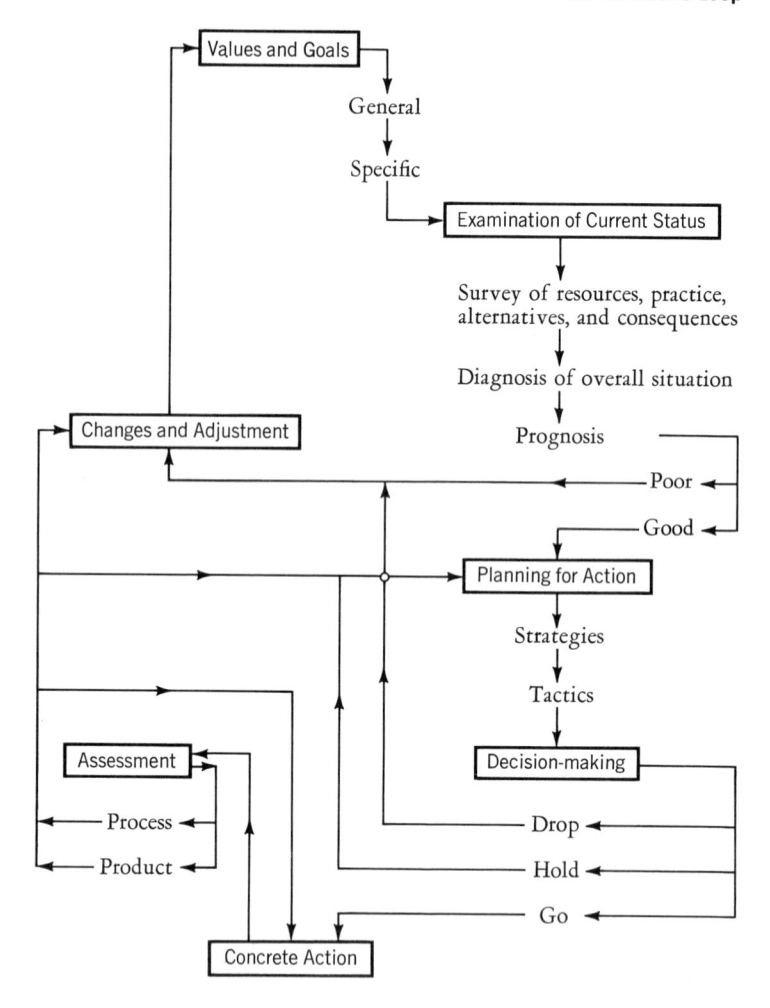

```
Values and Goals
      │
   General
      │
   Specific
      │
      └──→ Examination of Current Status
                    │
           Survey of resources, practice,
           alternatives, and consequences
                    │
           Diagnosis of overall situation
                    │
                 Prognosis
                    ├──── Poor ──→ Changes and Adjustment
                    └──── Good
                           │
                           ↓
                    Planning for Action
                           │
                       Strategies
                           │
                        Tactics
                           │
                    Decision-making
                    ├──── Drop
                    ├──── Hold
                    └──── Go
                           │
                    Concrete Action
                           │
                      Assessment
                    ├──── Process
                    └──── Product
```

lum. To arrive at a diagnosis of the situation, we survey our resources (what different curricula are available to be taught?), practice (what is actually being taught?), alternatives (what other choices are possible in curriculum material, structure, and sequence?), and consequences (what are the possible results of the current practice and of the alternatives?). On the basis of such diagnosis, we derive a prognosis for the original goal, forecasting the probability of reaching it.

Specifically, we may find that no attention has been paid to the possibility of communication difficulty between students of the poor who use a particular vernacular and teachers who use another.[5] No teaching material has been prepared in such informal dialects and a wholesale shifting to the informal language may entail confusion on the part of both teachers and students. It may be advisable for the teacher to find out the kind and extent of such communication gaps on both sides, that is, what he does not understand in children and what they do not understand in him.[6] If the gap is too large, the prognosis for the original intention to teach students to understand teachers' formal vernacular would be poor and, hence, would demand either reformulation of the values and goals or re-examination of the current status, or both.

If, on the other hand, the prognosis is good, we start planning for action, first the overall strategy and next the specific tactics. A gradual transition may be preferred to an outright showdown, while a frank and open comparison of the different languages may be a successful tactic (we call them "police"—you call them "fuzz," etc.).[7] We must use our imagination in making up plans since there is no safe and sure way which is applicable to every teaching situation.

When a plan is ready, we must make a final decision before plunging into action. A re-analysis of the plan and of the overall situation may reveal that we have to drop the particular blueprint at this point. If so, we have to go back to several earlier points and re-loop. Administrative, interpersonal, financial, health, and various other reasons may make it impracticable to execute the action plan. It may have to be held up temporarily, pending further revisions and elaboration.

On the other hand, the decision may be a "go" and the plan can be put into concrete action. Then, both the process and product (results) must be carefully observed and assessed. If things go well, keep the action up; if not, changes and adjustment are necessary to the operation, or its plan, or its goals. In this manner, the entire loop is closed and the self-corrective feature becomes clear. This is why we say evaluation is a crucial component in teaching. Without this closed loop, teaching is reduced to random, haphazard activities.

IN A LOOP

As we have seen, the closed nature of the evaluative loop is important because it provides the only way we can get any feedback from our action. The word, "feedback," should be a familiar one to us, since most physiological functions, mediated by the central nervous system, work on this principle. For example, it is important for a person to be able to hear what he is saying in order for him to adjust his speech continuously to the temporal and situational requirements. For another example, try to remember the feelings of powerlessness and panic you experienced if you have ever had to drive on solid ice at night; in that situation, a minimum of information is fed back through your tactile or visual sense organs, and you realize how much you normally use that feedback to guide you in making corrections.

Not only humans but other animals also depend on information feedback to guide their behavior. It is well known that bats and porpoises, among others, emit high-frequency signals and navigate by judging the feedback, the sounds reflected by other objects standing in their way. Needless to say, this is exactly the mechanism used in our sonars, radars, and guided missile systems. Without such feedback, neither these animals nor many scientific apparatuses would operate successfully.

Another familiar word is "reward" or "reinforcement" in learning. Something is reinforcing precisely because it gives the learner some information concerning his performance, namely, whether he is operating on a right level or plane, whether he is moving in the proper direction, and whether he is traveling at a satisfactory speed. Even though many of us disliked certain aspects of the grade system when we were students, we depended heavily on our teachers' grading to steer our course, and we used to complain bitterly when no information was made available because we could not know what was expected of us and how we were doing. Under the circumstances, our efforts were something like blasting a shotgun in the dark.

So, students need some information from teachers to set up their own goals, to examine their current status, to map out a plan for action, to assess their actual moves, and to make necessary changes and revisions. It is certainly one of our duties to provide whatever feedback is relevant to students' progress and development.

But let us keep in mind that the closed evaluative loop is indispensable, first and foremost, to teachers themselves in their teaching activities. It is not primarily for the sake of students that we ask the normative and descriptive questions. We evaluate teaching, not out of any immediately altruistic motives, but because we will be unable to function as teachers without it. If we think we can teach without engaging at the same time in evaluation, we are deceiving ourselves and we will soon be lost and useless.

It was earlier mentioned that many evaluative efforts are executed informally and even subconsciously. In fact, if evaluation becomes an automatic habit in teaching, and if we can forget about it just as we ordinarily do the presence and role of our autonomic or involuntary nervous system, this will be wonderful. Unfortunately, we tend to forget about evaluation long *before* we have established it as a habit. We must therefore make some conscious efforts to build such activities where there have been few and to recognize the loop clearly where its existence has, till now, been only implied.

By now it has grown apparent that the familiar appraisal activity of test administration and score-reporting is but a fraction of the entire evaluative function performed by teachers. More fundamental questions have to be asked first and any such part operations should be interpreted in the total context of an evaluative loop. The specific methods of assessment to be used are obviously determined by the full sequence and not by whims and fads.

For example, when we answer the normative question on instruction, "How should we teach?," our response may be phrased in terms of some rules (logical, evidential, or social), of certain criteria, or of personal preferences and desires.[8] In each case, a different loop will be planned and executed, and different assessment techniques will be employed. If, therefore, we decide that we should teach according to the rules of deductive logic or discovery method, our assessment will be different from one made in terms of the distribution of time among various subactivities (such as lecture, discussion, prompting, disciplining, etc.). Likewise, if our normative definition is made in reference to the proportion of students surpassing national norms of a standardized achievement-test battery, the techniques used will be quite dissimilar to those adopted when the definition is couched in terms of personal feelings.

Actually, most of these forms of answers are intermixed and, hence, evaluation is seldom complete with a single loop. Both quantitative and qualitative approaches are adopted and judgments are made on both (so-called) objective and subjective bases. Teacher and peer nominations, students' writings and oral reports, observation, anecdotal records, interview results, and projective techniques are as useful as standardized and nonstandardized tests, inventories, course examinations, and grades. A close working relationship with other teachers and parents, as well as with specialists, including remedial teachers, doctors, school nurses, social workers, school counselors, and school psychologists, is obviously desirable. Here, it can easily be seen that public and communicable evaluative efforts are necessary to facilitate each other's work for the ultimate benefit of our students.[9]

By all means, therefore, let us ask the basic questions on teaching and continue to ask them time and again to keep the evaluative loop working well. What, in your mind, is teaching?

FOOTNOTES

[1] See, for example:

Gordon C. Lee. *Education and Democratic Ideals.* New York: Harcourt, Brace & World, 1965.

Israel Scheffler. "Philosophical Models of Teaching," *Harvard Educational Review* 35: 131–143; Spring 1965.

Kaoru Yamamoto. "The Rewards and Results of Teaching," *Education* 87: 67–72; October 1966.

[2] See, for example:

Gunnar Myrdal. *An American Dilemma.* New York: Harper & Brothers, 1944.

Harry Passow, Ed. *Education in Depressed Areas.* New York: Teachers College Press, Teachers College, Columbia University, 1963.

W. Lloyd Warner. *American Life: Dream and Reality.* (rev. ed.) Chicago: University of Chicago Press, 1962.

[3] This presumes our treatment of another set of questions, namely, "Whom should we teach?" and, "Whom are we teaching?" It seems that we usually do well to think of more than one aspect of teaching.

[4] We may further wish to define what is meant by such concepts as "to understand," or "a formal version." The more specific our goals and intentions are, the easier it is to plan for an action, to carry it out, and to assess the results. Often, however, too specific efforts are rendered ineffective because of the absence of consideration of broader factors.

[5] Incidentally, this kind of information comes from activities labeled "research." Research can take many forms but here, in contrast with evaluation, we can ask various questions singly and in their own right. Thus, we can ask, "Who should teach?" or, "Who do you think should teach?," without coupling it with another question, "Who are teaching?" For this reason, it is sometimes said that evaluation needs criteria (the normative question), while research does not. Naturally, we can conduct research on evaluation or do research on research operations themselves.

[6] As for the specific form such a gap takes, see, for example:

Basil Bernstein. "Language and Social Class," *British Journal of Sociology* 11: 271–276; September 1960.

Martin Deutsch. "The Role of Social Class in Language Development and Cognition," *American Journal of Orthopsychiatry* 35: 78–88; January 1965.

Frank Riessman and Frank Alberts. "Digging 'The Man's' Language," *Saturday Review* 49: 80–81 & 98; September 17, 1966.

Estelle Cherry Peisach. "Children's Comprehension of Teacher and Peer Speech," *Child Development* 36: 467–480; June 1965.

[7] Here again we see the close relationships among different sets of questions. The matter of what-to-teach is actually intermeshed with that of how-to-teach and also with the question of whom-to-teach.

[8] The readers may be interested in consulting such references as the following for further discussion of this point:

Milton Meux. "The Evaluating Operation in the Classroom," In Arno A. Bellack, Ed. *Theory and Research in Teaching.* New York: Bureau of Publications, Teachers College, Columbia University, 1963. Pp. 11–24.

Hilda Taba. *Curriculum Development.* New York: Harcourt, Brace & World, 1962.

Fred T. Wilhelms, Ed. *Evaluation as Feedback and Guide.* (1967 ASCD Yearbook) Washington: Association for Supervision and Curriculum Development, 1967.

[9] Meaningful integration of all the information is a skill to be developed through practice. See, for example:

Robert L. Brackenbury. *Getting Down to Cases.* New York: G. P. Putnam's Sons, 1959.

James L. Hymes, Jr. *Behavior and Misbehavior.* Englewood Cliffs, N.J.: Prentice-Hall, 1955.

Bel Kaufman. *Up the Down Staircase.* New York: Avon Books, 1966. (N-130)

Sybil Marshall. *An Experiment in Education.* New York: Cambridge University Press, 1963.

Pauline Sears and Vivian Sherman. *In Pursuit of Self-Esteem.* Belmont, Calif.: Wadsworth Publishing, 1964.

Robert W. White. *Lives in Progress.* (2nd ed.) New York: Holt, Rinehart & Winston, 1966.

TEACHING STYLES AND LEARNING

Daniel Solomon

William E. Bezdek

Larry Rosenberg

There has been no shortage of firm statements about the constituents of good teaching. Their firmness, however, bears no relation to their validity. Some have appeared without benefit of empirical investigation altogether, while others have been nourished by untenable conclusions drawn from inadequate or simply nondefinitive research, or by ambitious generalizations from work in disparate areas—

From Daniel Solomon, William E. Bezdek and Larry Rosenberg. *Teaching Styles and Learning,* published in 1963 by the Center for the Study of Liberal Education for Adults, Chicago, Ill. The selection here is the monograph's Chapter 1, "General Introduction and Summary," pp. 1–9, and is reprinted here with permission. *Teaching Styles and Learning* was based on a Study of Teaching Style undertaken by the Center for the Study of Liberal Education for Adults.

animal psychology, psychoanalysis, group dynamics, nondirective counseling, and pragmatic philosophy. This is not to say that prescriptions for teaching from one or more of these sources may not turn out to be valid; merely that they have not been demonstrated sufficiently.

While much research on teaching has accumulated during the last two or three decades (some of it is reviewed briefly in the next chapter), results have been largely inconclusive. Perhaps it is this inconclusiveness which has encouraged the growth of a variety of different teaching dogmas—if a study can be found denying a position on teaching, another can usually be found which confirms it; if no position can be said to be clearly demonstrated, none can be said to be clearly wrong.

Many things may account for the relatively meager results of so much research. Possibly the teacher's behavior is simply not very important to the students' learning. Or perhaps, in spite of the large number of studies, the proper variables of teacher behavior have not yet been studied, in relation to the proper measures of learning. Our opinion (developed further in the following chapter) is that too many studies have followed along similar lines—with one variant or another of an experimental manipulation and comparison of "teacher-centered" and "student-centered" classes. This experimental approach may have occasioned the neglect of whole classes of behaviors which were neither built into the studies nor observed, because they did not fit within their theoretical frameworks. Thus, important variables may have been overlooked.

Not all studies of teaching have been "experimental," however. In recent years, a small number of studies have attempted to investigate the teacher's behavior as it occurs naturally in the classroom. These have obtained measures on relatively large numbers of specific characteristics of teacher behavior, sometimes with and sometimes without the aid of theoretical predisposition. Some of these studies have used factor analysis to determine underlying dimensions of teacher behavior. While the studies touch on different educational levels, some consistencies do show up in the identified dimensions. Little research exists, however, relating dimensions found in studies such as these to learning.

As far as adult education is concerned, knowledge about teacher behavior and its effects is even less developed than it is for other levels of education; for no research has been done which relates teaching behavior to *adult* learning. The uncertainty about teaching–learning connections which exists for education in general as a *result* of research is, for adult education, much greater due to a *lack* of research.

STRATEGY OF THIS STUDY

The study reported in this paper constitutes the second step in a program of research aimed at identifying the concomitants and determinants of effective teaching for adults.

The earlier study (described fully in Solomon and Miller, 1961*) analyzed interviews with a small number of teachers of adults (who were asked to describe their teaching) into a fairly large number of categories of specific behaviors, perceptions, motives, and objectives of teaching. These categories formed the nucleus of variables measured in the present study. Because part of the purpose was to identify significant dimensions of teacher behavior, a large number of categories of behavior was needed, and other variables derived from theory, our own expectations and hunches, and the results of other studies were therefore also added. The instruments used in the study (reproduced in Appendix C †) will suggest the range of categories involved.

This study looked at teachers in their "natural setting." But even after deciding on this milieu, at least two strategies were possible: to study teachers of many different courses, in many different types of adult classes; or to study a set of classes as similar as possible in all respects but the teacher. The first would be building on the earlier study, substituting more direct observation for the teachers' self-reports. Its primary advantage would be that it would be exposed to a broad range of teacher behaviors, and would lead to the development of hypotheses about similarities and differences in teacher behavior across quite different types and levels of adult education. Its major disadvantage would be the difficulty (with any but a huge, and

---

Editor's Notes

* D. Solomon and H. L. Miller. *Explorations in Teaching Styles*. Chicago: Center for the Study of Liberal Education for Adults, 1961.

† This appendix, here omitted, includes the following five exhibits.
　　　Exhibit 1—Teacher Behavior Rating Scale,
　　　　　　　2—Tape Analysis Dimensions and Instrument,
　　　　　　　3—Student Questionnaire,
　　　　　　　4—CSLEA Teacher Questionnaire, and
　　　　　　　5—American Government Examination.

therefore impracticable, sample) of obtaining comparable measures of learning across classes. The second strategy, allowing for control of more of the variables, and therefore for more precise comparisons of the outcomes of classes of various teachers, seemed more advisable, at the present stage of knowledge in this area. Once evidence of relationships between teaching behavior and student learning is relatively clear for one course, extensions can be made, in further research, to other courses, levels, student bodies, etc.

The requirement of a fairly large number of very similar adult classes sent us to evening colleges, to look for an introductory credit course. The hope was that we would find a sufficient number of sections of a single course at one school for the entire study. Since this did not turn out to be the case, we selected a course—introductory American Government—which had as many sections in a school as any other course, and which seemed to have more similarity in the material covered between the classes in different schools than did most other courses. The fact that there would be a great age range in these classes did not seem undesirable, since it would make possible comparisons of the effectiveness of various types of teacher behavior for students of different ages, findings which could be of great importance to adult education.

METHODS USED

Twenty-four teachers of evening courses in introductory American Government were involved in the study, ten of them from one school (a large, eastern, urban college), the rest distributed among various midwestern colleges and universities, with no more than two teachers at any one of them.

The general plan of the study was to obtain measures on a large number of specific behaviors of the teachers, as well as certain of their objectives for the course, and some motives relevant to teaching. These various measures were then analyzed for the groupings or patterns which occurred among them, as a means of reducing them to a smaller number of dimensions or *factors;* later, teachers' scores on each of the factors were related to learning measures.

Measures of the teachers' behaviors were obtained from three sources: the students, trained observers, and tape recordings. Teams of *two observers* each visited two classes of each instructor during the middle of the semester. They watched the teacher's behavior carefully, and made ratings on 38 items immediately after the class was over. The rating instrument (Appendix C, Exhibit 1) contained 8 point scales for such items as "teacher's direct control," "threatening behavior," "understanding," and "sensitivity." The second visit to each class was made by a different team of observers from the first, so that impressions gained on the first visit would not influence the observations on the second. A comparison of the ratings made on the two visits showed generally similar results between the two sets of ratings, indicating both that the measures were fairly reliable and that the teachers' behavior, as measured by this instrument, was relatively stable between these two sessions.

The same two class sessions were *tape recorded*. From these recordings, the speech of teacher and students was scored according to a limited number of categories (such as "interpretation statements," "factual statements," etc.), and various proportions and ratios involving these categories were computed. Examples of the instrument used, and the definitions of the categories can be found in Exhibit 2 of Appendix C.

Student descriptions of the teacher's behavior were requested in a fairly long questionnaire (Exhibit 3, Appendix C) distributed toward the close of the semester. The items in this questionnaire asked for statements about intensity or frequency of various behaviors of the teacher over the course of the entire semester. Some items in this questionnaire were: "Was the instructor usually easy-going and informal?" "Did he ever criticize students in class?" "Were the points he made clear and easy to understand?" There were 52 such descriptive items, and another eight items which asked the students to evaluate the instructor, the course, the amount of learning achieved, and the interest developed.

Although the emphasis in the study was on teachers' behavior, another, much shorter questionnaire was given to the *teachers* at the end of the semester to assess their feelings about possible objectives for the course and motivations toward teaching (see Exhibit 4, Appendix C).

FACTOR ANALYSIS

These instruments together produced 169 different items referring to the behavior of each of the teachers. A Univac factor analysis program handled the next phase of our analysis. Factor analysis is used to reduce a large number of variables to a relatively small number of hypothetical underlying constructs. The analysis shows which variables tend to cluster together and, assuming that variables cluster together because they all possess something in common, tries to determine (through inspection of these variables) how best to describe that "something."

In the present study the factor analysis produced eight factors, representing eight clusters of variables. The following factor "names" represent the descriptions which seemed best to encompass the variables in each of the clusters. (A detailed rationale for the label assigned to each factor appears in chapter four.)

Factor 1—*Permissiveness vs. Control*
Factor 2—*Lethargy vs. Energy*
Factor 3—*Aggressiveness vs. Protectiveness*
Factor 4—*Obscurity, Vagueness vs. Clarity, Expressiveness*
Factor 5—*Encouragement of Content-Related (factual) Student Participation vs. Nonencouragement of Participation; Emphasis on Student Growth*
Factor 6—*Dryness vs. Flamboyance*
Factor 7—*Encouragement of Students' Expressive Participation vs. Lecturing*
Factor 8—*Warmth vs. Coldness*

Scores were computed for each teacher on each factor. These show the extent to which the teacher manifests the behavior represented by the variables strongly associated with each of the factors. Finally, the scores were related to several measures of learning.

MEASURES OF LEARNING

In addition to the student evaluations already mentioned, the amount of learning achieved was measured by a multiple-choice test (Exhibit 5, Appendix C) given both at the beginning and end of the semester. This test had two parts: part one (35 items) measured factual information; part two (10 items) assessed the students' comprehension of a difficult passage. Students' scores on each part were derived by subtracting the post-test score from the pre-test score.

FINDINGS

The relationships between the elements of teaching style (represented by scores on the various factors) and the students' learning were explored in three kinds of analyses.

1. Teacher scores on each factor were correlated with class means for each of the learning measures to assess direct, linear

relationships between teacher behavior and student learning.

2. On the possibility that there might be nonlinear relationships between teachers' scores on some of the factors and student learning, a series of *chi*-square analyses were made using the students' individual scores instead of the class means used in the correlational analysis. This analysis divided the sample of teachers into upper, middle, and lower thirds according to their scores on each factor, and compared the relative amount of learning of students in each of these groups. A nonlinear relationship would exist, for example, if students did poorly with teachers at the two extremes on a factor, but well with those in the middle range; or, well with those at the extremes and poorly with those in the middle.

3. Finally, an analysis of variance enabled us to look for interactions between teachers' factor scores and certain student and classroom characteristics, in their influence on learning. In this way we hoped to find out whether students of certain types, or in certain types of classes, were affected more favorably than others by any of the kinds or styles of behavior represented in the factors. This analysis also gave additional evidence on those direct effects which were independent of interactions.

The *direct relationships* investigated in these analyses seemed generally to fit together plausibly. Gains in factual information were related to teachers' scores on Factors 4 ("... clarity, expressiveness") and 7 ("... lecturing"). (In each case the pole of the dimension mentioned is the one which proved to be effective.) In our judgment, these factors represent behaviors and qualities of behavior which provide the most efficient way for a teacher to present and transmit *factual* material. Gains on the *comprehension* test, on the other hand, were associated with a moderate position on the permissiveness-control continuum (Factor 1), and with the "energy," "aggressiveness" and "flamboyance" poles of Factors 2, 3 and 6. It is our opinion that these four factors may have in common the function of activating the student's personal involvement with the topic, thereby encouraging him to think about it, deal with it abstractly, and understand its complexities.

Students gave most favorable evaluations to teachers whose scores on Factors 4 and 8 indicated "warmth" and "clarity" respectively.

The analysis of the effect on learning of *interactions between teacher behaviors and certain individual and environmental characteristics* produced results somewhat more resistant to interpretation. With respect to comprehension, the measure of gains showed no significant relationships.

With regard to gains in factual learning, however, we found several significant interactions. Students with *jobs* did best with teachers who were relatively aggressive, and who emphasized students' factual participation. *Women* did best in classes of teachers who scored high on the "lecturing" dimension. Students below the *age* of 19 learned most factual information from teachers who emphasized student growth; those 19 and over, with teachers who emphasized student factual participation.

Class size was involved in a larger number of significant interactions than any of the other variables, and seemed to produce a more consistent pattern of relationships. Students in large classes learned factual material best with teachers who were permissive, who emphasized student growth, were "warm," and were "flamboyant"; while students in small classes did best with teachers who lectured, were relatively "dry," and emphasized student factual participation. In small classes, students can perhaps depend on each other for various social-emotional gratifications, and the teacher's appropriate role can be to lecture and give factual emphasis. In large classes, however, student social interaction may be less in evidence, and the effective teacher must take on himself some of these functions.

IMPLICATIONS AND LIMITATIONS

Although the results of this study are encouraging, it would be decidedly premature to attempt to make specific applications. A persistent thread in the skein of behavioral research is the failure of repeated studies to bear out original findings. The small sample in the present study requires that we maintain an attitude of some doubt as to the reliability and replicability of the findings, and the degree to which the findings are representative even of teachers of evening American Government courses.

Certain idiosyncracies in the conditions of the present study also suggest caution in dealing with the findings. The study was done at a particular time (during a presidential election), at particular schools, and with certain unavoidable discrepancies between the testing situations in the different classes. The degree to which any or all of these factors may have influenced the results is not known. The only way to achieve relative satisfaction on this point is to repeat the study in other situations, with other sets of idiosyncratic conditions.

The limitation of the sample to a particular kind of course also severely straitens the generalizations which can be made as a result of this study. In further research, we hope both to repeat and to extend the investigations initiated in this study, so that the reliability of the present findings can be specified with certainty, and the degree to which differences occur in different course areas, with different kinds of students, can be ascertained.

Should the present results hold up after further research, we believe they may well have interesting implications for practice in adult education, and perhaps for college instruction in general. The fact that gains in comprehension and in factual information tended to be influenced by different types of teacher behavior, seems to suggest strongly that teachers need to be very clear about their course objectives. Some of our results, particularly as developed in the case studies at the end of the report, seem to indicate that there are a number of ways to achieve a particular objective. Thus, one teacher, neither "flamboyant" nor "energetic," was within the intermediate range on the "permissiveness-control" dimension (a range associated with gains in comprehension in the statistical analysis), and had a class which ranked very high on comprehension learning. When the variety of relationships are known with greater assurance, it may be possible to help teachers develop those aspects of their natural behavior most compatible with one or more types of behavior, out of a larger number of possibilities, all of which relate to a particular objective. If it should be found that certain behaviors or styles are more suited for some groups of students than others (as for instance adults, and there are some indications of this in the present study), it may be possible eventually to select teachers particularly suitable for particular audiences, or to help teachers develop the styles most suited for particular audiences.

THEORIES OF TEACHING

N. L. Gage

The thesis of this chapter is that theories of learning will have greater usefulness to education when they are transformed into theories of teaching.[1] This thesis rests upon an assumption as to the present usefulness of learning theory in education and upon a distinction between theories of learning and theories of teaching. Let us examine each of these ideas.

First, the limited usefulness of learning theory in education has long been acknowledged. Estes, writing on "Learning" in the *Encyclopedia of Educational Research,* judged that "no convergence is imminent between the educator's and the laboratory scientist's approaches to learning," and he was able to report

---

From N. L. Gage, "Theories of Teaching." In Ernest Hilgard, Ed. *Theories of Learning and Instruction* (63rd Yearbook of the National Society for the Study of Education, Part I). Chicago: University of Chicago Press, 1964. Pp. 268–285.

little progress "toward bridging the gap between laboratory psychology and the study of school learning."[2] Near the close of his *Theories of Learning,* Hilgard stated, "... It is not surprising, therefore, that the person seeking advice from the learning theorist often comes away disappointed."[3] Educational psychology textbooks usually include treatments of learning that draw in general terms upon learning theories. But these treatments bear only slight resemblance to the elaborations of the theories as portrayed in Hilgard's book.

Second, our thesis embodies a basic distinction between theories of learning and theories of teaching. While theories of learning deal with the ways in which an organism learns, theories of teaching deal with the ways in which a person influences an organism to learn.

To rephrase the thesis: Although theories of learning are necessary to the understanding, prediction, and control of the learning process, they cannot suffice in education. The goal of education—to engender learning in the most desirable and efficient ways possible—would seem to require an additional science and technology of teaching. To satisfy the practical demands of education, theories of learning must be "stood on their head" so as to yield theories of teaching.

In this chapter, we shall attempt to support this thesis by considering (a) the need for theories of teaching, (b) the need for analysis and specification of teaching in developing such theories, (c) some illustrative analyses and specifications of teaching, and (d) the kinds of research that might yield improved empirical bases for theories of teaching.

THE NEED FOR THEORIES OF TEACHING

That theories of teaching are needed in addition to theories of learning may seem in the main to require no argument. Yet, the development of theories of teaching has been neglected. In comparison with learning, teaching goes almost unmentioned in the theoretical writings of psychologists. Many signs of this disregard can be observed. For example, *Psychological Abstracts* contains large sections on laboratory learning and school learning but only a small section on teaching, and that within the section on "Educational Personnel." The *Annual Review of Psychology* usually includes a chapter on learning but seldom more than a few paragraphs on teaching. Volumes have been devoted to theories of learning, but not a single book deals exclusively with theories of teaching. Textbooks of educational psychology give much more space to discussions of learning and the learner than to methods of teaching and the teacher. *A Comprehensive Dictionary of Psychological and Psychoanalytical Terms* has three pages, containing 50 entries, concerned with learning but devotes only five lines to "Teaching" as follows: "The art of assisting another to learn. It includes the providing of information (instruction) and of appropriate situations, conditions, or activities designed to facilitate learning."[4]

Reasons for the Neglect The reasons for the neglect of theories of teaching are in themselves of interest. Examining these reasons may help determine whether such theories are possible of formulation and are desirable.

Art vs. science—Sometimes the attempt to develop theories of teaching is seen as implying the development of a science of teaching. Yet, some writers reject the notion of a science of teaching. Highet entitled his book *The Art of Teaching,*

> ... because I believe that teaching is an art, not a science. It seems to me very dangerous to apply the aims and methods of science to human beings as individuals, although a statistical principle can often be used to explain their behavior in large groups and a scientific diagnosis of their physical structure is always valuable.... Of course it is necessary for any teacher to be orderly in planning his work and precise in his dealing with facts. But that does not make his teaching "scientific." Teaching involves emotions, which cannot be systematically appraised and employed, and human values, which are quite outside the grasp of science. "Scientific" teaching, even of scientific subjects, will be inadequate as long as both teachers and pupils are human beings. Teaching is not like inducing a chemical reation: It is much more like painting a picture or making a piece of music, or on a lower level like planting a garden or writing a friendly letter.[5]

Highet's argument would, of course, also militate against the development of a science of learning. His argument against a science of teaching need not be considered to apply to a theory of teaching. We should not equate the attempt to develop a theory about an activity with the attempt to eliminate its phenomenal, idiosyncratic, and artistic aspects. Painting and composing, and even friendly letter-writing and casual conversation, have inherent order and lawfulness that can be subjected to theoretical analysis. The painter, despite the artistry immanent in his work, often can be shown by students of his art to be behaving according to a theory—of color, perspective, balance, or abstraction. The artist whose lawfulnesses are revealed does not become an automaton; ample scope remains for his subtlety and individuality. His processes and products need not remain immune to attempts at rational understanding on the part of critics and scholars.

So it is with teaching. Although teaching requires artistry, it can be subjected to scientific scrutiny. The power to explain, predict, and control that may result from such scrutiny will not dehumanize teaching. Just as engineers can still exercise ingenuity within the theory of thermodynamics, teachers will have room for artistic variation on the theory that scientific study of teaching may establish. And for the work of those who train, hire, and supervise teachers, theory and empirical knowledge of teaching will provide scientific grounding.

Even if it had no practical value, a scientific understanding of teaching should still be sought. Like interstellar space and evolution, learning has been studied for its own sake. So teaching can be studied as a phenomenon of interest in its own right. Theories of teaching are desirable because of their practical value if it is forthcoming, but desirable in any case.

Presumed adequacy of learning theory—The need for theories of teaching stems also from the insufficiency *in principle* of theories of learning. Theories of learning deal with what the learner does. But changes in education must depend in large part upon what the teacher does. That is, changes in how learners go about their business of learning occur in response to the behavior of their teachers or others in the educational establishment. Much of our knowledge about learning can be put into practice only by teachers. And the ways in which these teachers would put this knowledge into effect constitute part of the subject of theories of teaching. Our position is that practical applications have not been gleaned from theories of learning largely because theories of teaching have not been developed. The implications of learning theory need to be translated into implications for the behavior of teachers. Teachers will then act on these implications in such ways as to improve learning. Theories of teaching and the empirical study of teaching may enable us to make better use of our knowledge about learning.

Is there any room for theory of teaching? Or, on the other hand, is theory of learning and behavior so all-encompassing as to preclude any valid concern with theory of teaching? Hilgard pointed out that Hull "scarcely distinguishes between a theory of learning and a theory of behavior, so important is learning in his conception of behavior.... Hence the systematic aspects of learning theory have come to be important to all psychologists interested in more general theories."[6] Because teaching is a form of behavior, adequate theories of learning, or general theories of behavior, would, in this view, encompass teaching as well. But this view applies only to teaching considered as the "dependent variable," the thing to be explained. In this sense, the behavior of teachers will indeed be understood by the same theories that apply to the behavior and learning of pupils. The kind of theory of teaching with which we are concerned places the behavior of teachers in the position of "independent variables" as a function of which the learning of pupils is to be explained. That is, theories of teaching should be concerned with explaining, predicting, and controlling the ways in which teacher behavior affects the learning of pupils. In this perspective there is ample room for theories of teaching. Such theories would deal with a whole realm of phenomena neglected by theories of learning.

It might be objected that, with learning as the dependent variable, theories of teaching become only a subclass of theories of learning: a subclass in which the independent variables consist of the behavior and characteristics of teachers. Such a conception of theories of teaching seems altogether admissible within the thesis of this chapter; it would not change the major argument. Theories of teaching would still need to be developed as a substantial discipline, even if not co-ordinate with theories of learning.

The two kinds of theory must ultimately, of course, be strongly connected; theories of learning will have many implications for theories of teaching. But that is another matter. These implications will become clear as the study of teaching develops. As will be illustrated, the psychology of learning has much to offer the person who attempts to formulate the ways in which teaching proceeds.

The Demands of Teacher Education Explicit concern with the theory of teaching should benefit teacher education. In training teachers, we often seem to rely on mere inference from theory of learning to the practice of teaching. Yet, what we know about learning is inadequate to tell us what we should do about teaching. This inadequacy is clearly evident in our educational psychology courses and textbooks. The irrepressible question of students in educational psychology courses is, "How should I teach?" While they may infer a partial answer from a consideration of how pupils learn, they cannot get all of it in this way. Much of what teachers must know about teaching does not directly follow from a knowledge of the learning process. Their knowledge must be acquired explicitly rather than by inference. Farmers need to know more than how plants grow. Mechanics need to know more than how a machine works. Physicians need to know more than how the body functions. Teachers need to know more than how a pupil learns.

Teachers must know how to manipulate the independent variables, especially their own behaviors, that determine learning. Such knowledge cannot be derived automatically from knowledge about the learning process. To explain and control the teaching act requires a science and technology of teaching in its own right. The student of educational psychology who complains that he has learned much about learning and learners, but not about teaching, is asking for the fruits of scientific inquiry, including theories of teaching.

THE NEED FOR ANALYSIS AND SPECIFICATION

How should work toward such theory proceed? In this section, we advocate the analysis and specification of teaching. Then we consider some sketches of what such analysis and specification might lead to.

The Misleadingly Generic Term, "Teaching" As a concept, teaching sorely needs analysis. Such analysis should clarify the concerns of theories of teaching. For "teaching" is a misleadingly generic term; it covers too much. It falsely suggests a single, unitary phenomenon that may fruitfully be made the subject of theory development.

It may fairly be argued that learning theory has long been hung up on a similar fallacy. Because the term "learning" has been applied to an enormous range of phenomena, psychologists have been misled into believing that a single theory can be developed to explain all these phenomena. Animal learning in puzzle boxes and Skinner boxes, human learning of nonsense syllables and eyelid responses in the laboratory, and the learning of school subjects in classrooms have all been termed "learning." And, because all these activities have been given the same name, psychologists have attempted to account for all of them by a single, unified, general theory.

Yet, as is well known, after more than a half-century of effort, no such unification of learning theory has materialized. Research and theorizing on learning have had three main foci—animal learning, human learning in the laboratory, and human learning in the classroom. (In recent years, a fourth focus has developed: programed learning. In time this new development may strengthen the connection between the laboratory and the school.) The various kinds of learning have not been embraced successfully by any single learning theory. And this failure may well stem from the false belief that a single term, "learning," guarantees that a single, universally applicable theory of learning can be found.

Some analogies to other processes may clarify this point. Medicine does not search for a single theory of illness or healing. Physicians long ago discovered that people can get sick in several basically different ways, such as being infected with germs or viruses, having organic malfunctions, suffering traumatic impacts of energy, or experiencing environmental deprivations. And, rather than a general theory of healing, physicians use several different approaches, such as giving medicines, using surgery, improving environments, or changing diets.

Another example is "getting rich," which is, like learning, concerned with the acquisition of something. Getting rich also takes place in many different ways—inheriting, gambling, stealing, making profits, or earning wages—and no one has tried to develop a general, unified theory of how to get rich. The concept of "getting rich" simply has no scientific value; it covers too many different processes. Perhaps we should consider the possibility that, as a unitary concept, school learning has no scientific value either, because it covers too many distinct phenomena and processes.

The same then might be said of teaching. The term "teaching" should not be taken to imply that teaching is a basic process to which a general theory may apply. For "teaching" embraces far too many kinds of process, of behavior, of activity, to be the proper subject of a single theory. We must not be misled by the one word, "teaching," into searching for one theory to explain it.

If this argument is valid, the concept of teaching must be analyzed to reveal processes or elements that might constitute the proper subject of theories. What kinds of analysis can be made? Several can be suggested.

First, teaching can be analyzed according to types of teacher *activities*. Teachers engage in explaining activities, mental hygiene activities, demonstrating activities, guidance activities, order-maintaining activities, housekeeping activities, record-keeping activities, assignment-making activities, curriculum-planning activities, testing and evaluation activities, and many other kinds of activities. If everything a teacher does *qua* teacher is teaching, then teaching consists of many kinds of activity. It is unreasonable to expect a single theory to encompass all of these.

Second, teaching can be analyzed according to the types of *educational objectives* at which it is aimed; examples of major types are affective, psychomotor, and cognitive objectives. Thus, teaching processes can be classified according to the domain of objectives to which they seem primarily relevant. When the teacher uses words to define, describe, or explain a concept, such as "extrapolation," his behavior may be primarily relevant to cognitive objectives. When he offers warmth and encouragement, we may consider him to be acting in ways primarily relevant to the affective domain. When he demonstrates the correct way to write a capital F, his behavior may be primarily relevant to psychomotor objectives. At any given moment, more than one of these domains of objectives may be affected. It may sometimes be difficult to distinguish the teacher's influence on cognitive change from his influence on affective change in pupils. So, when the teacher fails to explain something clearly, the pupil may become not only confused (cognitively) but discouraged (affectively) as well. Nonetheless, analyses of this kind may have strategic value. At any rate, we should not assume that a single theory of teaching will apply to all kinds of objectives.

A third way to analyze teaching stems from the notion that teaching can be viewed as the obverse, or "mirror image," of learning and therefore has *components corresponding to those of learning*. If the learning process can be analyzed into basic elements or components—let us use Neal Miller's "drive," "cue," "response," and "reward" as examples—then teaching can be analyzed similarly. Corresponding components of teaching might be "motivation-producing," "perception-directing," "response-eliciting," and "reinforcement-providing." For some elements of Miller's analysis of learning, there are well-established separate domains of theory, such as theories of motivation and theories of perception. Similarly, theories of motivating, perception-directing, response-eliciting, and rewarding, corresponding to such elements of the teaching process, may develop. In any event, it is questionable whether a single theory of teaching should be sought to encompass all these components of the teaching process.

A fourth way to analyze teaching, not entirely distinct from those already mentioned, derives from *families of learning theory*. These families may be illustrated by "conditioning theory," "identification theory," and "cognitive theory." Some theorists (e.g., Mowrer [7]) conceive learning, in all its forms, to be a matter of conditioning with punishment or rewards consisting of primary or secondary reinforcements associated with independent or response-dependent stimulation. Such a conditioning theory of learning may imply a corresponding kind of theory of teaching. Other theorists (e.g., Bandura [8]) emphasize that learning consists, at least in major part, of the learner's identification with a model, whom the learner imitates. In this case, a second kind of theory of teaching is implied. A third kind of theorist (e.g., Luchins [9]) holds that learning consists of the cognitive restructuring of problematical situations. Here, a third kind of theory of teaching is suggested.

It is conceivable that all three of these major families of learning theory are valid, for different kinds of persons learning different things in different situations. Any reductionism, or attempt to derive the other two from any one of these, may yield only a spurious parsimony. The three kinds of theory seem at present to be compatible, in the sense that they at least do not lead to different predictions about the same data. Rather, they seem to have been developed to account for different data—for the learning of different kinds of things in different situations. If so, all three approaches to the development of theory of teaching should be of some value.

Illustrative Specifications We have suggested the bases for four different analyses of teaching: (a) types of teacher activities, (b) types of educational objectives, (c) components of the learning process, and (d) families of learning theory. We have also suggested that no single theory of teaching should be offered that would attempt to account for all activities of teachers, would be aimed at all objectives of education, and would involve all components of the learning process, in a way that would satisfy all theories of learning. To comply with our call for specification, we should now at least sketch what a theory of teaching might be concerned with, if it is to become specific. To do so, we shall make various selections from among the products of our analyses.

Selection One—From the teacher's activities, let us select the one called explaining, leaving aside for the moment the mental hygiene, demonstrating, and other activities. Of the types of objectives, let us choose to focus on the cognitive domain, and, even more specifically, on the student's ability to extrapolate trends beyond the given data. Of the components of the learning process, let us choose the perceptual, or the teacher's corresponding function of directing the student's perceptions to the salient part of his environment, which, in the present instance, consists of the kinds of trends in data that we want him to learn to extrapolate. And finally, of the families of learning theory in accordance with which we wish to derive a theory of teaching, let us choose the cognitive restructuring approach.

At this point, having made these choices, we should be in a better position to develop a theory of teaching. Having eliminated many realms of phenomena from our concern, we have cut the problem down to size. We may still be a long way from our goal, but not so far as before.

Of the several choices we have made, the most arguable one is that of the cognitive restructuring as against the conditioning or the identification paradigms of learning and, hence, of teaching. The cognitive restructuring paradigm of learning holds that the learner arrives at knowledge and understanding by perceiving the situation (the problem) before him and then rearranging it, through central cognitive processes, in ways that yield meaning of a rational, logically consistent kind. The teacher can engender this restructuring by pointing to, either physically or verbally, and by manipulating the parts of the cognitive configuration so as to make the structure he wants learned stand out as a kind of figure against the ground of irrelevancies and distractions. The teacher manipulates the cognitive field in accordance with laws of cognition—analogous to the laws of perception governing the constancies, groupings, and whole-qualities in visual and auditory stimuli. Then the pupil apprehends the cognitive structure to be learned. He can no more avoid learning in this instance than he can avoid seeing phi-phenomenon (the appearance of motion when two lights are flashed in brief succession) under proper conditions.

This conception of teaching follows the metaphor of the manipulator of stimuli who *compels* perceivers to see the stimuli in certain ways. Following certain principles of, say, similarity and proximity, we can compel a person to see a configuration of dots as falling into rows rather than columns. Similarly, following certain principles of cognitive structure, the teacher can "compel" his students to understand the principles of extrapolation.

Can we justify the rejection of the conditioning and identification paradigms for this kind of teaching? The conditioning paradigm seems to fall short simply because such teaching does not proceed by successive approximation of responses to the

THEORIES OF TEACHING
N. L. Gage

objective, as is implied by the term "shaping behavior." The teacher does not get the pupil to move gradually toward correct extrapolating behavior by feeding him stimuli that gradually take on the form of the problem to be understood, eliciting responses that gradually approximate what is correct, and providing reinforcement appropriately along the way. Rather, the teacher can often produce the desired behavior all at once by judiciously restructuring the student's cognitive field.

As for the identification paradigm in this instance, it would hold that the teacher gets his results by being prestigious or positively cathected. Why do we reject this approach to understanding the teaching of a logically consistent set of ideas? The identification approach implies that prestigious models can succeed in teaching even logically inconsistent or invalid ideas. But it is unlikely that the model can get a learner to imitate behavior that the learner can plainly perceive to be logically or cognitively inconsistent. (Asch's conformity-producing group-pressure situations seem to produce mere compliance rather than learning, since much of the yielding disappears in private retests.[10]) Much of what we teach has an iron logic of its own; mathematics is a prime example. *To the degree that the content is logically structured,* the learner will be influenced by the structure rather than by his human model.

Selection Two—Let us now try another fairly likely combination of the components resulting from our analyses. From the teacher's activities, let us select his mental-hygiene function. From the types of educational objectives, let us select one from the affective domain, such as the pupil's emotional security in the classroom situation. Of the components of the learning process, let us choose the motivational one, or the teacher's corresponding function of arousing in the pupil a desire to learn what the teacher wants him to learn. And finally, of the families of learning theory, let us choose conditioning.

For this particular selection of specifications, we should pay particular attention to the teacher's acts of rewarding the pupil's provisional tries. Dispensing praise and warmth, almost without regard to what the pupil does so long as it remains within classroom requirements, the teacher positively reinforces the pupil's efforts to comply with the teacher's demands for effort and activity. Basking in a shower of laudatory remarks and approving glances, the pupil gradually comes out of his shell. He shows evidence of improved security.

Why do we select the conditioning approach here and reject cognitive restructuring or identification? In this instance, what has to be learned has no particular cognitive structure. No set of logically organized ideas has to be grasped by the pupil. The goal of getting the pupil to feel secure enough to respond in the classroom cannot readily be achieved, as we all know, through any process of rational explanation or intellectual argument.

We reject the identification approach because the goal in this instance is not to get the pupil to behave the way the teacher does. The kinds of emotional security and activity that the pupil should exhibit in the classroom cannot be achieved through a process of imitating the teacher's security and activity. Indeed, the teacher's confidence and high activity may be precisely what overwhelms the pupil and causes him to withdraw into nonparticipation. For this particular combination of (a) mental-hygiene activity, (b) affective objective, and (c) motivational component of the learning process, it is not the pupil's identification with the teacher that will bring about the security we want. It is rather the teacher's consistent reinforcement, by the conditioning paradigm of the teaching process, that will gradually "shape" the pupil's behavior into a form bespeaking emotional security.

Selection Three—A third selection from the components of our analyses of teaching will illustrate a still different version of a theory of teaching. Suppose we select the teacher's demonstrating activities, aimed at psychomotor objectives, with special concern for the response component of the learning process. For example, let us consider the teacher's activity in demonstrating the proper way to write the capital letter F in attempting to teach handwriting. Here it seems appropriate to emphasize the identification-imitation paradigm of the teaching process. The teacher goes to the blackboard and writes the letter F with the motions that he wants his pupils to adopt as their own. The teacher's prestige makes his way of performing this task unquestionably correct in the eyes of his pupils. His pupils watch him do it and then do it themselves. Depending on the maturity of their psychomotor skills, their success may be complete or partial. But given sufficient maturity, the pupils will write the letter F with the motions that the teacher wants them to use. The pupils make responses matching those of the teacher. Their imitation involves combining responses into relatively complex new patterns solely by observing the performance of another person.

In this instance, let us again assume that what is to be learned has no necessary logic. Many different ways of writing the letter

F could be defended on rational grounds. Thus, the teacher does not carry out his task by explaining the reasons for a particular solution of the problem of how to write the letter. He does not derive his solution by building on earlier conclusions or premises. He has no ideational structure for his pupils to incorporate into their own thinking. Hence, the notion of teaching by cognitive restructuring does not seem to apply to this particular form of teaching.

We reject the conditioning approach here because it would entail a highly inefficient kind of gradual approximation to the desired behavior. To proceed through a painstaking process of response differentiation and extinction, gradually reinforcing desired bits of writing behavior and extinguishing the undesired ones, would be a wearisome and ineffective undertaking. It seems better to characterize the teaching process in this instance as a matter of inducing imitation of what is demonstrated by a prestigious model with whom the pupil identifies.

The foregoing may not represent the most fruitful ways of analyzing the concept of teaching. Other analyses, yielding different components, are clearly possible. Other combinations of resulting components may be more interesting to other persons seeking to develop theories of teaching. The point is that some such analyses and choices must be made before the properly specified concern of a theory can be isolated. Otherwise, attempts to develop theories of teaching will founder on excessive generality. To avoid such analyses and choices is to assume that the single word *teaching* denotes a single process amenable to a single, general theory. That kind of assumption has led to the present chasm between the purportedly general theories of learning developed in psychological laboratories and the kind of learning that goes on in schools. Although learning the Morse code, learning political attitudes, and learning mathematics are all called "learning," they do not necessarily involve the same kind of process. And, because the teaching of all these things is called by the one name of teaching, it does not follow that a single theory of teaching will account for how the teacher does his work.

CONNECTIONS BETWEEN THEORY AND RESEARCH ON TEACHING

Theories not only reflect past experience but also shape future research. Often the main value of a theory lies in the new kinds of research it generates. Throughout the history of psychology, new empirical work, revealing new phenomena and processes, has followed upon new theories. Theories of motivation, perception, and learning have had this effect, and, similarly, the development of theories of teaching may stimulate new kinds of research with variables that have been neglected previously.

This kind of development can be seen in current research on programmed learning. Many new variables have been given experimental attention in studies of programed learning as a result of the development of reinforcement theory. Prompting, construction versus selection of responses, overtness of response, and a variety of reinforcement techniques are now being studied. Some of these variables had been identified previously, but they now take new forms, more relevant to meaningful learning in classrooms.

What impact will the development of theories of teaching have on research? Only research effort will tell. But some conjectures may be warranted. Such conjectures are intended to stimulate explicit concern with theories of teaching of the kind urged in this chapter. Some of the new research movements briefly described below are already under way and serve as illustrations of promising developments.

Teaching as cognitive restructuring—Theories of teaching as cognitive restructuring focus on the teacher's behavior as a manipulator of ideas. Such theories concentrate research attention on the intellectual structures that characterize what is to be taught. This emphasis was occasionally evident in the research on teaching done in the 1930's and '40's. Studies of cognitive development and learning, such as those by Piaget, have long been available. But manifestations of a growing concern with the teacher's role in fostering such learning have only recently begun to appear. As Ausubel and Fitzgerald put it, "The importance of cognitive structure variables has been generally underestimated in the past because preoccupation with noncognitive, rote, and motor types of learning has tended to focus attention on such current situational and intrapersonal factors as task, practice, drive, incentive, and reinforcement variables." [11]

Some recent research on teaching conceived as cognitive restructuring may be mentioned to illustrate the kinds of variables brought to the fore by such an orientation. Smith has directed a study [12] of the logical operations of secondary-school teachers and students; he and his co-workers have described and analyzed such logical operations as defining, designating, classifying, explaining, and evaluating.

Another kind of research concerned with cognitive variables in teaching is illustrated by the work of Runkel,[13] who was concerned with a relationship, termed "collinearity," between the teacher's dimensions of thought and those of his students. Collinearity differs from similarity in that it indicates whether the dimensions or factors used in evaluating a set of objects might be the same even though the rank order of the objects in the evaluations given by two persons might be quite different. For example, two persons might evaluate a number of suits of clothing on the same bases (color, cut, and price) as underlying dimensions, even though they assign quite different rank orders to the suits. Runkel found evidence that, the greater the collinearity of students and teachers, the higher the achievement of the students as judged by the teachers. The finding was attributed to better communication between teachers and students when their cognitive structures were collinear.

A third style of research on cognitive variables in teaching is exemplified in studies by Suchman, who has been developing methods of training children in scientific inquiry,[14] that is, methods of increasing the number of valid questions children ask in seeking explanations of elementary scientific phenomena demonstrated in a film.

A final example is provided by the work of Ausubel,[15] who used organizers (i.e., "advanced introductory material at a high level of abstraction, generality, and inclusiveness") to influence various attributes of cognitive structure and then ascertained the influence of this manipulation on learning, retention, and problem-solving.

Teaching as model-providing—As for research illustrating the identification approach to teaching, Bandura's recent work[16] seems noteworthy. He has conducted experiments dealing with (a) the effects on imitation of pairing a model with generalized reinforcers, (b) delayed imitation in the absence of the model, (c) the influence of the behavior of models in shaping frustration-reactions, and (d) the influence of social reinforcements and the behavior of models in shaping children's moral judgments. Bandura offers cogent arguments for greater concern with what we would characterize as teaching by model-providing than with teaching by conditioning.

Teaching as conditioning—The conditioning approach to teaching has been studied extensively in recent years—primarily through research on teaching machines and programed learning. Krumboltz's review[17] organized recent findings under four headings: (a) evoking the desired response, (b) reinforcing the desired response, (c) maintaining and improving the desired response, and (d) eliminating the undesired response. To the degree that such research can be translated into implications or teacher behavior rather than merely the design and administration of programed learning materials, it will bear upon theories of teaching conceived according to the conditioning approach.

SUMMARY

This chapter has developed the thesis that theories of learning will become more useful in education when they are transformed into theories of teaching. In support of this thesis, we examined the need for theories of teaching and sought to counter the arguments that teaching is an art and that learning theories make theories of teaching unnecessary. The demands of teacher education make theories of teaching especially important. In developing theories of teaching, a major step is analysis and specification. We offered analyses on the basis of (a) types of teacher activity, (b) types of educational objective, (c) components of the learning process, and (d) families of learning theory. Then we examined several selections of components from these analyses to illustrate how theories of teaching might be formulated when they were aimed at different combinations of *a, b, c,* and *d,* above. The sketches of these selections indicate that no single, unified, general theory of teaching should be sought to account for the various processes by which teachers engender learning. Rather, a number of theories of teaching, corresponding to major families of learning theory, will be necessary. Finally, the various approaches to the development of theories of teaching will influence research on teaching. Such influence has already appeared in a number of research movements that can be classified according to the three families of theory of teaching employed in the earlier discussion: cognitive structure theories, identification theories, and conditioning theories.

FOOTNOTES

[1] The author is very grateful to Philip W. Jackson and Romayne Ponleithner for valuable editorial suggestions.

[2] William K. Estes, "Learning." In Chester W. Harris, Ed. *Encyclopedia of Educational Research.* (3rd ed.) New York: Macmillan Co., 1960, p. 767.

[3] Ernest R. Hilgard, *Theories of Learning.* (2nd ed.) New York: Appleton-Century-Crofts, 1956, p. 485.

[4] Horace B. English and Ava C. English, *A Comprehensive Dictionary of Psychological and Psychoanalytical Terms.* New York: Longmans, Green & Co., 1958.

[5] Gilbert Highet, *The Art of Teaching.* New York: Vintage Books, 1955, pp. vii–viii.

[6] Hilgard, *op. cit.,* p. 2.

[7] O. Hobart Mowrer, *Learning Theory and Behavior.* New York: John Wiley & Sons, 1960, p. 213.

[8] Albert Bandura, "Social Learning Through Imitation." In M. R. Jones, Ed. *Nebraska Symposium of Motivation.* Lincoln: University of Nebraska Press, 1962. Pp. 211–269.

[9] Abraham S. Luchins, "Implications of Gestalt Psychology for AV Learning," *AV Communications Review,* IX, No. 5 (1961), 7–31.

[10] David Krech, Richard S. Crutchfield and Egerton L. Ballachey, *Individual in Society.* New York: McGraw-Hill Book Co., 1962, pp. 504–529.

[11] David P. Ausubel and Donald Fitzgerald, "Meaningful Learning and Retention: Interpersonal Cognitive Variables," *Review of Educational Research,* XXXI (December 1961), 500–510.

[12] B. Othanel Smith and Milton O. Meux, with the collaboration of Jerrold Coombs, Daniel Eierdam and Ronald Szoke, *A Study of the Logic of Teaching.* Urbana: Bureau of Educational Research, University of Illinois, 1962 (mimeographed).

[13] Philip J. Runkel, "Cognitive Similarity in Facilitating Communication," *Sociometry,* XIX (1956), 178–191.

[14] J. Richard Suchman, "Inquiry Training in the Elementary School," *Science Teacher,* XXVII (November 1960), 42–47.

[15] Ausubel and Fitzgerald, *op. cit.,* p. 505.

[16] Bandura, *op. cit.,* pp. 256–264.

[17] John D. Krumboltz, "Meaningful Learning and Retention: Practice and Reinforcement Variables," *Review of Educational Research,* XXXI (December 1961), 535–546.

ANALYSIS OF TEACHING— ANOTHER LOOK[1]

Kaoru Yamamoto

It was roughly ten years ago that Ackerman[2] called to our attention the futility of our search for a set of personality traits, possession of which was believed to make any teacher competent and effective. He emphasized that a complete picture of the teaching process would never be drawn without establishing a chain first from such antecedents to the teacher's classroom behavior and, in turn, from such behavior in the classroom to the effects on pupils. Likewise, Mitzel and Gross[3] stressed the multidimensional nature of teacher

---

From "Analysis of Teaching—Another Look," *School Review* 75: 205–215; Summer 1967. Reprinted by permission of The University of Chicago Press. [Copyright 1967 by The University of Chicago.]

effectiveness which, further, may vary from goal to goal and from situation to situation.

TEN YEARS OF PROGRESS

Within the following decade, the analysis of teacher-pupil interactions in the classroom has attracted much attention. Three major systems of observation and analysis have been developed or refined.[4] These are, first, cognitive systems such as those used by Bellack and Davitz,[5] Gallagher and Aschner,[6] and Smith and Meux,[7] or Taba;[8] second, affective systems such as those employed by Flanders,[9] Hughes,[10] or Withall;[11] and, finally, multidimensional systems such as those of Cornell, Lindvall, and Saupe,[12] or Medley and Mitzel.[13]

Similarly, our increased awareness of the various forces affecting the teaching process itself has forced our attention away from a simple conceptual scheme involving only a teacher and his pupils in a more or less isolated schoolroom to a far more complex, multivariate model inescapably involving the larger social contexts in which today's schools operate. For example, Biddle[14] proposed a system with five main sequence variables (formative experiences, teacher properties, teacher behaviors, immediate effects, and long-term consequences) and two contextual variables (classroom situations, and school and community contexts). One further step was taken by Siegel and Siegel[15] in their description of the comprehensive "instructional gestalt," or a three-dimensional model encompassing the environmental variables, teacher and student personality variables, method variables, and, finally, outcome variables. Also, an entire volume of the NSSE yearbook was devoted to the socio-psychological characteristics of the instructional group itself.[16]

Further, and at long last, we have come to the realization that theories of learning are not theories of teaching.[17] Understanding of learning, in and of itself, will not add much to our understanding of teaching. The relationship here is similar to that between, say, botany and horticulture. It is one thing to know all about how a plant's cells are structured, how its chromosomes look and behave, and how it achieves the crucial process of photosynthesis, while it is another to know what kind of soil is good for the plant, when to sow, how to fertilize when with what, and so on. A botanist may be able to tell us everyting about the mechanisms of a plant's life, but we must have a horticulturist to grow flowers and fruits.

A LONG WAY AHEAD

Indeed, the progress has been encouraging.[18] More than anything else, I would dare say, these and related efforts have made us realize that education, as an applied science, should develop its own unique philosophies, theories, techniques, and skills to perform its mission satisfactorily and proudly. As aptly put by Smith and Ennis,

> Whether to use or not to use knowledge and techniques developed in other fields in the study of educational problems is not at issue. The problems of education are broad and their solution often requires resources from many intellectual domains. But when knowledge from related fields is taken as though it were the answer to educational questions, or used to frame educational questions which require a conceptual framework of their own, the time has come for students of education to take stock.[19]

Such re-examination has begun, and education is trying constructively to find its identity again in the fast-changing world of the twentieth century.

Admittedly, it is a long way to go. We must understand a man as a man, being controlled by, and at the same time controlling, the physiological, ecological, historical, social, spiritual, and psychological forces. We must then look at what is really involved in transmitting knowledge to these humans through the vehicle of the school.[20]

We must build *prescriptive* theories of teaching [21] which cover both strategies and tactics of instructional behavior.[22] Somehow we must learn to arrange and manipulate instructional variables and to structure learning tasks so as to engender comprehension [23] and develop thinking.[24]

Without dwelling any further on the tasks confronting us, however, let me discuss one specific observation in the rest of this paper. Bluntly speaking, my thesis is that we have not really come to understand the peculiar nature of the classroom as a group. We are so accustomed to looking at the class as a group that we forget this aggregate of pupils is unique in many ways.

First of all, we talk as if we were after some "group goals" which are internally defined by the group members themselves, when the only real goals are all externally selected and specified. As Smith puts it, "Instructional influence is nonsymmetrical rather than symmetrical," and "at a more fundamental level instructional behavior is unidirectional." [25] The main objective of teaching is to change students' cognitive structure and attitude system according to a set of socially defined goals and expectations, and *not* to change teachers. Students do not have any say in this matter of goal setting.

Actually, the above observation is true not only with the goals of instruction but also with the materials, procedures, and personnel.[26] Students are usually powerless in the selection of curriculum, teaching methods and media, instructional personnel, and authority relationships. Indeed, below a certain level, even their group membership is compulsory and their participation, mandatory. Thus, "the roles of the two sides differ in teaching, if not in tennis." [27]

Granted the external determination of the so-called group goals, tasks, procedures, and members, it may still be argued by some that the same thing is true of many working groups in business, industry, and the military. They, too, do not often define their objectives. They, too, are often assigned tasks and methods not of their choice, and their membership is frequently defined for them by someone else.

Let us remember, however, that the latter groups will be rather directly affected by the results of their action *as a group*, or by their group performance. In sharp contrast, the classroom groups are seldom, if ever, affected *as a group* by their achievement *as a group*. In essence, students are competing against each other as individuals and not against other groups *as a group*. This point and its implications were observed and discussed in a slightly different context by Coleman in his study of high school climate,[28] and by Deutsch in his comparison of co-operative versus competitive college student groups in problem-solving experiments.[29]

In a strange twist of logic, moreover, many of us behave as if a teacher were influencing his class *as a group* through what he does, what he says, what he teaches, and who he is. Correspondingly, investigators often expect to judge this teacher's competence or effectiveness by the pseudocollective performance of his class, for example, the mean gains in achievement or the mean changes in personality.

The fact of the matter is that things happening *in* a group situation are not necessarily the same as things happening *to* the group as a group. A good example is the vicarious learning phenomenon upon which much of our classroom discourse depends. We have acted for a long time as if a teacher's work with a child would somehow generalize to other children in the class to the same extent. Serious studies on this topic are of quite recent origin and the results still fragmentary.[30] The importance and complex nature of differential feedback in the group performance and individual achievement was demonstrated in non-educational settings,[31] and there is a good possibility that this is also true in instructional situations.[32]

SCHEMES OF ANALYSIS

When we look at the available techniques of classroom observation and analysis, it is easy to realize that these and other unique features of the instructional group simply do not stand out in strong relief against the averaged-out background. Take, for example, Flanders' rule of two-thirds, which states that, "in the average classroom someone is talking two-thirds of the time; two-thirds of this is teacher talk; and two-thirds of teacher talk consists of direct influence (lecture, direction giving, or criticism)."[33] The teacher is talking—but to whom? His verbal communication may represent either the direct or indirect influence category, and he may indeed be influencing students—but specifically whom, why, and how? One third of the time, students talk—but which students and to whom?

The point I am raising here naturally transcends the criticism[34] that many of the current observation and analytical procedures concentrate on the affective or socio-psychological functions of teaching acts at the price of cognitive or logico-structural aspects of classroom interactions. The question could be asked equally validly of the "content-free" systems of Flanders[35] or Hughes,[36] the conceptual-referential systems of Bellack and Davitz[37] or Smith and Meux,[38] or even the non-interactional systems of Loban[39] or Sanders.[40]

All these schemes seem to ascribe to the entire "class" any verbal behavior revealed by individual children. Thus, any child may talk and the utterance is automatically regarded as an index of what is done by every member of the alleged group. Any experience by any single individual in the aggregate is recorded and interpreted as if it were equally shared by the group. Meanwhile, individual pupil perceptions remain unrecorded, and the increasingly important pupil-pupil patterns of interaction[41] (peers serving as models and resource persons for learning) are largely left unanalyzed.

One facet of this problem was skilfully described by Gage in the following words:

> None of these models has come to grips with the complication that teachers typically deal with more than one pupil at a time. In classroom lecturing, of course, the pupil side must be "aver-

aged" in some way by the teacher, who engages in most of the action, or overt behavior, shown in the paradigms. In classroom discussion, the pupil on the other side of the "net" from the teacher may change from volley to volley, and stable conceptions of the characteristics of the changing pupil may be hard to envisage.[42]

As another example of the uniqueness of the instructional group, a pupil's sociometric status in a classroom does not have the same significance as an employee's formal or informal position in an organization. In a very indirect way, a popular or high-status child may affect other children's development and learning, but his position in the classroom does not allow him to exert any task-oriented authority delegated by the teacher, nor hold him responsible for execution of certain specialized activities in the division of labor commonly found in many other types of the small group. As central as he may be in the power or communication structure of the group, the child is still a child pursuing his individual aims as an individual pupil according to the expectations and admonitions of the significant adults in his life and also according to whatever motives he has developed for himself.

In brief, then, the matter of structure and dynamics seems not directly comparable between the classroom and other types of the small group. To be sure, under certain circumstances, the teaching phenomena may be analyzed and explained on the basis of the records of collective verbal communication, and through application of the principles of general group processes. In many cases, however, a question, "Interaction really between whom and whom?" could be profitably raised. The three principal dimensions of individual variation, namely, activity, task ability, and likability,[43] may have to be closely observed for each participant and incorporated somehow into a new model of the instructional group.

Description of the communication process, however, is not the only problem in the analysis of teaching. A real difficulty arises when we try to relate the "process" variables obtained from such observation to the "presage"[44] or "concomitant"[45] variables and further with the "product" variables in the efforts to understand the whole instructional phenomenon.

First of all, even ignoring for the moment the unique nature of the classroom as a group, the current small-group theory and research would not appear to provide much help in clarifying the presage-process link in the teaching paradigm. Thus, for example, a recent review of conceptual orientations of such contemporary small-group theorists as Bales, Cartwright, Zander, Homans, Moreno, Newcomb, Thibaut, and Kelley came to the conclusion that "there are few occasions when variables at the individual process level are treated as the independent and those at the group level are treated as the dependent—that is, what characteristics of the individual affect the group?" [46]

When, further, we try to relate the process variables with some product variables, the situation becomes rather difficult mainly because of the fact that there are three kinds of properties associated with what Horwitz called the "group system." [47] Cartwright and Zander described these as (a) "properties of an individual," (b) "internal properties" of the group, and (c) "properties of an undifferentiated group." [48] The same three categories were named by Cattell as (a) "population variables," namely, means or other statistics of some measured characteristics of component individuals; (b) "structure variables," namely, the descriptions of the internal behavior of the group; and (c) "syntality variables," or the performance of the group acting as a whole.[49]

As I indicated earlier, most process data which the current techniques of observation and analysis give us are, correctly or incorrectly, at the group-as-a-whole level. In contrast, most product data we employ are nothing but the "population" variables, that is, some indexes of properties of individuals. Thus, for example, we find what proportion of the spoken lines is devoted to "structuring pedagogical move" and how much of the discourse concerns "substantive meanings." [50] We may be able to identify different instructional patterns in this manner, and we would then relate these with some pupil-performance variables, such as the mean change in achievement or personality.

But, at this stage of the game, do such efforts represent the most logical approach when the two indexes are measuring two facets of the underlying phenomenon at two different levels? Hopefully, sooner or later, advances in our knowledge will enable us to subsume results from different levels of observations under a unified formulation, but, for the moment, would it not be easier and more meaningful to work out some functional relationships among data on the same level?

It is possible, to a certain extent, to reconstruct patterns of group behavior from those of individuals, and vice versa.[51] Nevertheless, there always remains some covariation not accountable by either set of variables.[52] Have we progressed so far as to believe that we can make some sense out of heterogeneous measures of the individual-group-institutional system [53] to understand the instructional phenomena? This, then, is the question in the mind of a rather naïve but active participant in the act of teaching.

FOOTNOTES

[1] A revision of a paper originally delivered at the February, 1966, meeting of the American Educational Research Association in Chicago.

[2] W. I. Ackerman, "Teacher Competence and Pupil Change," *Teachers College Record,* XXIV (1954), 273-89.

[3] H. E. Mitzel and C. F. Gross, *A Critical Review of the Development of Pupil Growth Criteria in Studies of Teacher Effectiveness.* New York: Division of Teacher Education, City of New York, 1956.

[4] E. Amidon and Anita Simon, "Teacher-Pupil Interaction," *Review of Educational Research,* XXXV (1965), 130-39.

[5] A. A. Bellack and J. R. Davitz, *The Language of the Classroom: Meanings Communicated in High School Teaching* (Final Report, U.S. Office of Education, Cooperative Research Project No. 1497 [New York: Institute of Psychological Research, Teachers College, Columbia University, 1963]).

[6] J. J. Gallagher and Mary J. M. Aschner, "A Preliminary Report: Analyses of Classroom Interaction," *Merrill-Palmer Quarterly of Behavior and Development,* IX (1963), 183-94.

[7] B. O. Smith and M. O. Meux, *A Study of the Logic of Teaching* (Final Report, U.S. Office of Education, Cooperative Research Project No. 258 [Urbana: Bureau of Educational Research, University of Illinois, 1962]).

[8] Hilda Taba et al., *Thinking in Elementary School Children* (Final Report, U.S. Office of Education, Cooperative Research Project No. 1574 [San Francisco: San Francisco State College, California, 1964]).

[9] N. A. Flanders, *Teacher Influence, Pupil Attitudes, and Achievement* (OE-25040, Cooperative Research Monograph No. 12 [Washington, D.C.: Government Printing Office, 1965]).

[10] Marie Hughes, *Development of the Means for the Assessment of the Quality of Teaching in Elementary Schools* (Final Report, U.S. Office of Education, Cooperative Research Project No. 353 [Salt Lake City: University of Utah, 1959]).

[11] J. G. Withall, "The Development of a Technique for the Measurement of Social-Emotional Climate in the Classrooms," *Journal of Experimental Education,* XVII (1949), 347-61.

[12] F. G. Cornell, C. M. Lindvall and J. L. Saupe, *An Exploratory Measurement of Individualities of Schools and Classrooms.* Urbana: Bureau of Educational Research, University of Illinois, 1953.

[13] D. M. Medley and H. E. Mitzel, "A Technique for Measuring Classroom Behavior," *Journal of Educational Psychology,* XLIX (1958), 86-92.

[14] B. J. Biddle, "The Integration of Teacher Effectiveness Research." In B. J. Biddle, and W. J. Ellena, Eds. *Contemporary Research on Teacher Effectiveness.* New York: Holt, Rinehart & Winston, 1964, pp. 1-40.

[15] L. Siegel and Lila C. Siegel, "The Instructional Gestalt: A Conceptual Framework and Design for Educational Research," *AV Communication Review,* XII (1964), 16-45.

[16] N. B. Henry, Ed. *The Dynamics of Instructional Groups* (59th Yearbook of the National Society for the Study of Education, Part II). Chicago: University of Chicago Press, 1960.

[17] N. L. Gage, "Theories of Teaching." In E. R. Hilgard, Ed. *Theories of Learning and Instruction* (63rd Yearbook of the National Society for the Study of Education, Part I). Chicago: University of Chicago Press, 1964, pp. 268-285.

[18] D. G. Ryans, "Assessment of Teacher Behavior and Instruction," *Review of Educational Research,* XXXIII (1963), 415-41.

[19] B. O. Smith and R. H. Ennis, *Language and Concepts in Education.* Chicago: Rand McNally Co., 1961, p. iv.

[20] J. S. Bruner, "The Growth of Mind," *American Psychologist,* XX (1965), 1007-17. See also his *Toward a Theory of Instruction* (Cambridge, Mass.: Harvard University Press, 1966).

[21] J. S. Bruner, "Needed: A Theory of Instruction," *Educational Leadership,* XX (1963), 523-32.

[22] B. O. Smith, "A Conceptual Analysis of Instructional Behavior," *Journal of Teacher Education,* XIV (1963), 294-98.

[23] N. L. Gage, "Toward a Cognitive Theory of Teaching," *Teachers College Record,* LXV (1964), 408-12.

[24] Hilda Taba and F. F. Elzey, "Teaching Strategies and Thought Processes," *Teachers College Record,* LXV (1964), 524-34.

[25] Smith, *op. cit.,* p. 296.

[26] J. W. Getzels and H. A. Thelen, "The Classroom Group as a Unique Social System." In Henry, Ed., *op. cit.,* pp. 53-82.

[27] N. L. Gage, "Paradigms for Research on Teaching." In N. L. Gage, Ed. *Handbook of Research on Teaching.* Chicago: Rand McNally Co., 1963, p. 129.

[28] J. S. Coleman, "Academic Achievement and the Structure of Competition," *Harvard Educational Review,* XXIX (1959), 339-51.

[29] M. Deutsch, "The Effects of Cooperation and Competition upon Group Process." In D. Cartwright and A. Zander, Eds. *Group Dynamics.* (2d ed.) Evanston, Ill.: Row, Peterson, 1960, pp. 414-48.

[30] Adrienne Barnwell and L. Sechrest, "Vicarious Reinforcement in Children at Two Age Levels," *Journal of Educational Psychology,* LVI (1965), 100-06; I. J. Semler, *Concept Learning and Retention in a Simulated Classroom Situation* (Final Report, U.S. Office of Education, Cooperative Research Project No. S-225 [Cedar Rapids, Iowa: Cedar Rapids Community School District, 1965]); R. M. W. Travers and R. K. Van Wagenen, "Observational Learning in a Simulated Recitation Group," *American Educational Research Journal,* I (1964), 26-34; R. M . W. Travers, R. K. Van Wagenen, Danielle H. Haygood, and Mary McCormick, "Learning as a Consequence of the Learner's Task Involvement under Different Conditions of Feedback," *Journal of Educational Psychology,* LV (1964), 167-73; R. K. Van Wagenen and R. M. W. Travers, "Learning under Conditions of Direct and Vicarious Reinforcement," *Journal of Educational Psychology,* LIV (1963), 356-62.

[31] See, for example, R. B . Zajonc, "The Effects of Feedback and Probability of Group Success on Individual and Group Performance," *Human Relations,* XV (1962), 149-61.

[32] M. Horwitz, "Feedback Processes in Classroom Groups," in Henry, Ed., *op. cit.,* pp. 218-24.

[33] Amidon and Simon, *op. cit.,* p. 132.

[34] N. L. Gage, "Toward a Cognitive Theory of Teaching," *op. cit.;* B. O. Smith, "Concept of Teaching," *Teachers College Record,* LXI (1960), 229-41; Taba and Elzey, *op. cit.*

[35] N. A. Flanders, "Some Relationships among Teacher Influence, Pupil Attitudes, and Achievement," in Biddle and Ellena, Eds., *op. cit.,* pp. 196-231.

[36] Hughes, *op. cit.*

[37] Bellack and Davitz, *op. cit.*

[38] Smith and Meux, *op. cit.*

[39] W. Loban, "Language Proficiency and School Learning." In J. D. Krumboltz, Ed. *Learning and the Educational Process.* Chicago: Rand McNally Co., 1965, pp. 113-31.

[40] N. M. Sanders, *Classroom Questions: What Kinds?* New York: Harper & Row, 1965.

[41] See, for example, D. Schreiber, "Raising Aspirations of Youth: Implications for Community Organizations." In E. P. Torrance and R. D. Strom, Eds. *Mental Health and Achievement.* New York: John Wiley & Sons, 1965, pp. 63-69.

[42] Gage, "Paradigms for Research on Teaching," *op. cit.,* p. 129.

[43] R. Brown, *Social Psychology.* New York: Free Press, 1965, p. 683.

[44] H. E. Mitzel, "Criteria of Teacher Effectiveness." In C. W. Harris and M. R. Liba, Eds. *Encyclopedia of Educational Research.* (3d ed.) New York: Macmillan Co., pp 1481-86.

[45] D. G. Ryans, "Prediction of Teacher Effectiveness." In C. W. Harris and M. R. Liba, Eds., *op. cit.,* pp. 1486-91.

[46] J. DeLamater, C. G. McClintock, and G. Becker, "Conceptual Orientations of Contemporary Small Group Theory," *Psychological Bulletin,* LXIV (1965), 402-12.

[47] M. Horwitz, "The Conceptual Status of Group Dynamics," *Review of Educational Research,* XXIII (1953), 309-28.

[48] Cartwright and Zander, *op. cit.,* p. 642.

[49] R. B. Cattell, "New Concepts for Measuring Leadership, in Terms of Group Syntality," *Human Relations,* IV (1951), 161-84.

[50] Bellack and Davitz, *op. cit.*

[51] E. F. Borgatta and R. F. Bales, "Interaction of Individuals in Reconstituted Groups," *Sociometry,* XVI (1953), 302-20.

[52] E. F. Borgatta, L. S. Cottrell, Jr. and H. J. Meyer, "On the Dimensions of Group Behavior," *Sociometry.* XIX (1956), 222-40.

[53] Horwitz, "The Conceptual Status of Group Dynamics," *op. cit.*

DISCUSSION QUESTIONS
AND FURTHER READINGS

As mentioned earlier, evaluative judgments on teaching presuppose answers to both prescriptive and descriptive questions. Fortunately or unfortunately, these questions can be answered from many different points of reference. Thus, for example, a teacher can give one set of answers, his colleagues another, and his students still another. Answers given by individual students may or may not reflect their collective answers as a group. Curriculum directors, counselors, principals, superintendents, and board members may all give divergent answers. Moreover, these answers can be couched in either subjective or objective terms and expressed in qualitative or quantitative symbols. In the abundance of these potentially disparate answers, how are you going to appraise your own teaching? If you are to depend selectively on these sources of information, what rationale and guiding principles will you use for such differential evaluation?

Some of the more externally anchored attempts at evaluation of teaching are summarized in N. L. Gage, Ed., *Handbook of Research on Teaching* (Chicago: Rand McNally, 1963). In contrast, a more internally oriented approach is illustrated in Clark Moustakas, *The Authentic Teacher* (Cambridge, Mass.: Howard Doyle Publishing Co., 1966). What unique contributions do these objective and subjective orientations make to a teacher?

Your contemplation of this topic would undoubtedly reflect your own understanding of the image of man and its historical transformations, the human modes of knowing, and the fission and fusion of the "two cultures." Consult J. Bronowski, *The Identity of Man* (New York: The Museum of Natural History, 1965), Richard M. Jones, Ed., *Contemporary Educational Psychology* (New York: Torchbooks, Harper & Row, 1967), Floyd W. Matson, *The Broken Image* (Garden City, N.Y.: Anchor Books, Doubleday, 1966), Paul Nash, Ed., *Models of Man* (New York: John Wiley, 1968), and Charles P. Snow, *The Two Cultures and the Scientific Revolution* (New York: Cambridge University Press, 1959).

EPILOGUE

LOOKING BACK
AND AHEAD

By now, I hope you would agree with me when I say that to understand teaching is to understand man and society in their complex entirety. It may also be said that to learn to be a teacher is to search for identity, integrity, and compassion. The search is a life-long and often lonesome one although, as you have found, some of the greatest human minds are those of our fellow travellers. When we feel that Whitehead, James, or Dewey sound amazingly current and relevant and when we recall that Plato, Jesus, or Confucius are known first and foremost for their teaching activities, we realize that teaching is indeed one of the most lasting human endeavors—transcending time, space, and culture.

It follows that being a teacher places quite a responsibility on the individual. How can we find out more about great teachers so that we may emulate them? *The Art of Teaching* by Highet, from which a selection was reproduced in this book, contains a long chapter on some of these teachers and their varied methods of teaching. Similar analyses are found in John E. Colman's *The Master Teachers and the Art of Teaching* (New York: Pitman Publishing Corporation, 1967), Harry S. Broudy and John R. Palmer's *Exemplars of Teaching Method* (Chicago: Rand McNally, 1965), and Houston Peterson's *Great Teachers* (New Brunswick, N.J.: Rutgers University Press, 1946. Also available as a Vintage Book edition from Alfred A. Knopf, Inc., of New York.). Some of the philosophical models underlying various approaches in the tradition of Western education may be found in Paul Nash's *Models of Man* (New York: John Wiley & Sons, 1968).

As suggested all along, self-examination is crucial for teachers. Two books of different styles may be of help here. One is *Myself* by Sylvia Ashton-Warner (New York: Simon and Schuster, 1967) and the other is Clark Moustakas' *The Authentic Teacher* (Cambridge, Mass.: Howard A. Doyle Publishing Company, 1966). Each in its own way reminds us of the importance of close scrutiny of self and others in our efforts to sharpen sensitivity as a teacher and as a human being.

An example of such sensitivity is also found in John Holt's *How Children Learn* (New York: Pitman Publishing Corporation, 1967). The book is a sequel to the same author's *How Children Fail* from which a selection was reprinted in the present volume. What a sensitive and creative teacher may accomplish is clearly illustrated in Sybil Marshall's *An Experiment in Education* (New York: Cambridge University Press, 1966).

Granted the preventive values of a trusting and honest relationship between the teacher and the learner, it is still beneficial for a would-be teacher to know something of the dynamics of common behavior problems and learning deficiencies. A book by Rudolf Dreikurs, *Psychology in the Classroom* (New York: Harper and Row, 1968) is useful for this purpose. More extended and moving case descriptions are to be found in such works as Dorothy W. Baruch's *One Little Boy* (New York: Dell Publishing Company, 1964) and Virginia M. Axline's *Dibs in Search of Self* (Boston: Houghton Mifflin Company, 1964. Also available in paperback from Ballantine Books of New York.).

Some recent attempts at formulating theories of teaching may be found in *Instruction: Some Contemporary Viewpoints,* edited by Laurence Siegel (San Francisco: Chandler Publishing Company, 1967) and *Teaching: Vantage Points for Study,* edited by Ronald T. Hyman (Philadelphia: J. B. Lippincott, 1968). That no consensus has been reached in such efforts is obvious in two recent analyses of teaching: J. M. Stephens' *The Process of Schooling* (New York: Holt, Rinehart and Winston, 1967) and Philip W. Jackson's *Life in Classrooms* (New York: Holt, Rinehart and Winston, 1968). Students and teachers in the classroom are indeed a worthy subject of study for teachers with keen observational eyes and an open mind.

Finally, in our quest for maturity, we should consider such modern classics as Joshua Loth Liebman's *Peace of Mind* (New York: Simon and Schuster, 1946) and Anne Morrow Lindbergh's

Gift from the Sea (New York: Pantheon Books, 1955; also available from Vintage Books, Random House, of New York). Robert E. Nixon's *The Art of Growing* (New York: Random House, 1962) may also be helpful in your contemplation.

Please carry on your study of teaching. Just remember that teaching involves the whole person of the teacher every hour of the day and every day of the week. It is a tremendous challenge and privilege for any individual to be in a teaching position in relationship to another human being or a group of human beings. In the final analysis, what sustains a teacher in such a deeply involved vocation is nothing other than the familiar triad which is found in any other human enterprises of worth, namely, love, faith, and hope.